PLATO

REPUBLIC 5

with an introduction, translation and commentary
by

S. Halliwell

Aris & Phillips – Warminster – England

iv

ISBNS   085668 535 6 (cloth)
         085668 536 4 (limp)

ISSN   0953 – 7961

British Library Cataloguing - in - Publication Data
A Catalogue record for this book is available from the British Library

Printed and published in England by Aris & Phillips Ltd, Teddington House, Warminster, Wiltshire BA12 8PQ

Contents

Preface

Despite the variety and interest of its contents, *Republic* 5 has never before had a separate commentary devoted to it in English. In producing one, I have attempted to offer a wide-ranging treatment of the book's many remarkable aspects - its radical proposals for female Guardians, and for the abolition of the family within the ruling class of the just city; its bold ideas (both declared and implicit) about human nature, kinship, eugenics and sexuality; its extreme pursuit of the principle of social unity, especially in the Guardian class; its statement of a code of warfare, in relation to the division between Greeks and barbarians; its thesis that philosopher-rulers are needed for human happiness; and its controversial account of the difference between philosophical knowledge and non-philosophical belief. As regards this last topic, which represents the driest and toughest section of the book, I have endeavoured to give basic guidance to the analytical complexities which engage philosophical specialists here, though I have also questioned some of the assumptions made by such specialists.

My aim throughout has been to provide information, arguments and suggestions which will be of use to the many kinds of readers that bk. 5 continues to attract. I have tried to pay regular attention to philosophical, historical and linguistic matters, and to present these in ways which will make it possible for both less and more advanced students to derive assistance from my commentary, though individuals will still need, of course, to exercise appropriate discrimination in focussing on the details which are most helpful to them. I hope, however, that many will be induced to work through as much of my material as possible, and will share my conviction that the understanding of Plato is an enterprise which requires us to place his writings in history, and to read them with close, integrated attention to every facet of the extraordinarily rich medium in which he expressed and dramatised his thought.

In most respects, I have kept my practice consistent with what I offered in my edition of *Republic* bk. 10, published in this series in 1988, though I have cited a somewhat wider selection of secondary literature for the benefit of those who wish to pursue particular issues further. Grammatical material and untransliterated Greek have for the most part been either kept in separate notes, or placed at the end of comments.

University of Birmingham   S. H.

Abbreviations & References

Abbreviations for ancient authors and works, including Plato's, are not included here; in general, they follow familiar forms such as those used in LSJ or *OCD²* (below). References to passages in the *Republic* are normally given without the title of the work: the book number is supplied in all cases except for those in bk. 5 itself, though it is given only once for consecutive citations from the same book.

AJP   *American Journal of Philology*

CEG   P.A. Hansen (ed.) *Carmina Epigraphica Graeca* (Berlin, 1983–9)

CJ   *Classical Journal*

CP   *Classical Philology*

CQ   *Classical Quarterly*

CR   *Classical Review*

DK   H. Diels & W. Kranz (edd.) *Die Fragmente der Vorsokratiker⁷* (Berlin, 1954)

EG   D. Page (ed.) *Epigrammata Graeca Selecta* (Oxford, 1975)

FGrH   F. Jacoby (ed.) *Die Fragmente der griechischen Historiker* (Berlin, 1923–)

GRBS   *Greek Roman and Byzantine Studies*

Hense   O. Hense (ed.) *C. Musonius Rufus: Reliquiae* (Leipzig, 1905)

IG   *Inscriptiones Graecae* (Berlin, 1873–)

JHS   *Journal of Hellenic Studies*

K(ock)   T. Kock (ed.) *Comicorum Atticorum Fragmenta* (Leipzig, 1880–88)

Kaibel   G. Kaibel (ed.) *Comicorum Graecorum Fragmenta*, vol. 1 (Berlin, 1899)

Kroll   W. Kroll (ed.) *Procli Diadochi in Platonis Rem Publicam Commentarii*, vol. 1 (Leipzig, 1899)

KRS   G. S. Kirk, J. E. Raven, M. Schofield, *The Presocratic Philosophers²* (Cambridge, 1983)

LIMC   *Lexicon Iconographicum Mythologiae Classicae* (Zurich, 1981–)

LSJ   H. G. Liddell, R. Scott, H. S. Jones, *A Greek-English Lexicon⁹*, with Supplement (Oxford, 1968)

ML   R. Meiggs & D. Lewis (edd.) *A Selection of Greek Historical Inscriptions to the End of the Fifth Century B.C.* (Oxford, 1969)

Mnem.   *Mnemosyne*

N²   A. Nauck (ed.) *Tragicorum Graecorum Fragmenta²* (Leipzig, 1889)

OCD²   N. G. L. Hammond & H. H. Scullard (edd.) *The Oxford Classical Dictionary²* (Oxford, 1970)

P. Herc.   *Herculaneum Papyri*

P. Oxy.   *Oxyrynchus Papyri* (London, 1898–)

PCG   R. Kassel & C. Austin (edd.) *Poetae Comici Graeci* (Berlin, 1983–)

PMG   D. Page (ed.) *Poetae Melici Graeci* (Oxford, 1962)

Rose   V. Rose (ed.) *Aristotelis...Fragmenta* (Leipzig, 1886)

SVF   H. von Arnim (ed.) *Stoicorum Veterum Fragmenta* (Leipzig, 1903–5)

TAPA	*Transactions of the American Philological Association*
TrGF	*Tragicorum Graecorum Fragmenta* (Göttingen, 1971–)
W(est)	M. L. West (ed.) *Iambi et Elegi Graeci* (Oxford, 1971–2)
Wehrli	F. Wehrli (ed.) *Die Schule des Aristoteles* (Basle, 1944–59)
ZPE	*Zeitschrift für Papyrologie und Epigraphik*

Introduction

'If I were confident in myself that I know what I'm talking about, your reassurance would be a fine thing. For in a gathering of intelligent friends, in discussion of subjects that are of the greatest importance and dear to one's heart, to speak with knowledge of the truth gives one security and confidence. But to offer arguments in a doubtful and exploratory state of mind, as I'm doing, is something frightening and risky...' (450d8–451a1)

§1.1 Design & Discovery: Approaching Bk. 5

Plato's *Republic* is a philosophical enquiry into the nature of justice. But the work's richness is such as to convert that apparently clear-cut statement of theme into a peculiarly complex development of arguments, ideas and images. In the course of the dialogue, justice is given the status of the master-virtue both of individual souls and of human communities, and large parts of the *Republic* are framed as an attempt to explore the relationship between these two levels of ethical analysis, the psychological and the political. What begins in bk. 1 as a discussion (and rejection) of the traditional Greek ethic of 'helping friends and harming enemies', gradually unfolds so as to take on the dimensions of a comprehensive search for the values by which human beings ought to conduct both their personal and their social lives. If the *Republic* can be said to have a controlling thought lying at its core, it is that the goodness reflected by those values is the ultimate cause and explanation of reality, and therefore the key to human hopes of happiness. It is in order to affirm such ambitious and grandiose claims that the work eventually forsakes the medium of dialogue, and completes itself in bk. 10 with a visionary myth of the eternal destiny of the soul.

But though the *Republic* may find its way to a conclusion of unmistakable emphasis, it does so by a route that is philosophically intricate and far from linear. It is possible, of course, to demarcate and summarise certain large blocks of material encompassed by the dialogue – with bks. 2-4 outlining the social structure (Rulers, Auxiliaries, farmers/artisans) of the just city, bks. 2-3 concentrating on the education of the first two classes, and bk. 4 elaborating the parallelism between this civic structure and the internal forces (reason, spirit, desire) of the soul; bk. 5 expounding the special 'sharing' or 'communism' (*koinônia*) of the city's Guardians (comprising Rulers and Auxiliaries), and bks. 6-7 presenting the metaphysical framework to support an ideal of philosopher-rulers; bks. 8-9 examining the four main conditions of evil and injustice in both city and soul; and bk. 10 combining a critique of the claims of the poets to be teachers of wisdom, an argument for the immortality of the soul, and the final myth of Er, already mentioned. Quite apart from what this leaves out, however, no such résumé can begin to capture the particularly creative way in which Plato makes and shapes the progress of the dialogue. If we wish, therefore, to situate any single component – in this case, bk. 5 – in its context, we must approach the question of form and organisation from an appropriate angle.

Consideration of the structure of the *Republic* must take constant account of the double character of the work – as, simultaneously, an expression of sustained and deliberate processes of philosophical thought, and yet the dramatisation of a conversation which, like all encounters involving Socrates, is permeated by a spirit of intellectual discovery. The participants in the dialogue pursue lines of enquiry which carry them in directions they had not fully anticipated. This is even true of Socrates himself, who, despite his general dominance and relative control of the argument, is specifically shown at several junctures as less than fully prepared for the turn which the conversation takes. One of these junctures, and perhaps the most striking of all, is the beginning of bk. 5 itself, where the other members of the group insist that Socrates should elaborate upon a suggestion which he had made in passing at an earlier stage. Plato's handling of the dramatic scenario at the start of this book allows us to consider, in a particularly intriguing form, the broader question of the kind of design which it is legitimate to see, or to find, in the *Republic*.

No interpretation can afford to side-step the challenge posed by the *Republic*'s carefully shaped portrayal of a discourse which is improvisatory, unpredictable and heuristic in character. This is, of course, a general feature of Plato's Socratic dialogues. It is, indeed, one of the qualities which Aristotle had in mind when, in a context which follows on from an extensive analysis of *Republic* 5 itself, he lists 'the exceptional, the subtle, the novel, and the exploratory' as salient characteristics of these dialogues of Plato's.[1] It is easy to see how the last of these attributes, the exploratory or heuristic (*zêtêtikon*), picks out a style of enquiry and investigation (*zêtein*) which is depicted in the inconclusive ('aporetic') Socratic dialogues of Plato's earlier and shorter works. But the context suggests that Aristotle means his description to fit the *Republic* too, and I believe that he was right to do so.

The *Republic* may depict a Socrates who now, unlike his earlier self in Plato, has acquired positive ideas of his own to explain and defend. But it nevertheless continues to dramatise philosophy as an activity which, at the level of personal dialogue or dialectic (in one sense of that term), remains an unending quest for truth and understanding. It is in the nature of this quest that we can never be sure of anything like finality. That is a point embodied in the character of Plato's text, not least by Socratic expressions of self-doubt, but also by interventions (such as Adeimantus's at 6.487b ff.) which remind us of the possibility of resisting conclusions towards which Socrates guides the conversation. And if that is so, then the uncertainty involved in looking for design in the *Republic* may be one which we cannot definitively resolve, but which we must try to build, with constant adjustments, into our readings of the work.

Central to such reading should be the perception of Platonic dialogue as something which grows from the pursuit of arguments – not, therefore, the disclosure of preconceived or inevitable conclusions, but a provisional path of thought of the kind that might indeed be *discovered* by the parties to an intense discussion. Such a conception nonetheless allows for the controlling imagination of the philosophical 'dramatist', Plato, and for a multiplicity of means by which he is able to arouse and even manipulate the responses of his readers. It would certainly be misguided to suppose that the *Republic* lacks a purposeful structure; but it is equally true that the work reveals its design in a gradual, aggregative manner, as the argument moves through a sequence of phases. Hence, I think, the impression with which it is easy to be left that much of the material traversed by the conversation could have been explored in a different order or from other angles of approach. Within this combination of design and discovery, bk. 5 fulfils an especially subtle and important function. It adds in crucial respects to the political and social ideas broached in bks. 2-4 of the dialogue, yet at the same time it reorientates the argument in a direction which will lead on to the ambitious and visionary metaphysics of bks. 6-7. Bk. 5 forms a large and surprising hinge for the organisation of the work as a whole, and it is worth examining in a little more detail how this comes to be so.

§1.2 The Structure of Argument in Bk. 5

Bk. 5 begins with some typically Platonic touches of dramatic detail – a tug at the shoulder of Adeimantus's cloak, and some whispered words between him and Polemarchus. It ends with Socrates speaking of the realms of 'pure', immutable and (it seems) transcendent reality. In order to get a better purchase on a book which moves in this way between the mundane and the eternal, it will be useful to consider a schematic outline of the main stages of the conversation (cf. the section head-notes in the Commentary for a fuller summary):

449a-451b: Socrates reluctantly agrees to elaborate his conception of 'the sharing [koinônia] of women and children' in the Guardian class.

451c-453e: There are to be female Guardians who will be trained identically to the men, and will perform all duties, including warfare, alongside them. But does the 'nature' of women make such a proposal feasible?

454a-457c: If 'nature' is functionally analysed, it emerges that, though men as a class are superior to women, the two sexes do not differ in their essential capacities, and 'many women are better than many men at many things'. So the best women should indeed serve the city as Guardians.

457c-461e: The family will be abolished among the Guardians; breeding will be eugenically organised. Biological kinship will be concealed; the young will regard whole groups, not individuals, as their parents and siblings.

462a-466d: Unity is the overriding goal; individualism must be eliminated. Rulers and people will feel mutual dependence; the Guardians will be bonded by a sense of common kinship. The city will be free of all faction (stasis).

466d-471b: Young Guardians will be 'apprenticed' to war. Brave soldiers will be honoured during life and after death. The city must operate the principle that all Greeks are natural kin, Greeks and barbarians natural enemies.

471c-474b: But is all this really possible? The picture represents an ideal. Yet there is one condition which would make such a society feasible; the combination of power and philosophy in the same persons (philosopher-rulers).

474b-476d: The true philosopher must be distinguished from devotees of earthly arts and values. Unlike such people, who are limited to belief (doxa), the philosopher has knowledge of the immutable 'forms' of beauty, justice, etc.

476d-480a: Knowledge is of pure, perfect reality; 'ignorance' corresponds to that which has no reality. Belief occupies an intermediate position; it is concerned with that which is between reality and unreality.

Even in this minimal sketch, we can glimpse the combination of 'design and discovery' which I have already suggested is integral to the character of the *Republic* as whole. Bk. 5 does not supply an exhaustive account of the social arrangements which constitute 'the sharing of women and children'. Socrates unfolds his radical and challenging contentions in a suggestive and aggregative manner, using recurrent themes and emphases to link the arguments together, but without creating a sense of predetermined structure. These connections include the motif of Socrates' hesitation and self-doubt (p. 5 below); the scepticism (n. 450c 7) and laughter (n. 451a1) which are expected to greet the book's radical ideas; and the use of animal analogies for the social behaviour of humans (p. 17 below). Most important of all is the central theme of *koinônia*, a term which can be variously translated as 'sharing', 'community', 'partnership', and even 'equality'. Bk. 5 presents 'the sharing of women and children' as a composite idea embracing the joint participation of women in the duties of the Guardian class, a social organisation which makes the female Guardians 'common' (for procreative purposes) to the male members of the class,[2] and the attachment of the offspring of the Guardians to the whole group, rather than their containment within separate families.

Through the book's progressive exploration of these ideas, we are gradually taken from a plane of argument which is broadly social and political, and which has prevailed since the discussion of the ideal city began in bk. 2, to one which connects the philosophy of knowledge (epistemology) with the philosophy of being and reality (ontology, metaphysics), and which establishes the tone that will be sustained in bks. 6 and 7. In that sense, Socrates' interlocutors, who compelled him to change tack at the start of the book, get much more than they asked for; and so, by the same token, do Plato's readers. No wonder, then, that Aristotle, with this stretch of the *Republic* partly in mind, referred to 'the exceptional, the subtle, the novel, and the exploratory' as salient features of Plato's Socratic dialogues (p. 2 above) – before adding, with characteristically quiet irony, 'but it is somewhat difficult to do everything well' (*Pol.* 1265a12-13).

The shift of levels within bk. 5 conveys its own message: that the understanding of human beings, and the solution of human problems, cannot be carried to successful completion except by drawing on the knowledge which only the highest kind of philosophy can bring. This thesis is declared by Socrates in the famous statement of humanity's need for philosopher-rulers (473c-e); and everything that follows (up to the end of bk. 7)[3] is, in a sense, an attempt to specify how the term 'philosopher' is to be interpreted in that proposition. The thesis, therefore, is simultaneously the crowning point of the political argument that has been running since bk. 2, and the start of the metaphysics which will dominate the middle stretch of the entire dialogue. It is possible to see how Plato, while dramatising a conversation that springs several surprises on its readers, has designed bk. 5 so as to lead up to that grave and cardinal contention. He has done so, in part, by threading through the book one of the motifs mentioned above – that of scepticism about the possibility of ever realising Socrates' political and social proposals. Although the issue of feasibility seems to have been settled in biological and practical terms, it returns one final time, and with supreme emphasis, at 471c ff., and it is this which draws Socrates to pronounce philosopher-rulers to be the *sine qua non* for everything that he has earlier posited.

Yet this same shift of levels, within Plato's frame of reference, is also a source of interpretative difficulty. In sketching and defending his proposals for female Guardians, the abolition of the domestic family, and the rest, Socrates employs concepts and principles which lie within the realms of biology, psychology, and politics. Although contentious in many of their details, these sections of argument aim to supply answers to questions – about human nature, social relations, and so forth – which require no ultimate philosophical presuppositions for their understanding. But the same cannot be said of the latter parts of bk. 5, where the argument moves onto much more abstract ground. Here the tendency of Socrates' claims is towards a view which appears to require a sharp separation between the material and human world, on the one hand, and the sphere of pure, permanent reality, on the other. This view raises major doubts about the reliability of much human discourse, and especially about the judgements of value which occur in such discourse. But if that is so, these doubts might be thought to have some applicability to the arguments which have been so far constructed in the *Republic* itself, not least in bk. 5. This inference is strengthened by the fact that the philosophical knowledge of which Socrates speaks in the final pages of the book is not knowledge to which he lays claim himself: indeed, it is knowledge which, in his conspicuous self-doubt, he evidently disavows. If, therefore, Plato wishes the reader of bk. 5 to be guided towards a recognition that the true philosopher has access to ultimate standards of truth and value, he cannot do so without apparently undermining the very means which he uses to achieve this end. In this way, an enquiry into the structure of the book compels us to address, on a more fundamental level, the status of the arguments which Plato here attributes to Socrates.

§1.3 The Status of the Arguments in bk. 5
The arguments of bk. 5 are prefaced by a show of Socratic hesitation and even nervousness that reminds us of the Socrates of Plato's early, aporetic dialogues. The passage, though tinged with playfulness between Socrates and his companions, is a highly elaborate piece of characterisation, which we are entitled to suppose is a significant component of Plato's design of his dialogue. The whole subject of 'the sharing of women and children' is described as a 'hornet's nest' of arguments (450b 1); fear of ridicule, though dismissed as childish, is nonetheless allowed to lurk disconcertingly around the prospects of the discussion; and Socrates speaks of himself, a little later, as someone swimming for safety in very deep water (453d). This display of reluctance is so profuse that it involves elements which might be thought actually unsocratic in spirit (cf. nn. 449c2, 450b5, 7, d1). That particular anomaly is perhaps not hard to explain in terms of the humorously emphasised coyness of Socrates' self-doubt. But such an observation hardly exhausts the interest of this opening section of the book.

Far from being merely theatrical or ornamental, this initial drama of doubt and defensiveness creates repercussions at several subsequent points. The issue of credibility, with its associated fear of Utopianism, becomes a leitmotiv in the book, and continues to cause unease until the idea of philosopher-rulers is eventually formulated. But this solution to the problem of feasibility only widens the gap between the dialogue's hypothesis and the actualities of city politics. By saying that the necessary and sufficient condition for such a society is the existence of philosopher-rulers, Plato is hardly stipulating a practical means of bringing it about. He is, rather, stressing that the entire scheme depends on the acceptance of ultimate values which only specially trained philosophers can discover. In the end, therefore, the question of practical possibility is not so much answered as absorbed into a claim that all human values must be referred to a higher source of wisdom.

Socrates' statement of these ideas may seem a far cry from his original hesitancy. This discrepancy, which looks so acute if we juxtapose the beginning and the end of bk. 5, is a token of a more pervasive tension between the persona of Socrates and the controversial, idealistic nature of the programme for which he proceeds to argue. Two apparently clear-cut ways of resolving this tension (or similar tensions elsewhere in the *Republic*) have found some currency among modern interpreters. The first, which would now command wide approval from Platonic scholars, is to treat the Socratic persona, at this stage of Plato's life, as no more than a residue of the Socrates familiar from the earlier dialogues. Professions of ignorance or uncertainty, which had once been central to the Platonic portrayal of Socrates, have become no more than a superficial dramatic colouring; for we can see that Plato is now using this figure as a mouthpiece for audacious arguments of his own – arguments that culminate in the visionary metaphysics of bks. 6-7.[4] Entirely opposed to this way of reading is the view that bk. 5 deliberately draws attention to the far-fetched nature of its political and social proposals, in order to intimate that these should not be taken at face-value.[5] On this latter interpretation, the characterisation of Socrates helps to subvert the surface meaning of the arguments which are put into his mouth.

Neither of these approaches, it seems to me, can properly cope with the combination of drama and argument in bk. 5. The first view is right to see an important contrast between Plato's use of Socrates in the *Republic*, and the same figure in the shorter, aporetic dialogues. But it is implausible that as elaborate and sustained a scene as the opening of bk. 5 should amount to merely incidental decoration around the core of the discussion. To draw such an inference is surely to make Plato into a somewhat frivolous dramatist of philosophy. On the other hand, it is grossly unconvincing to suggest that substantial parts of the fabric of bk. 5 are, in effect, an exercise in heavy irony: this extreme reading renders Plato's text not only frivolous but utterly perverse. In addition to internal considerations (above all, the fact that Plato tries to *rebut,* not arouse, a sense of absurdity), such a hypothesis cannot explain why, as late as the *Laws*, Plato continues to commend sexual, social and political ideas of the kind advanced in *Republic* 5.[6] Nor can it be comfortably reconciled with the fact that Aristotle, in *Politics* 2, could criticise much of the contents of bk. 5 on the secure assumption that the book represented seriously entertained principles of politics and ethics.

If it is unrealistic either to ignore the dramatic indications of doubt and hesitation in bk. 5, or to take them as signs of a pervasive irony, what we need, I submit, is a way of seeing the work as poised between commitment and enquiry. This means that we need both to take the arguments seriously, and to allow our reading to be duly qualified by the signals, expressed through Socrates' prefatory and subsequent self-deprecation, that these same arguments are offered in a provisional, inconclusive spirit of philosophical investigation. It is possible to find some support for this balance of considerations in the reactions of Plato's earliest and most trenchant critic, Aristotle. For while Aristotle, as I have just mentioned, produces his own thorough critique of 'the constitution about which Socrates has spoken', as he calls the communistic politics of *Republic* 5 (*Pol.* 1264b24), he makes in this same context the general remark on Plato's dialogues which I quoted earlier in the Introduction (p. 2 above). And that is a remark which acknowledges the crucial element of exploration, search and enquiry (all covered by the term *zêtêtikon*) which marks those works, including *Republic* 5. It is only this element which can explain why Plato continues not only to use the persona of Socrates, but to highlight, at strategic points, the refusal of Socrates to claim the status of knowledge for anything that he puts forward.

To read bk. 5 (but not bk. 5 alone) as poised between commitment and enquiry is bound to be a delicate matter, calling for constant adjustment of assumptions and responses. It requires us to avoid slipping towards either extreme of treating the arguments as though they presumed definitive validity for themselves, or downgrading them to the level of a merely fanciful and non-committal 'thought experiment'. It cannot, however, and does not prevent us from following Aristotle in engaging actively and critically with the arguments of the book, to discover how far we might be persuaded by them, but also where we need to argue back against them, to fault them, or to reserve judgement. One consequence of this way of reading is a recognition that the value of Plato's writings need not be altogether diminished by particular shortcomings of argument, since any discernment of inadequacy by the reader will itself entail an engagement in the procedures of investigation which the text enacts. Nor should we have any fear that to approach a Platonic text in this fashion, with a mixture of sympathetic interest and critical independence, must be something very different from what its author hoped for. In the case of *Republic* 5, after all, we will be doing something not very far from what Socrates' immediate interlocutor, Glaucon, implicitly promises when he urges his mentor: 'Don't hesitate at all; your hearers will be neither undiscerning, nor full of doubt, nor ill-disposed towards you.' (450d3-4).

§2 Nature, Individuals & Society

'The sharing of women and children' comprises a set of proposals which are designed to promote the unity both of the Guardian class and of the city. Unity is a dominant principle of the city's organisation (esp. 462a-66d), and it is closely related to the work's central subject of justice. Civic justice was provisionally defined, in bk. 4, as a condition in which each person fulfils his proper and appropriate function, and thus contributes to the maintenance of the city as an integrated social entity. It has been assumed, since the start of the discussion of the just city in bk. 2, that a social organisation is a 'community', 'partnership' or 'shared enterprise' – all possible translations of *koinônia*. When bk. 5 raises the question of 'the sharing (*koinônia*) of women and children', therefore, it is pursuing one dimension of the larger theme of the city's cohesion.

Most Greeks could no doubt have assented to the general proposition that a city is, or should be, a *koinônia*, in the sense that it is bound together by common interests, needs and concerns: hence the established idea that a state, in its public structure and aspect, is 'the common/shared realm' (*to koinon*, cf. 461a4). But Plato presses for a bold extension of such ideas. He has already moved in this direction by his ascription to the Guardian class, at the end of bk. 3, of a 'shared' life (416e4), organised in central barracks (*sussitia*) and lived without any private property. This scenario is sustained and deepened by the consideration of women and children in bk. 5. The idea of *koinônia* is here elaborated in three interlocking ways: the women will 'share with/in' (*koinônein*) the duties of the male Guardians; they will not be the wives of individuals, but the 'common' (*koinai*) mates of the men; the Guardians' children will, likewise, be 'common' to the class as a whole, not to particular parents. Plato's thinking thus transforms ordinary notions of social and political unity, and elaborates a radically communistic or collectivist conception of the Guardian class. Moreover, although this communism is apparently exclusive to them, and is not duplicated in the lives of the city's third class of farmers and workers (n. 450c1), it is unequivocally clear that the organisation of the Guardians' lives is not directly for their own benefit, but for the good of the city as a whole (456d-7a, 465e-6a). There is no trace here of any concern for equality as a value worth pursuing for the sake of *individuals* – no egalitarianism, in other words (cf. p. 15 below). Indeed, it is a crucial part of bk. 5's programme that the force of individualism (*idiôsis*, 462b8) should be reduced to the very minimum within the community of the Guardians. This is a point which will recur below.

But if 'the sharing of women and children' is a supreme expression of collectivism, some qualifications need to be added. The first is that the enquiry into the ideally just city was intended from the outset to provide a model of justice in the individual soul: the city as social structure is, at the same time, a paradigm of 'the city within' (9.591e1). Latent in the political arguments of the *Republic*, therefore, there must remain many implications, both psychological and ethical, for the lives of individuals. Besides, we shall see, when we consider the case for female Guardians, that the concept of a human being's 'nature' is one which, for Plato, necessarily makes reference to individuals. This is reinforced by the further consideration that at a number of points in bk. 5 itself we can observe Plato taking account of the existence and strength of human individuality. One of these points is the highly paradoxical passage in which he uses the psycho-physical integrity of an individual as an analogy for the degree of social and emotional bonding which he wishes his Guardians to experience (462c10 ff.). But there are several other passages where the argument accepts the inescapably individual dynamics of important factors in the Guardians' lives: the focus in all these cases is the experience of erotic and sexual desire.

The significance of bk. 5's references to sexual desire will call for fuller examination later on. I have mentioned it here as an index of the underlying strain between the communistic spirit of the Guardian class, and the intense dynamics which Plato recognises within the individual soul. This strain might be redescribed as part of a complex relationship between 'nature' and 'value' in the account of the ideal state. Concepts of nature or the natural impinge in a number of ways upon the arguments of bk. 5: as the basic element in the case for female Guardians (p. 13); as the underpinning of the traditional polarity between Greeks and barbarians (§3 below); as the implicit justification for the repeated use of animal analogies and metaphors (p. 17); and as the essential characterisation of sexual passion (458d2-3). The case of sex illustrates very clearly that Plato is ready to appeal to 'nature' in so far as he can discern ways of channelling its impetus into valuable forms of social practice, but also that he does not treat it as an ultimate or indisputable authority: thus the sexual desires of the Guardians will sometimes be exploited (e.g. as an inducement to courage and to the creation of bonding between Auxiliaries, 468b-c); but they must equally be subject to general regulation, and thwarted when necessary (458d-e, 459d-e).

Nature, then, is a power to which Plato appeals in his challenge to existing traditions and conventions; but it is not a power which could ever be allowed simply to have its way. Rather, it is to be handled and controlled through new social structures. And these structures are to be justified not simply by reference to human nature, but on fundamentally ethical grounds. Ultimate ethical values, as the last part of bk. 5

ontends, are eternal and unchanging (§4 below): in that sense, they are, for Plato, a far
deeper source of authority than nature as manifested through biology, even if he is
prepared to use the term 'nature' on a different level to encompass transcendent reality
itself.[7] Although the earlier parts of bk. 5, where the programme of social and sexual
communism is set out, do not directly invoke the kind of transcendent values of which
we hear later on, the justification of that programme is entirely ethical, not naturalistic.
As such, it applies concepts of goodness and justice which require the knowledge of the
true philosopher for their understanding and application.

That means, of course, that the depicted practices of the ideal city would have
eventually to be referred to a framework of judgement which cannot be expounded in the
text of the dialogue itself. But that does not leave us with nothing more to say about bk.
5's programme of social proposals. For these proposals are described and defended by
arguments which, if not those of true philosophical knowledge, and if not meant as
necessarily definitive, are nonetheless serious and challenging. In the next two sections,
I shall attempt to address the substance of these arguments in closer detail.

2.1 Plato's Female Guardians

Since the latter part of the 19th century, discussion of the female Guardians of *Rep.* 5
has, perhaps unavoidably, become implicated in distinctively modern concerns with the
social and political status of women. The contemporary slant given to debate about the
book has often concentrated itself around the question whether Plato is entitled to be
called a feminist. It is understandable that Natalie Bluestone, in surveying more than a
century of such arguments, should discern a bifurcation of opinion into the two major
categories of 'misogynist' and 'feminist' readings of bk. 5.[8] But if Plato's views are to be
usefully compared with modern ideologies and social movements, it is appropriate to set
his proposals in as clear a historical perspective as possible – which means asking, in the
first place, how they were related to the ideas and practices of his own day.

Since Plato lived, wrote and taught in his native city for most of his career, it makes
obvious sense to measure his female Guardians against the norms of classical Athens.
The comparison yields a picture of extreme divergence; in all the following respects, the
proposals of bk. 5 form a radical contradiction of general Athenian practices (practices
which, to a considerable extent, were typical of the Greek world as a whole):[9]

   the female Guardians are to lead lives entirely unsegregated from men;
   they are not to be under the individual control of male kinsmen;
   they are to be relieved of virtually all child-rearing and domestic labours;
   they are to share precisely the same education as their male counterparts;
   they are to engage publicly in gymnastics, training naked alongside the men;
   they are to learn and employ all the same skills as men;
   they are to perform all the same duties as men, including those of warfare;
   they are to take part in philosophy, even to the highest levels;
   they are to be capable of rising even to supreme positions of political power.

In *Rep.* 5 itself, Plato makes no direct reference to the place of women in either Athens
or any other Greek state, though there are many details on which allusion to such
practice is implicit.[10] The radicalism of its proposals for women is justified, in Plato's
terms, not by any kind of comparative sociology, but by a sequence of abstract principles
and arguments. Yet Plato's reasons did not develop in a historical vacuum. So before

we examine the substance of bk. 5's arguments for female Guardians, it is well worth asking about their possible sources, models and affinities in Plato's world. There are six main areas which repay attention here, though I shall have to restrict myself to salient details. The aim of the exercise is not to contend that Plato was merely reworking elements which he had borrowed from others, but to clarify aspects of the cultural context within which the philosopher's concept of female Guardians was formed.

A. *Sparta*: Spartan citizen women lived lives that differed from conditions in Athens in several pertinent respects: their education was partly covered by state-organised activities; they were less restricted to domestic duties, and appeared in public with relative freedom; they took part in athletic training and competition; consideration was paid to their eugenic fitness as mothers; and they could bear legitimate children to more than one male citizen.[11]

Plato was unquestionably familiar with these social facts, and they have to be counted as a partial influence on his thinking. But the envisaged life of his female Guardians is much more remarkable than anything to be found in Doric communities, and Plato intended the difference to be understood. In the *Laws*, he twice contrasts his own proposals for women (which, in that work, use a moderated version of bk. 5's principles) with the customs of both Sparta and Crete: at 6.780d–81d he criticises these states for failing to carry through the organisation of communal messes (*sussitia*) to include women; and at 7.805e–6c he calls the Spartan system a 'compromise', praising its educational and athletic features, but complaining that it stops short of the necessary military training for women. Elsewhere, Plato is even prepared to echo a critical Athenian view of the 'licence' of Spartan women (*Laws* 1.637c2).

B. *'Anthroplogy'*: Several passages in Herodotus (the precise accuracy of which need not concern us) refer to types of sexual 'communism' among non-Greek peoples: the Massagetae marry, but share their wives sexually (1.216.1); the ?Thracian Agathyrsi have a common right to intercourse with their women, so that all the men live as 'brothers and kinsmen to one another' (4.104); the Libyan Nasamones practice polygyny, and share their wives like the Massagetae (4.172.2); the Auseës, also of Libya, do not make individual marriages at all, and their breeding is by 'common' mating (4.180.5-6). Herodotus intimates that hearsay about such alien customs circulated in the Greek world, since he corrects the general claim that the Scythians engage in sexual communism (1.216.1).[12] Similarly, it was becoming a familiar idea, at least by the later 5th century, that some of the typical social roles of men and women in the Greek world were found inverted in Egypt (Herod. 2.35; Soph. *OC* 337, with Jebb's n.; anon. *Dissoi Logoi* 2.17).

The issue here is not whether Plato knew specific sections of Herodotus's *Histories* (which he never cites explicitly), but whether he had heard of the *kind* of reports I have cited. Unquestionably he had, since in bk. 7 of the *Laws* he cites a Black Sea people, the Sauromatae (mentioned at Herod. 4.21, 110–17, etc.), as a contemporary proof that women can be accomplished horse-riders and can acquire military skills alongside their men (804e–5a, 806b5). Whether or not this information was derived from Herodotus, it is proof that Plato was actively interested in such comparative material, which, as I have indicated, was becoming well known among Greek thinkers (for the Sauromatae cf. Hippoc. *Aër.* 17, and note Aristotle's reference at *Pol.* 1262a18-21 to Libyan tribes like those at Herod. 4. 180.6, above).

C. *Contemporary Speculation*: This is a rough heading, to encompass the evidence that ideas pertinent to those of *Rep.* 5 were 'in the air' in the later 5th and early 4th century, especially in the intellectually exploratory atmosphere of Athenian culture.[13] It is obvious that some of the material indicated under A–B above must itself have helped to generate questions about the nature, potential and status of women, particularly in contrast to their social restrictions in Athens. Euripides and Socrates are two major figures who have often been linked with a 'free-thinking' reappraisal of traditional views of women, though there are problems of evidence and interpretation in both cases; the former's plays certainly contain reflections of changing attitudes towards women, but it is hard to ascribe particular beliefs to either of these men.[14] The most intriguing, though equally contentious, evidence is that of Aristophanes' *Ecclesiazusae* (see the Appendix). Since I think it is out of the question that Aristophanes derived his material from Plato, the play can reasonably be taken to owe something to contemporary trends of radical argument and utopian speculation. Among other suggestive hints of relevant ideas from the period are Eur. fr. 653 N[2] (an unknown character says 'a woman's/wife's bed ought to be shared/common [*koinon*]'); the unorthodox belief of Antisthenes, one of the founders of the Cynic tradition of philosophy, that virtue is the same for women and men (D. Laert. 6. 12);[15] and the dialogue *Aspasia* by Aeschines Socraticus, in which questions were raised about relations between husbands and wives (*apud* Cic. *De inv.* 1.52). We should probably see a deliberate allusion to the contemporary climate of thought in Adeimantus's remark that the sharing of women and children 'could take many forms' (449c8). But this remark should also be a warning to us: Plato is not simply echoing current speculations; his own proposals have a specificity and a philosophical character of their own.

D. *Myth and Legend*: In addition to the military imagery of Athena, which we know impinged on Plato's ideas about women (*Critias* 110b–c, *Laws* 7.806b3), Greek mythology contained a salient model – the legendary Amazons – of women who were highly proficient in military skills, and who did not, in most versions, marry individual husbands. Although apparently oblique (and underplayed by modern scholars),[16] the 'precedent' was not lost on Plato. At *Laws* 7.806b1, in faulting the inability of Spartan women to fight in defence of their city or children, he draws an explicit contrast with Amazons. Earlier in the same passage he makes the Athenian stranger, who is arguing that girls as well as boys should be trained in horse-riding and gymnastics, say that 'I was persuaded of this long ago by hearing certain ancient stories...' (804e4–5). This is surely another allusion to the Amazon legend, and it is followed by one of the references to the Sauromatae mentioned in B above. The juxtaposition is telling: the Sauromatae were sometimes regarded as descendants of the Amazons (see Herod. 4.110-17), so that Plato's speaker is matching up a mythical motif with contemporary reports of non-Greek peoples. This may strike us as a peculiar attitude to take (though belief in 'Amazon' societies has been recurrent in later periods too),[17] but it reveals something about the seriousness with which mythological paradigms could be taken by Greek minds, and it proves that Plato's thinking about women was coloured by potent images of his culture's mythology. This is all the more remarkable if we accept that the Amazon legend expressed deep-seated fears about the implications of a society in which women could live independently of men's control. If it is true that the story of the Amazons conveyed a warning 'that anyone who withdraws from or hates ordinary family life becomes dangerous to society as a whole', then this confirms that, at the very least, the scenario of *Rep.* 5 is hardly meant to be a comfortable one for the conventional Greek male psyche.[18]

It is likely, though unprovable, that Plato was also familiar with a variety of stories, partly or fully legendary, of occasions on which groups of Greek women had acted with special organisation and collective courage.[19]

E. *Pythagorean communities*: There is a possibility that contemporary Pythagorean groups in southern Italy and Sicily contained female members or associates.[20] Such groups seem to have approximated to self-contained, somewhat ascetic fraternities (*hetaireiai*), organised on the same communistic principle from which *Rep.* 5 sets out, that 'friends share everything' (n. 449c5). It is a further possibility that ideas on eugenics were current in Pythagorean circles (p. 17 below). Plato's exact familiarity with such communities is not reconstructible; but we know that he was acquainted with Pythagorean figures who visited Athens, that he paid three visits of his own (at least one of them before the likely composition date of bk. 5) to Magna Graecia, and that at some point he developed a friendship with the Pythagorean, Archytas of Tarentum.[21] The existence of more general affinities between Platonic thought and Pythagorean philosophy makes this an intriguing though obscure area of possible influence. However, there is no reason at all to suppose that any kind of *sexual* communism was ever attractive to Pythagoreans, whose views on women seem to have presupposed marriage and to have been highly moralising.[22]

F. *Animal breeding*: This is a field somewhat remote from the material cited in A–E, but it needs to be added to the list of possible influences on Plato's thinking. In addition to the specific reference at 459a–b, bk. 5 contains a series of images and metaphors which express the notion that the Guardians are equivalent to a 'herd' of animals which must be tended, and eugenically bred, for the good of the group as a whole (see p. 17 below). This is relevant to the idea of female Guardians, whose existence is justified in terms of the city's interests: it is best for the city that the most capable women should be bred, trained and used for the benefit of all (456e–7a).

Though it is hard to estimate the precise influence on Plato of each of these sources, there is in every case some concrete connection with bk. 5's materials. It emerges clearly enough that Plato did not develop the radical concept of female Guardians in isolation from ideas already current in his culture, and that he himself was conscious of the range of affinities – Greek and non-Greek, human and animal, actual and legendary – which I have illustrated. Yet none of this reduces the boldness of bk. 5's proposals. Aristotle, after his critique of the constitutions of both the *Republic* and the *Laws*, refers to other schemes for political reform, and describes all of them as being closer than Plato's to the existing forms of government in the Greek world: 'for no-one else has made the original suggestion of holding women and children in common, or for the inclusion of women in the common messes' (*Pol.* 1266a34-6). Plato, as he himself had emphasised in his criticisms of Sparta and Crete (A above), had gone beyond not only known practice, but any reformist programme propounded by theorists or philosophers.

To go this far, Plato felt obliged to confront the dominant cultural presumption that women had a nature different from, and inferior to, that of men. When Socrates, looking for a defence of the idea of female Guardians, first puts to Glaucon the objection of an imaginary interlocutor (in effect, any ordinary Greek male), that a woman's nature differs considerably from a man's, Glaucon's reaction is to concede the point automatically (453b7-9). Glaucon needs Socrates' guidance to find an answer to the problem, yet in the end it is Glaucon himself who produces the apparently simple consideration that answers the opponent. That consideration is no more, and no less, than that 'many women are better than many men at many things' (455d3-4). But what Plato wishes to infer from that observation is a principle that most Greeks could only have found audacious and unsettling.

The case for female Guardians involves two major components: a rebuttal of the belief that men and women have distinct natures, and should therefore fulfil separate social roles; and an appeal to the paramount value of the city's unity, to support the contention that it is in the interests of the society as a whole that the best women should perform the functions for which they are fitted. Plato incorporates into his case an emphatic denial that existing traditions and institutions are an authoritative guide to either what *could* or what *should* be the case. Instead, Plato relies on an alternative understanding of 'nature', to reveal the potential for different forms of life from those currently practised; and upon the principles of ethics, to establish what is best for a city or community.

Plato's argument postulates that social conventions are not only relative and changeable, but also highly plastic or malleable. For this reason, they can, it seems, just as easily contravene as agree with nature (cf. esp. 456c1-2), so that social conventions cannot themselves be safely invoked as evidence of nature. Where, then, is 'nature', in the relevant sense, to be found or located? The answer endorsed by bk. 5, with only marginal qualifications, is: in the potential of *individuals*. Although Plato allows Socrates and Glaucon to agree that the female sex (*genos*) as a whole exhibits a certain inferiority to the male (455c-d), the case for female Guardians revolves around the assumption of a distinct 'nature', a set of potential capacities of mind/soul and body (esp. 455b), in each person. It is by stripping down the issue to the level of essential abilities, both intellectual and physical, that Plato sees a way of contesting the generalisations and prejudices that base themselves merely on an existing framework of cultural norms. Only by recognising the specifically individual locus of human nature, he seems to suggest, can we escape from a crude failure to discover what particular women are truly capable of. And the seriousness with which he takes that failure is marked by the proposal that in the ideal city there would be women among the supreme philosopher-rulers of the state.

Plato's insistence on the individual natures of human beings reflects a wider belief that the psyche or soul is somehow prior to society, because it is the soul which contains the elemental forces (reason, spiritedness, desire) that supply the dynamics of behaviour: as bk. 4 clearly affirms, the character of a society derives from the forces present in each soul (4.435e).[23] The conception of female Guardians, accordingly, is the product of an argument for educating and utilising the mental, physical and moral qualities of particular women – those who, like their male counterparts, possess the 'best natures' available to the city (456e-7b, with 7.519c8-9). But this way of putting the point alerts us to one aspect of the tension, to which I have already drawn attention (p. 8), between individual and collective factors in the overall scheme of bk. 5. For if this scheme seeks to define the 'nature' of a person in terms of basic mental and physical capacities, and thus to escape from socially predetermined ideas of male and female roles (with the sole exception of reproductive function), it does so in the service of a cause that is collectivist and anti-individualist in character. The state needs to make the most of its women, not for the sake of giving particular women a chance for personal fulfilment, in the sense of an individually chosen form of life, but in order to pursue the common good and the greater unity (which is also the greater justice) of the city as a whole. It is quite misplaced to speak of 'opportunities' or 'freedom of action' for women in this context.[24] Freedom, in fact, is simply not a functioning value of the ideal city of the *Republic*, least of all for the Guardians or their top echelon, the Rulers. In bk. 7, the need to breed philosopher-rulers in the city is summed up by saying that the aim is not for the law 'to leave them free to do what each of them wants, but to use them to bind the city together' (520a3-4). That principle is germane to every aspect of the Guardians' lives treated in the preceding books of the dialogue.

What is true of the entire Guardian class is necessarily true of the women, both Rulers and Auxiliaries, within it. Plato's female Guardians, it has to be stressed, will not *choose* their form of life. For these women, individual satisfaction, as something peculiar or distinctive to a particular person, is not only not provided for, but utterly contrary to the ideology of their group. Everything about their upbringing, education and social behaviour is designed to instil in them, as in their male counterparts, a collectivist spirit and a denial of 'individualism' (*idiôsis*, 462b8). But this allows us to address head-on the question of whether Plato can be called at least a proto-feminist. For beneath its various forms, modern feminism is a phenomenon whose roots are essentially liberal, and to that extent individualist. But as we have seen, the principle of freedom is irrelevant to the existence of Plato's Guardians. Without such a principle, any strong notion of women's 'rights' becomes hard to sustain. Because of the role-equality for the Guardians envisaged in bk. 5, it might seem superficially plausible to say that the women of the class have the same rights as their male counterparts. But the concept of a 'right' is surely quite out of place here, since Guardians, whether male or female, have no choice but to perform the administrative, political and other functions that are expected of them.[25] It is deeply significant that the one passage in the *Republic* which does mention the freedom of women occurs in the context of a harsh criticism of democracy. for Plato, (alleged) 'equal legal rights (*isonomia*) and freedom' between the sexes can be cited alongside the degree of liberty allowed (again, allegedly) to slaves in democracies; both are symptoms of disorder and degeneracy.[26]

But if Plato should not be portrayed as a proponent of the rights or freedoms of women, it remains true and important that in one vital respect his proposal for female Guardians does represent a case for the equal treatment of women with men. This is because of the contention, already mentioned, that the nature of an individual should be interpreted in terms of basic or essential capacities, both mental and bodily. By arguing at this level, Plato is able to suggest that there is no intrinsic difference of aptitude between the sexes, other than that of reproductive functions (454d10 f.). It is a crucial element in the organisation of the Guardians' lives that even this biological difference will not be allowed to have extensive social consequences: thus, female Guardians will carry no special responsibility for child-care beyond that of breast-feeding, and the latter will be planned so as to control the demands made on the women; in all other matters, they will be relieved of domestic and parental burdens (460b-d). These and other arrangements are designed to create conditions in which the intellectual and physical abilities of female Guardians can be developed just as effectively as those of the men, to the maximum potential of each individual. And put in this way, Plato's position does indeed have some resemblance to feminism. But that is not because it *is* a feminist position; it is only because some of its considerations, and even some of its results, are *compatible* with feminism. So it is not surprising that we can find parallels at certain points between bk. 5's arguments and the contentions of later writers advocating specifically feminist theses.[27]

Such parallels do nothing, however, to affect the cardinal fact that the equality contained in bk. 5's proposals is a role-equality (employing women alongside men in all activities) which is entirely at the service of state-controlled collectivism. On Plato's scheme, the existence of female Guardians will be the result not of free choice or inclination, but of a stringently regulated system of social functions, to which individuals, with only rare exceptions (n. 456a8), are tied by birth and training, and compulsorily committed by ideology. If we wish to conclude, therefore, that there is indeed a particular kind of female equality enshrined in this programme, we must also recognise that it is an equality divorced from the value of individual liberty, and one which falls even further short of anything that can be called 'egalitarianism'.[28]

Moreover, the form of role-equality advocated in bk. 5 can most aptly be understood as a *minimisation of gender*. By attempting to reduce the impact of child-bearing, in the way described above, and by insisting on the capacity of women to participate alongside men in athletic, military and political activities, Plato constructs an ideal which ought to alter the intrinsic conception of women as a *genos*. Bk. 5 does not dispense with such a conception, but it implicitly reduces it to the single factor of reproductive function. (Even relative physical weakness should probably be regarded as a contingent feature, not a necessary characteristic.) The notion of women as forming a *genos* definable by essential intellectual or psychological differences from men is therefore discarded. This implication should not be obscured by the problem of (in)consistency with things said elsewhere in the *Republic* or in other works, nor by certain details in bk. 5 which seem to betray residual male prejudices.[29] Both of these considerations are real, and not unimportant; but they cannot detract from the argument's central impetus towards the minimisation of gender within the society of the Guardians. Bk. 5 presumes that in many activities, including the supreme fields of philosophy and politics, the lives of male and female Guardians could be almost indistinguishable; and it supposes that such an aim could be carried a very long way even in the sphere of military training and warfare (§3 below). For that reason, the radicalism of the idea of female Guardians resides not so much in the specifics of a way of life, as in the degree to which Plato's case approaches a gender-neutral interpretation of 'human nature'. And in that sense we have grounds for judging that what is really at issue in much of bk. 5 is not a view of women,[30] but a philosophical conception of human beings as creatures to whose lives biological gender can be made largely irrelevant.

But that judgement leaves room for one further question about Plato's position. If *Rep.* 5 seeks to minimise the social implications (within the Guardian class) of the different reproductive roles of men and women, its arguments nonetheless display a keen sense of the workings of individual sexual desire. Although there is some uncertainty whether Plato regards male and female as entirely 'symmetrical' in this respect, it is clear that he not only allows for the operation of sexual desire between particular Guardians, but even wishes to encourage and exploit this behaviour for certain purposes.[31] This might prompt one to ask where, in the final analysis, sexual desire and love might belong in the form of life planned for the Guardians. The question is potentially puzzling, because of one central fact – that while, within certain contexts and limits (as controlled by the Rulers), members of the Guardian class can seek overtly sexual encounters with one another, no two Guardians can be imagined as sharing, in anything *more* than a sexual act, a relationship that is theirs and theirs alone: for any such relationship would necessarily count as a symptom of individualism, and pose a threat to the unity of the group. But what this must mean, if Plato's designs are understood in strict consistency, is that the Guardians' sexuality will be severed from any other expression of personal affection or social intimacy. Instead, all erotic feelings and behaviour, however intensely individual they may be in their immediate physical manifestations, must be translated into a contribution to the bonding and the greater good of the class (and the city) as a whole. It is because of this that Plato's arguments for female Guardians are followed and reinforced in bk. 5 by a scheme of eugenics and reformed kinship relations; and it is to these, therefore, that we now need to turn.

§2.2 Eugenics and Kinship

The communistic life of the male Guardians had been sketched at the end of *Rep.* 3 (416-17), and bk. 5 submits that women too should be totally integrated into this arrangement. Plato takes it as following from this (457c7-8)[32] that marriages and families (i.e. the *oikos*, the most basic unit of Greek society) will have to be abolished in the Guardian class, since both institutions represent forms of individual or private interest which are incompatible with collectivist ideology and behaviour – in short, with maximum *koinônia* (cf. p. 7). The abolition of these institutions will be complemented by two pieces of positive policy: first, a scheme of eugenics, controlled by the Rulers, to ensure that only the 'best' of the Auxiliaries breed with one another, and that only fully fit offspring are allowed to be brought up by the class;[33] second, a conception of communal kinship, whereby the primary parent-child and sibling relationships connect extensive groups of people, rather than small groups and individuals. Both of these striking elements in Plato's programme merit closer scrutiny.

Attention to conditions and factors which will, or are believed to, conduce to production of fit offspring, is probably a feature of virtually all human societies. In ancient Greece, aristocratic ideas of the inherent quality (the *eugeneia*) of select families, or lineages, were widespread and influential; however arbitrary their rationale may have been, their effects were considerable and long-standing. The Guardians of the *Republic* can be regarded, to a degree, as a kind of in-breeding aristocracy, though one whose qualities are ultimately philosophical and entirely lacking in the inherited prestige or privileges of actual Greek aristocracies. In more concrete and *ad hoc* terms, we know that practical principles of eugenics, in a relatively basic sense of the term, had some currency in classical Athens; Plato himself, at *Tht.* 149d5-8, describes them as part of the medical or technical knowledge of midwives (cf. n. 460c8). Outside Athens, it is reasonably clear that the ruling class of Sparta held beliefs about the potential eugenic significance of factors such as age at marriage, parental diet, exercise and the regulation of intercourse.[34] Given the many other strands of Spartan influence on Plato's thinking, it is a ready inference that this precedent helped to shape bk. 5's conception of eugenics:

there are, in fact, some verbal hints to this effect in Plato's text.[35] A further though more conjectural source of influence may have been the existence of special tenets of 'breeding' (*gennêsis*), akin to those in Sparta, held or practised by some Pythagoreans.[36]

Whatever weight any of these models may have carried with Plato, there is another element which can be unequivocally identified as active in his eugenic arguments – the comparison of human beings with other social animals. This pattern of argument had been employed in fifth-century intellectual circles: its use by some Sophists is attested, and this will probably explain its echoes in a number of passages of Aristophanes.[37] What is at issue here is certainly nothing that could lay claim to scientific status, and it is arguably true that 'Plato knew virtually nothing about animals'.[38] But it is undoubtedly true that he believed certain things about them, and was prepared to deploy these beliefs in constructing philosophical arguments.[39] In the *Republic*, the very concept of a Guardian class is predicated from the outset upon an animal analogy: the younger Guardians, or Auxiliaries, are defined in terms of a mixture of aggressiveness and gentleness – equated with 'spirit', *thumos*, and 'philosophy' – which is supposed to be found in dogs, especially guard-dogs (*phulakes*, the same term as 'Guardians'), as well as some other animals.[40] This type of consideration recurs at a number of points in the course of the work, including bk. 5 itself. The following are the main examples of animal analogy and imagery to be found in bk. 5:

451c8-e2: the Guardians are guard-dogs or sheepdogs (cf. 466d1), the people are the 'flock' (cf. 459e1–3). Since dogs of both sexes can perform the same tasks, the analogy serves to symbolise the case for female Guardians.

459a-b: the practice of animal breeding (of dogs, birds, horses, etc.) is used to initiate the idea of eugenic breeding among the Guardians.

466d7: the full partnership or sharing, *koinônia*, of female with male Guardians is said to be of the kind found 'among other animals' (cf. dogs, 466d1).

467a10 f.: the willingness of parent animals to fight on behalf of their offspring is cited as a model for the courage of the Auxiliaries.

We can see from these passages that Plato introduces the example of animals in two distinct ways: first, as illustration of what naturally happens among social creatures, and could therefore, by presumed extrapolation, happen among human beings too; second, to make observations on ways in which animals are *used* by humans. The first of these aims supports Plato's general strategy in bk. 5 of contending, by appeal to 'nature', that many social practices are artificial and radically alterable. But the second aim is perhaps even more far-reaching. It is reinforced by other occurrences of animal breeding terminology at 454d10 f., 460a9, c1, 461b5 (see nn.), and its implication is that if men can improve and adapt other animals by selective breeding, they should equally be able to do so with themselves (cf. 4.424a5-b1). Upon the feasibility of this startlingly eugenic proposal depends the status of the Guardians as a military, political and philosophical élite.

The model of animal breeding takes us, of course, well beyond any ordinary desire to produce fine offspring, for it necessitates the translation of this desire into a systematic pursuit. But this translation raises large and formidable difficulties. Two fundamental requirements for organised eugenics of the kind envisaged by Plato are expertise and control. As to the first, *Rep.* 5 itself gives inadequate grounds for believing that the city's Rulers could reliably identify the qualities possessed by each and all of the Guardians under their authority, still less that they have a basis on which confidently to predict how these qualities will be transmitted to the Guardians' offspring.[41] Animals are bred for limited physical variables (speed, size, colour, etc.); the Guardians are required to possess a complex *combination* of attributes, physical, intellectual and moral. In positing such a compound ability, Plato's argument never faces the twin questions of how far these various qualities can be expected to occur in the same person, and whether they are all biologically transmissible (cf. n. 461a8 f.).

But even if such doubts about the scientific basis of the eugenic scheme were slighter, it would still be the case that Plato's use of animal analogies simply presupposes, rather than doing anything to justify, the ethical and political propriety of authoritarian manipulation of the Guardians' breeding habits. A defender of Plato might emphasise that the Rulers are not entirely analogous to animal breeders, since it is the good of the city, not of themselves, which they seek by eugenic means. (Whether animal breeding itself is for the good of the animals need not be pursued here.) But the fact remains that a political scheme of eugenics entails the control of the most personal and intimate aspects of human behaviour, and this is something which could readily lead, as twentieth-century readers of Plato are only too well aware, to ruthlessly sustained techniques of interference, prohibition and social engineering.

The price which Plato is prepared to contemplate for his eugenic system includes not only the general rigidities of the class structure itself, but also compulsory abortion (461c5), exposure (460c3-5), an elaborate use of political deception (459d-e), and the prevention of sexual pair-bonding. Everything about the lives of the Guardians is meant to make possible the absolute degree of control which the Rulers will need to exercise over them. But there remains one crucial weakness close to the very heart of this design. Whatever the chances that other aspects of human behaviour might yield to the extreme pressures of a collectivist ideology and social training, Plato himself accepts that sexuality represents a universal instinct of human nature (458d), and that it is irreducibly located in the desires of individuals (468c2-3). Such desires can be manipulated by both impediments and encouragements, but not even Plato believes that humans are infinitely manipulable in this respect. The risk of sexually caused resentment and frustration, acknowledged at 459e3, is something which could hardly be avoided or suppressed by propaganda alone, as the argument there implausibly envisages.

It is, besides, a vital element in bk. 5's programme that sexual desires will be expected to operate strongly in some Guardians, at least some of the time. Yet the book leaves it uncertain how these desires could be consistently aligned with the eugenic policies of the Rulers. There is here, in short, a huge and intractable gap between the principles sketched in bk. 5, and the practical means indicated for their implementation. I think we are bound to conclude that, at the very least, the successful maintenance of the Guardian class would depend much more upon the training of its members for particular military and political duties, than upon the capacity of the Rulers to supervise and predict the outcome of the Auxiliaries' sexual unions.

The problems just identified within bk. 5's eugenics are partly a matter of inadequate knowledge on the part of the Rulers: as Plato himself virtually acknowledges (8.546a-b, cf. 3.415b1-3), it would be all too easy for misjudgements to be made. But they also reflect tensions between nature and society, the individual and the community – or, to use terms often preferred by Plato, the soul and the city.[42] Such tensions remain of central significance when we turn to the collective kinship outlined in bk. 5. As with Plato's case for female Guardians, the abolition of the family is a proposal which appears to anticipate the arguments of some modern feminists. But this resemblance is superficial.[43] Plato's motivation here has nothing to do with improving the lives of women *per se*. It is true that the duties of female Guardians necessitate that they be relieved of child-rearing work (460c-d). But that practical aim could have been achieved without the abolition of the family, which is independently motivated on two grounds: first, as part of the eugenic programme, already considered, which requires the 'best' men and women to breed for the state;[44] secondly, and more fundamentally, by the goal of engendering the maximum sense of unity among the Guardians (462a ff.). The family, with its related patterns of kinship, is treated in *Rep.* 5 as an obstacle to such unity; it is a major manifestation of 'individualism' (*idiôsis*, 462b8), which divides a class or a city by fragmenting it into separate units of private property (cf. the faintly satirical images of family and property at 464c-e, 465c).

The institution of the domestic family is therefore incompatible with the ideology of the Guardian class. If this class is to experience the fullest *koinônia*, the deepest sense of shared pleasures and pains, it must be turned into a large, single 'family' in its own right – that is the thrust of Plato's programme of kinship for the Guardians. But this programme, which would make all relations hold between extended bands of people, is open to objection on two levels, the practical and the theoretical. On the practical level, the arrangements necessary for the operation of any such network of collective kinship would need to be much more complex than Plato's sketch seems to recognise. There are, for one thing, problems in the definition and regulation of incest which are left unclear at 461b-e (n. 461e1-2). But there are also much wider difficulties with the application of kinship terminology to groups of Guardians. If, as certain passages seem to suggest, the only recognised relationships are to be those between parents and children (extendable to grandparents/children) and between siblings, there are certainly definitional and administrative intricacies of which the text gives no hint. But if these relationships are not exhaustive, then the kinship scheme would necessarily contain varying degrees of affinity, and this would amount to a flaw in the desired homogeneity of attachment among the members of the class.[45]

It would be a mistake to suppose that such objections are merely pedantic, or fail to address the spirit of Plato's proposals. It cannot be pedantic to question the practical obscurities or even incoherences of what is put forward as a workable plan. Moreover, recognition of detailed difficulties is one way of drawing attention to the theoretical problems that beset Plato's arguments for a collective kinship. For the details I have mentioned stem from the fact, so awkward for Plato's purposes, that kinship must have *exclusive* as well as inclusive implications. It is central to the argument of bk. 5 that collective kinship will be a means of binding *all* members of the Guardian class together: within the projected system, no Guardian will be able to regard any other as alien or unrelated (463b-c). Even if the unity of the Guardians, a group of perhaps a thousand people (n. 458b9 f.), could be effected through a radical conception of common kinship, it could surely only be at the expense of making members of the class perceive themselves as more closely related to one another than to the rest of the population. Since the ultimate and overriding aim is the unity of the city as a whole, this consequence looks like a grave weakness in the argument (n. 465b9-10). But how, in any case, can a scheme of collective kinship be achieved without introducing gradations of affinity (see above)? Plato's answer, namely to transfer onto groups of Guardians the structural categories of the family, is irreducibly paradoxical, given that it is the character and consequences of the family as an institution which his entire design is intended to eradicate.

That the kinship proposed for the Guardians represents not so much a new system of relationships as the projection of existing relations onto larger groups, emerges most clearly from 463c-d (cf. 465a11 f.). There Plato explicitly suggests that the feelings and behaviour prescribed by customary morality (*nomos*) for the treatment of (e.g.) fathers, would be carried over into a context where people would regard many others, not specific individuals, as their parents. Such considerations highlight the paradoxical nature of Plato's case. This case depends, for its larger force, upon acceptance of the cultural malleability of kinship, as of other social practices. Bk. 5 even proposes the remoulding of what might be thought to be the most directly biological component of kinship, the relation between mother and child (460c-d). It is as if, in other words, the entire fabric of kinship could be fashioned and determined by purely social arrangements, and by the ideology which supports them. Yet at the centre of the revised kinship envisaged for the Guardians lie precisely the psychological and ethical dynamics – the affective and behavioural bonds between parents and children, brothers and sisters, etc. – which are currently manifested within the individual family. If, as Plato's argument presupposes, the forms of kinship shape the emotional loyalties of the lives to which they apply, how can we know that a bond between those who call one another (e.g.) 'father' and 'son' will mean the same thing within a communistic group as it does within a nuclear family? To sustain this and similar objections against the Platonic scheme for the Guardians, we do not have to appeal to 'nature' (which is not to say that we *cannot*). We need only to observe that Plato assumes, without any argument, that he can identify psychological components of kinship which would survive transplantation from the family to the collective organisation within which all Guardians will live.

Thus Plato proposes to abolish the family while relying on an interpretation of kinship behaviour which is modelled directly on the family itself. But there is an even more fundamental level at which this critique of his proposal can be pursued. Bk. 5's paradigm for the unity of feeling desired among the Guardians is the individual – both in his sense of identity (signalled by the use of 'mine', 462c, 463e), and in the psycho-physical integration of his awareness (462c10 ff.). In addition to the logical difficulties, commented upon by Aristotle (n. 462c4-8), which attach to the first of these points, it is conceptually remarkable that Plato should emphasise the nature of individual identity and consciousness in the very passage where he is arguing for the effacement of individualism, *idiôsis* (462b8), from the lives of his Guardians. As with the family, so with the individual: Plato's thesis implicitly hypothesises the transference of certain psychological and ethical forces from existing patterns of mentality onto new social structures and the ideology that informs them. The Guardians are to lose, so far as possible, their identity as individuals, and are to acquire a new identity as members of a collective class (cf. *Laws* 12.942a-d for a militaristic model of this). But the social entity which will bestow this new identity is conceived of in terms of the very institutions from which the Guardians are purportedly to be free: the Guardian class is itself to be a family and an individual writ large.

There is, of course, a crucial distinction between the status of family and individual for Plato's argument. The former may function as a source of kinship categories and principles, but as a separate form of life it would indeed be abolished from the Guardian class. Individuality cannot be so abolished, and, as I have stressed in previous sections of this Introduction, it is a force which Plato acknowledges at several important points in his account of the Guardians' lives. A collective system of kinship is a crucial element of the proposal to reduce and limit individualism among the Guardians, but it cannot alter the fact – which lies at the heart of Plato's psychology throughout the *Republic* – that human societies are conceivable only if there are individual humans to inhabit them.

§3 War, Greeks & Barbarians

The issue of practical 'possibility' is a *leitmotiv* in bk. 5 (n. 471c6 'put aside'). Plato is at pains to emphasise that his imaginary city ('Kallipolis', the beautiful/ noble city: 7.527c2) represents a structure and organisation which, however ambitious, *are* within the scope of an actual human society: in that respect, the *Republic* purports to be idealistic but not utopian. One index of Plato's anxiety to avoid the charge of utopianism is the fact that he wishes the city to be imagined as existing in the actual, i.e. non-ideal, Greek world, and as maintaining a variety of relations with other Greek cities, as well as with barbarian peoples outside Greece. Right from the start of the 'founding' of the imaginary city in bk. 2, it was hypothesised that its people would engage in trade (2.370e5 ff.), and bk. 5 itself assumes that inhabitants of the city will attend Panhellenic festivals (470e10 f.), such as those at Delphi or Olympia.[46] But contact between an ideally just society and its neighbours could scarcely be guaranteed to be free of conflict, and parts of bk. 5 contemplate the implications of this for the city.

Plato gives the governing class of his city the name of 'Guardians' in part because it is their function to protect the city from outside attack (3.414b2, cf. *Tim.* 17d). Hence the lower and younger section of the class, the Auxiliaries, can be referred to as 'the military' (*to polemikon*, e.g. 4.434b2-3): they are conceived of as a kind of standing army, and a good deal of their education is to be devoted to the development of physical strength, as well as to the acquisition of specifically military skills. One of the Auxiliaries' two principal characteristics, the possession of keen 'spirit' or 'mettle' (*thumos*), is a quality with an aggressive aspect to it (n. 456a4), though it has to be tempered, in their behaviour as a whole, by the gentler attributes of philosophical virtue. It is the latter part of this combination, with the intellectual and cultural pursuits designed to foster it, which is meant to save Plato's conception of the Auxiliaries' life from the criticism that he himself brings against the excessively militaristic soldiers of Sparta and Crete.[47] So the Auxiliaries will be *more* than soldiers, though that does not diminish the fact that they will be highly trained to fight and kill, when called on by their Rulers to do so.

Because the arguments of bk. 5 depend, as we have seen (§2.1), on the principle that women have essentially the same human nature as men, it follows that (some) women are just as well endowed as (some) men for the duties of Auxiliaries: that women might be, for example, naturally less aggressive than men, is an idea which Plato seems not to entertain. The joint participation of women and men in these duties is an aspect of the *koinônia*, the 'sharing' and communal existence, that has been stressed in earlier sections of the Introduction: Guardians of both sexes will receive the same physical education and training, they will share the same life in communal messes or barracks (458c8-9), and they will campaign together (466e4). Although Glaucon voices a residual uncertainty about the exact details of women's role in warfare, the cause of this is probably only the assumption of relative physical 'weakness' (n. 471d3-5). The crucial principle of the women's participation in military training and combat is not put in doubt: for practical purposes, everything said in bk. 5 about war and the Auxiliaries should apply equally to women and to men.

Since Plato believes that the root causes of war are a sense of one's own property, and a desire for increased wealth (2.373d-e, cf. *Phdo* 66c-d), war is not something which the Guardians will seek or pursue. Yet warfare can still be regarded as a kind of 'craft' or 'profession' for the Auxiliaries, and one to which their children must be collectively 'apprenticed' (466e-7a). In this last respect, Plato has in mind something very radical – a kind of youth corps, of children (girls as well as boys) from perhaps as young as seven (n. 466e5), travelling with the army on certain campaigns, and organised with two aims in view: first, that they should become used to the whole military way of life (467a1-2), including at least a taste of the danger of it (467c1-3); second, that by watching warfare and witnessing celebrations of victory, they should learn to appreciate and in time to emulate the bravery of their collective 'parents'. Such experience is obviously most important for adolescents who are approaching the age of service themselves. These will be the object of erotic feelings from the adult Auxiliaries (468b-c), and such feelings are evidently held to contribute to the creation of bonds between the members of the class, especially in the intense atmosphere of a campaign. Here Plato is adapting an idea which was already associated with homosexuality among soldiers, though he suggests that heterosexual relations too could function in this way.[48]

In any case, there is a potential source of difficulty here, since the intensity of individual erotic attachments needs to be harnessed to the unity of the group as a whole. This is a problem which does not peculiarly concern the life of the Auxiliaries on campaign; the tension between individual and collective values is one which affects the conditions of their entire existence as a class (see §§2, 2.2). It has a certain salience in the military context, however, because it is there that Plato lays some stress on the scope for the distinctive courage of individuals. He conceives of such heroism (cf. the comparison to Homeric heroes at 468c10 ff.) as something which, for the sake of honour, encouragement, and the creation of role-models for the younger relations of the Auxiliaries, deserves to be publicly recognised with rewards that include sexual privileges (468b-c). If we ask why Plato should argue for such a state of affairs, there are perhaps two main elements to be incorporated into an answer. The first is that he must assume the benefits are ones which effectively accrue to the Guardians, and the city, as a whole, not just to the individuals involved: in both practical terms (military success, the preservation of the city) and ethical terms (the enhancement of virtue among the Guardians), the beneficiary is the entire community and its collective preservation. The second point is that, insofar as sexual privileges give scope for heterosexual desires, Plato may here once more be concerned with eugenics – i.e. with promoting breeding between the 'best natures' among the Auxiliaries, in the belief that genetic transmission of more than strictly physical attributes is possible (n. 461a8 f.). These suggestions do not solve all the difficulties that beset the provisions for intense erotic attachments between Auxiliaries. But they do identify conceivable justifications for the otherwise paradoxical promotion of individual passions within the context of a highly collectivist ideology.

But it is unquestionably this ideology which defines both the need for, and the nature of, courage on the part of the soldiers. The role of 'defenders of the city' which both Rulers and Auxiliaries fulfil is built, as we saw, into the the very conception of their identity as 'Guardians', *phulakes*. Although the point is nowhere made explicit, this must provide the main reason for the Rulers ever to send the city to war (cf. the Commentary, p. 182). Once at war, the Auxiliaries are expected to fight with unconditional commitment to the communal cause: failure to do so will bring demotion from the Guardian class (468a5-7); and surrender to the enemy is intended to be unthinkable, since, unlike the warriors of ordinary Greek cities, the Auxiliaries have no hope of ever being ransomed from captivity (468a9-10). These principles are not wholly unprecedented; they have some affinities with established Greek ideas of fighting for one's city or community.[49] But the status of the Guardians in relation to their city demands of them a thoroughness of virtue which goes beyond anything easily imaginable in a historical Greek society. That is because the Guardians will always, by definition, be fighting in a just cause, and will always be fighting to vindicate the entire 'philosophy' which they represent. If they fail to live up to the highest standards of virtue, which in this context means an unwavering readiness to die for the city, they will not only be jeopardising the city's safety, they will be denying *their own identity* as embodiments of courage.

If that last observation pitches the expectations on the Auxiliaries at an idealistically high level, Plato's sketch of principles for the city's attitudes towards its opponents brings us down to an all-too-mundane level of thinking. Bk. 5 gives hardly anything in the way of concrete suggestions for how, when and where the city would resort to military force, but it does supply certain basic 'ethics' of war, and these all depend on a traditional distinction between Greeks and non-Greeks (barbarians). Here it is important to stress that the only definition of justice endorsed in the *Republic*, namely 'each to his own function' (n. 453b5), applies to the internal relations either of the city or of the individual soul; if it is applicable at all to inter-state relations, this is something we are never told. By contrast, the principles which are supplied for the city's dealings with others perfectly fit a definition of justice which was rejected in bk. 1 (332a-5a), i.e. the traditional ethic of helping friends and harming enemies. Bk. 5 reinstates this antithesis, and correlates it directly to the dichotomy between Greeks and barbarians: the equation, it is suggested, is rooted in nature (470c6-8). What was taken to be inadequate as an account of justice *within* a community, where shared civic bonds make the friend/enemy distinction (ideally) inappropriate,[50] is now regarded as a suitable basis for a city's dealings with its fellow-countrymen and with foreign peoples.

With the premise of 'natural' friends and enemies in place, P. offers a set of clear guidelines for military action and conduct. The city can, in fact, be truly at 'war' only with its *enemies*, the barbarians; any conflict with other Greeks must be understood as a lapse into internal 'faction', *stasis*, a term usually reserved for civil unrest within a city (470c, 471a). The pursuit of military action must be regulated in accordance with this fundamental attitude. Force and the destruction of property may be used intensively against non-Greeks, but they must be limited to what is strictly necessary to bring about a peaceful resolution of any dispute with Greeks (470a-71b). Above all, although it would be perfectly acceptable for the city to enslave barbarians, it should never inflict slavery upon fellow-Greeks; indeed, it should actually try to bring about a general change of Greek practice in this respect (469b-c). These tenets might well strike us now as a mixture of humane decency, in their promotion of non-belligerent norms of behaviour between Greeks, and blunt chauvinism, in their insistence on the natural enmity of Greeks and barbarians. But the second part of this judgement should be tempered by the realisation that Plato's city could have little if any motivation for an *offensive* war against foreign enemies, and is probably to be envisaged only as fighting in self-defence.[51] Similarly, a historical appraisal of Plato's position in relation to the practices of his own world, could reasonably combine admiration with disappointment.[52] But it is also possible to ask what implications bk. 5's discussion of warfare has for Plato's broader beliefs about human beings and their lives. Here, two main lines of thought can be briefly suggested.

The first is that bk. 5 juxtaposes, without fully clarifying the relation between, the internal loyalties of inhabitants of the just city, and the sense of 'ethnic' or 'national' kinship (470c2) which is expected to control the conduct of hostilities with other Greek cities. This is a problem which arises especially for the Guardian class, who comprise the soldiers as well as the rulers, and would therefore have to integrate the proposed attitudes into their own decisions and behaviour. I have already mentioned that the Guardians face a tension between the collectivist kinship of their own class, and the looser kinship which needs to bind them to the city's farmers and artisans (p. 19 above). To this tension is added the requirement that the Guardians should feel, and act on, a deep affinity with other Greeks too. It is true, of course, that human beings can feel many different types and degrees of attachment. But it is also observably true that the maintenance of any one allegiance may limit the possible scope for others. In the case of the Guardians, the question is whether their own corporate sense of class-identity, and the extent of their obligations to the city, are compatible with a strongly developed feeling of ethnic patriotism. This objection has a practical as well as a psychological side. The *Republic* does not make it easy to see what practices or institutions would be conducive to bonding between Guardians and other Greeks: panhellenic festivals are the only thing of this kind ever mentioned (470e10). Nor can this be a casual silence. Everything about the life of the Guardians requires that they should be absorbed in, and controlled by, their shared existence. The possibilities of social contact with other Greeks are drastically limited by the political, cultural, and ideological conditions of the city's régime. If, then, patriotism is to take root in the mentality of the Guardians, it could only, one might suppose, be for abstract, philosophical reasons, not because of socially expressible forms of kinship.

But that, after all, is precisely as it should be, given that Plato's entire scheme depends on the subordination of human beings to the demands of philosophical reasoning. This, however, brings us to the second major difficulty with bk. 5's presentation of the Greek-barbarian dichotomy. Plato himself, in other passages and other works, seems to acknowledge, as other Greek thinkers had also done, that the barbarian world is not simply inferior to the Greek world: above all (from his own point of view), it is a world which might even contain special sources of philosophical wisdom (n. 470c1-3). In the largest perspective of Platonic thought, what matters about human beings is not such contingent things as their local attachments or cultural backgrounds, but the fact that they have immortal souls: and on this view, barbarian souls ought presumably to matter just as much as Greek souls. Yet the proposition, emphatically affirmed in *Rep*. 5, that barbarians are 'natural enemies' to Greeks is one which belongs at the level of merely traditional chauvinism, and it is not exposed to the rigorous interrogation which Socrates gave to a friends/enemies ethic at 1.334c-5e. Put another way, this part of bk. 5 conspicuously fails to overcome conventional, culturally relative *prejudice* of just the same kind, so one might well think, as was radically challenged in the case of women (§2.1 above). The charge, in short, is that Plato here fails to live up to his own highest standards of philosophical questioning, instead resting content with attitudes and assumptions which reflect nothing deeper than the readiest preconceptions of his own society.

Whether or not Plato can be defended against this charge, it may be worth adding a broader comment on this aspect of bk. 5. The *Republic*'s entire enquiry into justice centres on the civic framework of a Greek polis, which is taken to represent a largely self-sufficient form of political and social community (as well as an appropriate paradigm for the internal relations of the soul). Such a framework does not in itself predetermine the extent or nature of consideration that might be given to a city's dealings with other states, whether Greek or barbarian. In this connection, it is pertinent that Aristotle, whose *Politics* belongs to the same polis-centred phase of political theory as the *Republic*, is able to criticise Plato, with bk. 5 very much in mind, for giving inadequate attention to his ideal city's relations with its neighbours.[53] So we cannot conclude that the shortcomings of this part of the book are entirely due to limitations inherent in the city-state model of political philosophy. What we can say, however, is that this model has helped to lock Plato into a pattern of argument which focuses with great intensity on the internal politics of the community; and as a result, questions of inter-state politics become relegated to a zone where they can be taken care of by a conventional ethic of 'friends' and 'enemies', superimposed on the Greek-barbarian dichotomy. We can also say that when, later in the fourth century, Greek philosophy began to develop concepts of man that allowed such categories to be transcended, it did so by breaking out of a polis-centred conception of political life.[54]

§4 Philosophy, Knowledge and Value

After the discussion of military organisation has been completed, Glaucon challenges Socrates to address once more the crucial question of 'possibility' (471c-e). From the outset of bk. 5 (450c6-8), Socrates has been concerned to avoid the charge of outright utopianism. Glaucon's renewed challenge on that front indicates the seriousness with which Plato wishes this issue to be taken. Socrates' new response to the question, 'could such a city ever really be brought about?', is in two parts. He starts by saying that the purpose of the imagined city is to provide an ideal or paradigm, *paradeigma*, against which the moral lives of individuals can be tested. It is in the nature of such an ideal not that it should directly match anything already present in the world, but that it should embody standards which can be used to judge real people and things. But Socrates then proceeds to argue that there is one essential condition which *would* anyway make the realisation of the just city truly feasible – namely, philosopher-rulers.

The first of Socrates' two points has its own importance, since it reminds us that the dialogue is an exercise in philosophical enquiry and exploration (p. 2 above), that its concern lies more on the side of guiding principles than of recommendations for immediate action, and that the structure of the city is in part an analogue for the internal relations of the soul. But Plato is not content with that answer, and he allows Socrates to unfold what will turn out to be a long, elaborate and ambitious case for the feasibility of the ideally just city: a case which, with its various ramifications, fills the entirety of bks. 6-7 of the *Republic*. It is not possible here to pursue those subsequent ramifications, but we do need to pay some close attention to how the concept of the 'true philosopher' (475e3) is elucidated in the final pages of bk. 5. If, as Socrates tells us with such intense conviction, the entire happiness of mankind depends upon philosopher-rulers (473c-d), we can reasonably expect to be given a clear, compelling account of the nature of a 'philosopher', and that for at least two reasons: first, because the term was not one which possessed an undisputed significance or applicability in Plato's time (p. 201 below); secondly, because most of those currently called 'philosophers' are disqualified by their apolitical interests from consideration as philosopher-rulers (473d3-5). Without a cogent statement of who *can* count as truly philosophical, then, 'happiness depends on philosopher-rulers' may have a resounding ring, but is unlikely to be a more enlightening proposition than (say) 'happiness depends on those with the political wisdom necessary to create good governement'.

But there seems to be a more specific risk of circularity in Plato's position at this point. From the earlier discussion of the city, it has already emerged that its rulers would need to be people of 'wisdom', *sophia* (esp. 4.428a-e), and that their nature would need to be 'philosophical' (2.375e10 f., 376b-c, 3.410e1). Yet Socrates is now, at the end of bk. 5, contending that the one condition that would make such a city possible is the existence of philosopher-rulers – precisely such people, on a *prima facie* reading, as those posited *within* the sketch of the city's political constitution. Does not Socrates' reponse to Glaucon's challenge, therefore, involve a large *petitio principii*?

The answer to this question, I think, is 'no'. Bks. 2-4 did indeed posit a body of Rulers (and, to that extent, an entire Guardian class from which they would be chosen) endowed with philosophical characters; and the passages cited above indicate that such characters would include intellectual, psychological and ethical qualities. We can say, to that extent, that the discussion has already adumbrated a conception of philosopher-rulers. But that conception has so far functioned as only a sketchy assumption, and Plato's return to the matter at the end of bk. 5 shows that he is aware of this fact. It is only in the argument that now begins to develop that we are told much of what is truly essential to the nature of a philosopher. Between 474 and the end of bk. 7 we will be supplied with a picture of the true philosopher that adds in fundamental ways to the brief hints offered in earlier books. So the final section of bk. 5 initiates a fresh and radical section of the dialogue, and in that sense Socrates is here doing much more than reaffirming a premise previously stated.[55] The pivotal difference between bks. 5-7 and bks. 2-4 can perhaps be most concisely formulated in the following way. Those earlier books presupposed that the Rulers would possess the 'wisdom' required for the just government of the city, but they did not tell us what would make a body of rulers uniquely qualified for this task: bks. 5-7 attempt, in a complex and momentous manner, to supply that so far missing component for the understanding of the *Republic*'s account of justice.

The status of the missing component can be broadly indicated by bringing together some of the hints which will be given in bk. 6 about the nature of ideal philosopher-rulers. They are said to carry with them a mental model, *paradeigma*, of the standards to apply in their political and ethical work (484c-d). For all their capacity to apply themselves to practical matters (484d ff.), they are people concerned with the contemplation of 'all time and being' (486a8-9), and their experience has a visionary quality to it (500b-d). They are capable of a mystical, quasi-sexual union with 'reality' (490b) and the divine (500c9 f., 501b7-c1). And the highest level of their philosophical achievement is knowledge of the transcendent source of all value, 'the form of goodness' (505a ff.). Even these few references are enough to suggest that the account of philosopher-rulers is less an attempt to describe certain human attributes, than a metaphysical and religiously coloured doctrine of the nature of reality itself. Throughout bks. 5-7 this doctrine is partly couched in terms of the rare individuals who are capable of apprehending the ultimate character of reality. We are told, for example, that philosophers are people with a visionary access to 'unchanging being' or 'the truth'. But the most pressing question this raises is surely not, *who* are such people?, but, *what* is this 'being' or this 'truth'?

The last section of bk. 5 lays the foundations for this grandly metaphysical attempt to explicate the proposal that human societies require philosopher-rulers if they are ever to find true justice and happiness. Although it contains numerous difficult details, the basic strategy behind this section of argument is not in doubt. Plato's guiding aim here is to identify philosophers as possessors of special knowledge, the kind of knowledge that could guarantee the political fulfilment of human justice and well-being. *If* the existence of such people – or, rather, of such knowledge – can be established, then it will be evident that they should provide the rulers of society.

The foundations laid by bk. 5 must be understood, I believe, as a combination of imagery and argument, or (even) of rhetoric and logic. Plato begins, and thus sets the tone for, his description of the 'true philosophers' by exploiting emotive metaphors and evocative analogies for their nature. In ways that anticipate recurrent motifs in bks. 6-7 (see above), he suggests that philosophers are indeed *'lovers* of wisdom', whose lives are suffused with a quasi-erotic passion and an insatiable appetite for truth. Their highest apprehensions, Plato implies, have a visionary or mystical quality which carries them beyond the experiences of the rest of mankind (see p. 207). Philosophy stands to ordinary life as does waking to dreaming (476c-d), and as such involves a surer and clearer contact with what is real. These claims and ideas are accompanied by arguments of extreme logical dryness and intricacy; but if we try to interpret the latter in isolation from the former, we run the risk of misrepresenting the motives of Plato's entire conception of philosophy in the *Republic*. When the final arguments of bk. 5 are complete, the visionary and erotic notes previously sounded are recalled and reinforced (479e-80 a). It is this imagery which gives us a crucial clue to the spirit of the whole enterprise, and which must therefore be borne in mind throughout the arguments with which it is associated.[56]

These arguments are notable for their density of ontological terms, i.e. of the language of 'being' used to express abstract and general propositions about what 'exists', 'is x', 'is true' (all possible senses of the verb 'be').[57] Modern philosophical analysis of the arguments, it is fair to say, has been substantially preoccupied with finding a rigorous and consistent interpretation of the ontology of the passage. Yet the difficulty of Plato's use of ontological language in this context – a difficulty reflected in the failure of scholars to agree on such an interpretation – is that it is mostly presented in phrasing and statements of extreme spareness, which oscillate, in their possible meanings, between thoughts of utter simplicity and outright metaphysical rarefaction. The same is true, and for the same reasons, of the terminology of 'knowledge' and 'belief' around which the arguments are built. Depending, then, on one's assumptions and one's overall reading of the passage, there are sentences which one can take either as formulating ideas of uncontentious obviousness, or of profoundly obscure philosophical significance. But even where there may be ostensible grounds for seeking the simpler or more uncomplicated meaning, as in parts of the conversation with an imaginary opponent at 476e6 ff., the fabric of the text continues to pose problems at every turn (see head-note to 476d-480a).

As a result, it is impossible to produce even provisional translations of Plato's meanings without becoming involved in complex issues of interpretation. To take only one example of detail: are we to treat 477a2-4 ('the completely real is completely knowable') as merely affirming a necessary connection between knowledge and truth/existence (in line with ordinary Greek uses of the verb 'to be': see n. *ad loc.*), or as hinting at an esoteric doctrine of 'degrees of reality' that goes far beyond common assumptions and understanding? When such questions are multiplied many times, as they are by other details of the passage, we might wish to conclude that normal interpretative criteria have been thrown into a state of peculiar uncertainty. Although my commentary will address the individual details of argument, and will adopt tentative positions on some of them, my general approach is one which does not attempt to produce a 'solution' of the puzzles they contain.

I remain, therefore, highly sceptical about the chances of discovering a reading of 475e-480a that will succeed in imposing a uniform, unambiguous significance on Plato's ontological language. It seems to me more realistic to suppose that we need to keep in mind more than one sense of the verb 'to be', in order to cope with the interlocking ideas that knowledge is concerned with that which 'is' (476e-7a, 478a 6), while belief attaches to that which simultaneously 'is' and 'is not', and is thus midway between 'being' and 'non-being', or 'reality' and 'unreality' (478d-e). There are specific points in the course of the argument where it is plausible to see one particular sense of 'be' as making better sense than others;[58] but it is hard if not impossible to read the entire passage with a single, strictly limited sense of 'be' in mind, still less to solve the challenge by adopting a consistent decision about translation.[59] And the main reason for this, I suggest, is that Plato's aims in the final section of bk. 5 cannot be *reduced* to the establishment of logically precise distinctions of the kind that might find favour with modern philosophical analysis: if they could, we might expect the distinctions in question to figure a little more explicitly in the text. This is not to deny that Plato's thought has an analytical dimension to it, or that part of his concern is with logical problems which he was to tackle further, and perhaps more successfully, in later works.[60] But we should be encouraged, by what I have called Plato's mixture of imagery and argument, to read the passage as a whole in a way which does justice to its function within the dialogue, and this means recognising the more-than-logical centre of Plato's interests here.

The discussion seeks to contrast true philosophers with non-philosophers. The contrast hinges on the claim that to terms such as 'beautiful' and 'just' there corresponds, in each case, a single entity ('beauty itself', 'justice itself', etc.) which is uniform and immutable (476b, 479a, e). Only philosophers can grasp this; others neither believe it, nor are capable of understanding it (476c, 479a, 479e-80 a). Accordingly, only philosophers have knowledge of such things, while the rest have no more than belief, opinion or judgement (*doxa*: n. 476d6). 'Knowledge' and 'belief' here figure in propositions some of which could be construed as applying to everything to which these names belong: Plato says nothing specifically to the contrary. There are good reasons, however, for not taking the argument as a whole to have so wide a scope. Above all, the terms and concepts with which the argument is concerned appear to be limited to the types from which examples are given at 475e-6a and 479b (see nn.). But we can go further than this, for the avowed aim of justifying the suggestion of philosopher-rulers requires the argument to focus not on knowledge in general, but on knowledge of beauty, justice, goodness.[61] These are the qualities which inform and motivate human action; they are therefore the values that must be realised and maintained by the policies of a city's rulers. Since there are said to be forms of these values which are single, eternal and changeless, it transpires that philosophy is here being defined as, in part at any rate, the knowledge of absolute moral values. And these values, we have to remember, are not accessible to the minds of most people, but only to the 'vision' of the few (476b).

It is suggested at 479a that all particular moral judgements, as applying to individual persons or things, are necessarily relative and unstable. The absolutes which the philosopher knows must therefore be independent of all experience of the material and human world. But this means that, by its own definitions, Plato's text cannot *tell* us what it is that philosophers know, or how it is that they know it: all it can do, as I have already stressed, is resort to mystical and erotic metaphors to evoke an order or dimension of intellectual 'vision' which is not available to most human beings. These observations will remain true even after bks. 6-7 have developed a much fuller scheme of metaphysical arguments (and imagery), and have indicated the shape of philosophical education that would lead the most gifted Guardians to the level of thought (called 'dialectic' in bk. 7) at which they will enjoy their knowledge of unchanging reality.

If Plato's text cannot, and does not purport to, tell us the nature of philosophical knowledge of absolute moral values, then it clearly cannot explain in any detail how philosopher-rulers would bring such knowledge to bear on the society which they govern. This is a critical factor, given the overarching aim that Plato has set himself of justifying the very concept of philosopher-rulers. In bk. 6, Plato will be at pains to stress that his Guardians, contrary to prevailing Greek stereotypes of the philosopher (as unworldly and unpractical), would be capable of full and scrupulous management of the city's affairs. Yet such management will be guided by the knowledge of transcendent moral values. The relationship between absolute and relative values, between ethical knowledge and ethical belief or opinion, is therefore of the essence of government by philosophers, in a way that is not the case with other types of knowledge which the philosopher may possess.[62] But Plato's arguments, in bk. 5 at least, offer little elucidation of how that relationship would function. We have to suppose that the philosopher would judge moral particulars in the light of moral universals, and would be actively aware of how the latter underlie the former. In that sense, philosopher-rulers would fulfil the image of 476c-d: they would be like people who see dreams for what they are worth, not mistaking them for reality but grasping the ways in which they resemble (but also fall short of) it.

This image, however, accentuates the difficulty of construing the philosopher's treatment of moral particulars in the light of – by reference to his inner model or vision of – moral absolutes. It is impossible for those who are awake to explain dreams to those who are experiencing them: on this analogy, philosopher-rulers could never give an account of their moral knowledge to non-philosophers. Accordingly, it cannot simply be that the philosopher has knowledge of general principles – such as definitions of virtues – by which particular cases must be judged. Plato's whole argument rests on the premise that most people do not believe in the existence of such entities as 'justice itself', and are incapable of apprehending them; while the capacity to rise to knowledge of transcendent absolutes is the culmination of a long, arduous process for which only very few minds are equipped (cf. 476b11). This position supplies us with at least three good grounds for inferring that the moral knowledge of the true philosopher amounts to something more than knowledge of general principles or definitions: first, many non-philosophical Greeks *did* believe in some such principles; second, such principles could be at least explained to many people, without the need for years of philosophical training; third, as far as the cardinal virtue of justice is concerned, the *Republic* has already put forward a definition of the virtue (4.433a ff.), yet that definition made no reference to absolute or transcendent standards.

This leaves us, I believe, in a position to say virtually nothing of substance about the (moral) knowledge ascribed to philosophers in the final section of bk. 5. The ascription is made in an argument which removes this knowledge from the realm of normal human experience, and which compounds the consequent impediments to interpretation by applying the imagery of mystical vision and illumination to the philosopher's awareness of entities such as 'beauty itself' and 'justice itself'. Plato's own argument is intrinsically designed so as to leave the reader with a choice between accepting condemnation to the ranks of the *philodoxoi*, 'the lovers of belief' (480a6), or of assenting to an account of philosophical enlightenment which argues by a series of seemingly logical steps for a conclusion that cannot be grasped by logic (at least, the logic of the text) alone. If the *Republic* can supply something more, or something more compelling, than this, to persuade us of the rationale of linking human happiness with philosopher-rulers, it requires its readers to progress to the fuller arguments – and the more graphic imagery – of bks. 6-7.

Notes to the Introduction

1   Arist. *Pol.* 1265a10–12. Of the four terms here, the first three (*peritton, kompson, kainotomon*) are all capable of ambiguous nuances (for P.'s own use of *kompsos* see n. 460a8): Aristotle's remark is a compliment, but it also has overtones of detachment from some of P.'s ways of writing. For Aristotle's critique of bk. 5, see Simpson's article and my Index s.v. Aristotle.

2   This is P.'s formulation at 457c10f.; cf. e.g. Herod. 4.104 (see p. 10). On such phrasing see nn. 451c6 ('possession'), 456b9.

3   8.543c–4b shows that P. thinks of the whole of bks. 5–7 as a section of the dialogue. It is true that 6.502d marks a kind of winding-up of the 'women and children' discussion, but that does not affect the larger point: the discussion of philosopher-rulers *emerges* from the topic of *koinônia*.

4   Vlastos (1991) is a recent and powerful statement of the distinction between Soc. in P.'s early and 'middle' dialogues. But his approach leaves unexplained, to my mind, the elements of *dramatic* continuity between the two groups.

5   This view has been developed by Leo Strauss, *The City and the Man* (Chicago, 1964), and some of his followers: see esp. the 'Interpretive Essay' in A. Bloom, *The Republic of Plato* (New York, 1968), at 379–89, with Bluestone 41–50, 154–62, for criticisms. Z. Planinc, *Plato's Political Philosophy* (London, 1991), finds the argument for female Guardians 'unjust and even ridiculous' (280), and Saxonhouse 45–52 thinks the proposals deliberately unrealisable. More subtly, H.D. Rankin, 'The Comic *Republic*', *Polis* 2.2 (1979) 11–18, suggests that P. evokes comedy as 'a corrective to over-commitment' (18).

6   *Laws* 5.739b–c (cf. 7.807b) identifies the ideal state with one based on 'friends share everything' (see n. 449c5); this is, in effect, a ref. back to the guiding principles of *Rep.* 5. The *Laws*' own proposals for women belong to the 'second best' city, though they still show a leaning towards the ideas of *Rep.* 5: see e.g. nn. 450c1, 452a4–5, 456b2, and cf. Lacey 178–94.

7   For the suggestion that transcendent values exist 'by nature', see n. 476b7–8. The rule of philosophers also involves an appeal to nature: 474c1–2, cf. 6.485a.

8   Bluestone's book provides a lively survey of earlier writings on the subject.

9   On Athenian women see Gould, Just, Lacey ch. 7, Pomeroy (1976) chs. 4–6, Powell ch. 8. Many specific points are taken up in my Commentary.

10   See e.g. nn. 451d6, 452a2, 11, 455c6–7.

11   See Cartledge's article, Michell 45–61, Powell 243–6, and my Index s.v. Sparta. Other Doric states did not follow much of this pattern: cf. Willetts chs. 7–13, Lacey 208–16. Spartan 'sharing' of wives for eugenics: Xen. *Lac.* 1.7–8, with MacDowell (1986) 82–8, Cartledge 102–4. On P.'s general relation to Sparta: E. Rawson, *The Spartan Tradition in European Culture* (Oxford, 1969) 61–72, E.N. Tigerstedt, *The Legend of Sparta in Classical Antiquity*, vol. 1 (Stockholm, 1965) 244–76.

12   The passages of Herod. are discussed in S. Pembroke, 'Women in Charge:...The Ancient Idea of Matriarchy', *J. of the Warburg & Courtauld Institutes* 30 (1967) 1–35, at 3–18. Further Greek texts on communism of women and children are cited by J. Ferguson, *Utopias of the Classical World* (London, 1975) 19–21.

13   On 'utopian' thought in the 5th and early 4th centuries: see F. Solmsen, *Intellectual Experiments of the Greek Enlightenment* (Princeton, 1975) ch. 3. M. Hadas, *CP* 30 (1935) 120–1, posits utopian literature to explain connections between P., Herodotus, and Aristophanes' *Ecclesiazusae*.

14   The evidence of Eur.'s plays, esp. *Medea*, was used to argue for a 'women's liberation' movement by I. Bruns, *Frauenemancipation in Athen* (Kiel, 1900); for qualifications see e.g. Vogt 20–1 (228–9). It is generally accepted that Eur. at least echoes current questions about women. As regards Soc., I dissent from the common ascription to him of radical views on women, e.g. by Vogt 21–2 (229–30), Adam I 280, Wender 84–6, Cantarella 53–4, and, in a popular sketch, F.A. Wright, *Feminism in Greek Literature* (London, 1923) 135–49. Neither Xen. *Symp.* 2.8–9 (women's nature is no worse than men's, 'except for intelligence and strength') nor *Oec.* 3.14–15 (equal importance of wives and husbands for the *oikos*), even if reliable evidence, amounts to a radical divergence from common views; it is significant that Wender 85 treats *Symp.* 2.9 as a *distortion* of Soc.'s own views. Lefkowitz 497 regards Xen. *Oec.* 7.23–4 and 10.1 as evidence for the views of 'Socrates and his followers': this seems to be tenuous (10.1 is merely a response to Ischomachus's description). As for *Meno* 72d–3b, (i) it cannot be safely cited for the attitudes of the historical Soc., (ii) a careful reading (n.b. 73a1–2, b5–c1) shows no radical import for the status of women.

15   The relationship between P. and the early Cynics is obscure. Diogenes of Sinope probably did not come to Athens much before 350, but Antisthenes was some 20 years older than P. On particular details see nn. 449c4, 8, 461e2–3.

16   The Amazons are cited in the (?Platonising) arguments of the 1st cent. A.D. Stoic, Musonius Rufus, for the common education of the sexes (p. 15, 15–18 Hense); also by Proclus, 242.1–4, 253.17–26 Kroll. Their relevance was appreciated in the 19th cent.: e.g. by G. Grote, *Plato and the Other Companions of Sokrates*[2] (London, 1888) IV 196–7, and J.S. Mill, 'On the Subjection of Women' (1869), §I. W.B. Tyrrell, *Amazons* (Baltimore, 1984) 31–3, cites *Rep.* 5, but his book makes no mention of the *Laws*' refs. to the Amazons.

17   Examples are cited by S. Goldberg, *The Inevitability of Patriarchy*[2] (London, 1977) 29–34; Goldberg's own thesis is a controversial defence of physiologically based differences between the mental and behavioural natures of men and women.

18   Quotation: M.R. Lefkowitz, *Women in Greek Myth* (London, 1986) ch. 1, at 27. On the Amazons cf. also Just 241–51, and Tyrrell (n. 16 above). Visual images of these women would have been widely familiar in P.'s time: see *LIMC* I.2 440 ff.

19   There is a collection in Plut., 'Virtues of Women', *Mor.* 242e–263c. Some post-date P., but he could have known e.g. the story of the Argive women manning the walls against Spartan Cleomenes, c.494 (245c–f; absent from Herodotus's narrative of this campaign). That such stories were aetia for religious rituals is argued by F. Graf, *ZPE* 55 (1984) 245–54; cf. also Vidal-Naquet 209–10.

20   That Pythagoras had female followers is claimed by Porph. *Vita Pyth.* 18–19 (DK I 100) = Dicaearchus fr. 33 Wehrli, and Justinus *Epitome* 20.4.8; but these texts, as well as refs. to Pythagoras's wife and/or daughter (e.g. D. Laert. 8.41–2), are subject to severe uncertainties: see Burkert (1972) 114–5, Morrison, *CQ* 6 (1956) 145–6, and KRS 225–7. Later Pythagorean women are discussed by S. Pomeroy, *Women in Hellenistic Egypt* (New York, 1984) 61–71.

21   See Morrison, esp. 201–2, Theslef f 29, 36; cf. *Epist.* 13.360b. Important Platonic affinities with Pythagoreanism are recognised as early as Arist. (e.g.) *Met.* 987b10–13: see Burkert (1972) 15–28, 83–96. P.'s relations with Archytas are reassessed by G.E.R. Lloyd, *Phronesis* 35 (1990) 159–74.

22   For some evidence see de Vogel 110–11, 130–38 (though the treatment of details is unreliable). The 'Speeches of Pythagoras' (Iambl. *Vita Pyth.* 39–57), which may be of 4th cent. origin, contain an injunction against separating parents and children (Iambl. ib. 49): see Demand's article for a speculative argument here.

23   Annas (1981) 179 ascribes to P. the view that '"the city is brave" precisely does not reduce to "there are brave citizens in it"...' But that is exactly what *is* asserted at 4.429a–b. This does not mean that P. is blind to the power of social forces to shape individuals: the *Rep.*'s critique of existing societies, and its identification of the political conditions necessary for justice, presuppose a recognition of just such power.

24   Talk of women's '(equal) opportunities' is extremely common in this context: e.g. Cantarella 58–9, Pierce 2–3, Wender 75–6, Bluestone 11; Wender's claim (76) that 'any woman' will have a chance to become a Guardian, is especially mistaken. But the term 'opportunity' has become inescapably linked with liberal ideals and policies, and should therefore be avoided in describing P.'s position. See Annas (1976) 311–15 for good arguments on this point.

25   Vlastos (1989) characterises *Rep.* 5 entirely in terms of the female Guardians' equality of 'rights', despite admitting (289) that 'liberty' is irrelevant to the scheme. Lefkowitz (1989), while rejecting much of Vlastos's case, continues to talk of 'equal rights' (497). Against this, see Annas (last n.) and Lucas 223 (who denies the applicability of 'rights', but still calls P. a feminist).

26   8.563b: that this freedom falls far short of the goals of modern, democratic feminism, only confirms the gap between Platonic and feminist politics. Cf. also the criticism of Spartan women's freedom cited in section A, p. 10 above.

27   Cf. p. 147 (Mill), and n. 44 below.

28   'Egalitarian' is inapplicable to the female Guardians for two main reasons: one, the term is inextricable from some notion of 'rights' (n. 25 above); two, it is an extremely general, even universal, concept, whereas the Guardians represent a special élite: for the lower class, the scope for development of individual abilities will be largely circumscribed by the system (promotion to the Guardians, n. 456a8, necessarily being a rarity). Yet Calvert, in an otherwise useful article, can speak of parts of bk. 5 as 'completely egalitarian' (243), and characterises P. as, with qualifications, 'an enlightened liberal' (233). See, by contrast, Vidal-Naquet 5: 'Plato did not advocate the equality of men and women, but insofar as possible an equal use of them'.

29   See my nn. on 451c6, 456b9, 457c11, 469d7.

30   When (e.g.) Annas (1981) 185 complains about the involvement of female Guardians in 'fighting and other "macho" pursuits', she intimates that there is something wrong with P.'s ideas for *women*; but if her criticism is worth making, it ought, I suggest, to be aimed at P.'s ideas for the Guardians as a whole. Analogously, a complaint that P. has ignored the lives of non-Guardian women in his city, ought rather to be a complaint about his neglect (if it is that) of the third class as a whole. Nor can I agree with Lefkowitz (1989) 484 that female Guardians are 'for the use and benefit of *men*': the Guardian class as such is conceived for the benefit of the city as a whole. The idea of the Guardians as quasi-men is at least as old as Rousseau's *Émile*, bk. 5.

31   Male and female desire: see nn. 458d2–3, 468c3. Annas (1976) 319 says that 'no importance at all is given to individuals' choices' in sex, but cf. 460b, 468c.

32   457c7–8 indicates the relationship; cf. W.S. Jacobs, *Apeiron* 12 (1978) 29–31. Okin ch. 2 argues a different view: for good criticism see Bluestone 102–8.

33   See my nn. on 459d9 f., 460c4–5.

34   See Critias fr. 32 DK (diet and exercise of both parents), from his *Constitution of the Lacedaimonians*; Xen. *Lac.* 1.3–10 (diet, exercise, regulation of intercourse, occasional sharing of wives for eugenic purposes: cf. n. 11 above).

35   See n. 459e3 on the use of the term *agelê*.

36   Such tenets occur in Aristoxenus fr. 39 Wehrli, Iambl. *Vita Pyth.* 209–13 (DK I 475–6), covering age at marriage, the importance of exercise for girls as well as boys, and regulation of intercourse; cf. de Vogel 179–80, 236–7, 269–70.

37   See Xen. *Mem.* 4.4.20 (Hippias), Ar. *Clouds* 1427–31, *Birds* 755–9, 1347–50.

38   Dover (1978) 167.

39   Some other examples: *Critias* 110b–c (equality of tasks between the sexes of social animals); *Laws* 1.636b5–6 (sexual pleasure), 3.690b7 (rule by the stronger), 7.789b–4 (effects of movement), 8.836c3–6, 840d (the unnaturalness of homosexuality). Fortenbaugh (1975a) 295–6 suggests that *Laws* lacks the *Rep*'s use of animal analogy to reinforce a conception of breeding for functional specialisation. On bk. 5's analogies cf. e.g. Rankin (1964) 53–4, id. (1965) 417–20, Lefkowitz (1989) 484/497 (comparing Theogn. 183–8). Wender 76 is prepared to accept that P.'s ideas were genuinely influenced by his observation of dogs. P. nowhere expresses concern for the lives of animals as such: see the satirical view of animals under democracy at 8.563c.

40   2.375a ff.; for 'other animals' see 375d10.

41   See n. 461a8 f. for one acute problem about P.'s idea of 'genetics'.

42   Part of the problem is an asymmetry between social classes and parts of the soul: thus, the Auxiliaries are, above all, the embodiment of *thumos*, the middle part of the soul; yet their individual souls also contain reason and desire, the latter being principally at work in their sexuality. Cf. n. 466b1.

43   For comparison of P.'s abolition of the family with the same proposal by feminists, see Annas (1976) 319, and M. Midgley & J. Hughes, *Women's Choices* (London, 1983) ch. 3, esp. 87–93.

44   Although P. might have posited permanent marriages between couples of 'the best', he presumably wishes to keep open the possibility of individuals who will breed with more than one of the opposite sex (cf. Sparta, n. 11 above).

45   For the complexities inherent in P.'s proposals, see nn. 461d4, e1–2, 463c5–7.

46   One topic nowhere mentioned is the admittance of outsiders. Given the strictness of the social system, it is hard to see how the city could tolerate much of this, and P. probably takes for granted a quasi-Spartan exclusivity (cf. my n. on 10.595a5, 'refusal'): this point is made explicit at *Laws* 12.952d–3e.

47   See esp. *Laws* 2.666e–7b; cf. n. 458c8–9.

48   See n. 468c3 for the question whether P. intends symmetry between the sexes in this context. Greek refs. to military homosexuality: Dover (1978) ch. IV.

49   See e.g. n. 468a5–6, on laws concerning deserters etc. in Athens and elsewhere.

50   If a city is a true unity, then all its citizens must be 'friends', *philoi*: cf. 3.412d, 8.547c2, 9.590d6, *Tim.* 17d, and n. 463b1.

51   Note that, after the point about slaves (469b–c), the following prohibitions on booty seem to refer to *all* military contexts, as 469e8 indicates: in any case, the Guardians could never countenance a war designed to bring wealth to the city. It is true that G.'s remark at 469c6–7 might imply the idea of an offensive campaign, but the argument as a whole leaves it unclear why the city should ever undertake such an action. Cf. head-note to 466d–471c.

52   See n. 469c5.

53   Arist. *Pol.* 1265a20 ff.

54   M. Schofield, *The Stoic Idea of the City* (Cambridge, 1991) chs. 3–4, argues that the difference between classical and Hellenistic modes of political thinking can be nicely seen within early Stoicism, in the transition from Zeno's *Politeia* (which was influenced by P. himself, ch. 2) to the new ideals of 'cosmic citizenship' and 'natural rights' that transcend the city-state model.

55   We need, in any case, to distinguish two ways of construing the question about 'possibility': one, focussing on bringing the city into being; the other, on the sustainability of such a city. It is true that the concept of philosopher-rulers cannot give a decisive answer to the first of these problems – hence P.'s further thoughts at 7.540d–41b. But the new account of the philosopher *is* meant to underpin the sustainable coherence of the just city.

56   The imagery has sometimes been played down by modern, analytically-minded scholars: see, for example, the suggestions of Penner 96–8. A recent book which tries to take P.'s visionary language seriously is M. Morgan, *Platonic Piety* (New Haven, 1990): see ch. 5.

57   These three uses (respectively: existential, predicative/copular, veridical) are extensively studied in Kahn's book. The question is examined by virtually every modern philosophical study of the last part of bk. 5: for proponents of readings based on each of the three senses of 'be', in the order given, see F.C. White, *Australasian Journal of Philosophy* 62 (1984) 339–54; Annas (1981) 196–9; Fine (1978). Cf. n. 476e10, and Jordan 59–60.

58   For passages where one might press particular senses of 'be', cf. my nn. on 478b 6–7 (existential), 479b9–10 (predicative), 477a3 (veridical).

59   Annas (1986) 6 recommends translation by 'is' and 'is not'. Such locutions may indeed serve for partial analysis, but they cannot dissolve problems: other considerations aside, they involve an oddity which is not true to P.'s Greek, which for the most part is, linguistically speaking, unremarkable. Indeed, the use of ordinary Greek idioms for special philosophical ends is precisely one source of difficulty for us: cf. e.g. nn. 476b6–7, 477a3.

60   On being/non-being in later dialogues, see Owen ch. 6, whose first sentence ('Platonists who doubt that they are Spectators of Being must settle for the knowledge that they are investigators of the verb "to be"') makes a shrewd point about the difference between P.'s metaphysics and its modern analysis.

61   See n. 476a5. 479b adds some non-moral qualities (see nn. there): these raise various questions about the larger nature of P.'s so-called 'theory of Forms', but they are not so pertinent to philosopher-rulers (see n. 62 below).

62   Including knowledge of the attributes cited at 479b: thus, philosophers might have knowledge of absolute 'doubleness' or 'heaviness', but this would not lead them to reform the city's arithmetic or weights and measures. Nor, in any case, can we suppose philospher-rulers to possess *all* knowledge (in ordinary senses of the term), despite the wording of 475b8–9 (see n.), c6.

36

Bibliography

Listed here are those works which are cited in the introduction, notes and commentary by author's name alone (with date of publication where appropriate); not included are items whose bibliographic details are given at citation.

Adam, J. *The Republic of Plato*² (Cambridge, 1963)
Annas, J. 'Plato's *Republic* and Feminism', *Philosophy* 51 (1976) 307-21
–, *An Introduction to Plato's Republic* (Oxford, 1981)
–, 'Plato, *Republic* V-VII', in G. Vesey (ed.) *Philosophers Ancient & Modern* (Cambridge, 1986)
Arends, J.F.M. *Die Einheit der Polis: Eine Studie über Platons Staat* (*Mnem.* Suppl. 106: Leiden, 1988)
Baldry, H.C. *The Unity of Mankind in Greek Thought* (Cambridge, 1965)
Bérard, C. 'The Order of Women', in C. Bérard et al., *A City of Images*, Eng. tr. (Princeton, 1989) 89-107
Bluestone, N.H. *Women & the Ideal Society: Plato's Republic & Modern Myths of Gender* (Oxford, 1987)
Boardman, J. *Athenian Red Figure Vases: the Archaic Period* (London, 1975)
–, *Athenian Red Figure Vases: the Classical Period* (London, 1989)
Boter, G. *The Textual Tradition of Plato's Republic* (*Mnem.* Suppl. 107: Leiden, 1989)
Brandwood, L. *A Word Index to Plato* (Leeds, 1976)
Burkert, W. *Lore & Science in Ancient Pythagoreanism*, Eng. tr. (Cambridge Mass., 1972)
–, *Greek Religion*, Eng. tr. (Oxford, 1985)
Calvert, B. 'Plato and the Equality of Women', *Phoenix* 29 (1975) 231-43
Cameron, A. & Kuhrt, A. (edd.) *Images of Women in Antiquity* (London, 1983)
Cantarella, E. *Pandora's Daughters*, Eng. tr. (Baltimore, 1987)
Cartledge, P. 'Spartan Wives: Liberation or Licence?', *CQ* 31 (1981) 84-105
Clark, G. *Women in the Ancient World*, Greece & Rome New Surveys in the Classics no. 21 (Oxford, 1989)
Cooper, N. 'Between Knowledge & Ignorance', *Phronesis* 31 (1986) 229-42
Crombie, I.M. *An Examination of Plato's Doctrines* (London, 1962-63)
Cross, R.C. & Woozley, A.D. *Plato's Republic: a Philosophical Commentary* (London, 1964)
David, E. *Aristophanes & Athenian Society of the Early Fourth Century B.C.* (*Mnem.* Suppl. 81: Leiden, 1984)
Davies, J.K. *Athenian Propertied Families 600-300 B.C.* (Oxford, 1971)
Demand, N. 'Plato, Aristophanes, and the *Speeches of Pythagoras*', *GRBS* 23 (1982) 179-84
Denniston, J.D. *The Greek Particles*² (Oxford, 1954)
Dover, K.J. *Greek Popular Morality in the time of Plato and Aristotle* (Oxford, 1974)
–, *Greek Homosexuality* (London, 1978)

Fine, G. 'Knowledge and Belief in *Republic* V', *Archiv für Geschichte der Philosophie* 60 (1978) 121-39

–, 'Knowledge and Belief in *Republic* V-VII', in S. Everson (ed.) *Epistemology* (Companions to Ancient Thought, 1: Cambridge, 1990) 85-115

Fortenbaugh, W.W. 'Plato: Temperament and Eugenic Policy', *Arethusa* 8 (1975a) 283-305

–, 'On Plato's Feminism in *Republic* V', *Apeiron* 9 (1975b) 1-4

Gallop, D. *Plato Phaedo* (Oxford, 1975)

Garner, R. *The Greek Way of Life: from Conception to Old Age* (London, 1990)

Golden, M. *Children & Childhood in Classical Athens* (Baltimore, 1990)

Goodwin, W.W. *Syntax of the Moods & Tenses of the Greek Verb*, rev. edn. (London, 1912)

Gosling, J. '*Republic* Book V: τὰ πολλὰ καλὰ', *Phronesis* 5 (1960) 116-28

–, *Plato* (London, 1973)

Greene, G.C. *Scholia Platonica* (Haverford, 1938)

Grube, G.M.A. 'The Marriage Laws in Plato's *Republic*', *CQ* 21 (1927) 95-9

Hanson, V.D. *Warfare & Agriculture in Classical Greece* (Pisa, 1983)

Harrison, A.R.W. *The Law of Athens* (Oxford, 1968-71)

Huby, P. *Plato and Modern Morality* (London, 1972)

Jordan, R.W. *Plato's Arguments for Forms* (Cambridge, 1983)

Just, R. *Women in Athenian Law and Life* (London, 1989)

Kahn, C.H. *The Verb 'Be' in Ancient Greek*, Foundations of Language, Suppl. Series, vol. 16 (Dordrecht, 1973)

Lacey, W.K. *The Family in Classical Greece* (London, 1968)

Lefkowitz M.R. & Fant, M.B. *Women's Life in Greece & Rome* (London, 1982)

Lefkowitz, M. 'Only the Best Girls Get to', *Times Literary Supplement* May 5-11, 1989, 484/497

Lesser, H. 'Plato's Feminism', *Philosophy* 54 (1979) 113-17

Lucas, J. 'Plato's Philosophy of Sex', in E. Craik (ed.) '*Owls to Athens*': *Essays on Classical Subjects Presented to Sir Kenneth Dover* (Oxford, 1990) 223-31

MacDowell, D.M. *The Law in Classical Athens* (London, 1978)

–, *Spartan Law* (Edinburgh, 1986)

Michell, H. *Sparta* (Cambridge, 1952)

Morrison, J.S. 'The Origins of Plato's Philosopher-Statesman', *CQ* 8 (1958) 198-218

Morrow, G.R. *Plato's Cretan City* (Princeton, 1960)

Mulhern, J.J. 'Population and Plato's *Republic*', *Arethusa* 8 (1975) 265-81

Okin, S.M. *Women in Western Political Thought* (Princeton, 1979)

Owen, G.E.L. *Logic Science & Dialectic* (London, 1986)

Penner, T. *The Ascent from Nominalism: Some Existence Arguments in Plato's Middle Dialogues* (Dordrecht, 1987)

Pierce, C. 'Equality: *Republic* V', *The Monist* 57 (1973) 1-11

Pomeroy, S.B. 'Feminism in Book V of Plato's *Republic*', *Apeiron* 8 (1974) 33-5

–, *Goddesses Whores Wives & Slaves* (London, 1976)

–, 'Plato and the Female Physician (*Republic* 454d2)', *AJP* 99 (1978) 496-500

Popper, K. *The Open Society & its Enemies*[4], vol. 1 (London, 1962)

Powell, A. *Athens and Sparta* (London, 1988)

Preus, A. 'Biomedical Techniques for Influencing Human Reproduction in the Fourth Century B.C.', *Arethusa* 8 (1975) 237-63

Pritchett, W.K. *The Greek State at War* (Berkeley, 1971-91)

Rankin, H.D. *Plato and the Individual* (London, 1964)

–, 'Plato's Eugenic ΕΥΦΗΜΙΑ and ΑΠΟΘΕΣΙΣ in *Republic*, Book V', *Hermes* 93 (1965) 407-20

Reeve, C.D.C. *Philosopher-Kings: the Argument of Plato's Republic* (Princeton, 1988)

Reverdin, O. *La Religion de la Cité Platonicienne* (Paris, 1945)

Richards, H. *Platonica* (London, 1911)

Robinson, R. *Plato's Earlier Dialectic*[2] (Oxford, 1953)

Saxonhouse, A.W. *Women in the History of Political Thought* (New York, 1985)

Simpson, P. 'Aristotle's Criticisms of Socrates' Communism of Wives and Children', *Apeiron* 24 (1991) 99-113

Thesleff, H. *Studies in Platonic Chronology* (Helsinki, 1982)

Ussher, R.G. *Aristophanes Ecclesiazusae* (Oxford, 1973)

Vidal-Naquet, P. *The Black Hunter*, Eng. tr. (Baltimore, 1986)

Viljoen, G. van N. 'Plato and Aristotle on the Exposure of Infants at Athens', *Acta Classica* 2 (1959) 58-69

Vlastos, G. *Platonic Studies*[2] (Princeton, 1981)

–, 'Was Plato a Feminist?', *Times Literary Supplement* March 17-23, 1989, 276/288-9

–, *Socrates: Ironist and Moral Philosopher* (Cambridge, 1991)

Vogel, C.J. de *Pythagoras & Early Pythagoreanism* (Assen, 1966)

Vogt, J. *Von der Gleichwertigkeit der Geschlechter in der bürgerlichen Gesellschaft der Griechen* (Wiesbaden, 1960: Akademie der Wissenschaften und der Literatur in Mainz, Abhandlungen der Geistes- und Sozialwissenschaftlichen Klasse, nr. 2)

Vretska, K. 'Platonica', *Wiener Studien* 66 (1953) 76-91

Weir Smyth, H. *Greek Grammar*, rev. G. M. Messing (Cambridge Mass., 1956)

Wender, D. 'Plato: Misogynist, Paedophile, and Feminist', *Arethusa* 6 (1973) 75-90

White, F.C. 'J. Gosling on τὰ πολλὰ καλά', *Phronesis* 23 (1978a) 127-32

–, 'The *Phaedo* & *Republic* V on Essences', *JHS* 98 (1978b) 142-56

White, N.P. *A Companion to Plato's Republic* (Indianapolis, 1979)

Wilkinson, L.P. *Classical Attitudes to Modern Issues* (London, 1979)

Willetts, R.F. *Aristocratic Society in Ancient Crete* (London, 1955)

Woodruff, P. *Plato Hippias Major* (Oxford, 1982)

–, 'Plato's Early Theory of Knowledge', in S. Everson (ed.) *Epistemology* (Companions to Ancient Thought, 1: Cambridge, 1990) 60-84

Note on the Text and Translation

The Greek text is reprinted from J. Burnet (ed.) *Platonis Res Publica* (Oxford, 1902). I have replaced Burnet's apparatus criticus with a deliberately minimal apparatus (printed on p. 130) which provides details only of (i) passages where Burnet diverges from the main mss. ADF, except when the latter contain simple and certain scribal errors; (ii) conjectures printed by Burnet; (iii) alternative readings of some note. Wherever possible, I have checked Burnet's apparatus against other sources of information, and in a few places I have supplemented it. For the readings of minor manuscripts, I have sometimes referred the reader to Boter's monograph (see Bibliography); the following is a list of abbreviations of the main mss. cited, together with page references to Boter's descriptions of them:

A   Parisinus gr. 1807 (9th cent.: Boter 45-8)
D   Venetus gr. 185 (12th cent.: Boter 57-8)
E   Venetus gr. 184 (15th cent.: Boter 56-7)
F   Vindobonesis supp. gr. 39 (14th cent.: Boter 62-4)
N   Venetus gr. 187 (15th cent.: Boter 58-9)
β   Florentinus Laurentianus 80, 19 (?12th/14th cent.: Boter 34-5)

The translation is intended in the first instance as a reasonably close guide to the sense of the Greek, though I have tried to balance this consideration against the aim of providing a version that is tolerably readable. But the translation is not, at any rate, meant to be used independently of my commentary, which contains explanations of many of the choices I have made: this is especially important with occasional variations in translating particular Greek words, or with the treatment of difficult philosophical points in the last section of the book.

With the exceptions of 449b6-8 and 451b2, I have omitted the phrases 'I said' and 'he said' throughout, and replaced them with the initial letters of the speakers (Adeimantus, Glaucon, Socrates and Thrasymachus).

REPUBLIC 5

E

Ἀγαθὴν μὲν τοίνυν τὴν τοιαύτην πόλιν τε καὶ πολιτείαν a
καὶ ὀρθὴν κς.λῶ καὶ ἄνδρα τὸν τοιοῦτον· κακὰς δὲ τὰς ἄλλας
καὶ ἡμαρτημένας, εἴπερ αὕτη ὀρθή, περί τε πόλεων διοικήσεις
καὶ περὶ ἰδιωτῶν ψυχῆς τρόπου κατασκευήν, ἐν τέτταρσι
πονηρίας εἴδεσιν οὔσας. 5
Ποίας δὴ ταύτας; ἔφη.
Καὶ ἐγὼ μὲν ᾖα τὰς ἐφεξῆς ἐρῶν, ὥς μοι ἐφαίνοντο
ἕκασται ἐξ ἀλλήλων μεταβαίνειν· ὁ δὲ Πολέμαρχος— b
σμικρὸν γὰρ ἀπωτέρω τοῦ Ἀδειμάντου καθῆστο—ἐκτείνας
τὴν χεῖρα καὶ λαβόμενος τοῦ ἱματίου ἄνωθεν αὐτοῦ παρὰ
τὸν ὦμον, ἐκεῖνόν τε προσηγάγετο καὶ προτείνας ἑαυτὸν
ἔλεγεν ἄττα προσκεκυφώς, ὧν ἄλλο μὲν οὐδὲν κατηκούσαμεν, 5
τόδε δέ· Ἀφήσομεν οὖν, ἔφη, ἢ τί δράσομεν;
Ἥκιστά γε, ἔφη ὁ Ἀδείμαντος μέγα ἤδη λέγων.
Καὶ ἐγώ, Τί μάλιστα, ἔφην, ὑμεῖς οὐκ ἀφίετε;
Σέ, ἦ δ᾽ ὅς.
Ὅτι, ἐγὼ εἶπον, τί μάλιστα; c
Ἀπορραθυμεῖν ἡμῖν δοκεῖς, ἔφη, καὶ εἶδος ὅλον οὐ τὸ
ἐλάχιστον ἐκκλέπτειν τοῦ λόγου ἵνα μὴ διέλθῃς, καὶ λήσειν
οἰηθῆναι εἰπὼν αὐτὸ φαύλως, ὡς ἄρα περὶ γυναικῶν τε καὶ
παίδων παντὶ δῆλον ὅτι κοινὰ τὰ φίλων ἔσται.
Οὐκοῦν ὀρθῶς, ἔφην, ὦ Ἀδείμαντε; 5
Ναί, ἦ δ᾽ ὅς. ἀλλὰ τὸ ὀρθῶς τοῦτο, ὥσπερ τἆλλα, λόγου
δεῖται τίς ὁ τρόπος τῆς κοινωνίας· πολλοὶ γὰρ ἂν γένοιντο.
μὴ οὖν παρῇς ὅντινα σὺ λέγεις· ὡς ἡμεῖς πάλαι περιμένομεν d
οἰόμενοί σέ που μνησθήσεσθαι παιδοποιίας τε πέρι, πῶς
παιδοποιήσονται, καὶ γενομένους πῶς θρέψουσιν, καὶ ὅλην
ταύτην ἣν λέγεις κοινωνίαν γυναικῶν τε καὶ παίδων· μέγα
γάρ τι οἰόμεθα φέρειν καὶ ὅλον εἰς πολιτείαν ὀρθῶς ἢ μὴ 5
ὀρθῶς γιγνόμενον. νῦν οὖν, ἐπειδὴ ἄλλης ἐπιλαμβάνῃ

Translation

449a S.   Well then, it is this kind of city and régime which I call good and correct, and likewise with the individual of the same kind. And given that this kind is correct, I regard the others as bad and flawed, in both the government of cities and the state of individuals' souls: they belong to four types of deficiency.

G.   What are they?

(S.)   I was going to describe these in turn, according to what I thought to
b   be their development from one another. But Polemarchus, who was sitting a little distance from Adeimantus, stretched out his hand, gripped the latter's cloak at the shoulder, drew Adeimantus towards him and leaned forwards to say something with his head close to Adeimantus. We heard nothing of what was said other than: 'Shall we let it pass, then, or what?' 'Certainly not', said Adeimantus, now speaking aloud. So I said:
Precisely *what* is it that you won't let pass?

A.   *You.*

c S.   Why exactly?

A.   We think you're shirking, and are tricking your way out of discussing a whole and substantial aspect of the argument. You thought you'd escape by just making the remark casually, as though indeed it were clear to anyone that as regards women and children it will be a case of 'friends share everything'.

S.   Well isn't that correct, Adeimantus?

A.   Yes. But the correctness of this point, as with the rest of the argument, calls for an explanation of the nature of the 'sharing'; for
d   it could take many forms. So don't fail to say which one you mean, as we've all been long waiting in the expectation that you would surely discuss how they will organise procreation, how they will rear the children who are born, and the whole of what you mean by 'sharing' of women and children. We think it makes a fundamental difference to the régime whether this matter is correctly organised or not. So now that you've started to broach a different régime

πολιτείας πρὶν ταῦτα ἱκανῶς διελέσθαι, δέδοκται ἡμῖν τοῦτο
ὃ σὺ ἤκουσας, τὸ σὲ μὴ μεθιέναι πρὶν ἂν ταῦτα πάντα ὥσπερ **450**
τἆλλα διέλθῃς.

Καὶ ἐμὲ τοίνυν, ὁ Γλαύκων ἔφη, κοινωνὸν τῆς ψήφου
ταύτης τίθετε.

Ἀμέλει, ἔφη ὁ Θρασύμαχος, πᾶσι ταῦτα δεδογμένα ἡμῖν 5
νόμιζε, ὦ Σώκρατες.

Οἷον, ἦν δ' ἐγώ, εἰργάσασθε ἐπιλαβόμενοί μου. ὅσον
λόγον πάλιν, ὥσπερ ἐξ ἀρχῆς, κινεῖτε περὶ τῆς πολιτείας·
ἣν ὡς ἤδη διεληλυθὼς ἔγωγε ἔχαιρον, ἀγαπῶν εἴ τις ἐάσοι
ταῦτα ἀποδεξάμενος ὡς τότε ἐρρήθη. ἃ νῦν ὑμεῖς παρα- 10
καλοῦντες οὐκ ἴστε ὅσον ἑσμὸν λόγων ἐπεγείρετε· ὃν ὁρῶν b
ἐγὼ παρῆκα τότε, μὴ παράσχοι πολὺν ὄχλον.

Τί δέ; ἢ δ' ὃς ὁ Θρασύμαχος· χρυσοχοήσοντας οἴει
τούσδε νῦν ἐνθάδε ἀφῖχθαι, ἀλλ' οὐ λόγων ἀκουσομένους;

Ναί, εἶπον, μετρίων γε. 5

Μέτρον δέ γ', ἔφη, ὦ Σώκρατες, ὁ Γλαύκων, τοιούτων
λόγων ἀκούειν ὅλος ὁ βίος νοῦν ἔχουσιν. ἀλλὰ τὸ μὲν
ἡμέτερον ἔα· σὺ δὲ περὶ ὧν ἐρωτῶμεν μηδαμῶς ἀποκάμῃς ἢ
σοι δοκεῖ διεξιών, τίς ἡ κοινωνία τοῖς φύλαξιν ἡμῖν παίδων c
τε πέρι καὶ γυναικῶν ἔσται καὶ τροφῆς νέων ἔτι ὄντων, τῆς
ἐν τῷ μεταξὺ χρόνῳ γιγνομένης γενέσεώς τε καὶ παιδείας,
ἣ δὴ ἐπιπονωτάτη δοκεῖ εἶναι. πειρῶ οὖν εἰπεῖν τίνα
τρόπον δεῖ γίγνεσθαι αὐτήν. 5

Οὐ ῥᾴδιον, ὦ εὔδαιμον, ἦν δ' ἐγώ, διελθεῖν· πολλὰς γὰρ
ἀπιστίας ἔχει ἔτι μᾶλλον τῶν ἔμπροσθεν ὧν διήλθομεν.
καὶ γὰρ ὡς δυνατὰ λέγεται, ἀπιστοῖτ' ἄν, καὶ εἰ ὅτι μάλιστα
γένοιτο, ὡς ἄριστ' ἂν εἴη ταῦτα, καὶ ταύτῃ ἀπιστήσεται.
διὸ δὴ καὶ ὄκνος τις αὐτῶν ἅπτεσθαι, μὴ εὐχὴ δοκῇ εἶναι ὁ d
λόγος, ὦ φίλε ἑταῖρε.

Μηδέν, ἦ δ' ὅς, ὄκνει· οὔτε γὰρ ἀγνώμονες οὔτε ἄπιστοι
οὔτε δύσνοι οἱ ἀκουσόμενοι.

without having analysed these things adequately, we've decided
450a   what you heard us saying just now – not to let you go, until you
discuss all these topics in the same way as everything else.

G.   Count me too as a supporter of this proposal!

T.   You can naturally take it that we *all* share this view, Socrates.

S.   What a thing to do, apprehending me like this! What a new argument
you're provoking about our régime, as if we were making a fresh
start. I was feeling satisfied at having by now, as I thought, described
the whole régime, and would have been content if anyone should
leave the matter at that and accept my earlier account of it. But by
b   now invoking those points, you don't realise what a hornet's nest of
argument you're stirring up. It was because I could see this that I left
the subject on one side earlier, so that it shouldn't cause us a lot of
trouble.

T.   What! Do you think we've all come here to indulge our fancies,
rather than to listen to arguments?

S.   Arguments, certainly – but within limits!

G.   Yet the limit, Socrates, on listening to such arguments, for those who
are thoughtful, is surely a whole lifetime. But forget about *our*
convenience. In answer to our questions, *you* mustn't tire in fol-
c   lowing your own line of argument to explain what form our
Guardians' 'sharing' will take, in relation to children and women
and the child-rearing that belongs to the period between birth and
formal education – something which is thought of as involving a
very heavy burden. So try to tell us how this ought to be organised.

S.   It's not easy, good friend, to discuss this subject, since it contains
even more grounds for scepticism than the earlier stages of our
discussion. It could be doubted whether my proposals are possible,
and it will also be doubted whether, even if they were completely
d   realised, they would be for the best. That's why there is a certain
hesitation on my part to broach the subject, in case the argument
should seem emptily utopian, my dear companion.

G.   Don't hesitate at all; your hearers will be neither undiscerning, nor
full of doubt, nor ill-disposed towards you.

Καὶ ἐγὼ εἶπον· Ὦ ἄριστε, ἦ που βουλόμενός με παρα- 5
θαρρύνειν λέγεις;

Ἔγωγ᾽, ἔφη.

Πᾶν τοίνυν, ἦν δ᾽ ἐγώ, τοὐναντίον ποιεῖς. πιστεύοντος
μὲν γὰρ ἐμοῦ ἐμοὶ εἰδέναι ἃ λέγω, καλῶς εἶχεν ἡ παραμυθία·
ἐν γὰρ φρονίμοις τε καὶ φίλοις περὶ τῶν μεγίστων τε καὶ 10
φίλων τἀληθῆ εἰδότα λέγειν ἀσφαλὲς καὶ θαρραλέον, ἀπι-   e
στοῦντα δὲ καὶ ζητοῦντα ἅμα τοὺς λόγους ποιεῖσθαι, ὃ δὴ
ἐγὼ δρῶ, φοβερόν τε καὶ σφαλερόν, οὔ τι γέλωτα ὀφλεῖν—   451
παιδικὸν γὰρ τοῦτό γε—ἀλλὰ μὴ σφαλεὶς τῆς ἀληθείας οὐ
μόνον αὐτὸς ἀλλὰ καὶ τοὺς φίλους συνεπισπασάμενος κείσομαι περὶ ἃ ἥκιστα δεῖ σφάλλεσθαι. προσκυνῶ δὲ Ἀδρά-
στειαν, ὦ Γλαύκων, χάριν οὗ μέλλω λέγειν· ἐλπίζω γὰρ 5
οὖν ἔλαττον ἁμάρτημα ἀκουσίως τινὸς φονέα γενέσθαι ἢ
ἀπατεῶνα καλῶν τε καὶ ἀγαθῶν καὶ δικαίων νομίμων πέρι.
τοῦτο οὖν τὸ κινδύνευμα κινδυνεύειν ἐν ἐχθροῖς κρεῖττον ἢ
φίλοις, ὥστε εὖ με παραμυθῇ.   b

Καὶ ὁ Γλαύκων γελάσας, Ἀλλ᾽, ὦ Σώκρατες, ἔφη, ἐάν τι
πάθωμεν πλημμελὲς ὑπὸ τοῦ λόγου, ἀφίεμέν σε ὥσπερ
φόνου καὶ καθαρὸν εἶναι καὶ μὴ ἀπατεῶνα ἡμῶν. ἀλλὰ
θαρρήσας λέγε.   5

Ἀλλὰ μέντοι, εἶπον, καθαρός γε καὶ ἐκεῖ ὁ ἀφεθείς, ὡς
ὁ νόμος λέγει· εἰκὸς δέ γε, εἴπερ ἐκεῖ, κἀνθάδε.

Λέγε τοίνυν, ἔφη, τούτου γ᾽ ἕνεκα.

Λέγειν δή, ἔφην ἐγώ, χρὴ ἀνάπαλιν αὖ νῦν, ἃ τότε ἴσως
ἔδει ἐφεξῆς λέγειν· τάχα δὲ οὕτως ἂν ὀρθῶς ἔχοι, μετὰ   c
ἀνδρεῖον δρᾶμα παντελῶς διαπερανθὲν τὸ γυναικεῖον αὖ
περαίνειν, ἄλλως τε καὶ ἐπειδὴ σὺ οὕτω προκαλῇ.

Ἀνθρώποις γὰρ φύσι καὶ παιδευθεῖσιν ὡς ἡμεῖς διήλθομεν, κατ᾽ ἐμὴν δόξαν οὐκ ἔστ᾽ ἄλλη ὀρθὴ παίδων τε καὶ   5
γυναικῶν κτῆσίς τε καὶ χρεία ἢ κατ᾽ ἐκείνην τὴν ὁρμὴν
ἰοῦσιν, ἥνπερ τὸ πρῶτον ὡρμήσαμεν· ἐπεχειρήσαμεν δέ
που ὡς ἀγέλης φύλακας τοὺς ἄνδρας καθιστάναι τῷ λόγῳ.

S. My fine friend, are you saying this out of a desire to encourage me?

G. Of course.

S. Well you're having exactly the opposite effect! If I were confident in myself that I know what I'm talking about, your reassurance would be a fine thing. For in a gathering of intelligent friends, in discussion of subjects that are of the greatest significance and dear to one's heart, to speak with knowledge of the truth gives one security and confidence. But to offer arguments in a doubtful and exploratory state of mind, as I'm doing, is something frightening and risky – not because I might incur laughter (that's a childish fear), but in case I slip, miss the truth, and not only fall myself but bring my friends down with me too, in an area where avoiding mistakes is of supreme importance. I supplicate the goddess Adrasteia, Glaucon, on account of what I'm going to say; for I actually think it's a lesser fault to be an accidental killer than a deliberate deceiver about the principles of beauty, goodness and justice. So it would be better to run this risk among enemies rather than friends – which makes your reassurance a fine thing!

Glaucon laughed and said:

(G.) Well, Socrates, if we suffer anything untoward from the argument, we acquit you (as we would with a murder charge) as both free from responsibility and innocent of deceiving us. Come, speak with confidence.

S. Well it's true, the acquitted in a court is free from responsibility, so the law says; and it's reasonable, if that's true there, that the same should apply here too.

G. Continue then, now that that point is settled.

S. I now need to explain afresh what I perhaps should have explained in the proper order at that earlier point. But perhaps it will make good sense this way, after the completion of a male drama, to perform the women's next – especially since you invite me so forcefully.

For people who have been bred and educated as we earlier discussed, it's my view that there is no other correct possession and use of children and women than to follow the impetus which we gave them in the first place. Surely we tried to establish the men, in our argument, as guard-dogs of their flock.

48

Ναί.

Ἀκολουθῶμεν τοίνυν καὶ τὴν γένεσιν καὶ τροφὴν παρα- d
πλησίαν ἀποδιδόντες, καὶ σκοπῶμεν εἰ ἡμῖν πρέπει ἢ οὔ.

Πῶς; ἔφη.

Ὧδε. τὰς θηλείας τῶν φυλάκων κυνῶν πότερα συμφυλάττειν οἰόμεθα δεῖν ἅπερ ἂν οἱ ἄρρενες φυλάττωσι καὶ 5
συνθηρεύειν καὶ τἆλλα κοινῇ πράττειν, ἢ τὰς μὲν οἰκουρεῖν
ἔνδον ὡς ἀδυνάτους διὰ τὸν τῶν σκυλάκων τόκον τε καὶ
τροφήν, τοὺς δὲ πονεῖν τε καὶ πᾶσαν ἐπιμέλειαν ἔχειν περὶ
τὰ ποίμνια;

Κοινῇ, ἔφη, πάντα· πλὴν ὡς ἀσθενεστέραις χρώμεθα, e
τοῖς δὲ ὡς ἰσχυροτέροις.

Οἷόν τ᾽ οὖν, ἔφην ἐγώ, ἐπὶ τὰ αὐτὰ χρῆσθαί τινι ζῴῳ, ἂν
μὴ τὴν αὐτὴν τροφήν τε καὶ παιδείαν ἀποδιδῷς;

Οὐχ οἷόν τε. 5

Εἰ ἄρα ταῖς γυναιξὶν ἐπὶ ταὐτὰ χρησόμεθα καὶ τοῖς
ἀνδράσι, ταὐτὰ καὶ διδακτέον αὐτάς.

Ναί. 452

Μουσικὴ μὴν ἐκείνοις γε καὶ γυμναστικὴ ἐδόθη.

Ναί.

Καὶ ταῖς γυναιξὶν ἄρα τούτω τὼ τέχνα καὶ τὰ περὶ τὸν
πόλεμον ἀποδοτέον καὶ χρηστέον κατὰ ταὐτά. 5

Εἰκὸς ἐξ ὧν λέγεις, ἔφη.

Ἴσως δή, εἶπον, παρὰ τὸ ἔθος γελοῖα ἂν φαίνοιτο πολλὰ
περὶ τὰ νῦν λεγόμενα, εἰ πράξεται ᾗ λέγεται.

Καὶ μάλα, ἔφη.

Τί, ἦν δ᾽ ἐγώ, γελοιότατον αὐτῶν ὁρᾷς; ἢ δῆλα δὴ ὅτι 10
γυμνὰς τὰς γυναῖκας ἐν ταῖς παλαίστραις γυμναζομένας μετὰ
τῶν ἀνδρῶν, οὐ μόνον τὰς νέας, ἀλλὰ καὶ ἤδη τὰς πρεσβυ- b
τέρας, ὥσπερ τοὺς γέροντας ἐν τοῖς γυμνασίοις, ὅταν ῥυσοὶ
καὶ μὴ ἡδεῖς τὴν ὄψιν ὅμως φιλογυμναστῶσιν;

Νὴ τὸν Δία, ἔφη· γελοῖον γὰρ ἄν, ὥς γε ἐν τῷ παρεστῶτι,
φανείη. 5

G.   Yes.

d   S.   Then let's proceed by giving them a system of breeding and rearing children that corresponds with that, and see whether we think it suits them or not.

G.   How?

S.   As follows. Do we think that female guard-dogs should share the guard duties of the males, and hunt alongside them, and share all other activities with them; or that the females should stay indoors and look after the house, on the grounds that bearing and rearing the puppies incapacitates them, while the males should do the hard work and undertake the entire supervision of the flocks?

e   G.   They should share all activities – except that we employ the females as weaker animals, the males as stronger.

S.   Now is it possible to employ any animal for the same purposes as another, if you don't give it the same nurture and training?

G.   It isn't possible.

S.   If, then, we intend to employ the women for the same tasks as the men, we must also teach them the same things.

452a   G.   Yes.

S.   Well, we assigned music and gymnastics to the men.

G.   Yes.

S.   So we must give the women too these skills, as well as military training, and must employ them on the same principles as the men.

G.   It makes sense, given your arguments.

S.   Perhaps many details of what we're now saying, because they contradict tradition, would seem ridiculous, if they could be realised precisely as proposed.

G.   That's certainly true.

S.   What do you see as the most ridiculous aspect of them? Isn't it obvious that it's the idea of the women exercising naked in the

b   wrestling schools alongside the men – not just the young women, but the older ones too, just as we now see the old men in the gymnasia, when, despite their wrinkled and ugly appearance, they still insist on training enthusiastically?

G.   Absolutely; it *would* appear ridiculous, by the standard of present practice.

50

Οὐκοῦν, ἦν δ' ἐγώ, ἐπείπερ ὡρμήσαμεν λέγειν, οὐ φοβητέον τὰ τῶν χαριέντων σκώμματα, ὅσα καὶ οἷα ἂν εἴποιεν εἰς τὴν τοιαύτην μεταβολὴν γενομένην καὶ περὶ τὰ γυμνάσια καὶ περὶ μουσικὴν καὶ οὐκ ἐλάχιστα περὶ τὴν τῶν ὅπλων c
σχέσιν καὶ ἵππων ὀχήσεις.

Ὀρθῶς, ἔφη, λέγεις.

Ἀλλ' ἐπείπερ λέγειν ἠρξάμεθα, πορευτέον πρὸς τὸ τραχὺ τοῦ νόμου, δεηθεῖσίν τε τούτων μὴ τὰ αὑτῶν πράττειν ἀλλὰ 5
σπουδάζειν, καὶ ὑπομνήσασιν ὅτι οὐ πολὺς χρόνος ἐξ οὗ τοῖς
Ἕλλησιν ἐδόκει αἰσχρὰ εἶναι καὶ γελοῖα ἅπερ νῦν τοῖς πολλοῖς
τῶν βαρβάρων, γυμνοὺς ἄνδρας ὁρᾶσθαι, καὶ ὅτε ἤρχοντο
τῶν γυμνασίων πρῶτοι μὲν Κρῆτες, ἔπειτα Λακεδαιμόνιοι,
ἐξῆν τοῖς τότε ἀστείοις πάντα ταῦτα κωμῳδεῖν. ἢ οὐκ οἴει; d
Ἔγωγε.

Ἀλλ' ἐπειδὴ οἶμαι χρωμένοις ἄμεινον τὸ ἀποδύεσθαι τοῦ
συγκαλύπτειν πάντα τὰ τοιαῦτα ἐφάνη, καὶ τὸ ἐν τοῖς ὀφθαλ-
μοῖς δὴ γελοῖον ἐξερρύη ὑπὸ τοῦ ἐν τοῖς λόγοις μηνυθέντος 5
ἀρίστου· καὶ τοῦτο ἐνεδείξατο, ὅτι μάταιος ὃς γελοῖον ἄλλο
τι ἡγεῖται ἢ τὸ κακόν, καὶ ὁ γελωτοποιεῖν ἐπιχειρῶν πρὸς
ἄλλην τινὰ ὄψιν ἀποβλέπων ὡς γελοίου ἢ τὴν τοῦ ἄφρονός
τε καὶ κακοῦ, καὶ καλοῦ αὖ σπουδάζει πρὸς ἄλλον τινὰ e
σκοπὸν στησάμενος ἢ τὸν τοῦ ἀγαθοῦ.

Παντάπασι μὲν οὖν, ἔφη.

Ἆρ' οὖν οὐ πρῶτον μὲν τοῦτο περὶ αὐτῶν ἀνομολογητέον,
εἰ δυνατὰ ἢ οὔ, καὶ δοτέον ἀμφισβήτησιν εἴτε τις φιλο- 5
παίσμων εἴτε σπουδαστικὸς ἐθέλει ἀμφισβητῆσαι, πότερον
δυνατὴ φύσις ἡ ἀνθρωπίνη ἡ θήλεια τῇ τοῦ ἄρρενος γένους **453**
κοινωνῆσαι εἰς ἅπαντα τὰ ἔργα ἢ οὐδ' εἰς ἕν, ἢ εἰς τὰ μὲν
οἷά τε, εἰς δὲ τὰ οὔ, καὶ τοῦτο δὴ τὸ περὶ τὸν πόλεμον
ποτέρων ἐστίν; ἆρ' οὐχ οὕτως ἂν κάλλιστά τις ἀρχόμενος
ὡς τὸ εἰκὸς καὶ κάλλιστα τελευτήσειεν; 5

Πολύ γε, ἔφη.

Βούλει οὖν, ἦν δ' ἐγώ, ἡμεῖς πρὸς ἡμᾶς αὐτοὺς ὑπὲρ τῶν

S. Yet now that we've broached the subject, we musn't be intimidated by all the various jokes that the facetious would make against such
c a radical change in the gymnasia, in musical education, and, not least, in the holding of weapons and horse-riding.

G. You're quite right.

S. But now that we've started to dicuss it, we must move on to the rough ground of these regulations, asking these people to eschew their usual behaviour but to be serious instead, and reminding them that it's not so long since the Greeks found shameful and ridiculous something which most barbarians still find so – the sight of *men* unclothed – and that when first the Cretans, and then the Spartans,
d instituted naked gymnastics, the wits of the time were able to mock all these things. Don't you think so?

G. Certainly.

S. But when experience, so I believe, showed them that it was preferable to strip off than to keep all such parts covered, what had struck the eyes as ridiculous faded away, because of what had been rationally shown to be best. And this demonstrated that it is a fool who finds ridiculous anything other than bad things, as also the man who tries to arouse laughter by treating any appearance as ridiculous other
e than that of what is stupid and bad – and likewise, moreover, with anyone whose seriousness aims at, and takes for itself, any other standard of beauty than that of goodness.

G. Absolutely.

S. Well then, should we not first seek agreement on whether these ideas are possible or not, and give anyone who wishes to, whether a
453a humorist or someone serious, a chance to dispute whether the nature of the human female is able to share in *all* tasks with that of the male sex, or in none at all, or in some but not in others; and, in particular, to which of these categories military activity belongs? Wouldn't one, by making in this way the finest of starts, probably also reach the finest of conclusions?

G. Very much so.

S. So would you like us to dispute with one another on behalf of the

52

ἄλλων ἀμφισβητήσωμεν, ἵνα μὴ ἔρημα τὰ τοῦ ἑτέρου λόγου πολιορκῆται;

Οὐδέν, ἔφη, κωλύει.　　　　　　　　　　　　　　　　　　　　b

Λέγωμεν δὴ ὑπὲρ αὐτῶν ὅτι "Ὦ Σώκρατές τε καὶ Γλαύκων, οὐδὲν δεῖ ὑμῖν ἄλλους ἀμφισβητεῖν· αὐτοὶ γὰρ ἐν ἀρχῇ τῆς κατοικίσεως, ἣν ᾠκίζετε πόλιν, ὡμολογεῖτε δεῖν κατὰ φύσιν ἕκαστον ἕνα ἐν τὸ αὑτοῦ πράττειν."　　5

Ὡμολογήσαμεν οἶμαι· πῶς γὰρ οὔ;

"Ἔστιν οὖν ὅπως οὐ πάμπολυ διαφέρει γυνὴ ἀνδρὸς τὴν φύσιν;"

Πῶς δ' οὐ διαφέρει;

"Οὐκοῦν ἄλλο καὶ ἔργον ἑκατέρῳ προσήκει προστάττειν　10
τὸ κατὰ τὴν αὑτοῦ φύσιν;"　　　　　　　　　　　　　　　c

Τί μήν;

"Πῶς οὖν οὐχ ἁμαρτάνετε νυνὶ καὶ τἀναντία ὑμῖν αὐτοῖς λέγετε φάσκοντες αὖ τοὺς ἄνδρας καὶ τὰς γυναῖκας δεῖν τὰ αὐτὰ πράττειν, πλεῖστον κεχωρισμένην φύσιν ἔχοντας;"　5
ἕξεις τι, ὦ θαυμάσιε, πρὸς ταῦτ' ἀπολογεῖσθαι;

Ὡς μὲν ἐξαίφνης, ἔφη, οὐ πάνυ ῥᾴδιον· ἀλλὰ σοῦ δεήσομαί τε καὶ δέομαι καὶ τὸν ὑπὲρ ἡμῶν λόγον, ὅστις ποτ' ἐστίν, ἑρμηνεῦσαι.

Ταῦτ' ἐστίν, ἦν δ' ἐγώ, ὦ Γλαύκων, καὶ ἄλλα πολλὰ　10
τοιαῦτα, ἃ ἐγὼ πάλαι προορῶν ἐφοβούμην τε καὶ ὤκνουν　d
ἅπτεσθαι τοῦ νόμου τοῦ περὶ τὴν τῶν γυναικῶν καὶ παίδων κτῆσιν καὶ τροφήν.

Οὐ μὰ τὸν Δία, ἔφη· οὐ γὰρ εὐκόλῳ ἔοικεν.

Οὐ γάρ, εἶπον. ἀλλὰ δὴ ὧδ' ἔχει· ἄντε τις εἰς κολυμ-　5
βήθραν μικρὰν ἐμπέσῃ ἄντε εἰς τὸ μέγιστον πέλαγος μέσον, ὅμως γε νεῖ οὐδὲν ἧττον.

Πάνυ μὲν οὖν.

Οὐκοῦν καὶ ἡμῖν νευστέον καὶ πειρατέον σῴζεσθαι ἐκ τοῦ λόγου, ἤτοι δελφῖνά τινα ἐλπίζοντας ἡμᾶς ὑπολαβεῖν ἂν ἢ　10
τινα ἄλλην ἄπορον σωτηρίαν.

others, in order that the other side of the argument shouldn't go by default?

b G. Why not?

S. Let us, then, say on their behalf: "Socrates and Glaucon, you don't need *others* to dispute with you; you yourselves, when you were beginning to found your city, agreed that it was a natural principle that each individual should perform his own function."

G. I believe we did agree that, surely.

S. "Now, isn't it necessarily the case that a woman's nature differs utterly from a man's?"

G. Of course it differs.

c S. "Should the task assigned to each of them not be different too, then, to suit their own natures?"

G. What else?

S. "How then can you now not be making a mistake and contradicting yourselves, by saying at this point that men and women should perform the *same* activities, when they have natures that are completely distinct?" Will you have any defence against these objections, my remarkable friend?

G. To find one impromptu is far from easy. But I shall and do ask *you* to explain what our own argument should be.

S. These are the problems, Glaucon, and there are many others of the
d same kind, which I anticipated long ago and which made me anxious and hesitant about broaching the regulations concerning the possession and maintenance of women and children.

G. No wonder! It's no simple matter.

S. It certainly isn't. But, still, the situation is this: whether one falls into a small water-tank or into the middle of the largest sea, it makes no difference – one tries to swim, just the same.

G. Of course.

S. So we too have to swim and have to try to find a way of getting safely out of the argument, whether by hoping for the support of a dolphin, or for some other unlikely salvation!

Ἔοικεν, ἔφη.

Φέρε δή, ἦν δ᾽ ἐγώ, ἐάν πῃ εὕρωμεν τὴν ἔξοδον. ὁμολογοῦμεν γὰρ δὴ ἄλλην φύσιν ἄλλο δεῖν ἐπιτηδεύειν, γυναικὸς δὲ καὶ ἀνδρὸς ἄλλην εἶναι· τὰς δὲ ἄλλας φύσεις τὰ αὐτά φαμεν νῦν δεῖν ἐπιτηδεῦσαι. ταῦτα ἡμῶν κατηγορεῖται;

Κομιδῇ γε.

Ἡ γενναία, ἦν δ᾽ ἐγώ, ὦ Γλαύκων, ἡ δύναμις τῆς ἀντιλο- **454** γικῆς τέχνης.

Τί δή;

Ὅτι, εἶπον, δοκοῦσί μοι εἰς αὐτὴν καὶ ἄκοντες πολλοὶ ἐμπίπτειν καὶ οἴεσθαι οὐκ ἐρίζειν ἀλλὰ διαλέγεσθαι, διὰ τὸ μὴ δύνασθαι κατ᾽ εἴδη διαιρούμενοι τὸ λεγόμενον ἐπισκοπεῖν, ἀλλὰ κατ᾽ αὐτὸ τὸ ὄνομα διώκειν τοῦ λεχθέντος τὴν ἐναντίωσιν, ἔριδι, οὐ διαλέκτῳ πρὸς ἀλλήλους χρώμενοι.

Ἔστι γὰρ δή, ἔφη, περὶ πολλοὺς τοῦτο τὸ πάθος· ἀλλὰ μῶν καὶ πρὸς ἡμᾶς τοῦτο τείνει ἐν τῷ παρόντι;

Παντάπασι μὲν οὖν, ἦν δ᾽ ἐγώ· κινδυνεύομεν γοῦν ἄκοντες ἀντιλογίας ἅπτεσθαι.

Πῶς;

Τὸ ⟨μὴ⟩ τὴν αὐτὴν φύσιν ὅτι οὐ τῶν αὐτῶν δεῖ ἐπιτηδευμάτων τυγχάνειν πάνυ ἀνδρείως τε καὶ ἐριστικῶς κατὰ τὸ ὄνομα διώκομεν, ἐπεσκεψάμεθα δὲ οὐδ᾽ ὁπηοῦν τί εἶδος τὸ τῆς ἑτέρας τε καὶ τῆς αὐτῆς φύσεως καὶ πρὸς τί τεῖνον ὡριζόμεθα τότε, ὅτε τὰ ἐπιτηδεύματα ἄλλῃ φύσει ἄλλα, τῇ δὲ αὐτῇ τὰ αὐτὰ ἀπεδίδομεν.

Οὐ γὰρ οὖν, ἔφη, ἐπεσκεψάμεθα.

Τοιγάρτοι, εἶπον, ἔξεστιν ἡμῖν, ὡς ἔοικεν, ἀνερωτᾶν ἡμᾶς αὐτοὺς εἰ ἡ αὐτὴ φύσις φαλακρῶν καὶ κομητῶν καὶ οὐχ ἡ ἐναντία, καὶ ἐπειδὰν ὁμολογῶμεν ἐναντίαν εἶναι, ἐὰν φαλακροὶ σκυτοτομῶσιν, μὴ ἐᾶν κομήτας, ἐὰν δ᾽ αὖ κομῆται, μὴ τοὺς ἑτέρους.

Γελοῖον μεντἂν εἴη, ἔφη.

e G. It seems so.

S. Come then, let's see if we can somehow find the means of escape. For we agree that different natures ought to practice different activities, and that the natures of a woman and a man *are* different; yet we now find ourselves asserting that different natures should practice the *same* activities. Is this the charge against us?

G. Precisely.

454a S. What a grand power belongs to the art of altercation!

G. Why?

S. Because many people seem to succumb to it even against their will, and to think that they are not bickering but engaging in dialectic. The reason is their failure to examine the topic of argument by drawing distinctions of kind; instead, it's on a purely verbal level that they pursue the contradiction in what is said, and thereby indulge in bickering rather than dialectic with one another.

G. Yes, that *is* what happens to many people. But surely this doesn't apply to us too at the moment?

b S. It certainly does; at least, we're in danger of unwittingly dealing in mere altercation.

G. How?

S. We're vigorously and contentiously pursuing, on a verbal level, the principle that different natures should not be given the same activities; but we didn't at all consider what we earlier meant to define as the *kinds* of difference or identity of nature, or the bearings of these differences, when we were assigning different activities to different natures, and the same ones to the same nature.

G. No, we didn't consider that.

c S. Accordingly, it's open to us, so it seems, to ask ourselves afresh whether bald people and long-haired people have the same nature or opposite ones; and when we agree that they are opposite, to forbid the long-haired to be cobblers, if that is what the bald are to be, or *vice versa.*

G. But that would be ridiculous!

Ἆρα κατ' ἄλλο τι, εἶπον ἐγώ, γελοῖον, ἢ ὅτι τότε οὐ πάντως τὴν αὐτὴν καὶ τὴν ἑτέραν φύσιν ἐτιθέμεθα, ἀλλ' ἐκεῖνο τὸ εἶδος τῆς ἀλλοιώσεώς τε καὶ ὁμοιώσεως μόνον ἐφυλάττομεν τὸ πρὸς αὐτὰ τεῖνον τὰ ἐπιτηδεύματα; οἷον **d** ἰατρικὸν μὲν καὶ ἰατρικὴν τὴν ψυχὴν [ὄντα] τὴν αὐτὴν φύσιν ἔχειν ἐλέγομεν· ἢ οὐκ οἴει;

Ἔγωγε.

Ἰατρικὸν δέ γε καὶ τεκτονικὸν ἄλλην;   5

Πάντως που.

Οὐκοῦν, ἦν δ' ἐγώ, καὶ τὸ τῶν ἀνδρῶν καὶ τὸ τῶν γυναικῶν γένος, ἐὰν μὲν πρὸς τέχνην τινὰ ἢ ἄλλο ἐπιτήδευμα διαφέρον φαίνηται, τοῦτο δὴ φήσομεν ἑκατέρῳ δεῖν ἀποδιδόναι· ἐὰν δ' αὐτῷ τούτῳ φαίνηται διαφέρειν, τῷ τὸ μὲν θῆλυ τίκτειν, 10 τὸ δὲ ἄρρεν ὀχεύειν, οὐδέν τί πω φήσομεν μᾶλλον ἀποδε- **e** δεῖχθαι ὡς πρὸς ὃ ἡμεῖς λέγομεν διαφέρει γυνὴ ἀνδρός, ἀλλ' ἔτι οἰησόμεθα δεῖν τὰ αὐτὰ ἐπιτηδεύειν τούς τε φύλακας ἡμῖν καὶ τὰς γυναῖκας αὐτῶν.

Καὶ ὀρθῶς γ', ἔφη.   5

Οὐκοῦν μετὰ τοῦτο κελεύομεν τὸν τὰ ἐναντία λέγοντα τοῦτο αὐτὸ διδάσκειν ἡμᾶς, πρὸς τίνα τέχνην ἢ τί ἐπιτήδευμα **455** τῶν περὶ πόλεως κατασκευὴν οὐχ ἡ αὐτὴ ἀλλὰ ἑτέρα φύσις γυναικός τε καὶ ἀνδρός;

Δίκαιον γοῦν.

Τάχα τοίνυν ἄν, ὅπερ σὺ ὀλίγον πρότερον ἔλεγες, εἴποι 5 ἂν καὶ ἄλλος, ὅτι ἐν μὲν τῷ παραχρῆμα ἱκανῶς εἰπεῖν οὐ ῥᾴδιον, ἐπισκεψαμένῳ δὲ οὐδὲν χαλεπόν.

Εἴποι γὰρ ἄν.

Βούλει οὖν δεώμεθα τοῦ τὰ τοιαῦτα ἀντιλέγοντος ἀκολου- θῆσαι ἡμῖν, ἐάν πως ἡμεῖς ἐκείνῳ ἐνδειξώμεθα ὅτι οὐδέν ἐστιν **b** ἐπιτήδευμα ἴδιον γυναικὶ πρὸς διοίκησιν πόλεως;

Πάνυ γε.

Ἴθι δή, φήσομεν πρὸς αὐτόν, ἀποκρίνου· ἆρα οὕτως

S. Ridiculous for any other reason than because in our earlier argument we weren't positing similar and different natures in simply *any* sense,

d but were only looking for that kind of difference and sameness which bears upon activities themselves? For example, we meant that a man and a woman with medical talents have the same nature – don't you agree?

G. Certainly.

S. But a doctor and a builder have different natures?

G. Completely so.

S. So, with both the male and the female sex, if one of them is shown to have a distinct capacity for some skill or other activity, we will declare that we should assign this to it. But if they seem to differ in

e this respect alone, that the female bears offspring, while the male begets, we will declare that we have not yet been brought nearer a proof that a woman is different from a man in the sense relevant to our argument, but we will continue to believe that our Guardians and their women should perform the same activities.

G. Quite correct.

455a S. So next we urge our opponent to enlighten us on precisely this: for what skill, or which of the activities involved in the organisation of the city, are the natures of woman and man different?

G. That's right.

S. Now, perhaps someone else too, just as you did a short while ago, might say that it isn't easy to give an adequate account on the spur of the moment, but that it wouldn't be difficult after further reflection.

G. Yes, he might say that.

S. Do you want us, then, to ask our opponent to follow our discussion,

b in the hope that we might somehow demonstrate to him that there is no activity which is peculiar to a woman as regards the running of a city?

G. Certainly.

S. "Come then," we'll say to him, "answer this: did you mean that one

58

ἔλεγες τὸν μὲν εὐφυῆ πρός τι εἶναι, τὸν δὲ ἀφυῆ, ἐν ᾧ ὁ 5
μὲν ῥᾳδίως τι μανθάνοι, ὁ δὲ χαλεπῶς; καὶ ὁ μὲν ἀπὸ
βραχείας μαθήσεως ἐπὶ πολὺ εὑρετικὸς εἴη οὗ ἔμαθεν, ὁ δὲ
πολλῆς μαθήσεως τυχὼν καὶ μελέτης μηδ' ἃ ἔμαθε σῴζοιτο;
καὶ τῷ μὲν τὰ τοῦ σώματος ἱκανῶς ὑπηρετοῖ τῇ διανοίᾳ, τῷ
δὲ ἐναντιοῖτο; ἆρ' ἄλλα ἄττα ἐστὶν ἢ ταῦτα, οἷς τὸν εὐφυῆ c
πρὸς ἕκαστα καὶ τὸν μὴ ὡρίζου;
Οὐδείς, ἦ δ' ὅς, ἄλλα φήσει.

Οἶσθά τι οὖν ὑπὸ ἀνθρώπων μελετώμενον, ἐν ᾧ οὐ πάντα
ταῦτα τὸ τῶν ἀνδρῶν γένος διαφερόντως ἔχει ἢ τὸ τῶν 5
γυναικῶν; ἢ μακρολογῶμεν τήν τε ὑφαντικὴν λέγοντες καὶ
τὴν τῶν ποπάνων τε καὶ ἑψημάτων θεραπείαν, ἐν οἷς δή τι
δοκεῖ τὸ γυναικεῖον γένος εἶναι, οὗ καὶ καταγελαστότατόν
ἐστι πάντων ἡττώμενον; d

Ἀληθῆ, ἔφη, λέγεις, ὅτι πολὺ κρατεῖται ἐν ἅπασιν ὡς
ἔπος εἰπεῖν τὸ γένος τοῦ γένους. γυναῖκες μέντοι πολλαὶ
πολλῶν ἀνδρῶν βελτίους εἰς πολλά· τὸ δὲ ὅλον ἔχει ὡς σὺ
λέγεις. 5

Οὐδὲν ἄρα ἐστίν, ὦ φίλε, ἐπιτήδευμα τῶν πόλιν διοι-
κούντων γυναικὸς διότι γυνή, οὐδ' ἀνδρὸς διότι ἀνήρ,
ἀλλ' ὁμοίως διεσπαρμέναι αἱ φύσεις ἐν ἀμφοῖν τοῖν
ζῴοιν, καὶ πάντων μὲν μετέχει γυνὴ ἐπιτηδευμάτων κατὰ
φύσιν, πάντων δὲ ἀνήρ, ἐπὶ πᾶσι δὲ ἀσθενέστερον γυνὴ e
ἀνδρός.

Πάνυ γε.

Ἦ οὖν ἀνδράσι πάντα προστάξομεν, γυναικὶ δ' οὐδέν;
Καὶ πῶς; 5
Ἀλλ' ἔστι γὰρ οἶμαι, ὡς φήσομεν, καὶ γυνὴ ἰατρική, ἡ δ'
οὔ, καὶ μουσική, ἡ δ' ἄμουσος φύσει.

Τί μήν;

[Καὶ] γυμναστικὴ δ' ἄρα οὔ, οὐδὲ πολεμική, ἡ δὲ ἀπόλεμος 456
καὶ οὐ φιλογυμναστική;

Οἶμαι ἔγωγε.

person has a natural aptitude for something, and another lacks it, whenever the one finds it easy to learn something, and the other difficult? And the one, after a short process of learning, is good at making further discoveries in the subject of his learning, while the other, even if he receives a great deal of instruction and attention, doesn't even retain what he was taught? And the one has his mind adequately supported by his bodily condition, while the other's is

c   obstructed by his? Are there any other factors than these, by which you meant to define both the person with, and the one lacking, a natural aptitude for each thing?"

G. No-one will disagree with these factors.

S. Well now, are you aware of any practice cultivated by humans in which the male sex is not superior to the female in all the ways just mentioned? Or do we have to spend time discussing weaving and the preparation of cakes and vegetables – activities in which the female sex seems to have some distinction, and where it looks utterly

d   ridiculous if it's inferior to all men?

G. It's true that the one sex is greatly surpassed by the other in virtually everything. Yet there are many women who are better at many things than many men; but overall it is as you describe.

S. So, my friend, there is no activity in the governing of a city which belongs to a woman *qua* woman, nor any to a man *qua* man; but natural capacities are distributed similarly among both creatures, and women

e   can participate naturally in all activities, and likewise men, though women are weaker than men for all of them.

G. Entirely true.

S. So shall we assign everything to men, and nothing to a woman?

G. How could we?

S. No, because, as we'll agree, one woman has a natural ability for medicine, and another not, and one for music, another not?

G. Yes.

456a S. Then, isn't one woman gymnastic, and fitted for soldiering, while another is unmilitary and lacking in inclination for gymnastics?

G. I certainly think so.

Τί δέ; φιλόσοφός τε καὶ μισόσοφος; καὶ θυμοειδής, ἡ δ᾽ ἄθυμός ἐστι;

Καὶ ταῦτα.

Ἔστιν ἄρα καὶ φυλακικὴ γυνή, ἡ δ᾽ οὔ. ἦ οὐ τοιαύτην καὶ τῶν ἀνδρῶν τῶν φυλακικῶν φύσιν ἐξελεξάμεθα;

Τοιαύτην μὲν οὖν.

Καὶ γυναικὸς ἄρα καὶ ἀνδρὸς ἡ αὐτὴ φύσις εἰς φυλακὴν πόλεως, πλὴν ὅσα ἀσθενεστέρα, ἡ δὲ ἰσχυροτέρα ἐστίν.

Φαίνεται.

Καὶ γυναῖκες ἄρα αἱ τοιαῦται τοῖς τοιούτοις ἀνδράσιν b ἐκλεκτέαι συνοικεῖν τε καὶ συμφυλάττειν, ἐπείπερ εἰσὶν ἱκαναὶ καὶ συγγενεῖς αὐτοῖς τὴν φύσιν.

Πάνυ γε.

Τὰ δ᾽ ἐπιτηδεύματα οὐ τὰ αὐτὰ ἀποδοτέα ταῖς αὐταῖς φύσεσιν;

Τὰ αὐτά.

Ἥκομεν ἄρα εἰς τὰ πρότερα περιφερόμενοι, καὶ ὁμολογοῦμεν μὴ παρὰ φύσιν εἶναι ταῖς τῶν φυλάκων γυναιξὶ μουσικήν τε καὶ γυμναστικὴν ἀποδιδόναι.

Παντάπασιν μὲν οὖν.

Οὐκ ἄρα ἀδύνατά γε οὐδὲ εὐχαῖς ὅμοια ἐνομοθετοῦμεν, ἐπείπερ κατὰ φύσιν ἐτίθεμεν τὸν νόμον· ἀλλὰ τὰ νῦν παρὰ c ταῦτα γιγνόμενα παρὰ φύσιν μᾶλλον, ὡς ἔοικε, γίγνεται.

Ἔοικεν.

Οὐκοῦν ἡ ἐπίσκεψις ἡμῖν ἦν εἰ δυνατά γε καὶ βέλτιστα λέγοιμεν;

Ἦν γάρ.

Καὶ ὅτι μὲν δὴ δυνατά, διωμολόγηται;

Ναί.

Ὅτι δὲ δὴ βέλτιστα, τὸ μετὰ τοῦτο δεῖ διωμολογηθῆναι;

Δῆλον.

Οὐκοῦν πρός γε τὸ φυλακικὴν γυναῖκα γενέσθαι, οὐκ ἄλλη μὲν ἡμῖν ἄνδρας ποιήσει παιδεία, ἄλλη δὲ γυναῖκας, ἄλλως

S. And mustn't there be a philosophical and an unphilosophical woman? And one woman with a spirited nature, and another who lacks it?

G. Also true.

S. So there is also a woman equipped to be a Guardian, and another who isn't. Isn't that the sort of natural potential that we selected in our male Guardians too?

G. Precisely so.

S. Then a woman and a man can possess the same natures for Guardianship of a city, except in so far as the former is weaker, the latter stronger.

G. It seems so.

b S. Therefore such women must be selected to live with men of the same kind, and share Guardian duties with them, given that they are equivalent and kindred to them in nature.

G. Very true.

S. And must we not assign the same activities to the same natures?

G. Yes.

S. Then we have been brought back round to our earlier claim, and we agree that it is not contrary to nature to assign music and gymnastics to the female Guardians.

G. Absolutely.

S. So what we were legislating was not impossible, nor merely utopian, since the law we were prescribing was in keeping with nature. But it is the opposite social practices occurring at present which turn out, it seems, to be more unnatural.

c

G. So it seems.

S. Now our enquiry was to establish whether our proposals were both possible and for the best?

G. It was.

S. And that they are possible has now been agreed?

G. Yes.

S. And we must next agree whether they are for the best?

G. Clearly.

S. Well, as regards producing women equipped for Guardianship, it won't be two different kinds of education that will produce our men

τε καὶ τὴν αὐτὴν φύσιν παραλαβοῦσα;　　　　　d

Οὐκ ἄλλη.

Πῶς οὖν ἔχεις δόξης τοῦ τοιοῦδε πέρι;

Τίνος δή;

Τοῦ ὑπολαμβάνειν παρὰ σεαυτῷ τὸν μὲν ἀμείνω ἄνδρα,　5
τὸν δὲ χείρω· ἢ πάντας ὁμοίους ἡγῇ;

Οὐδαμῶς.

Ἐν οὖν τῇ πόλει ἣν ᾠκίζομεν, πότερον οἴει ἡμῖν ἀμείνους
ἄνδρας ἐξειργάσθαι τοὺς φύλακας, τυχόντας ἧς διήλθομεν
παιδείας, ἢ τοὺς σκυτοτόμους, τῇ σκυτικῇ παιδευθέντας;　10

Γελοῖον, ἔφη, ἐρωτᾷς.

Μανθάνω, ἔφην.　τί δέ; τῶν ἄλλων πολιτῶν οὐχ οὗτοι
ἄριστοι;　　　　　e

Πολύ γε.

Τί δέ; αἱ γυναῖκες τῶν γυναικῶν οὐχ αὗται ἔσονται
βέλτισται;

Καὶ τοῦτο, ἔφη, πολύ.　　　　　5

Ἔστι δέ τι πόλει ἄμεινον ἢ γυναῖκάς τε καὶ ἄνδρας ὡς
ἀρίστους ἐγγίγνεσθαι;

Οὐκ ἔστιν.

Τοῦτο δὲ μουσική τε καὶ γυμναστικὴ παραγιγνόμεναι, ὡς
ἡμεῖς διήλθομεν, ἀπεργάσονται;　　　　　457

Πῶς δ’ οὔ;

Οὐ μόνον ἄρα δυνατὸν ἀλλὰ καὶ ἄριστον πόλει νόμιμον
ἐτίθεμεν.

Οὕτως.　　　　　5

Ἀποδυτέον δὴ ταῖς τῶν φυλάκων γυναιξίν, ἐπείπερ ἀρετὴν
ἀντὶ ἱματίων ἀμφιέσονται, καὶ κοινωνητέον πολέμου τε καὶ
τῆς ἄλλης φυλακῆς τῆς περὶ τὴν πόλιν, καὶ οὐκ ἄλλα
πρακτέον· τούτων δ’ αὐτῶν τὰ ἐλαφρότερα ταῖς γυναιξὶν
ἢ τοῖς ἀνδράσι δοτέον διὰ τὴν τοῦ γένους ἀσθένειαν. ὁ　10
δὲ γελῶν ἀνὴρ ἐπὶ γυμναῖς γυναιξί, τοῦ βελτίστου ἕνεκα　b
γυμναζομέναις, ἀτελῆ τοῦ γελοίου σοφίας δρέπων καρ-

d and our women for us, especially since it will be entrusted with people of the same nature?

G. It must be the same education.

S. So what is your view about this –

G. What?

S. The assumption you make that one man is superior to another – or do you think they're all equal?

G. Not at all.

S. In the city which we were founding, who do you think have been turned out the better men: our Guardians, after receiving the education we described, or the cobblers, when they've been trained in their leather-craft?

G. What a ridiculous question!

e S. I realise that. Aren't these Guardians the best of the entire citizen body?

G. By far.

S. Well – and won't the female Guardians be the best of all the women?

G. By far, once more.

S. Is there anything better for a city than that it should produce the best possible women and men?

G. No there isn't.

S. And this result will be achieved by the availability of music and
457a gymnastics, in the way we described?

G. Of course.

S. So the regulation we were laying down was not just possible but also best for the city.

G. Yes.

S. Then the female Guardians must be strip off their clothing, since they will clothe themselves in excellence rather than cloaks. And they must share in both warfare and the rest of the civic duties of the Guardians, and not be given different activities; but within these areas, the women must be allotted lighter tasks than the men,
b because of the weakness of their sex. As for the person who laughs at the sight of naked women, when their athletic training is all for the best - 'plucking an unripe fruit of humour's cleverness', he has no

πόν, οὐδὲν οἶδεν, ὡς ἔοικεν, ἐφ' ᾧ γελᾷ οὐδ' ὅτι πράττει·
κάλλιστα γὰρ δὴ τοῦτο καὶ λέγεται καὶ λελέξεται, ὅτι τὸ μὲν
ὠφέλιμον καλόν, τὸ δὲ βλαβερὸν αἰσχρόν.   5

Παντάπασι μὲν οὖν.

Τοῦτο μὲν τοίνυν ἓν ὥσπερ κῦμα φῶμεν διαφεύγειν τοῦ
γυναικείου πέρι νόμου λέγοντες, ὥστε μὴ παντάπασι κατα-
κλυσθῆναι τιθέντας ὡς δεῖ κοινῇ πάντα ἐπιτηδεύειν τούς τε
φύλακας ἡμῖν καὶ τὰς φυλακίδας, ἀλλά πῃ τὸν λόγον αὐτὸν   c
αὐτῷ ὁμολογεῖσθαι ὡς δυνατά τε καὶ ὠφέλιμα λέγει;

Καὶ μάλα, ἔφη, οὐ σμικρὸν κῦμα διαφεύγεις.

Φήσεις γε, ἦν δ' ἐγώ, οὐ μέγα αὐτὸ εἶναι, ὅταν τὸ μετὰ
τοῦτο ἴδῃς.   5

Λέγε δή, ἴδω, ἔφη.

Τούτῳ, ἦν δ' ἐγώ, ἕπεται νόμος καὶ τοῖς ἔμπροσθεν τοῖς
ἄλλοις, ὡς ἐγῷμαι, ὅδε.

Τίς;

Τὰς γυναῖκας ταύτας τῶν ἀνδρῶν τούτων πάντων πάσας   10
εἶναι κοινάς, ἰδίᾳ δὲ μηδενὶ μηδεμίαν συνοικεῖν· καὶ τοὺς   d
παῖδας αὖ κοινούς, καὶ μήτε γονέα ἔκγονον εἰδέναι τὸν αὑτοῦ
μήτε παῖδα γονέα.

Πολύ, ἔφη, τοῦτο ἐκείνου μεῖζον πρὸς ἀπιστίαν καὶ τοῦ
δυνατοῦ πέρι καὶ τοῦ ὠφελίμου.   5

Οὐκ οἶμαι, ἦν δ' ἐγώ, περί γε τοῦ ὠφελίμου ἀμφισβη-
τεῖσθαι ἄν, ὡς οὐ μέγιστον ἀγαθὸν κοινὰς μὲν τὰς γυναῖκας
εἶναι, κοινοὺς δὲ τοὺς παῖδας, εἴπερ οἷόν τε· ἀλλ' οἶμαι περὶ
τοῦ εἰ δυνατὸν ἢ μὴ πλείστην ἂν ἀμφισβήτησιν γενέσθαι.

Περὶ ἀμφοτέρων, ἦ δ' ὅς, εὖ μάλ' ἂν ἀμφισβητηθείη.   e

Λέγεις, ἦν δ' ἐγώ, λόγων σύστασιν· ἐγὼ δ' ᾤμην ἔκ γε
τοῦ ἑτέρου ἀποδράσεσθαι, εἴ σοι δόξειεν ὠφέλιμον εἶναι,
λοιπὸν δὲ δή μοι ἔσεσθαι περὶ τοῦ δυνατοῦ καὶ μή.

Ἀλλ' οὐκ ἔλαθες, ἦ δ' ὅς, ἀποδιδράσκων, ἀλλ' ἀμφοτέρων 5
πέρι δίδου λόγον.

Ὑφεκτέον, ἦν δ' ἐγώ, δίκην. τοσόνδε μέντοι χάρισαί

notion, so it seems, what he is laughing at or how he is behaving. For it is, and always will be, the finest saying, that 'what brings benefit is beautiful, what brings harm is ugly'.

G. Absolutely.

S. Should we say, then, that in our proposed regulation for women we are avoiding one sort of 'wave', and thus escaping being entirely

c engulfed for the suggestion that our male and female Guardians should share all their activities, while our argument manages to maintain a consistent claim to be asserting what is both possible and for the best?

G. It's certainly no small wave you're avoiding!

S. But you won't say it's so large when you see the next one!

G. Tell me, then – let me see.

S. This next regulation follows on from the one just discussed, and from all our previous proposals.

G. What is it?

S. That all these women should be shared between all these men, and

d that no individual woman and man should live together; and the children too should be shared between them, without a parent knowing its own offspring, or a child its parent.

G. This provides much greater grounds for doubt, as regards both possibility and benefit, than the last proposal.

S. I don't think that as regards the benefit of it, at least, anyone would argue that it isn't the greatest good for both women and children to be shared, *if* it's possible; but I suppose there would be a great deal of dispute about whether it is or isn't possible.

e G. There would be strenuous disagreement about *both*!

S. You're suggesting a massive argument! But I was hoping to escape the first point, namely whether you thought it beneficial, and that I would just be left with the argument about possibility.

G. Well, you didn't make your escape successfully! You must provide your arguments on both points.

458a S. I must face the charge. But grant me this much favour: let me pamper

μοι· ἔασόν με ἑορτάσαι, ὥσπερ οἱ ἀργοὶ τὴν διάνοιαν εἰώ- **458**
θασιν ἑστιᾶσθαι ὑφ᾽ ἑαυτῶν, ὅταν μόνοι πορεύωνται. καὶ
γὰρ οἱ τοιοῦτοί που, πρὶν ἐξευρεῖν τίνα τρόπον ἔσται τι ὧν
ἐπιθυμοῦσι, τοῦτο παρέντες, ἵνα μὴ κάμνωσι βουλευόμενοι
περὶ τοῦ δυνατοῦ καὶ μή, θέντες ὡς ὑπάρχον εἶναι ὃ βού- 5
λονται, ἤδη τὰ λοιπὰ διατάττουσιν καὶ χαίρουσιν διεξιόντες
οἷα δράσουσι γενομένου, ἀργὸν καὶ ἄλλως ψυχὴν ἔτι
ἀργοτέραν ποιοῦντες. ἤδη οὖν καὶ αὐτὸς μαλθακίζομαι, καὶ **b**
ἐκεῖνα μὲν ἐπιθυμῶ ἀναβαλέσθαι καὶ ὕστερον ἐπισκέψασθαι,
ᾗ δυνατά, νῦν δὲ ὡς δυνατῶν ὄντων θεὶς σκέψομαι, ἄν μοι
παριῇς, πῶς διατάξουσιν αὐτὰ οἱ ἄρχοντες γιγνόμενα, καὶ
ὅτι πάντων συμφορώτατ᾽ ἂν εἴη πραχθέντα τῇ τε πόλει καὶ 5
τοῖς φύλαξιν. ταῦτα πειράσομαί σοι πρότερα συνδιασκοπεῖ-
σθαι, ὕστερα δ᾽ ἐκεῖνα, εἴπερ παριεῖς.

Ἀλλὰ παρίημι, ἔφη, καὶ σκόπει.

Οἶμαι τοίνυν, ἦν δ᾽ ἐγώ, εἴπερ ἔσονται οἱ ἄρχοντες ἄξιοι
τούτου τοῦ ὀνόματος, οἵ τε τούτοις ἐπίκουροι κατὰ ταὐτά, **c**
τοὺς μὲν ἐθελήσειν ποιεῖν τὰ ἐπιταττόμενα, τοὺς δὲ ἐπι-
τάξειν, τὰ μὲν αὐτοὺς πειθομένους τοῖς νόμοις, τὰ δὲ καὶ
μιμουμένους, ὅσα ἂν ἐκείνοις ἐπιτρέψωμεν.

Εἰκός, ἔφη. 5

Σὺ μὲν τοίνυν, ἦν δ᾽ ἐγώ, ὁ νομοθέτης αὐτοῖς, ὥσπερ τοὺς
ἄνδρας ἐξέλεξας, οὕτω καὶ τὰς γυναῖκας ἐκλέξας παραδώσεις
καθ᾽ ὅσον οἷόν τε ὁμοφυεῖς· οἱ δέ, ἅτε οἰκίας τε καὶ συσ-
σίτια κοινὰ ἔχοντες, ἰδίᾳ δὲ οὐδενὸς οὐδὲν τοιοῦτον κεκτη-
μένου, ὁμοῦ δὴ ἔσονται, ὁμοῦ δὲ ἀναμεμειγμένων καὶ ἐν **d**
γυμνασίοις καὶ ἐν τῇ ἄλλῃ τροφῇ ὑπ᾽ ἀνάγκης οἶμαι τῆς
ἐμφύτου ἄξονται πρὸς τὴν ἀλλήλων μεῖξιν. ἢ οὐκ ἀναγκαῖά
σοι δοκῶ λέγειν;

Οὐ γεωμετρικαῖς γε, ἦ δ᾽ ὅς, ἀλλ᾽ ἐρωτικαῖς ἀνάγκαις, αἳ 5
κινδυνεύουσιν ἐκείνων δριμύτεραι εἶναι πρὸς τὸ πείθειν τε
καὶ ἕλκειν τὸν πολὺν λεών.

Καὶ μάλα, εἶπον. ἀλλὰ μετὰ δὴ ταῦτα, ὦ Γλαύκων,

myself in the way in which lazy-minded people like to entertain themselves when they're walking alone. Such people omit to discover *how* they'll obtain any of the things they desire, so as to avoid the trouble of taking decisions about what is and isn't possible. They assume as available what it is that they want, and then they make all the other arrangements, and enjoy going through what they'll do when it comes about – thus rendering their already lazy

b minds lazier still. Well, I too am feeling self-indulgent at the moment, and I want to postpone for later consideration the question of how these things might be possible; and, on the assumption that they *are* possible, I'll now consider (if you'll let me) how the Rulers will arrange these things when they come about, and I'll argue that, if put into practice, they would be the most advantageous conditions for both the city and the Guardians. This is what I'll try to examine with you first, leaving the other question for later – if you'll allow this.

G. I do allow it; proceed with the enquiry.

c S. I believe that if the Rulers are to be worthy of this title, and likewise with their Auxiliaries, the latter will be prepared to carry out orders, and the Rulers to frame the orders, partly by themselves heeding the laws, and partly by emulating them, in so far as we give them leave to do so.

G. That seems reasonable.

S. So you, as their lawgiver, when you've selected the women, just as you did the men, will hand them over as people who have, so far as possible, the same nature. These Guardians, because they have shared dwellings and dining-halls, and none of them has any private

d property of this kind, will therefore spend their lives together; and as they are mixed together in the gymnasia as well as the rest of their daily lives, they will be brought by natural necessity, I think, to a desire for sexual intercourse with one another. Don't you agree that I'm referring to something necessary?

G. Not by logical but by erotic necessity, which probably has a keener power to persuade and draw most people.

S. Indeed. But by this stage, Glaucon, for the Guardians' sexual

ἀτάκτως μὲν μείγνυσθαι ἀλλήλοις ἢ ἄλλο ὁτιοῦν ποιεῖν οὔτε
ὅσιον ἐν εὐδαιμόνων πόλει οὔτ' ἐάσουσιν οἱ ἄρχοντες.　　　e

Οὐ γὰρ δίκαιον, ἔφη.

Δῆλον δὴ ὅτι γάμους τὸ μετὰ τοῦτο ποιήσομεν ἱεροὺς εἰς
δύναμιν ὅτι μάλιστα· εἶεν δ' ἂν ἱεροὶ οἱ ὠφελιμώτατοι.

Παντάπασι μὲν οὖν.　　　5

Πῶς οὖν δὴ ὠφελιμώτατοι ἔσονται; τόδε μοι λέγε, ὦ 459
Γλαύκων· ὁρῶ γάρ σου ἐν τῇ οἰκίᾳ καὶ κύνας θηρευτικοὺς
καὶ τῶν γενναίων ὀρνίθων μάλα συχνούς· ἆρ' οὖν, ὦ πρὸς
Διός, προσέσχηκάς τι τοῖς τούτων γάμοις τε καὶ παιδο-
ποιίᾳ;　　　5

Τὸ ποῖον; ἔφη.

Πρῶτον μὲν αὐτῶν τούτων, καίπερ ὄντων γενναίων, ἆρ'
οὐκ εἰσί τινες καὶ γίγνονται ἄριστοι;

Εἰσίν.

Πότερον οὖν ἐξ ἁπάντων ὁμοίως γεννᾷς, ἢ προθυμῇ ὅτι 10
μάλιστα ἐκ τῶν ἀρίστων;

Ἐκ τῶν ἀρίστων.

Τί δ'; ἐκ τῶν νεωτάτων ἢ ἐκ τῶν γεραιτάτων ἢ ἐξ b
ἀκμαζόντων ὅτι μάλιστα;

Ἐξ ἀκμαζόντων.

Καὶ ἂν μὴ οὕτω γεννᾶται, πολύ σοι ἡγῇ χεῖρον ἔσεσθαι
τό τε τῶν ὀρνίθων καὶ τὸ τῶν κυνῶν γένος;　　　5

Ἔγωγ', ἔφη.

Τί δὲ ἵππων οἴει, ἦν δ' ἐγώ, καὶ τῶν ἄλλων ζῴων; ἢ
ἄλλῃ πῃ ἔχειν;

Ἄτοπον μεντἂν, ἦ δ' ὅς, εἴη.

Βαβαῖ, ἦν δ' ἐγώ, ὦ φίλε ἑταῖρε, ὡς ἄρα σφόδρα ἡμῖν 10
δεῖ ἄκρων εἶναι τῶν ἀρχόντων, εἴπερ καὶ περὶ τὸ τῶν
ἀνθρώπων γένος ὡσαύτως ἔχει.

Ἀλλὰ μὲν δὴ ἔχει, ἔφη· ἀλλὰ τί δή;　　　c

Ὅτι ἀνάγκη αὐτοῖς, ἦν δ' ἐγώ, φαρμάκοις πολλοῖς χρῆσθαι. ἰατρὸν δέ που μὴ δεομένοις μὲν σώμασι φαρμάκων,

intercourse, or anything else that they do, to be unregulated, wouldn't
e   be a pious thing in a city of the happy, and the Rulers won't allow
it.

G.   No, it wouldn't be just.

S.   So clearly we shall next have to ensure marriages that are as sacred
as possible; and sacred marriages will be those that are most
beneficial.

G.   Absolutely.

459a S.   How, then, will the most beneficial marriages come about? Tell me
this, Glaucon – I notice that in your house there are hunting dogs and
very many well-bred birds: have you, in the name of Zeus, paid any
attention to the marriages and procreation of these animals?

G.   What do you mean!

S.   In the first place, although these animals as a group are well-bred,
isn't it the case that some of them are, or turn out to be, the very best?

G.   They are.

S.   So do you breed from all of them equally, or are you keen to breed
most of all from the best?

G.   From the best.

b S.   And most of all from the youngest, the oldest, or those who are in
their prime?

G.   Those in their prime.

S.   And if not bred in this way, do you think that your breed of birds and
dogs will turn out much lower in quality?

G.   Certainly.

S.   And what do you think about horses and other creatures? Is the
situation at all different with them?

G.   It would be remarkable if it were.

S.   Good heavens, my dear companion! We need our Rulers to be of the
highest quality, then, if the same holds true for the human species as
well.

c G.   Well it *does* hold – but what follows?

S.   That the Rulers are obliged to use many drugs. And when a doctor
has to treat bodies that don't require drugs, but the patients are

ἀλλὰ διαίτῃ ἐθελόντων ὑπακούειν, καὶ φαυλότερον ἐξαρκεῖν
ἡγούμεθα εἶναι· ὅταν δὲ δὴ καὶ φαρμακεύειν δέῃ, ἴσμεν ὅτι 5
ἀνδρειοτέρου δεῖ τοῦ ἰατροῦ.

Ἀληθῆ· ἀλλὰ πρὸς τί λέγεις;

Πρὸς τόδε, ἦν δ' ἐγώ· συχνῷ τῷ ψεύδει καὶ τῇ ἀπάτῃ
κινδυνεύει ἡμῖν δεήσειν χρῆσθαι τοὺς ἄρχοντας ἐπ' ὠφελίᾳ
τῶν ἀρχομένων. ἔφαμεν δέ που ἐν φαρμάκου εἴδει πάντα d
τὰ τοιαῦτα χρήσιμα εἶναι.

Καὶ ὀρθῶς γε, ἔφη.

Ἐν τοῖς γάμοις τοίνυν καὶ παιδοποιίαις ἔοικε τὸ ὀρθὸν
τοῦτο γίγνεσθαι οὐκ ἐλάχιστον. 5

Πῶς δή;

Δεῖ μέν, εἶπον, ἐκ τῶν ὡμολογημένων τοὺς ἀρίστους ταῖς
ἀρίσταις συγγίγνεσθαι ὡς πλειστάκις, τοὺς δὲ φαυλοτάτους
ταῖς φαυλοτάταις τοὐναντίον, καὶ τῶν μὲν τὰ ἔκγονα τρέφειν,
τῶν δὲ μή, εἰ μέλλει τὸ ποίμνιον ὅτι ἀκρότατον εἶναι, καὶ e
ταῦτα πάντα γιγνόμενα λανθάνειν πλὴν αὐτοὺς τοὺς ἄρχοντας,
εἰ αὖ ἡ ἀγέλη τῶν φυλάκων ὅτι μάλιστα ἀστασίαστος ἔσται.

Ὀρθότατα, ἔφη.

Οὐκοῦν δὴ ἑορταί τινες νομοθετητέαι ἐν αἷς συνάξομεν 5
τάς τε νύμφας καὶ τοὺς νυμφίους καὶ θυσίαι, καὶ ὕμνοι
ποιητέοι τοῖς ἡμετέροις ποιηταῖς πρέποντες τοῖς γιγνομένοις 460
γάμοις· τὸ δὲ πλῆθος τῶν γάμων ἐπὶ τοῖς ἄρχουσι ποιήσομεν, ἵν' ὡς μάλιστα διασῴζωσι τὸν αὐτὸν ἀριθμὸν τῶν
ἀνδρῶν, πρὸς πολέμους τε καὶ νόσους καὶ πάντα τὰ τοιαῦτα
ἀποσκοποῦντες, καὶ μήτε μεγάλη ἡμῖν ἡ πόλις κατὰ τὸ 5
δυνατὸν μήτε σμικρὰ γίγνηται.

Ὀρθῶς, ἔφη.

Κλῆροι δή τινες οἶμαι ποιητέοι κομψοί, ὥστε τὸν φαῦλον
ἐκεῖνον αἰτιᾶσθαι ἐφ' ἑκάστης συνέρξεως τύχην ἀλλὰ μὴ
τοὺς ἄρχοντας. 10

Καὶ μάλα, ἔφη.

Καὶ τοῖς ἀγαθοῖς γέ που τῶν νέων ἐν πολέμῳ ἢ ἄλλοθί b

prepared to follow a regimen, we regard even a rather poor practitioner as good enough. But when it's actually necessary to give drugs, we know that we need the doctor to be rather acute.

G. True; but what's your point?

S. This: it is frequent falsehood and deception which our Rulers will probably have to use for the benefit of those under their control. We surely agreed that when serving as a sort of drug, all such means are useful.

d

G. And we were correct to agree.

S. Well, in the case of marriages and procreation, this principle of correctness seems especially in place.

G. In just what way?

S. It's necessary, given our agreed premises, that the best men should mate with the best women in as many cases as possible, while the reverse should hold for the worst men and women; and we should rear the offspring of the former, but not of the latter, if our flock is to be of the highest quality. And all this should happen without the knowledge of anyone but the Rulers, if our Guardians' herd is to be as free from faction as it can be.

e

G. Entirely correct.

S. So then, we must legislate for festivals and sacrifices at which we shall bring together brides and bridegrooms, and our poets must compose hymns that befit the weddings which take place. The number of weddings we shall leave the Rulers to decide, in order that they can keep the number of males as constant as possible, making allowance for wars, diseases and everything of that sort, and in order that our city may, so far as possible, become neither too great nor too small.

460a

G. Correct.

S. I think, then, that specious lotteries must be created, so that the kind of inferior person we mentioned blames chance, and not the Rulers, at each act of pairing.

G. Very true.

S. And to those young men who show ability in war or in any other

b

που γέρα δοτέον καὶ ἆθλα ἄλλα τε καὶ ἀφθονεστέρα ἡ
ἐξουσία τῆς τῶν γυναικῶν συγκοιμήσεως, ἵνα καὶ ἅμα μετὰ
προφάσεως ὡς πλεῖστοι τῶν παίδων ἐκ τῶν τοιούτων
σπείρωνται.

'Ορθῶς.

Οὐκοῦν καὶ τὰ ἀεὶ γιγνόμενα ἔκγονα παραλαμβάνουσαι
αἱ ἐπὶ τούτων ἐφεστηκυῖαι ἀρχαὶ εἴτε ἀνδρῶν εἴτε γυναικῶν
εἴτε ἀμφότερα—κοιναὶ μὲν γάρ που καὶ ἀρχαὶ γυναιξί τε
καὶ ἀνδράσιν—

Ναί.

Τὰ μὲν δὴ τῶν ἀγαθῶν, δοκῶ, λαβοῦσαι εἰς τὸν σηκὸν c
οἴσουσιν παρά τινας τροφοὺς χωρὶς οἰκούσας ἔν τινι μέρει
τῆς πόλεως· τὰ δὲ τῶν χειρόνων, καὶ ἐάν τι τῶν ἑτέρων
ἀνάπηρον γίγνηται, ἐν ἀπορρήτῳ τε καὶ ἀδήλῳ κατακρύψουσιν
ὡς πρέπει.

Εἴπερ μέλλει, ἔφη, καθαρὸν τὸ γένος τῶν φυλάκων
ἔσεσθαι.

Οὐκοῦν καὶ τροφῆς οὗτοι ἐπιμελήσονται τάς τε μητέρας
ἐπὶ τὸν σηκὸν ἄγοντες ὅταν σπαργῶσι, πᾶσαν μηχανὴν
μηχανώμενοι ὅπως μηδεμία τὸ αὑτῆς αἰσθήσεται, καὶ ἄλλας d
γάλα ἐχούσας ἐκπορίζοντες, ἐὰν μὴ αὐταὶ ἱκαναὶ ὦσι, καὶ
αὐτῶν τούτων ἐπιμελήσονται ὅπως μέτριον χρόνον θηλάσον-
ται, ἀγρυπνίας δὲ καὶ τὸν ἄλλον πόνον τίτθαις τε καὶ τροφοῖς
παραδώσουσιν;

Πολλὴν ῥᾳστώνην, ἔφη, λέγεις τῆς παιδοποιίας ταῖς τῶν
φυλάκων γυναιξίν.

Πρέπει γάρ, ἦν δ' ἐγώ. τὸ δ' ἐφεξῆς διέλθωμεν ὃ
προυθέμεθα. ἔφαμεν γὰρ δὴ ἐξ ἀκμαζόντων δεῖν τὰ ἔκγονα
γίγνεσθαι.

'Αληθῆ.

'Αρ' οὖν σοι συνδοκεῖ μέτριος χρόνος ἀκμῆς τὰ εἴκοσι e
ἔτη γυναικί, ἀνδρὶ δὲ τὰ τριάκοντα;

Τὰ ποῖα αὐτῶν; ἔφη.

context, we must surely give privileges and rewards, among them a more generous chance of sleeping with the women, in order that simultaneously a pretext may be created for producing as many children as possible from such people.

G. Correct.

S. Well then, whenever offspring are born, they'll be taken by the officials responsible for these matters, whether male, female or both – for surely the magistracies too will be shared by women and men –

G. Yes.

c S. The offspring of the good, I think, they'll take and remove to the compound, into the care of nurses who live separately in one area of the city. But those of inferior parents, as well as any deformed offspring from the others, they'll dispose of in a prohibited and secret place, as is fitting.

G. Yes, if the breed of the Guardians is to remain pure.

S. And will these magistrates also make arrangements for feeding by bringing the mothers to the compound when they are lactating

d (taking every precaution to see that none of them recognises her own child), and supplying other women as wet-nurses if there aren't enough of the former? And will they supervise these women, to make sure that they spend only a moderate period breast-feeding, while leaving broken nights and other troubles for the wet-nurses?

G. You're describing a great deal of relief for the female Guardians in their child-bearing!

S. Which is as it should be. But let us follow through our earlier suggestion; for we said that offspring should be bred from parents in their prime.

G. True.

e S. Well, do you agree that a reasonable period for a woman's prime is twenty years, and thirty for a man's?

G. Which particular ones?

Γυναικὶ μέν, ἦν δ' ἐγώ, ἀρξαμένῃ ἀπὸ εἰκοσιέτιδος μέχρι
τετταρακονταέτιδος τίκτειν τῇ πόλει· ἀνδρὶ δέ, ἐπειδὰν τὴν 5
ὀξυτάτην δρόμου ἀκμὴν παρῇ, τὸ ἀπὸ τούτου γεννᾶν τῇ
πόλει μέχρι πεντεκαιπεντηκονταέτους.

Ἀμφοτέρων γοῦν, ἔφη, αὕτη ἀκμὴ σώματός τε καὶ 461
φρονήσεως.

Οὐκοῦν ἐάντε πρεσβύτερος τούτων ἐάντε νεώτερος τῶν
εἰς τὸ κοινὸν γεννήσεων ἅψηται, οὔτε ὅσιον οὔτε δίκαιον
φήσομεν τὸ ἁμάρτημα, ὡς παῖδα φιτύοντος τῇ πόλει, ὅς, ἂν 5
λάθῃ, γεννήσεται οὐχ ὑπὸ θυσιῶν οὐδ' ὑπὸ εὐχῶν φύς, ἃς
ἐφ' ἑκάστοις τοῖς γάμοις εὔξονται καὶ ἱέρειαι καὶ ἱερεῖς καὶ
σύμπασα ἡ πόλις ἐξ ἀγαθῶν ἀμείνους καὶ ἐξ ὠφελίμων
ὠφελιμωτέρους ἀεὶ τοὺς ἐκγόνους γίγνεσθαι, ἀλλ' ὑπὸ b
σκότου μετὰ δεινῆς ἀκρατείας γεγονώς.

Ὀρθῶς, ἔφη.

Ὁ αὐτὸς δέ γ', εἶπον, νόμος, ἐάν τις τῶν ἔτι γεννώντων
μὴ συνέρξαντος ἄρχοντος ἅπτηται τῶν ἐν ἡλικίᾳ γυναικῶν· 5
νόθον γὰρ καὶ ἀνέγγυον καὶ ἀνίερον φήσομεν αὐτὸν παῖδα
τῇ πόλει καθιστάναι.

Ὀρθότατα, ἔφη.

Ὅταν δὲ δὴ οἶμαι αἵ τε γυναῖκες καὶ οἱ ἄνδρες τοῦ γεννᾶν
ἐκβῶσι τὴν ἡλικίαν, ἀφήσομέν που ἐλευθέρους αὐτοὺς συγ- 10
γίγνεσθαι ᾧ ἂν ἐθέλωσι, πλὴν θυγατρὶ καὶ μητρὶ καὶ ταῖς c
τῶν θυγατέρων παισὶ καὶ ταῖς ἄνω μητρός, καὶ γυναῖκας αὖ
πλὴν ὑεῖ καὶ πατρὶ καὶ τοῖς τούτων εἰς τὸ κάτω καὶ ἐπὶ τὸ
ἄνω, καὶ ταῦτά γ' ἤδη πάντα διακελευσάμενοι προθυμεῖσθαι
μάλιστα μὲν μηδ' εἰς φῶς ἐκφέρειν κύημα μηδέ γ' ἕν, ἐὰν 5
γένηται, ἐὰν δέ τι βιάσηται, οὕτω τιθέναι, ὡς οὐκ οὔσης
τροφῆς τῷ τοιούτῳ.

Καὶ ταῦτα μέν γ', ἔφη, μετρίως λέγεται· πατέρας δὲ καὶ
θυγατέρας καὶ ἃ νυνδὴ ἔλεγες πῶς διαγνώσονται ἀλλήλων; d

Οὐδαμῶς, ἦν δ' ἐγώ· ἀλλ' ἀφ' ἧς ἂν ἡμέρας τις αὐτῶν
νυμφίος γένηται, μετ' ἐκείνην δεκάτῳ μηνὶ καὶ ἑβδόμῳ δὴ ἃ

S. A woman should bear children for the city from the age of twenty to that of forty; while a man should beget children for the city from the age when he loses his sharpest fitness for running, until he is fifty-five.

461a G. Yes, in both cases this is the period of physical and intellectual prime.

S. So if anyone engages in breeding for the state at an age either older or younger than this, we shall declare his offence to be both impious and unjust, since he is propagating for the city a child which, if it goes undetected, will be begotten and born independently of the sacrifices and prayers which priestesses, priests and the entire city will make at every wedding ceremony (prayers that from good and

b beneficial parents even better and more beneficial offspring should be produced), and instead will come into being under cover of darkness and through a terrible act of irresponsibility.

G. Correct.

S. The same regulation should apply if a male of breeding age liaises with a woman in her prime without a Ruler pairing them: we shall declare that he is creating an illegitimate, uncertified and unholy child for the city.

G. Quite correct.

S. But I think that when women and men pass the age of breeding, we

c shall leave the men free to mate with anyone they wish, except for daughter, mother, daughters' female children, and women in the generation before the mother's; and correspondingly in the case of the women, the exceptions here being son, father, and males in the generations either before or after these. And we shall allow all this only after instructing them to take care, if at all possible, not to let a single foetus that might be conceived reach birth, but if one does force its way out, to arrange things on the principle that no nurture is available for such a child.

G. These proposals are reasonable. But how will they recognise their

d fathers, daughters, and the other relatives you mentioned just now?

S. They won't at all. Instead, from the day on which someone becomes a bridegroom, he will call all offspring subsequently born in the

ἂν γένηται ἔκγονα, ταῦτα πάντα προσερεῖ τὰ μὲν ἄρρενα
υἱεῖς, τὰ δὲ θήλεα θυγατέρας, καὶ ἐκεῖνα ἐκεῖνον πατέρα, καὶ 5
οὕτω δὴ τὰ τούτων ἔκγονα παίδων παῖδας, καὶ ἐκεῖν' αὖ
ἐκείνους πάππους τε καὶ τηθάς, τὰ δ' ἐν ἐκείνῳ τῷ χρόνῳ
γεγονότα, ἐν ᾧ αἱ μητέρες καὶ οἱ πατέρες αὐτῶν ἐγέννων,
ἀδελφάς τε καὶ ἀδελφούς, ὥστε, ὃ νυνδὴ ἐλέγομεν, ἀλλήλων e
μὴ ἅπτεσθαι. ἀδελφοὺς δὲ καὶ ἀδελφὰς δώσει ὁ νόμος συνοικεῖν, ἐὰν ὁ κλῆρος ταύτῃ συμπίπτῃ καὶ ἡ Πυθία προσαναιρῇ.

Ὀρθότατα, ἦ δ' ὅς.

Ἡ μὲν δὴ κοινωνία, ὦ Γλαύκων, αὕτη τε καὶ τοιαύτη 5
γυναικῶν τε καὶ παίδων τοῖς φύλαξί σοι τῆς πόλεως· ὡς
δὲ ἑπομένη τε τῇ ἄλλῃ πολιτείᾳ καὶ μακρῷ βελτίστη, δεῖ
δὴ τὸ μετὰ τοῦτο βεβαιώσασθαι παρὰ τοῦ λόγου. ἢ πῶς
ποιῶμεν;

Οὕτω νὴ Δία, ἦ δ' ὅς.   462

Ἆρ' οὖν οὐχ ἥδε ἀρχὴ τῆς ὁμολογίας, ἐρέσθαι ἡμᾶς
αὐτοὺς τί ποτε τὸ μέγιστον ἀγαθὸν ἔχομεν εἰπεῖν εἰς πόλεως
κατασκευήν, οὗ δεῖ στοχαζόμενον τὸν νομοθέτην τιθέναι τοὺς
νόμους, καὶ τί μέγιστον κακόν, εἶτα ἐπισκέψασθαι ἆρα ἃ 5
νυνδὴ διήλθομεν εἰς μὲν τὸ τοῦ ἀγαθοῦ ἴχνος ἡμῖν ἁρμόττει,
τῷ δὲ τοῦ κακοῦ ἀναρμοστεῖ;

Πάντων μάλιστα, ἔφη.

Ἔχομεν οὖν τι μεῖζον κακὸν πόλει ἢ ἐκεῖνο ὃ ἂν αὐτὴν
διασπᾷ καὶ ποιῇ πολλὰς ἀντὶ μιᾶς; ἢ μεῖζον ἀγαθὸν τοῦ ὃ b
ἂν συνδῇ τε καὶ ποιῇ μίαν;

Οὐκ ἔχομεν.

Οὐκοῦν ἡ μὲν ἡδονῆς τε καὶ λύπης κοινωνία συνδεῖ, ὅταν
ὅτι μάλιστα πάντες οἱ πολῖται τῶν αὐτῶν γιγνομένων τε καὶ 5
ἀπολλυμένων παραπλησίως χαίρωσι καὶ λυπῶνται;

Παντάπασι μὲν οὖν, ἔφη.

Ἡ δέ γε τῶν τοιούτων ἰδίωσις διαλύει, ὅταν οἱ μὲν
περιαλγεῖς, οἱ δὲ περιχαρεῖς γίγνωνται ἐπὶ τοῖς αὐτοῖς
παθήμασι τῆς πόλεώς τε καὶ τῶν ἐν τῇ πόλει;   c

tenth month, and even the seventh, his 'sons', if male, and 'daughters', if female, and they will call him 'father'; on the same principle, he will call *their* offspring his 'grandchildren', and the latter in turn will call the others their 'grandfathers' and 'grandmothers'; while they will regard all those born in the period when their 'mothers' and

e 'fathers' were breeding, as 'sisters' and 'brothers', and thus, as we mentioned just now, will avoid sexual relations with one another. But brothers and sisters the law *will* allow to form unions in cases where the lottery falls out this way and the Pythian priestess agrees.

G. Quite correct.

S. This then, or something like it, is the 'sharing' of women and children for the Guardians of your city. But that this is consistent with the rest of the régime, and by far the best arrangement possible, is what we must next get securely established by our argument – should we not?

462a G. Yes, by Zeus!

S. Well, shouldn't we start to seek agreement by asking ourselves what the greatest good is that we can name for the condition of a city – one which the lawgiver should have his sights on in framing its laws – and what the greatest evil is; and then consider whether what we have just discussed fits our pattern of the good, and is incompatible with that of the evil?

G. Absolutely.

S. Now, can we name any greater evil for a city than that which pulls

b it apart and turns it into many cities rather than one? Or a greater good than whatever binds it together and makes it unified?

G. We can't.

S. Well, does a sharing of pleasure and pain bind it together, whenever all the citizens, so far as possible, feel similar joy or pain at the same gains or losses?

G. Undoubtedly so.

S. While individualism in such matters breaks up the city, whenever some people are highly distressed, others highly delighted, at the

c same experiences for the city and its inhabitants?

Τί δ' οὔ;

Ἆρ' οὖν ἐκ τοῦδε τὸ τοιόνδε γίγνεται, ὅταν μὴ ἅμα φθέγ-
γωνται ἐν τῇ πόλει τὰ τοιάδε ῥήματα, τό τε ἐμὸν καὶ τὸ οὐκ
ἐμόν; καὶ περὶ τοῦ ἀλλοτρίου κατὰ ταὐτά;   5

Κομιδῇ μὲν οὖν.

Ἐν ᾗτινι δὴ πόλει πλεῖστοι ἐπὶ τὸ αὐτὸ κατὰ ταὐτὰ τοῦτο
λέγουσι τὸ ἐμὸν καὶ τὸ οὐκ ἐμόν, αὕτη ἄριστα διοικεῖται;

Πολύ γε.

Καὶ ἥτις δὴ ἐγγύτατα ἑνὸς ἀνθρώπου ἔχει; οἷον ὅταν που   10
ἡμῶν δάκτυλός του πληγῇ, πᾶσα ἡ κοινωνία ἡ κατὰ τὸ σῶμα
πρὸς τὴν ψυχὴν τεταμένη εἰς μίαν σύνταξιν τὴν τοῦ ἄρχοντος ἐν αὐτῇ ᾔσθετό τε καὶ πᾶσα ἅμα συνήλγησεν μέρους   d
πονήσαντος ὅλη, καὶ οὕτω δὴ λέγομεν ὅτι ὁ ἄνθρωπος τὸν
δάκτυλον ἀλγεῖ· καὶ περὶ ἄλλου ὁτουοῦν τῶν τοῦ ἀνθρώπου
ὁ αὐτὸς λόγος, περί τε λύπης πονοῦντος μέρους καὶ περὶ
ἡδονῆς ῥαΐζοντος;   5

Ὁ αὐτὸς γάρ, ἔφη· καὶ τοῦτο ὃ ἐρωτᾷς, τοῦ τοιούτου
ἐγγύτατα ἡ ἄριστα πολιτευομένη πόλις οἰκεῖ.

Ἑνὸς δὴ οἶμαι πάσχοντος τῶν πολιτῶν ὁτιοῦν ἢ ἀγαθὸν
ἢ κακὸν ἡ τοιαύτη· πόλις μάλιστά τε φήσει ἑαυτῆς εἶναι τὸ   e
πάσχον, καὶ ἢ συνησθήσεται ἅπασα ἢ συλλυπήσεται.

Ἀνάγκη, ἔφη, τήν γε εὔνομον.

Ὥρα ἂν εἴη, ἦν δ' ἐγώ, ἐπανιέναι ἡμῖν ἐπὶ τὴν ἡμετέραν
πόλιν, καὶ τὰ τοῦ λόγου ὁμολογήματα σκοπεῖν ἐν αὐτῇ, εἰ   5
αὐτὴ μάλιστ' ἔχει εἴτε καὶ ἄλλη τις μᾶλλον.

Οὐκοῦν χρή, ἔφη.

Τί οὖν; ἔστι μέν που καὶ ἐν ταῖς ἄλλαις πόλεσιν   463
ἄρχοντές τε καὶ δῆμος, ἔστι δὲ καὶ ἐν ταύτῃ;

Ἔστι.

Πολίτας μὲν δὴ πάντες οὗτοι ἀλλήλους προσεροῦσι;

Πῶς δ' οὔ;   5

Ἀλλὰ πρὸς τῷ πολίτας τί ὁ ἐν ταῖς ἄλλαις δῆμος τοὺς
ἄρχοντας προσαγορεύει;

G.   Of course.

S.   Does this come about, then, when people in the city fail to apply such expressions as 'mine' and 'not mine' in the same way? And likewise with 'another's'?

G.   Entirely true.

S.   So the best organised city is one in which the greatest majority apply 'mine' and 'not mine' to the same things and on the same principles?

G.   Certainly.

S.   And one whose condition is closest to that of a single individual? For example, whenever one of us knocks, say, a finger, the whole shared awareness extending through the body to the mind, and creating an
d   interdependence with the ruling element in it, feels a single, simultaneous and unified sensation of pain at the trouble of one part of the body; and in this way we say that 'the person has a pain in his finger'. And doesn't the same principle apply with any other part of the person, in cases both of pain and of pleasurable relief?

G.   Yes, the same. And to answer your question, the best governed city does have a life that is as close as possible to such a condition.

S.   I think, then, that when an individual citizen experiences anything
e   good or bad, such a city will emphatically say that the experience belongs to part of itself, and the entire city will share in either the pleasure or the pain.

G.   That must be so, with the well-governed city.

S.   It's time for us to return to our own city, and to look to see whether it possesses in the highest degree the points agreed on in our discussion, or if some other city does so to a greater extent.

G.   Yes, we should.

463a S.   Well now, surely there exists, both in other cities and in ours, a combination of magistrates and people?

G.   There does.

S.   And all these people will call one another 'citizens'?

G.   Of course.

S.   But what else, apart from 'citizens', do the people in other cities call their magistrates?

Ἐν μὲν ταῖς πολλαῖς δεσπότας, ἐν δὲ ταῖς δημοκρατου-
μέναις αὐτὸ τοὔνομα τοῦτο, ἄρχοντας.

Τί δ’ ὁ ἐν τῇ ἡμετέρᾳ δῆμος; πρὸς τῷ πολίτας τί τοὺς 10
ἄρχοντάς φησιν εἶναι;

Σωτῆράς τε καὶ ἐπικούρους, ἔφη.   b

Τί δ’ οὗτοι τὸν δῆμον;

Μισθοδότας τε καὶ τροφέας.

Οἱ δ’ ἐν ταῖς ἄλλαις ἄρχοντες τοὺς δήμους;

Δούλους, ἔφη.   5

Τί δ’ οἱ ἄρχοντες ἀλλήλους;

Συνάρχοντας, ἔφη.

Τί δ’ οἱ ἡμέτεροι;

Συμφύλακας.

Ἔχεις οὖν εἰπεῖν τῶν ἀρχόντων τῶν ἐν ταῖς ἄλλαις 10
πόλεσιν, εἴ τίς τινα ἔχει προσειπεῖν τῶν συναρχόντων τὸν
μὲν ὡς οἰκεῖον, τὸν δ’ ὡς ἀλλότριον;

Καὶ πολλούς γε.

Οὐκοῦν τὸν μὲν οἰκεῖον ὡς ἑαυτοῦ νομίζει τε καὶ λέγει,
τὸν δ’ ἀλλότριον ὡς οὐχ ἑαυτοῦ;   c

Οὕτω.

Τί δὲ οἱ παρὰ σοὶ φύλακες; ἔσθ’ ὅστις αὐτῶν ἔχοι ἂν
τῶν συμφυλάκων νομίσαι τινὰ ἢ προσειπεῖν ὡς ἀλλότριον;

Οὐδαμῶς, ἔφη· παντὶ γὰρ ᾧ ἂν ἐντυγχάνῃ, ἢ ὡς ἀδελφῷ 5
ἢ ὡς ἀδελφῇ ἢ ὡς πατρὶ ἢ ὡς μητρὶ ἢ υἱεῖ ἢ θυγατρὶ ἢ
τούτων ἐκγόνοις ἢ προγόνοις νομιεῖ ἐντυγχάνειν.

Κάλλιστα, ἦν δ’ ἐγώ, λέγεις, ἀλλ’ ἔτι καὶ τόδε εἰπέ·
πότερον αὐτοῖς τὰ ὀνόματα μόνον οἰκεῖα νομοθετήσεις, ἢ
καὶ τὰς πράξεις πάσας κατὰ τὰ ὀνόματα πράττειν, περί τε d
τοὺς πατέρας, ὅσα νόμος περὶ πατέρας αἰδοῦς τε πέρι καὶ
κηδεμονίας καὶ τοῦ ὑπήκοον δεῖν εἶναι τῶν γονέων, ἢ μήτε
πρὸς θεῶν μήτε πρὸς ἀνθρώπων αὐτῷ ἄμεινον ἔσεσθαι, ὡς
οὔτε ὅσια οὔτε δίκαια πράττοντος ἄν, εἰ ἄλλα πράττοι ἢ 5
ταῦτα; αὗταί σοι ἢ ἄλλαι φῆμαι ἐξ ἁπάντων τῶν πολιτῶν

G. In most, they call them 'masters', but in democratic cities they use this very term, 'magistrates'.

S. And what of the people in *our* city? In addition to 'citizens', what do they call the magistrates?

b G. 'Saviours' and 'helpers'.

S. And what do *these* call the people?

G. 'Paymasters' and 'providers'.

S. And what do the magistrates in the other cities call their peoples?

G. 'Slaves'.

S. And what do these magistrates call one another?

G. 'Fellow-magistrates'.

S. And our magistrates?

G. 'Fellow-guardians'.

S. Now, can you say whether any magistrate in the other cities is able to address one of his fellow-magistrates as a kinsman, but another as unrelated to him?

G. Many of them do!

S. So does he regard and speak of the kinsman as belonging to himself,

c and the unrelated person as not doing so?

G. Yes.

S. But what about the Guardians in *your* city? Could any of them regard or address one of his fellow-guardians as unrelated to him?

G. Certainly not! For with everyone that he meets, he will believe that he is meeting a brother, sister, father, mother, son, daughter, or someone from the generation below or above these.

S. A very fine answer; but tell me this too. Will you lay down that they

d should merely use the *terms* of kinship, or that they should also make all their behaviour conform to these terms – in the case of fathers, doing everything that custom requires in the way of respect, care, and the obligation of obedience to one's parents – or that otherwise things will not be well between an individual and either gods or men, since it would be neither pious nor just should he behave differently from this? Are these or other statements the ones which all your citizens will constantly reiterate in the hearing of the young, from

ὑμνήσουσιν· εὐθὺς περὶ τὰ τῶν παίδων ὦτα καὶ περὶ πατέρων,
οὓς ἂν αὐτοῖς τις ἀποφήνῃ, καὶ περὶ τῶν ἄλλων συγγενῶν;

Αὗται, ἔφη· γελοῖον γὰρ ἂν εἴη εἰ ἄνευ ἔργων οἰκεῖα e
ὀνόματα διὰ τῶν στομάτων μόνον φθέγγοιντο.

Πασῶν ἄρα πόλεων μάλιστα ἐν αὐτῇ συμφωνήσουσιν
ἑνός τινος ἢ εὖ ἢ κακῶς πράττοντος ὃ νυνδὴ ἐλέγομεν τὸ
ῥῆμα, τὸ ὅτι τὸ ἐμὸν εὖ πράττει ἢ ὅτι τὸ ἐμὸν κακῶς.   5

Ἀληθέστατα αὖ, ἦ δ᾽ ὅς.

Οὐκοῦν μετὰ τούτου τοῦ δόγματός τε καὶ ῥήματος ἔφαμεν 464
συνακολουθεῖν τάς τε ἡδονὰς καὶ τὰς λύπας κοινῇ;

Καὶ ὀρθῶς γε ἔφαμεν.

Οὐκοῦν μάλιστα τοῦ αὐτοῦ κοινωνήσουσιν ἡμῖν οἱ πολῖται,
ὃ δὴ ἐμὸν ὀνομάσουσιν; τούτου δὲ κοινωνοῦντες οὕτω δὴ 5
λύπης τε καὶ ἡδονῆς μάλιστα κοινωνίαν ἕξουσιν;

Πολύ γε.

Ἆρ᾽ οὖν τούτων αἰτία πρὸς τῇ ἄλλῃ καταστάσει ἡ τῶν
γυναικῶν τε καὶ παίδων κοινωνία τοῖς φύλαξιν;

Πολὺ μὲν οὖν μάλιστα, ἔφη.   10

Ἀλλὰ μὴν μέγιστόν γε πόλει αὐτὸ ὡμολογήσαμεν ἀγαθόν, b
ἀπεικάζοντες εὖ οἰκουμένην πόλιν σώματι πρὸς μέρος αὐτοῦ
λύπης τε πέρι καὶ ἡδονῆς ὡς ἔχει.

Καὶ ὀρθῶς γ᾽, ἔφη, ὡμολογήσαμεν.

Τοῦ μεγίστου ἄρα ἀγαθοῦ τῇ πόλει αἰτία ἡμῖν πέφανται 5
ἡ κοινωνία τοῖς ἐπικούροις τῶν τε παίδων καὶ τῶν γυναικῶν.

Καὶ μάλ᾽, ἔφη.

Καὶ μὲν δὴ καὶ τοῖς πρόσθεν γε ὁμολογοῦμεν· ἔφαμεν
γάρ που οὔτε οἰκίας τούτοις ἰδίας δεῖν εἶναι οὔτε γῆν οὔτε
τι κτῆμα, ἀλλὰ παρὰ τῶν ἄλλων τροφὴν λαμβάνοντας, c
μισθὸν τῆς φυλακῆς, κοινῇ πάντας ἀναλίσκειν, εἰ μέλλοιεν
ὄντως φύλακες εἶναι.

Ὀρθῶς, ἔφη.

Ἆρ᾽ οὖν οὐχ, ὅπερ λέγω, τά τε πρόσθεν εἰρημένα καὶ τὰ 5
νῦν λεγόμενα ἔτι μᾶλλον ἀπεργάζεται αὐτοὺς ἀληθινοὺς

their earliest days, in regard both to those who are designated as their 'fathers', and to the rest of their kinsmen?

e G. Precisely these; since it would be ridiculous if they were merely to mouth the terms of kinship, without the actions to match.

S. So of all cities it is in this one that there will be the maximum agreement, when any individual prospers or suffers, in the use of the language we mentioned earlier – namely, that it is '*my*' prosperity or '*my*' suffering.

G. That's also very true.

464a S. Well, did we agree that this attitude and way of speaking is accompanied by shared experience of pleasures and pains?

G. Yes, and we were right to.

S. Then our citizens will share to the highest degree in the same enterprise, which they will call 'mine'? And through their share in this, they will consequently experience to the highest degree a sharing of pain and pleasure?

G. Certainly.

S. Is the reason for these things, in addition to the rest of their system, the Guardians' sharing of women and children?

G. Absolutely so.

b S. Now, we agreed that this is the greatest good for a city, when we compared a well-run city to the way that a body relates to the pain and pleasure of one of its parts.

G. And we were right to agree.

S. So the cause of the city's greatest good has been shown by us to be the Auxiliaries' sharing of children and women.

G. Yes, indeed.

S. What's more, we're also being consistent with our earlier arguments. For we said that these people should have no private dwellings or

c land or any other property, but should receive their maintenance from the other citizens, as the wages of their Guardianship; and that all should use their resources for shared purposes, if they are really to be Guardians.

G. Correct.

S. As I say, then, doesn't the combination of our previous and present arguments make them all the more into true Guardians, and prevent

φύλακας, καὶ ποιεῖ μὴ διασπᾶν τὴν πόλιν τὸ ἐμὸν ὀνομάζοντας μὴ τὸ αὐτὸ ἀλλ' ἄλλον ἄλλο, τὸν μὲν εἰς τὴν ἑαυτοῦ
οἰκίαν ἕλκοντα ὅτι ἂν δύνηται χωρὶς τῶν ἄλλων κτήσασθαι,
τὸν δὲ εἰς τὴν ἑαυτοῦ ἑτέραν οὖσαν, καὶ γυναῖκά τε καὶ d
παῖδας ἑτέρους, ἡδονάς τε καὶ ἀλγηδόνας ἐμποιοῦντας ἰδίων
ὄντων ἰδίας, ἀλλ' ἑνὶ δόγματι τοῦ οἰκείου πέρι ἐπὶ τὸ αὐτὸ
τείνοντας πάντας εἰς τὸ δυνατὸν ὁμοπαθεῖς λύπης τε καὶ
ἡδονῆς εἶναι;   5

Κομιδῇ μὲν οὖν, ἔφη.

Τί δέ; δίκαι τε καὶ ἐγκλήματα πρὸς ἀλλήλους οὐκ
οἰχήσεται ἐξ αὐτῶν ὡς ἔπος εἰπεῖν διὰ τὸ μηδὲν ἴδιον
ἐκτῆσθαι πλὴν τὸ σῶμα, τὰ δ' ἄλλα κοινά; ὅθεν δὴ ὑπάρχει
τούτοις ἀστασιάστοις εἶναι, ὅσα γε διὰ χρημάτων ἢ παίδων e
καὶ συγγενῶν κτῆσιν ἄνθρωποι στασιάζουσιν;

Πολλὴ ἀνάγκη, ἔφη, ἀπηλλάχθαι.

Καὶ μὴν οὐδὲ βιαίων γε οὐδ' αἰκίας δίκαι δικαίως ἂν
εἶεν ἐν αὐτοῖς· ἥλιξι μὲν γὰρ ἥλικας ἀμύνεσθαι καλὸν καὶ 5
δίκαιόν που φήσομεν, ἀνάγκην σωμάτων ἐπιμελείᾳ τιθέντες.

Ὀρθῶς, ἔφη.

Καὶ γὰρ τόδε ὀρθὸν ἔχει, ἦν δ' ἐγώ, οὗτος ὁ νόμος· εἰ 465
πού τίς τῳ θυμοῖτο, ἐν τῷ τοιούτῳ πληρῶν τὸν θυμὸν ἧττον
ἐπὶ μείζους ἂν ἴοι στάσεις.

Πάνυ μὲν οὖν.

Πρεσβυτέρῳ μὴν νεωτέρων πάντων ἄρχειν τε καὶ κολάζειν 5
προστετάξεται.

Δῆλον.

Καὶ μὴν ὅτι γε νεώτερος πρεσβύτερον, ἂν μὴ ἄρχοντες
προστάττωσιν, οὔτε ἄλλο βιάζεσθαι ἐπιχειρήσει ποτὲ οὔτε
τύπτειν, ὡς τὸ εἰκός. οἶμαι δ' οὐδὲ ἄλλως ἀτιμάσει· ἱκανὼ 10
γὰρ τὼ φύλακε κωλύοντε, δέος τε καὶ αἰδώς, αἰδὼς μὲν ὡς
γονέων μὴ ἅπτεσθαι εἴργουσα, δέος δὲ τὸ τῷ πάσχοντι τοὺς b
ἄλλους βοηθεῖν, τοὺς μὲν ὡς ὑεῖς, τοὺς δὲ ὡς ἀδελφούς,
τοὺς δὲ ὡς πατέρας.

them from pulling the city apart by applying 'mine' not to the same thing but to a whole variety of things, with each individual dragging off to his own house any possession which he can take away from
d   the rest, and all of them calling a different wife and children their own, who create for them private pleasures and pains in their private affairs? Instead of this, don't our Guardians share a single attitude about what is theirs, all strive for the same goal, and all have common experiences, so far as is possible, of pain and pleasure?

G.   Entirely so.

S.   Well now. Won't legal charges and accusations virtually vanish from their dealings with one another, because they lack any private possessions apart from their bodies, and share everything else between them? As a result of this, is it possible for them to live
e   without faction, in so far as it is the possession of wealth or of children and kin which causes such faction among men?

G.   They are bound to escape from such things.

S.   Besides, legal charges of violence or assault could find no just place among them, since we shall surely declare that it is fine and just behaviour for coevals to defend one another, and thus compel them to look after their bodies.

G.   Correct.

465a S.   And this regulation also has this further advantage: if, say, one individual were angry with another, by venting his anger in such a context he would be less likely to advance to greater acts of faction.

G.   Quite so.

S.   Moreover, an older Guardian will be ordered to control and reprimand all younger ones.

G.   Clearly.

S.   It's also clear that, without an order from some of the Rulers, a younger man will never attempt to use any force against an older man, nor to strike him, surely. And I think he won't insult him in any other way either, since two 'guardians' – fear and respect – are
b   sufficient to prevent this: respect, by inhibiting him from laying his hands on those regarded as his parents; and fear that the others will come to assist the victim, some as sons, some as brothers, some as fathers.

Συμβαίνει γὰρ οὕτως, ἔφη.

Πανταχῇ δὴ ἐκ τῶν νόμων εἰρήνην πρὸς ἀλλήλους οἱ ἄνδρες· ἄξουσι;

Πολλήν γε.

Τούτων μὴν ἐν ἑαυτοῖς μὴ στασιαζόντων οὐδὲν δεινὸν μή ποτε ἡ ἄλλη πόλις πρὸς τούτους ἢ πρὸς ἀλλήλους διχοστατήσῃ.

Οὐ γὰρ οὖν.

Τά γε μὴν σμικρότατα τῶν κακῶν δι' ἀπρέπειαν ὀκνῶ καὶ λέγειν, ὧν ἀπηλλαγμένοι ἂν εἶεν, κολακείας τε πλουσίων πένητες ἀπορίας τε καὶ ἀλγηδόνας ὅσας ἐν παιδοτροφίᾳ καὶ χρηματισμοῖς διὰ τροφὴν οἰκετῶν ἀναγκαίαν ἴσχουσι, τὰ μὲν δανειζόμενοι, τὰ δ' ἐξαρνούμενοι, τὰ δὲ πάντως πορισάμενοι θέμενοι παρὰ γυναῖκάς τε καὶ οἰκέτας, ταμιεύειν παραδόντες, ὅσα τε, ὦ φίλε, περὶ αὐτὰ καὶ οἷα πάσχουσι, δῆλά τε δὴ καὶ ἀγεννῆ καὶ οὐκ ἄξια λέγειν.

Δῆλα γάρ, ἔφη, καὶ τυφλῷ.

Πάντων τε δὴ τούτων ἀπαλλάξονται, ζήσουσί τε τοῦ μακαριστοῦ βίου ὃν οἱ ὀλυμπιονῖκαι ζῶσι μακαριώτερον.

Πῇ;

Διὰ σμικρόν που μέρος εὐδαιμονίζονται ἐκεῖνοι ὧν τούτοις ὑπάρχει. ἥ τε γὰρ τῶνδε νίκη καλλίων, ἥ τ' ἐκ τοῦ δημοσίου τροφὴ τελεωτέρα. νίκην τε γὰρ νικῶσι συμπάσης τῆς πόλεως σωτηρίαν, τροφῇ τε καὶ τοῖς ἄλλοις πᾶσιν ὅσων βίος δεῖται αὐτοί τε καὶ παῖδες ἀναδοῦνται, καὶ γέρα δέχονται παρὰ τῆς αὑτῶν πόλεως ζῶντές τε καὶ τελευτήσαντες ταφῆς ἀξίας μετέχουσιν.

Καὶ μάλα, ἔφη, καλά.

Μέμνησαι οὖν, ἦν δ' ἐγώ, ὅτι ἐν τοῖς πρόσθεν οὐκ οἶδα ὅτου λόγος ἡμῖν ἐπέπληξεν ὅτι τοὺς φύλακας οὐκ εὐδαίμονας ποιοῖμεν, οἷς ἐξὸν πάντα ἔχειν τὰ τῶν πολιτῶν οὐδὲν ἔχοιεν; ἡμεῖς δέ που εἴπομεν ὅτι τοῦτο μέν, εἴ που παραπίπτοι, εἰς αὖθις σκεψοίμεθα, νῦν δὲ τοὺς μὲν φύλακας

G.   Yes, that makes sense.

S.   In every respect, then, the laws will induce our men to live peace-
     fully towards one another?

G.   Very much so.

S.   And if the Guardians are free from internal faction, there is no fear
     that the rest of the city will ever be at odds either with them or with
     one another.

G.   None at all.

S.   As for the most insignificant kinds of difficulties from which they
     would escape, their pettiness makes me hesitate even to mention
c   them: flatterings of the rich by the poor, and all the painful shortages
     of resources which people experience in rearing families and in their
     financial affairs, through the necessary cost of feeding household
     slaves, so that they borrow money, and refuse to pay back loans, and
     resort to every means of getting hold of cash, which they then hand
     over to their wives and slaves for housekeeping - all the many and
     various problems, my friend, which they suffer in these matters, are
     obvious, rather vulgar and not worth discussing.

d G.   They're obvious even to the blind!

S.   So they will escape from all these things, and they will lead more
     fortunate lives than the fêted existence of Olympic victors.

G.   In what way?

S.   Surely these victors are deemed happy for only a fraction of what our
     Guardians possess: the victory of the latter is a much finer one, and
     their maintenance at public expense is more complete. For the
     victory they win consists in the salvation of the entire city; the
     crowns with which they and their children are wreathed are made
     both of their maintenance and of all other requirements of life; and
e   they receive privileges from their city during their lifetime, as well
     as obtaining a fitting burial after their death.

G.   Fine rewards indeed!

S.   Now, do you remember that earlier in our conversation we were
     reproved by the argument (I forget whose) that we were failing to
466a make the Guardians happy, since, although they were in a position
     to appropriate all the citizens' property, they actually had none at
     all? Didn't we say that, if the chance arose, we would consider this
     point at a later stage, but for the time being it really was *guardians*

φύλακας ποιοῖμεν, τὴν δὲ πόλιν ὡς οἷοί τ' εἶμεν εὐδαι-
μονεστάτην, ἀλλ' οὐκ εἰς ἓν ἔθνος ἀποβλέποντες ἐν αὐτῇ 5
τοῦτο εὔδαιμον πλάττοιμεν;

Μέμνημαι, ἔφη.

Τί οὖν; νῦν ἡμῖν ὁ τῶν ἐπικούρων βίος, εἴπερ τοῦ γε
τῶν ὀλυμπιονικῶν πολύ τε καλλίων καὶ ἀμείνων φαίνεται,
μή πῃ κατὰ τὸν τῶν σκυτοτόμων φαίνεται βίον ἢ τινων b
ἄλλων δημιουργῶν ἢ τὸν τῶν γεωργῶν;

Οὔ μοι δοκεῖ, ἔφη.

᾿Αλλὰ μέντοι, ὅ γε καὶ ἐκεῖ ἔλεγον, δίκαιον καὶ ἐνταῦθα
εἰπεῖν, ὅτι εἰ οὕτως ὁ φύλαξ ἐπιχειρήσει εὐδαίμων γίγνεσθαι, 5
ὥστε μηδὲ φύλαξ εἶναι, μηδ' ἀρκέσει αὐτῷ βίος οὕτω μέτριος
καὶ βέβαιος καὶ ὡς ἡμεῖς φαμεν ἄριστος, ἀλλ' ἀνόητός τε
καὶ μειρακιώδης δόξα ἐμπεσοῦσα εὐδαιμονίας πέρι ὁρμήσει
αὐτὸν διὰ δύναμιν ἐπὶ τὸ ἅπαντα τὰ ἐν τῇ πόλει οἰκειοῦσθαι, c
γνώσεται τὸν Ἡσίοδον ὅτι τῷ ὄντι ἦν σοφὸς λέγων πλέον
εἶναί πως ἥμισυ παντός.

᾿Εμοὶ μέν, ἔφη, συμβούλῳ χρώμενος μενεῖ ἐπὶ τούτῳ τῷ
βίῳ. 5

Συγχωρεῖς ἄρα, ἦν δ' ἐγώ, τὴν τῶν γυναικῶν κοινωνίαν
τοῖς ἀνδράσιν, ἣν διεληλύθαμεν, παιδείας τε πέρι καὶ
παίδων καὶ φυλακῆς τῶν ἄλλων πολιτῶν, κατά τε πόλιν
μενούσας εἰς πόλεμόν τε ἰούσας καὶ συμφυλάττειν δεῖν καὶ
συνθηρεύειν ὥσπερ κύνας, καὶ πάντα πάντῃ κατὰ τὸ δυνατὸν d
κοινωνεῖν, καὶ ταῦτα πραττούσας τά τε βέλτιστα πράξειν καὶ
οὐ παρὰ φύσιν τὴν τοῦ θήλεος πρὸς τὸ ἄρρεν, ᾗ πεφύκατον
πρὸς ἀλλήλω κοινωνεῖν;

Συγχωρῶ, ἔφη. 5

Οὐκοῦν, ἦν δ' ἐγώ, ἐκεῖνο λοιπὸν διελέσθαι, εἰ ἄρα καὶ
ἐν ἀνθρώποις δυνατόν, ὥσπερ ἐν ἄλλοις ζῴοις, ταύτην τὴν
κοινωνίαν ἐγγενέσθαι, καὶ ὅπῃ δυνατόν;

Ἔφθης, ἔφη, εἰπὼν ᾗ ἔμελλον ὑπολήψεσθαι.

that we were fashioning our Guardians to be, and it was the *city* that we were making as happy as possible, rather than setting our sights on creating the happiness of just one particular group within the city?

G. I do remember.

S. Well then. If the life of our Auxiliaries can now be seen to be much
b finer and better than that of Olympic victors, surely it isn't just on the same level as that of the cobblers or any other artisans, or that of the farmers?

G. I don't think it is.

S. Yet it's right to say again here what I said on that earlier occasion too; that if a Guardian tries to achieve a happiness which means he no longer *is* a Guardian at all; and if he isn't satisfied with a life that is so moderate, stable and, as we claim, supremely good, but is afflicted by a foolish and immature belief about happiness which
c impels him to try by force to take private possession of everything in the city – then he will come to realise that Hesiod was truly wise in saying that 'the half is in a sense more than the whole'.

G. If he takes my advice, he will adhere to the way of life we have given him.

S. So you agree, then, about the sharing of women with men that we have discussed, in regard to education, children, and Guardianship of the other citizens – that the women, whether in the city or on military campaign, should perform the Guardians' duties jointly,
d should 'go hunting' with the males, just as dogs do, and should share in all activities in every way possible; and that by behaving this way, they will act for the very best and will not be contravening the natural relation of female to male, by which they are naturally fitted to share their lives with one another?

G. I agree.

S. Then it's left for us to determine *whether* it is also possible among human beings, as it is among other creatures, for this degree of sharing to come into being, and *how* it would be possible.

G. You anticipated the response I was about to make.

Περὶ μὲν γὰρ τῶν ἐν τῷ πολέμῳ οἶμαι, ἔφην, δῆλον ὃν **e**
τρόπον πολεμήσουσιν.

Πῶς; ἦ δ' ὅς.

Ὅτι κοινῇ στρατεύσονται, καὶ πρός γε ἄξουσι τῶν
παίδων εἰς τὸν πόλεμον ὅσοι ἁδροί, ἵν' ὥσπερ οἱ τῶν ἄλλων 5
δημιουργῶν θεῶνται ταῦτα ἃ τελεωθέντας δεήσει δημιουργεῖν·
πρὸς δὲ τῇ θέᾳ διακονεῖν καὶ ὑπηρετεῖν πάντα τὰ περὶ τὸν **467**
πόλεμον, καὶ θεραπεύειν πατέρας τε καὶ μητέρας. ἢ οὐκ
ᾔσθησαι τὰ περὶ τὰς τέχνας, οἷον τοὺς τῶν κεραμέων παῖδας,
ὡς πολὺν χρόνον διακονοῦντες θεωροῦσι πρὶν ἅπτεσθαι τοῦ
κεραμεύειν; 5

Καὶ μάλα.

Ἦ οὖν ἐκείνοις ἐπιμελέστερον παιδευτέον ἢ τοῖς φύλαξι
τοὺς αὑτῶν ἐμπειρίᾳ τε καὶ θέᾳ τῶν προσηκόντων;

Καταγέλαστον μεντἄν, ἔφη, εἴη.

Ἀλλὰ μὴν καὶ μαχεῖταί γε πᾶν ζῷον διαφερόντως 10
παρόντων ὧν ἂν τέκῃ. **b**

Ἔστιν οὕτω. κίνδυνος δέ, ὦ Σώκρατες, οὐ σμικρὸς
σφαλεῖσιν, οἷα δὴ ἐν πολέμῳ φιλεῖ, πρὸς ἑαυτοῖς παῖδας ἀπο-
λέσαντας ποιῆσαι καὶ τὴν ἄλλην πόλιν ἀδύνατον ἀναλαβεῖν.

Ἀληθῆ, ἦν δ' ἐγώ, λέγεις. ἀλλὰ σὺ πρῶτον μὲν ἡγῇ 5
παρασκευαστέον τὸ μή ποτε κινδυνεῦσαι;

Οὐδαμῶς.

Τί δ'; εἴ που κινδυνευτέον, οὐκ ἐν ᾧ βελτίους ἔσονται
κατορθοῦντες;

Δῆλον δή. 10

Ἀλλὰ σμικρὸν οἴει διαφέρειν καὶ οὐκ ἄξιον κινδύνου **c**
θεωρεῖν ἢ μὴ τὰ περὶ τὸν πόλεμον παῖδας τοὺς ἄνδρας
πολεμικοὺς ἐσομένους;

Οὔκ, ἀλλὰ διαφέρει πρὸς ὃ λέγεις.

Τοῦτο μὲν ἄρα ὑπαρκτέον, θεωροὺς πολέμου τοὺς παῖδας 5
ποιεῖν, προσμηχανᾶσθαι δ' αὐτοῖς ἀσφάλειαν, καὶ καλῶς
ἕξει· ἦ γάρ;

e S. First, as regards warfare, I think it's clear how they'll campaign.

G. How?

S. They'll share jointly in expeditions; and, what's more, they'll take with them to war those children who are robust enough, in order that, just like the children of other craftsmen, they may observe the craft which they will have to practise when they are grown up. And in 467a addition to watching, they should give help and assistance with everything connected with warfare, and attend on their fathers and mothers. Or haven't you noticed what happens with crafts – how, for example, the children of potters assist and watch the work for a long time, before they try their hand at making pots?

G. Of course.

S. Well, ought the Guardians to show less care than potters in training their own children by experience and observation of what is necessary?

G. It would be ludicrous!

S. Besides, every creature will actually fight better when its own b offspring are present.

G. That's right. But there's a large danger, Socrates, that if they suffer a reversal, as tends to happen in war, they'll lose their children as well as their own lives, and will render the city incapable of recovery.

S. True. But, in the first place, do you think that they should take steps to avoid *ever* running a risk?

G. Not at all.

S. Well then. If risks must sometimes be run, shouldn't it be in a situation where success will make them better people?

G. Obviously.

c S. But do you think it makes hardly any difference, and isn't worth any risk, whether or not those destined to be military men should as children observe the affairs of war?

G. I don't; it does make a difference in the respect you mention.

S. Then means must be found of making the children observers of war, and of procuring their safety; then all will be well, won't it?

92

Ναί.

Οὐκοῦν, ἦν δ' ἐγώ, πρῶτον μὲν αὐτῶν οἱ πατέρες, ὅσα ἄνθρωποι, οὐκ ἀμαθεῖς ἔσονται ἀλλὰ γνωμονικοὶ τῶν στρατειῶν ὅσαι τε καὶ μὴ ἐπικίνδυνοι;   10   d

Εἰκός, ἔφη.

Εἰς μὲν ἄρα τὰς ἄξουσιν, εἰς δὲ τὰς εὐλαβήσονται.

Ὀρθῶς.

Καὶ ἄρχοντάς γέ που, ἦν δ' ἐγώ, οὐ τοὺς φαυλοτάτους 5 αὐτοῖς ἐπιστήσουσιν ἀλλὰ τοὺς ἐμπειρίᾳ τε καὶ ἡλικίᾳ ἱκανοὺς ἡγεμόνας τε καὶ παιδαγωγοὺς εἶναι.

Πρέπει γάρ.

Ἀλλὰ γάρ, φήσομεν, καὶ παρὰ δόξαν πολλὰ πολλοῖς δὴ ἐγένετο.   10

Καὶ μάλα.

Πρὸς τοίνυν τὰ τοιαῦτα, ὦ φίλε, πτεροῦν χρὴ παιδία ὄντα εὐθύς, ἵν', ἄν τι δέῃ, πετόμενοι ἀποφεύγωσιν.

Πῶς λέγεις; ἔφη.   e

Ἐπὶ τοὺς ἵππους, ἦν δ' ἐγώ, ἀναβιβαστέον ὡς νεωτάτους, καὶ διδαξαμένους ἱππεύειν ἐφ' ἵππων ἀκτέον ἐπὶ τὴν θέαν, μὴ θυμοειδῶν μηδὲ μαχητικῶν, ἀλλ' ὅτι ποδωκεστάτων καὶ εὐηνιωτάτων. οὕτω γὰρ κάλλιστά τε θεάσονται τὸ αὑτῶν 5 ἔργον, καὶ ἀσφαλέστατα, ἄν τι δέῃ, σωθήσονται μετὰ πρεσβυτέρων ἡγεμόνων ἑπόμενοι.

Ὀρθῶς, ἔφη, μοι δοκεῖς λέγειν.

Τί δὲ δή, εἶπον, τὰ περὶ τὸν πόλεμον; πῶς ἑκτέον σοι **468** τοὺς στρατιώτας πρὸς αὑτούς τε καὶ τοὺς πολεμίους; ἆρ' ὀρθῶς μοι καταφαίνεται ἢ οὔ;

Λέγ', ἔφη, ποῖ' αὖ.

Αὑτῶν μέν, εἶπον, τὸν λιπόντα τάξιν ἢ ὅπλα ἀποβαλόντα 5 ἤ τι τῶν τοιούτων ποιήσαντα διὰ κάκην ἆρα οὐ δημιουργόν τινα δεῖ καθιστάναι ἢ γεωργόν;

Πάνυ μὲν οὖν.

Τὸν δὲ ζῶντα εἰς τοὺς πολεμίους ἁλόντα ἆρ' οὐ δωρεὰν

G. Yes.

S. Now, in the first place, surely their fathers, within human limits, will
d   not make mistakes about, but will have good judgement of, which
     military campaigns are and are not dangerous?

G. Presumably.

S. So they will take the children to some, but will be cautious about
     taking them to others.

G. Correct.

S. And in charge of them they'll place not the worst people but those
     whose experience and age make them fit to be leaders and tutors to
     the children.

G. That's appropriate.

S. Yet, we'll agree, things often happen unexpectedly to many people.

G. Certainly.

S. So, with a view to such contingencies, my friend, they ought to give
     the young children wings at the outset, in order that, if ever
e   necessary, they can escape by flight.

G. What do you mean?

S. They must sit them on horses at as early an age as possible, and after
     training them to ride they should take them on horseback to watch
     warfare – not on spirited or fighting horses, but the swiftest and most
     amenable kind. In this way, the children will get a fine view of the
     function that will be theirs, and will be able to make their escape in
     the safest fashion, if every necessary, under the leadership of older
     men.

468a G. I agree with your suggestion.

S. And what of warfare itself? How ought your soldiers to behave both
     to one another and towards the enemy? Are my views correct or not?

G. Tell me what they are.

S. If any of them abandons rank, discards his weapons, or does
     anything of that sort out of cowardice, shouldn't he be demoted to
     the status of artisan or farmer?

G. Undoubtedly.

S. If anyone is captured alive by the enemy, shouldn't they make a gift

94

διδόναι τοῖς ἑλοῦσι χρῆσθαι τῇ ἄγρᾳ ὅτι ἂν βούλωνται;   10

Κομιδῇ γε.   b

Τὸν δὲ ἀριστεύσαντά τε καὶ εὐδοκιμήσαντα οὐ πρῶτον μὲν ἐπὶ στρατιᾶς ὑπὸ τῶν συστρατευομένων μειρακίων τε καὶ παίδων ἐν μέρει ὑπὸ ἑκάστου δοκεῖ σοι χρῆναι στεφανωθῆναι; ἢ οὔ;   5

Ἔμοιγε.

Τί δέ; δεξιωθῆναι;

Καὶ τοῦτο.

Ἀλλὰ τόδ' οἶμαι, ἦν δ' ἐγώ, οὐκέτι σοι δοκεῖ.

Τὸ ποῖον;   10

Τὸ φιλῆσαί τε καὶ φιληθῆναι ὑπὸ ἑκάστου.

Πάντων, ἔφη, μάλιστα· καὶ προστίθημί γε τῷ νόμῳ, ἕως ἂν ἐπὶ ταύτης ὦσι τῆς στρατιᾶς, καὶ μηδενὶ ἐξεῖναι   c ἀπαρνηθῆναι ὃν ἂν βούληται φιλεῖν, ἵνα καί, ἐάν τίς του τύχῃ ἐρῶν ἢ ἄρρενος ἢ θηλείας, προθυμότερος ᾖ πρὸς τὸ τἀριστεῖα φέρειν.

Καλῶς, ἦν δ' ἐγώ. ὅτι μὲν γὰρ ἀγαθῷ ὄντι γάμοι τε   5 ἕτοιμοι πλείους ἢ τοῖς ἄλλοις καὶ αἱρέσεις τῶν τοιούτων πολλάκις παρὰ τοὺς ἄλλους ἔσονται, ἵν' ὅτι πλεῖστοι ἐκ τοῦ τοιούτου γίγνωνται, εἴρηται ἤδη.

Εἴπομεν γάρ, ἔφη.

Ἀλλὰ μὴν καὶ καθ' Ὅμηρον τοῖς τοιοῖσδε δίκαιον τιμᾶν   10 τῶν νέων ὅσοι ἀγαθοί. καὶ γὰρ Ὅμηρος τὸν εὐδοκιμή-   d σαντα ἐν τῷ πολέμῳ νώτοισιν Αἴαντα ἔφη διηνεκέεσσι γεραίρεσθαι, ὡς ταύτην οἰκείαν οὖσαν τιμὴν τῷ ἡβῶντί τε καὶ ἀνδρείῳ, ἐξ ἧς ἅμα τῷ τιμᾶσθαι καὶ τὴν ἰσχὺν αὐξήσει.   5

Ὀρθότατα, ἔφη.

Πεισόμεθα ἄρα, ἦν δ' ἐγώ, ταῦτά γε Ὁμήρῳ. καὶ γὰρ ἡμεῖς ἔν τε θυσίαις καὶ τοῖς τοιούτοις πᾶσι τοὺς ἀγαθούς, καθ' ὅσον ἂν ἀγαθοὶ φαίνωνται, καὶ ὕμνοις καὶ οἷς νυνδὴ ἐλέγομεν τιμήσομεν, πρὸς δὲ τούτοις ἕδραις τε καὶ κρέα-   10

of him to his captors, to use their 'catch' in any way they wish?

b G.   Quite so

S.   But if someone shows prowess and wins glory, don't you agree that in the first place, while still on campaign, he should be crowned in turn by each of the adolescents and children who are with the army?

G.   I do.

S.   And also congratulated by hand?

G.   That too.

S.   But I don't think you'll agree with this -

G.   What?

S.   That he should kiss, and be kissed by, each of them.

c G.   Absolutely! And I would add to this regulation that, while they're still on campaign, no-one whom he wants to kiss should be allowed to refuse him, so that, if anyone feels sexual desire for another, whether male or female, he will be even keener to strive for military prizes.

S.   Excellent! Because, that a good warrior will get more opportunities for marriage than the rest, and that such men will be more often chosen than others, so that as many offspring as possible can be produced from such a person – those are points we made earlier.

G.   We did.

S.   Moreover, according to Homer too it's right to give such honours to
d   those of our young who prove themselves good warriors. For Homer said that Ajax, when glorious in the war, was 'rewarded with prime cuts of beef', on the principle that this was a suitable honour for a brave young man, as one which would build up his strength as well as honouring him.

G.   Quite correct.

S.   So we'll follow Homer in *this* instance, at any rate. We too, at sacrifices and other such occasions, will honour good warriors, in so far as they *show* their goodness, with both hymns and the other rewards we mentioned a moment ago, and in addition with 'first

σιν ἰδὲ πλείοις δεπάεσσιν, ἵνα ἅμα τῷ τιμᾶν ἀσκῶμεν e
τοὺς ἀγαθοὺς ἄνδρας τε καὶ γυναῖκας.

Κάλλιστα, ἔφη, λέγεις.

Εἶεν· τῶν δὲ δὴ ἀποθανόντων ἐπὶ στρατιᾶς ὃς ἂν εὐδο-
κιμήσας τελευτήσῃ ἆρ' οὐ πρῶτον μὲν φήσομεν τοῦ χρυσοῦ 5
γένους εἶναι;

Πάντων γε μάλιστα.

Ἀλλ' οὐ πεισόμεθα Ἡσιόδῳ, ἐπειδάν τινες τοῦ τοιούτου
γένους τελευτήσωσιν, ὡς ἄρα—

   οἱ μὲν δαίμονες ἁγνοὶ ἐπιχθόνιοι τελέθουσιν,   **469**
   ἐσθλοί, ἀλεξίκακοι, φύλακες μερόπων ἀνθρώπων;

Πεισόμεθα μὲν οὖν.

Διαπυθόμενοι ἄρα τοῦ θεοῦ πῶς χρὴ τοὺς δαιμονίους
τε καὶ θείους τιθέναι καὶ τίνι διαφόρῳ, οὕτω καὶ ταύτῃ 5
θήσομεν ᾗ ἂν ἐξηγῆται;

Τί δ' οὐ μέλλομεν;

Καὶ τὸν λοιπὸν δὴ χρόνον ὡς δαιμόνων, οὕτω θεραπεύ-
σομέν τε καὶ προσκυνήσομεν αὐτῶν τὰς θήκας; ταὐτὰ δὲ b
ταῦτα νομιοῦμεν ὅταν τις γήρᾳ ἤ τινι ἄλλῳ τρόπῳ τελευτήσῃ
τῶν ὅσοι ἂν διαφερόντως ἐν τῷ βίῳ ἀγαθοὶ κριθῶσιν;

Δίκαιον γοῦν, ἔφη.

Τί δέ; πρὸς τοὺς πολεμίους πῶς ποιήσουσιν ἡμῖν οἱ 5
στρατιῶται;

Τὸ ποῖον δή;

Πρῶτον μὲν ἀνδραποδισμοῦ πέρι, δοκεῖ δίκαιον Ἕλληνας
Ἑλληνίδας πόλεις ἀνδραποδίζεσθαι, ἢ μηδ' ἄλλῃ ἐπιτρέ-
πειν κατὰ τὸ δυνατὸν καὶ τοῦτο ἐθίζειν, τοῦ Ἑλληνικοῦ 10
γένους φείδεσθαι, εὐλαβουμένους τὴν ὑπὸ τῶν βαρβάρων c
δουλείαν;

Ὅλῳ καὶ παντί, ἔφη, διαφέρει τὸ φείδεσθαι.

Μηδὲ Ἕλληνα ἄρα δοῦλον ἐκτῆσθαι μήτε αὐτούς, τοῖς τε
ἄλλοις Ἕλλησιν οὕτω συμβουλεύειν; 5

Πάνυ μὲν οὖν, ἔφη· μᾶλλόν γ' ἂν οὖν οὕτω πρὸς τοὺς

e   seats and cuts of meat and full cups of wine', in order that in the act of honouring them we may also help to train our good men and women.

G.   An excellent proposal.

S.   So far, so good. But when someone who has won glory dies on campaign, won't we, to begin with, declare that he belongs to the Golden Race?

G.   Absolutely.

S.   Well, won't we follow Hesiod, who says that when people of this race die,

469a   'Some become sacred spirits living on the earth,
Noble creatures, protectors against evil, guardians of mortal men'?

G.   We *will* follow him.

S.   So, once we have enquired from the god how, and with what distinction, we should bury those who are akin to spirits and god-like, we shall perform their burial in whatever way he prescribes?

G.   How could we not?

b S.   And thereafter, in the belief that they are spirits, shall we tend and revere their graves? And shall we follow these same rites whenever anyone else judged outstandingly good during his lifetime dies from old age or in any other way?

G.   Justice requires it.

S.   Well now, how will our soldiers behave towards their enemies?

G.   In what respect?

S.   In the first place, as regards enslavement; do you think it is just for Greek cities to enslave fellow-Greeks, or should they try so far as possible to prevent any other city from doing so, and accustom them to this practice of sparing members of the Greek race while taking

c   all precautions against enslavement by non-Greeks?

G.   Sparing other Greeks is of supreme importance.

S.   So our own people will not possess a single Greek slave, and will urge other Greeks to do the same?

G.   Certainly; this would make Greeks turn all the more keenly against

βαρβάρους τρέποιντο, ἑαυτῶν δ᾽ ἀπέχοιντο.

Τί δέ; σκυλεύειν, ἦν δ᾽ ἐγώ, τοὺς τελευτήσαντας πλὴν ὅπλων, ἐπειδὰν νικήσωσιν, ἢ καλῶς ἔχει; ἢ οὐ πρόφασιν μὲν τοῖς δειλοῖς ἔχει μὴ πρὸς τὸν μαχόμενον ἰέναι, ὥς τι d τῶν δεόντων δρῶντας ὅταν περὶ τὸν τεθνεῶτα κυπτάζωσι, πολλὰ δὲ ἤδη στρατόπεδα διὰ τὴν τοιαύτην ἁρπαγὴν ἀπώλετο;

Καὶ μάλα. 5

Ἀνελεύθερον δὲ οὐ δοκεῖ καὶ φιλοχρήματον νεκρὸν συλᾶν, καὶ γυναικείας τε καὶ σμικρᾶς διανοίας τὸ πολέμιον νομίζειν τὸ σῶμα τοῦ τεθνεῶτος ἀποπταμένου τοῦ ἐχθροῦ, λελοι- πότος δὲ ᾧ ἐπολέμει; ἢ οἴει τι διάφορον δρᾶν τοὺς τοῦτο ποιοῦντας τῶν κυνῶν, αἳ τοῖς λίθοις οἷς ἂν βληθῶσι e χαλεπαίνουσι, τοῦ βάλλοντος οὐχ ἁπτόμεναι;

Οὐδὲ σμικρόν, ἔφη.

Ἐατέον ἄρα τὰς νεκροσυλίας καὶ τὰς τῶν ἀναιρέσεων διακωλύσεις; 5

Ἐατέον μέντοι, ἔφη, νὴ Δία.

Οὐδὲ μήν που πρὸς τὰ ἱερὰ τὰ ὅπλα οἴσομεν ὡς ἀναθή- σοντες, ἄλλως τε καὶ τὰ τῶν Ἑλλήνων, ἐάν τι ἡμῖν μέλῃ τῆς πρὸς τοὺς ἄλλους Ἕλληνας εὐνοίας· μᾶλλον δὲ καὶ 470 φοβησόμεθα μή τι μίασμα ᾖ πρὸς ἱερὸν τὰ τοιαῦτα ἀπὸ τῶν οἰκείων φέρειν, ἐὰν μή τι δὴ ὁ θεὸς ἄλλο λέγῃ.

Ὀρθότατα, ἔφη.

Τί δὲ γῆς τε τμήσεως τῆς Ἑλληνικῆς καὶ οἰκιῶν ἐμ- 5 πρήσεως; ποῖόν τί σοι δράσουσιν οἱ στρατιῶται πρὸς τοὺς πολεμίους;

Σοῦ, ἔφη, δόξαν ἀποφαινομένου ἡδέως ἂν ἀκούσαιμι.

Ἐμοὶ μὲν τοίνυν, ἦν δ᾽ ἐγώ, δοκεῖ τούτων μηδέτερα ποιεῖν, ἀλλὰ τὸν ἐπέτειον καρπὸν ἀφαιρεῖσθαι. καὶ ὧν ἕνεκα, βούλει b σοι λέγω;

Πάνυ γε.

Φαίνεταί μοι, ὥσπερ καὶ ὀνομάζεται δύο ταῦτα ὀνόματα,

non-Greeks, and refrain from conflict among themselves.

S. What about stripping the corpses of the dead after a victory (I make an exception for weapons) – is this an acceptable practice? Doesn't

d it give the cowardly an excuse for failing to confront the enemy, on the grounds that they're doing a necessary duty in hanging back to deal with the dead; and hasn't such plundering often been the downfall of armies in the past?

G. Certainly.

S. Don't you agree that it's base and greedy to strip a corpse, and a sign of a womanly, petty mind to imagine that the *body* of the dead is a hostile thing, even after the enemy's life has flown from it and all that is left is the means with which the person formerly fought? Do you think that those who do this are behaving any differently from

e bitches which get indignant at the stones thrown at them, but don't touch the person throwing them?

G. No differently at all.

S. So they should eschew the stripping of corpses, as well as refusals to let the enemy take up their dead?

G. They should undoubtedly eschew these things.

S. Nor indeed, surely, will we take captured weapons into our temples to dedicate them, especially the weapons of Greeks, if we have any

470a concern for good relations with the rest of the Greeks. On the contrary, we'll actually be afraid of causing pollution by taking into a temple things of this kind that belong to people of our own race, unless of course the god pronounces otherwise.

G. Quite correct.

S. What about ravaging Greek territory, and burning its buildings? What kind of behaviour will your soldiers adopt towards the enemy?

G. I'd like to hear *your* view!

S. Well my view is that they should practise neither of these things, but

b should only destroy the annual crops. Would you like me to explain why?

G. Of course.

S. I believe that, corresponding to the two names 'war' and 'faction',

πόλεμός τε καὶ στάσις, οὕτω καὶ εἶναι δύο, ὄντα ἐπὶ δυοῖν 5
τινοιν διαφοραῖν. λέγω δὲ τὰ δύο τὸ μὲν οἰκεῖον καὶ
συγγενές, τὸ δὲ ἀλλότριον καὶ ὀθνεῖον. ἐπὶ μὲν οὖν τῇ
τοῦ οἰκείου ἔχθρᾳ στάσις κέκληται, ἐπὶ δὲ τῇ τοῦ ἀλλοτρίου
πόλεμος.

Καὶ οὐδέν γε, ἔφη, ἀπὸ τρόπου λέγεις.   10

Ὅρα δὴ καὶ εἰ τόδε πρὸς τρόπου λέγω. φημὶ γὰρ τὸ c
μὲν Ἑλληνικὸν γένος αὐτὸ αὑτῷ οἰκεῖον εἶναι καὶ συγγενές,
ᾧ δὲ βαρβαρικῷ ὀθνεῖόν τε καὶ ἀλλότριον.

Καλῶς γε, ἔφη.

Ἕλληνας μὲν ἄρα βαρβάροις καὶ βαρβάρους Ἕλλησι 5
πολεμεῖν μαχομένους τε φήσομεν καὶ πολεμίους φύσει
εἶναι, καὶ πόλεμον τὴν ἔχθραν ταύτην κλητέον· Ἕλληνας
δὲ Ἕλλησιν, ὅταν τι τοιοῦτον δρῶσιν, φύσει μὲν φίλους
εἶναι, νοσεῖν δ' ἐν τῷ τοιούτῳ τὴν Ἑλλάδα καὶ στασιάζειν,
καὶ στάσιν τὴν τοιαύτην ἔχθραν κλητέον.   d

Ἐγὼ μέν, ἔφη, συγχωρῶ οὕτω νομίζειν.

Σκόπει δή, εἶπον, ὅτι ἐν τῇ νῦν ὁμολογουμένῃ στάσει,
ὅπου ἄν τι τοιοῦτον γένηται καὶ διαστῇ πόλις, ἐὰν ἑκάτεροι
ἑκατέρων τέμνωσιν ἀγροὺς καὶ οἰκίας ἐμπιμπρῶσιν, ὡς 5
ἀλιτηριώδης τε δοκεῖ ἡ στάσις εἶναι καὶ οὐδέτεροι αὐτῶν
φιλοπόλιδες—οὐ γὰρ ἄν ποτε ἐτόλμων τὴν τροφόν τε καὶ
μητέρα κείρειν—ἀλλὰ μέτριον εἶναι τοὺς καρποὺς ἀφαιρεῖσθαι τοῖς κρατοῦσι τῶν κρατουμένων, καὶ διανοεῖσθαι ὡς e
διαλλαγησομένων καὶ οὐκ ἀεὶ πολεμησόντων.

Πολὺ γάρ, ἔφη, ἡμερωτέρων αὕτη ἡ διάνοια ἐκείνης.

Τί δὲ δή; ἔφην· ἣν σὺ πόλιν οἰκίζεις, οὐχ Ἑλληνὶς
ἔσται;   5

Δεῖ γ' αὐτήν, ἔφη.

Οὐκοῦν καὶ ἀγαθοί τε καὶ ἥμεροι ἔσονται;

Σφόδρα γε.

Ἀλλ' οὐ φιλέλληνες; οὐδὲ οἰκείαν τὴν Ἑλλάδα ἡγήσονται, οὐδὲ κοινωνήσουσιν ὧνπερ οἱ ἄλλοι ἱερῶν;   10

there really are two distinct things, representing disagreements between two elements. The two elements I mean are, first, that of affinity and kinship, and, second, that of the alien and foreign. 'Faction' applies to enmity within a relationship of affinity, 'war' to one between alien elements.

G. Your point is an apt one.

c S. Then consider whether this too is apt. I claim that the Greek race has an affinity and kinship with itself, but is foreign and alien to the barbarian race.

G. Well said!

S. We shall declare that when Greeks fight with barbarians, or barbarians with Greeks, it is warfare they are engaging in, and they are natural enemies, and 'war' is the name we should give to this hostility. But in conflict between Greeks, whenever they resort to such behaviour, we shall say that Greeks are one another's natural friends, and that Greece suffers from sickness and faction in such a situation; and

d 'faction' is the name we should give to such hostility.

G. I agree with these views.

S. Consider, then, that in what is currently agreed to be faction, whenever any such thing comes about and a city is internally divided, if both sides ravage the other's lands and burn their houses, the faction is regarded as heinous and neither side is thought devoted to the city (they would otherwise never dare to devastate their own nurse and mother), but it is thought acceptable for those with the

e military advantage to deprive their opponents of their crops, and to work on the assumption that a time of reconciliation will come and the fighting will not go on forever.

G. This latter attitude is much more civilised than the other.

S. Now, won't the city which you're founding be a Greek city?

G. It has to be.

S. So its people will be good and civilised?

G. Extremely.

S. Well, won't they have affection for all Greeks? Won't they regard Greece as their own land, and share in the same religious festivals as other Greeks?

Καὶ σφόδρα γε.

Οὐκοῦν τὴν πρὸς τοὺς Ἕλληνας διαφοράν, ὡς οἰκείους, 471
στάσιν ἡγήσονται καὶ οὐδὲ ὀνομάσουσιν πόλεμον;

Οὐ γάρ.

Καὶ ὡς διαλλαγησομενοι ἄρα διοίσονται;

Πάνυ μὲν οὖν. 5

Εὐμενῶς δὴ σωφρονιοῦσιν, οὐκ ἐπὶ δουλείᾳ κολάζοντες
οὐδ' ἐπ' ὀλέθρῳ, σωφρονισταὶ ὄντες, οὐ πολέμιοι.

Οὕτως, ἔφη.

Οὐδ' ἄρα τὴν Ἑλλάδα Ἕλληνες ὄντες κεροῦσιν, οὐδὲ
οἰκήσεις ἐμπρήσουσιν, οὐδὲ ὁμολογήσουσιν ἐν ἑκάστῃ πόλει 10
πάντας ἐχθροὺς αὐτοῖς εἶναι, καὶ ἄνδρας καὶ γυναῖκας καὶ
παῖδας, ἀλλ' ὀλίγους ἀεὶ ἐχθροὺς τοὺς αἰτίους τῆς διαφορᾶς.
καὶ διὰ ταῦτα πάντα οὔτε τὴν γῆν ἐθελήσουσιν κείρειν b
αὐτῶν, ὡς φίλων τῶν πολλῶν, οὔτε οἰκίας ἀνατρέπειν,
ἀλλὰ μέχρι τούτου ποιήσονται τὴν διαφοράν, μέχρι οὗ ἂν
οἱ αἴτιοι ἀναγκασθῶσιν ὑπὸ τῶν ἀναιτίων ἀλγούντων δοῦναι
δίκην. 5

Ἐγὼ μέν, ἔφη, ὁμολογῶ οὕτω δεῖν πρὸς τοὺς ἐναντίους
τοὺς ἡμετέρους πολίτας προσφέρεσθαι· πρὸς δὲ τοὺς βαρβάρους, ὡς νῦν οἱ Ἕλληνες πρὸς ἀλλήλους.

Τιθῶμεν δὴ καὶ τοῦτον τὸν νόμον τοῖς φύλαξι, μήτε γῆν
τέμνειν μήτε οἰκίας ἐμπιμπράναι; c

Θῶμεν, ἔφη, καὶ ἔχειν γε καλῶς ταῦτά τε καὶ τὰ
πρόσθεν.

Ἀλλὰ γάρ μοι δοκεῖς, ὦ Σώκρατες, ἐάν τίς σοι τὰ
τοιαῦτα ἐπιτρέπῃ λέγειν, οὐδέποτε μνησθήσεσθαι ὃ ἐν τῷ 5
πρόσθεν παρωσάμενος πάντα ταῦτα εἴρηκας, τὸ ὡς δυνατὴ
αὕτη ἡ πολιτεία γενέσθαι καὶ τίνα τρόπον ποτὲ δυνατή·
ἐπεὶ ὅτι γε, εἰ γένοιτο, πάντ' ἂν εἴη ἀγαθὰ πόλει ᾗ γένοιτο,
καὶ ἃ σὺ παραλείπεις ἐγὼ λέγω, ὅτι καὶ τοῖς πολεμίοις
ἄριστ' ἂν μάχοιντο τῷ ἥκιστα ἀπολείπειν ἀλλήλους, γιγνώ- d
σκοντές τε καὶ ἀνακαλοῦντες ταῦτα τὰ ὀνόματα ἑαυτούς,

G. Absolutely.

471a S. So, they will regard disagreements with Greeks, their own people, as a matter of faction, and will refuse even to call it 'war'?

G. They will refuse to.

S. And they will pursue their disagreements, therefore, with the intention of finding reconciliation?

G. Certainly.

S. Then it will be a benign control that they will impose, without any punitive aim of enslaving or destroying – behaving as 'controllers', not as enemies.

G. Exactly.

S. So, as Greeks, they will not devastate Greece, nor will they burn its dwellings, nor will they agree that the entire population of each city – men, women and children – is its enemies, but only the few who b are in each case responsible for the conflict. For all these reasons they will be prepared neither to devastate another city's land, since most of its people are their friends, nor to raze its houses; but they will pursue the disagreement only to the point where those responsible for it are compelled by the distress of the innocent to pay for their offence.

G. I agree that this is how our citizens should conduct themselves towards their opponents, but that towards barbarians they should act in the way in which Greeks currently deal with each other.

S. Are we, then, to establish this law too for the Guardians, that they c should neither ravage Greek land nor burn its houses?

G. Let us establish it, and accept that both these and our earlier proposals are the right ones. Yet I suspect, Socrates, that if you're allowed to go on discussing such points, you'll never recall the issue which you put aside before making all these proposals – namely, to show that this régime could come into being, and how it could ever do so. I agree that, *if* it came about, everything would be advantageous for the city which possessed it; and I would add details which d you haven't mentioned: that they would fight supremely well against their enemies by never abandoning one another, because they would recognise, and call each other by, the names of 'broth-

ἀδελφούς, πατέρας, ὑεῖς· εἰ δὲ καὶ τὸ θῆλυ συστρατεύοιτο,
εἴτε καὶ ἐν τῇ αὐτῇ τάξει εἴτε καὶ ὄπισθεν ἐπιτεταγμένον,
φόβων τε ἔνεκα τοῖς ἐχθροῖς καὶ εἴ ποτέ τις ἀνάγκη βοη- 5
θείας γένοιτο, οἶδ᾽ ὅτι ταύτῃ πάντῃ ἄμαχοι ἂν εἶεν· καὶ
οἴκοι γε ἃ παραλείπεται ἀγαθά, ὅσα ἂν εἴη αὐτοῖς, ὁρῶ.
ἀλλ᾽ ὡς ἐμοῦ ὁμολογοῦντος πάντα ταῦτα ὅτι εἴη ἂν καὶ e
ἄλλα γε μυρία, εἰ γένοιτο ἡ πολιτεία αὕτη, μηκέτι πλείω
περὶ αὐτῆς λέγε, ἀλλὰ τοῦτο αὐτὸ ἤδη πειρώμεθα ἡμᾶς
αὐτοὺς πείθειν, ὡς δυνατὸν καὶ ᾗ δυνατόν, τὰ δ᾽ ἄλλα
χαίρειν ἐῶμεν.

Ἐξαίφνης γε σύ, ἦν δ᾽ ἐγώ, ὥσπερ καταδρομὴν ἐποίησω 472
ἐπὶ τὸν λόγον μου, καὶ οὐ συγγιγνώσκεις στραγγευομένῳ.
ἴσως γὰρ οὐκ οἶσθα ὅτι μόγις μοι τὼ δύο κύματε ἐκφυγόντι
νῦν τὸ μέγιστον καὶ χαλεπώτατον τῆς τρικυμίας ἐπάγεις,
ὃ ἐπειδὰν ἴδῃς τε καὶ ἀκούσῃς, πάνυ συγγνώμην ἕξεις, ὅτι 5
εἰκότως ἄρα ὤκνουν τε καὶ ἐδεδοίκη οὕτω παράδοξον λόγον
λέγειν τε καὶ ἐπιχειρεῖν διασκοπεῖν.

Ὅσῳ ἄν, ἔφη, τοιαῦτα πλείω λέγῃς, ἧττον ἀφεθήσῃ
ὑφ᾽ ἡμῶν πρὸς τὸ μὴ εἰπεῖν πῇ δυνατὴ γίγνεσθαι αὕτη ἡ b
πολιτεία.   ἀλλὰ λέγε καὶ μὴ διάτριβε.

Οὐκοῦν, ἦν δ᾽ ἐγώ, πρῶτον μὲν τόδε χρὴ ἀναμνησθῆναι,
ὅτι ἡμεῖς ζητοῦντες δικαιοσύνην οἷόν ἐστι καὶ ἀδικίαν δεῦρο
ἥκομεν. 5

Χρή· ἀλλὰ τί τοῦτο; ἔφη.

Οὐδέν· ἀλλ᾽ ἐὰν εὕρωμεν οἷόν ἐστι δικαιοσύνη, ἆρα καὶ
ἄνδρα τὸν δίκαιον ἀξιώσομεν μηδὲν δεῖν αὐτῆς ἐκείνης
διαφέρειν, ἀλλὰ πανταχῇ τοιοῦτον εἶναι οἷον δικαιοσύνη
ἐστίν; ἢ ἀγαπήσομεν ἐὰν ὅτι ἐγγύτατα αὐτῆς ᾖ καὶ c
πλεῖστα τῶν ἄλλων ἐκείνης μετέχῃ;

Οὕτως, ἔφη· ἀγαπήσομεν.

Παραδείγματος ἄρα ἔνεκα, ἦν δ᾽ ἐγώ, ἐζητοῦμεν αὐτό τε
δικαιοσύνην οἷόν ἐστι, καὶ ἄνδρα τὸν τελέως δίκαιον εἰ 5
γένοιτο, καὶ οἷος ἂν εἴη γενόμενος, καὶ ἀδικίαν αὖ καὶ τὸν

ers', 'fathers', 'sons'; and if women too were in the army (whether in the same ranks or in a separate unit in the rear), in order to cause panic among the enemy and to give support in an emergency, I'm sure that in this respect they would be altogether invincible. And at home, too, I can see how many advantages there would be for them which haven't been mentioned. But since you're assured of my agreement that all these and countless other benefits would accrue to the city, *if* this régime came into being, please don't discuss it any further; but let us now try to convince ourselves on this particular point, *that* it is possible and *how* it is possible, and leave the other topics aside.

472a S. All of a sudden you've made a kind of assault against my argument, and you're showing no sympathy for my vacillation! Perhaps you don't realise that, after my narrow escape from the two earlier waves, you're now confronting me with the biggest and harshest of the three. When you see and hear this one, you'll understand more sympathetically that I was right after all to hesitate and be nervous about putting forward and trying to examine so unlikely an argument.

b G. The more you speak like that, the less we'll let you get away without explaining how this régime could come into being. Come, explain without further delay.

S. Well, in the first place we have to recall that we've reached where we are by searching for the nature of justice and injustice.

G. True – but what of it?

S. Nothing. But if we discover the nature of justice, will we claim that the just man too should differ in no way from justice itself, but should have entirely the same nature? Or shall we be satisfied if he approximates to it as closely as possible, and has a much greater share in it than other men do?

G. Yes, we'll be satisfied with this.

S. So it was for the sake of having an ideal that we were searching for the nature of justice itself, as well as of the perfectly just man (if he *could* exist, and what he would be like if he did), and likewise with

ἀδικώτατον, ἵνα εἰς ἐκείνους ἀποβλέποντες, οἷοι ἂν ἡμῖν φαίνωνται εὐδαιμονίας τε πέρι καὶ τοῦ ἐναντίου, ἀναγκαζώμεθα καὶ περὶ ἡμῶν αὐτῶν ὁμολογεῖν, ὃς ἂν ἐκείνοις ὅτι ὁμοιότατος ᾖ, τὴν ἐκείνης μοῖραν ὁμοιοτάτην ἕξειν, ἀλλ' **d** οὐ τούτου ἔνεκα, ἵν' ἀποδείξωμεν ὡς δυνατὰ ταῦτα γίγνεσθαι.

Τοῦτο μέν, ἔφη, ἀληθὲς λέγεις.

Οἴει ἂν οὖν ἧττόν τι ἀγαθὸν ζωγράφον εἶναι ὃς ἂν γράψας παράδειγμα οἷον ἂν εἴη ὁ κάλλιστος ἄνθρωπος καὶ 5 πάντα εἰς τὸ γράμμα ἱκανῶς ἀποδοὺς μὴ ἔχῃ ἀποδεῖξαι ὡς καὶ δυνατὸν γενέσθαι τοιοῦτον ἄνδρα;

Μὰ Δί' οὐκ ἔγωγ', ἔφη.

Τί οὖν; οὐ καὶ ἡμεῖς, φαμέν, παράδειγμα ἐποιοῦμεν λόγῳ ἀγαθῆς πόλεως; **e**

Πάνυ γε.

Ἧττόν τι οὖν οἴει ἡμᾶς εὖ λέγειν τούτου ἕνεκα, ἐὰν μὴ ἔχωμεν ἀποδεῖξαι ὡς δυνατὸν οὕτω πόλιν οἰκῆσαι ὡς ἐλέγετο;

Οὐ δῆτα, ἔφη. 5

Τὸ μὲν τοίνυν ἀληθές, ἦν δ' ἐγώ, οὕτω· εἰ δὲ δὴ καὶ τοῦτο προθυμηθῆναι δεῖ σὴν χάριν, ἀποδεῖξαι πῇ μάλιστα καὶ κατὰ τί δυνατώτατ' ἂν εἴη, πάλιν μοι πρὸς τὴν τοιαύτην ἀπόδειξιν τὰ αὐτὰ διομολόγησαι.

Τὰ ποῖα; 10

Ἆρ' οἷόν τέ τι πραχθῆναι ὡς λέγεται, ἢ φύσιν ἔχει **473** πρᾶξιν λέξεως ἧττον ἀληθείας ἐφάπτεσθαι, κἂν εἰ μή τῳ δοκεῖ; ἀλλὰ σὺ πότερον ὁμολογεῖς οὕτως ἢ οὔ;

Ὁμολογῶ, ἔφη.

Τοῦτο μὲν δὴ μὴ ἀνάγκαζέ με, οἷα τῷ λόγῳ διήλθομεν, 5 τοιαῦτα παντάπασι καὶ τῷ ἔργῳ δεῖν γιγνόμενα ⟨ἂν⟩ ἀποφαίνειν· ἀλλ', ἐὰν οἷοί τε γενώμεθα εὑρεῖν ὡς ἂν ἐγγύτατα τῶν εἰρημένων πόλις οἰκήσειεν, φάναι ἡμᾶς ἐξηυρηκέναι ὡς δυνατὰ ταῦτα γίγνεσθαι ἃ σὺ ἐπιτάττεις. ἢ **b** οὐκ ἀγαπήσεις τούτων τυγχάνων; ἐγὼ μὲν γὰρ ἂν ἀγαπῴην.

Καὶ γὰρ ἐγώ, ἔφη.

injustice and the unjust man; in order that by looking to see how these people struck us in terms of happiness or its contrary, we would be forced to agree that in our own case too the person who most closely resembles them would have the fortune most like theirs. But it was never our purpose to demonstrate that these things could actually come into being.

d

G. What you say is true.

S. Now, do you think that it would be a failing on the part of a good painter if he were to paint an ideal of the most beautiful human being, and were to give the picture everything befitting it, but weren't able to demonstrate that such a man could actually exist?

G. I certainly don't.

e S. Well, weren't we too producing in our argument an ideal of the good city?

G. Of course.

S. So do you think that our argument is any the less satisfactory if we're unable to show that it's possible for a city to be organised in the way we've described?

G. Certainly not.

S. As regards strict truth, then, that is our position. However, if, in order to please you, we must also give serious effort to demonstrating precisely how and by what means these things would prove most possible, then for the sake of such a demonstration you must again see whether you can agree in the same way with my argument.

G. Which argument?

473a S. Is it possible for anything to be carried out precisely in the way it can be stated, or is it natural that action makes less contact with the truth than does speech, whether or not anyone thinks this? Do *you* agree with this or not?

G. I do.

S. Then don't compel me to show that the details we've covered in our discussion could precisely and entirely come about in practice. Rather, if we can find how a city could live in a way closely approximating to what we've specified, be prepared to affirm that

b

we've discovered how all your instructions could be brought about. Won't you be satisfied with that result? *I* certainly would.

G. Yes, so will I.

Τὸ δὲ δὴ μετὰ τοῦτο, ὡς ἔοικε, πειρώμεθα ζητεῖν τε καὶ
ἀποδεικνύναι τί ποτε νῦν κακῶς ἐν ταῖς πόλεσι πράττεται 5
δι’ ὃ οὐχ οὕτως οἰκοῦνται, καὶ τίνος ἂν σμικροτάτου μεταβαλόντος ἔλθοι εἰς τοῦτον τὸν τρόπον τῆς πολιτείας πόλις,
μάλιστα μὲν ἑνός, εἰ δὲ μή, δυοῖν, εἰ δὲ μή, ὅτι ὀλιγίστων
τὸν ἀριθμὸν καὶ σμικροτάτων τὴν δύναμιν.

Παντάπασι μὲν οὖν, ἔφη.   c

Ἑνὸς μὲν τοίνυν, ἦν δ’ ἐγώ, μεταβαλόντος δοκοῦμέν μοι
ἔχειν δεῖξαι ὅτι μεταπέσοι ἄν, οὐ μέντοι σμικροῦ γε οὐδὲ
ῥᾳδίου, δυνατοῦ δέ.

Τίνος; ἔφη.   5

Ἐπ’ αὐτῷ δή, ἦν δ’ ἐγώ, εἰμὶ ὃ τῷ μεγίστῳ προσῃκάζομεν
κύματι. εἰρήσεται δ’ οὖν, εἰ καὶ μέλλει γέλωτί τε ἀτεχνῶς
ὥσπερ κῦμα ἐκγελῶν καὶ ἀδοξίᾳ κατακλύσειν. σκόπει δὲ
ὃ μέλλω λέγειν.

Λέγε, ἔφη.   10

Ἐὰν μή, ἦν δ’ ἐγώ, ἢ οἱ φιλόσοφοι βασιλεύσωσιν ἐν
ταῖς πόλεσιν ἢ οἱ βασιλῆς τε νῦν λεγόμενοι καὶ δυνάσται d
φιλοσοφήσωσι γνησίως τε καὶ ἱκανῶς, καὶ τοῦτο εἰς ταὐτὸν
συμπέσῃ, δύναμίς τε πολιτικὴ καὶ φιλοσοφία, τῶν δὲ
νῦν πορευομένων χωρὶς ἐφ’ ἑκάτερον αἱ πολλαὶ φύσεις ἐξ
ἀνάγκης ἀποκλεισθῶσιν, οὐκ ἔστι κακῶν παῦλα, ὦ φίλε 5
Γλαύκων, ταῖς πόλεσι, δοκῶ δ’ οὐδὲ τῷ ἀνθρωπίνῳ γένει,
οὐδὲ αὕτη ἡ πολιτεία μή ποτε πρότερον φυῇ τε εἰς τὸ e
δυνατὸν καὶ φῶς ἡλίου ἴδῃ, ἣν νῦν λόγῳ διεληλύθαμεν.
ἀλλὰ τοῦτό ἐστιν ὃ ἐμοὶ πάλαι ὄκνον ἐντίθησι λέγειν,
ὁρῶντι ὡς πολὺ παρὰ δόξαν ῥηθήσεται· χαλεπὸν γὰρ ἰδεῖν
ὅτι οὐκ ἂν ἄλλη τις εὐδαιμονήσειεν οὔτε ἰδίᾳ οὔτε δημοσίᾳ. 5

Καὶ ὅς, Ὦ Σώκρατες, ἔφη, τοιοῦτον ἐκβέβληκας ῥῆμά
τε καὶ λόγον, ὃν εἰπὼν ἡγοῦ ἐπὶ σὲ πάνυ πολλούς τε καὶ
οὐ φαύλους νῦν οὕτως, οἷον ῥίψαντας τὰ ἱμάτια, γυμνοὺς 474
λαβόντας ὅτι ἑκάστῳ παρέτυχεν ὅπλον, θεῖν διατεταμένους
ὡς θαυμάσια ἐργασομένους· οὓς εἰ μὴ ἀμυνῇ τῷ λόγῳ καὶ

S. Then next, it seems, we should try to seek out and show what it is which is currently wrong with cities and prevents them being organised in the way we've discussed, and what the smallest change would be which would enable a city to attain to this type of régime – a single change, preferably; otherwise, two; and failing that, as few changes as possible, and ones with the smallest scope.

c G. Absolutely.

S. Well, there is a single change which I think would allow us to show that the transition could be made: but it isn't a small or easy change, though it *is* possible.

G. What is it?

S. I'm at the very point of facing what we compared to the greatest wave. Yet the subject cannot be evaded, even if the result is that I'm deluged by a kind of wave of outright laughter and contempt. Consider carefully what I'm about to say.

G. Tell us.

d S. Unless either philosophers come to power in cities, or else those who are currently called kings and princes become authentic and proper philosophers, so that political power and philosophy become combined, while the various natures of those who currently engage separately in one or other of these activities are compulsorily barred from them – without this condition, there will be no respite from evil, dear Glaucon, for cities, nor, I think, for the entire human race; and

e unless that happens, the constitution which we have discussed in our argument will never have any chance of coming into being or existing in the light of the sun. This is the claim which originally made me hesitate to start the discussion, because I could see how very implausible it would sound: it's difficult for people to see that no other city could possibly enjoy happiness, whether in its private or its social life.

G. What a suggestion and argument you've produced, Socrates! Now that you've uttered it, you can expect a great throng of people, no

474a riff-raff either, without further ado to throw off their cloaks, snatch any weapon that's to hand, and race up to you determined to do you some mischief: if you don't defend yourself, and fight them off, by

ἐκφεύξῃ, τῷ ὄντι τωθαζόμενος δώσεις δίκην.

Οὐκοῦν σύ μοι, ἦν δ' ἐγώ, τούτων αἴτιος;   5

Καλῶς γ', ἔφη, ἐγὼ ποιῶν. ἀλλά τοί σε οὐ προδώσω, ἀλλ' ἀμυνῶ οἷς δύναμαι· δύναμαι δὲ εὐνοίᾳ τε καὶ τῷ παρακελεύεσθαι, καὶ ἴσως ἂν ἄλλου του ἐμμελέστερόν σοι ἀποκρινοίμην. ἀλλ' ὡς ἔχων τοιοῦτον βοηθὸν πειρῶ τοῖς **b** ἀπιστοῦσιν ἐνδείξασθαι ὅτι ἔχει ᾗ σὺ λέγεις.

Πειρατέον, ἦν δ' ἐγώ, ἐπειδὴ καὶ σὺ οὕτω μεγάλην συμμαχίαν παρέχῃ. ἀναγκαῖον οὖν μοι δοκεῖ, εἰ μέλλομέν πῃ ἐκφεύξεσθαι οὓς λέγεις, διορίσασθαι πρὸς αὐτοὺς τοὺς   5 φιλοσόφους τίνας λέγοντες τολμῶμεν φάναι δεῖν ἄρχειν, ἵνα διαδήλων γενομένων δύναταί τις ἀμύνεσθαι, ἐνδεικνύμενος ὅτι τοῖς μὲν προσήκει φύσει ἅπτεσθαί τε φιλοσοφίας **c** ἡγεμονεύειν τ' ἐν πόλει, τοῖς δ' ἄλλοις μήτε ἅπτεσθαι ἀκολουθεῖν τε τῷ ἡγουμένῳ.

Ὥρα ἂν εἴη, ἔφη, ὁρίζεσθαι.

Ἴθι δή, ἀκολούθησόν μοι τῇδε, ἐὰν αὐτὸ ἀμῇ γέ πῃ   5 ἱκανῶς ἐξηγησώμεθα.

Ἄγε, ἔφη.

Ἀναμιμνήσκειν οὖν σε, ἦν δ' ἐγώ, δεήσει, ἢ μέμνησαι ὅτι ὃν ἂν φῶμεν φιλεῖν τι, δεῖ φανῆναι αὐτόν, ἐὰν ὀρθῶς λέγηται, οὐ τὸ μὲν φιλοῦντα ἐκείνου, τὸ δὲ μή, ἀλλὰ πᾶν   10 στέργοντα;

Ἀναμιμνήσκειν, ἔφη, ὡς ἔοικεν, δεῖ· οὐ γὰρ πάνυ γε **d** ἐννοῶ.

Ἄλλῳ, εἶπον, ἔπρεπεν, ὦ Γλαύκων, λέγειν ἃ λέγεις· ἀνδρὶ δ' ἐρωτικῷ οὐ πρέπει ἀμνημονεῖν ὅτι πάντες οἱ ἐν ὥρᾳ τὸν φιλόπαιδα καὶ ἐρωτικὸν ἀμῇ γέ πῃ δάκνουσί τε   5 καὶ κινοῦσι, δοκοῦντες ἄξιοι εἶναι ἐπιμελείας τε καὶ τοῦ ἀσπάζεσθαι. ἢ οὐχ οὕτω ποιεῖτε πρὸς τοὺς καλούς; ὁ μέν, ὅτι σιμός, ἐπίχαρις κληθεὶς ἐπαινεθήσεται ὑφ' ὑμῶν, τοῦ δὲ τὸ γρυπὸν βασιλικὸν φατε εἶναι, τὸν δὲ δὴ διὰ μέσου τούτων ἐμμετρώτατα ἔχειν, μέλανας δὲ ἀνδρικοὺς **e** your arguments, you'll really pay with mockery for your offence.

S.   But isn't it *you* who is to blame for my predicament?

G.   And I'm glad about it too! But I certainly won't desert you; I'll defend you with whatever means I can find. And what I can find is good will and encouragement, and perhaps more careful answers to

b   your questions than another person might give. Come, with me to help you in this way, try to demonstrate to the disbelievers that things are as you claim.

S.   I have no choice but to try, when you offer me such a staunch alliance. Now, if we're to fight off the people you mention, I think it's essential to define for them just whom we mean by the 'philosophers' that we dare to say ought to be rulers; so that, once their identity is clear, one can defend oneself by showing that there are

c   some people who are naturally fitted to engage in philosophy and to be the leaders of cities, while there are others who should not engage in it and who need to *be* led.

G.   Now is the time to give the definition.

S.   Come then, accompany me along the following route, to see whether we can somehow explain the point satisfactorily.

G.   Lead on.

S.   I'll have to remind you – or do you remember? – that whenever we say that someone is a 'lover' of something, it's necessary, if the description is to apply correctly, that he should be seen not to love only certain parts of the thing in question, but to love the whole of it.

d G.   You do, apparently, need to remind me; I certainly don't recall the point.

S.   That's not something one expected *you* to say, Glaucon! A devotee of sexual passion shouldn't forget that it's *all* young men of the right age who somehow bite and sting the passionate lover of boys, and seem to merit his attention and embraces. Isn't this how people like you behave towards your favourites? One boy, because he's snub-nosed, you'll praise with the description of 'charming'; another's

e   hooked nose you call 'royal'; while the one in between you regard as just right. You call the dark-skinned 'manly' to look at, and the

ἰδεῖν, λευκοὺς δὲ θεῶν παῖδας εἶναι· μελιχλώρους δὲ καὶ
τοὔνομα οἴει τινὸς ἄλλου ποίημα εἶναι ἢ ἐραστοῦ ὑποκορι-
ζομένου τε καὶ εὐχερῶς φέροντος τὴν ὠχρότητα, ἐὰν ἐπὶ
ὥρᾳ ᾖ; καὶ ἑνὶ λόγῳ πάσας προφάσεις προφασίζεσθέ τε 5
καὶ πάσας φωνὰς ἀφίετε, ὥστε μηδένα ἀποβάλλειν τῶν **475**
ἀνθούντων ἐν ὥρᾳ.

Εἰ βούλει, ἔφη, ἐπ' ἐμοῦ λέγειν περὶ τῶν ἐρωτικῶν ὅτι
οὕτω ποιοῦσι, συγχωρῶ τοῦ λόγου χάριν.

Τί δέ; ἦν δ' ἐγώ· τοὺς φιλοίνους οὐ τὰ αὐτὰ ταῦτα 5
ποιοῦντας ὁρᾷς; πάντα οἶνον ἐπὶ πάσης προφάσεως ἀσπαζομένους;

Καὶ μάλα.

Καὶ μὴν φιλοτίμους γε, ὡς ἐγῷμαι, καθορᾷς ὅτι, ἂν μὴ
στρατηγῆσαι δύνωνται, τριττυαρχοῦσιν, κἂν μὴ ὑπὸ μειζόνων 10
καὶ σεμνοτέρων τιμᾶσθαι, ὑπὸ σμικροτέρων καὶ φαυλοτέρων **b**
τιμώμενοι ἀγαπῶσιν, ὡς ὅλως τιμῆς ἐπιθυμηταὶ ὄντες.

Κομιδῇ μὲν οὖν.

Τοῦτο δὴ φάθι ἢ μή· ἆρα ὃν ἄν τινος ἐπιθυμητικὸν
λέγωμεν, παντὸς τοῦ εἴδους τούτου φήσομεν ἐπιθυμεῖν, ἢ 5
τοῦ μέν, τοῦ δὲ οὔ;

Παντός, ἔφη.

Οὐκοῦν καὶ τὸν φιλόσοφον σοφίας φήσομεν ἐπιθυμητὴν
εἶναι, οὐ τῆς μέν, τῆς δ' οὔ, ἀλλὰ πάσης;

Ἀληθῆ. 10

Τὸν ἄρα περὶ τὰ μαθήματα δυσχεραίνοντα, ἄλλως τε
καὶ νέον ὄντα καὶ μήπω λόγον ἔχοντα τί τε χρηστὸν καὶ **c**
μή, οὐ φήσομεν φιλομαθῆ οὐδὲ φιλόσοφον εἶναι, ὥσπερ
τὸν περὶ τὰ σιτία δυσχερῆ οὔτε πεινῆν φαμεν οὔτ' ἐπιθυμεῖν
σιτίων, οὐδὲ φιλόσιτον ἀλλὰ κακόσιτον εἶναι.

Καὶ ὀρθῶς γε φήσομεν. 5

Τὸν δὲ δὴ εὐχερῶς ἐθέλοντα παντὸς μαθήματος γεύεσθαι
καὶ ἀσμένως ἐπὶ τὸ μανθάνειν ἰόντα καὶ ἀπλήστως ἔχοντα,
τοῦτον δ' ἐν δίκῃ φήσομεν φιλόσοφον· ἦ γάρ;

fair-skinned 'children of the gods'. Do you think that the term 'honey-fresh' too was the coinage of anyone other than a lover who was using affectionate euphemism and making light of a boy's pallor, provided he was of the right age? In a word, you people adopt every kind of excuse, and utter every kind of language, to avoid rejecting a single young man in his prime.

475a

G.   If you want to use *me* as a basis for describing such behaviour by passionate lovers, I'll play along with you for the sake of the argument!

S.   Well now, don't you notice that lovers of wine behave in just this same way, using every excuse to indulge their fondness for every wine?

G.   Very much so.

S.   And again you observe, I think, how lovers of honour, if they're unable to become generals, occupy minor military offices; and if they can't obtain honours from people of great and august importance, they're content to be honoured by the insignificant and paltry, since it's *every* kind of honour that they love.

b

G.   Quite so.

S.   Then confirm or deny this: when we say that someone has a constant desire for something, shall we agree that it is for the *whole* of this class of things that he has a desire, or only for some instances of it?

G.   The whole class.

S.   So with the philosopher too, we'll agree that he has a desire for wisdom – not for this piece of wisdom rather than that, but *all* wisdom?

G.   True.

S.   Then we'll describe the person who has a strong dislike for studies, especially when he's young and doesn't yet have a rational grasp of good and evil, as no lover of learning and no philosopher; just as we say that the person who is difficult about food has no appetite or desire for it, and isn't a lover of food but rather 'faddy'.

c

G.   And our description will be right.

S.   Whereas the person who shows a ready willingness to taste every form of study, who has a positive inclination towards learning and is insatiable for it – *this* is the one we'll be justified in calling a philosopher. Isn't that so?

Καὶ ὁ Γλαύκων ἔφη· Πολλοὶ ἄρα καὶ ἄτοποι ἔσονταί σοι **d**
τοιοῦτοι. οἵ τε γὰρ φιλοθεάμονες πάντες ἔμοιγε δοκοῦσι τῷ
καταμανθάνειν χαίροντες τοιοῦτοι εἶναι, οἵ τε φιλήκοοι ἀτοπώ-
τατοί τινές εἰσιν ὥς γ᾽ ἐν φιλοσόφοις τιθέναι, οἳ πρὸς μὲν λόγους
καὶ τοιαύτην διατριβὴν ἑκόντες οὐκ ἂν ἐθέλοιεν ἐλθεῖν, ὥσπερ 5
δὲ ἀπομεμισθωκότες τὰ ὦτα ἐπακοῦσαι πάντων χορῶν περιθέ-
ουσι τοῖς Διονυσίοις οὔτε τῶν κατὰ πόλεις οὔτε τῶν κατὰ κώμας
ἀπολειπόμενοι. τούτους οὖν πάντας καὶ ἄλλους τοιούτων τινῶν
μαθητικοὺς καὶ τοὺς τῶν τεχνυδρίων φιλοσόφους φήσομεν; **e**

Οὐδαμῶς, εἶπον, ἀλλ᾽ ὁμοίους μὲν φιλοσόφοις.

Τοὺς δὲ ἀληθινούς, ἔφη, τίνας λέγεις;

Τοὺς τῆς ἀληθείας, ἦν δ᾽ ἐγώ, φιλοθεάμονας.

Καὶ τοῦτο μέν γ᾽, ἔφη, ὀρθῶς· ἀλλὰ πῶς αὐτὸ λέγεις; 5

Οὐδαμῶς, ἦν δ᾽ ἐγώ, ῥᾳδίως πρός γε ἄλλον· σὲ δὲ οἶμαι
ὁμολογήσειν μοι τὸ τοιόνδε.

Τὸ ποῖον;

Ἐπειδή ἐστιν ἐναντίον καλὸν αἰσχρῷ, δύο αὐτὼ εἶναι.

Πῶς δ᾽ οὔ; **476**

Οὐκοῦν ἐπειδὴ δύο, καὶ ἓν ἑκάτερον;

Καὶ τοῦτο.

Καὶ περὶ δὴ δικαίου καὶ ἀδίκου καὶ ἀγαθοῦ καὶ κακοῦ
καὶ πάντων τῶν εἰδῶν πέρι ὁ αὐτὸς λόγος, αὐτὸ μὲν ἓν 5
ἕκαστον εἶναι, τῇ δὲ τῶν πράξεων καὶ σωμάτων καὶ ἀλλήλων
κοινωνίᾳ πανταχοῦ φανταζόμενα πολλὰ φαίνεσθαι ἕκαστον.

Ὀρθῶς, ἔφη, λέγεις.

Ταύτῃ τοίνυν, ἦν δ᾽ ἐγώ, διαιρῶ, χωρὶς μὲν οὓς νυνδὴ
ἔλεγες φιλοθεάμονάς τε καὶ φιλοτέχνους καὶ πρακτικούς, 10
καὶ χωρὶς αὖ περὶ ὧν ὁ λόγος, οὓς μόνους ἄν τις ὀρθῶς **b**
προσείποι φιλοσόφους.

Πῶς, ἔφη, λέγεις;

Οἱ μέν που, ἦν δ᾽ ἐγώ, φιλήκοοι καὶ φιλοθεάμονες τάς
τε καλὰς φωνὰς ἀσπάζονται καὶ χρόας καὶ σχήματα καὶ 5
πάντα τὰ ἐκ τῶν τοιούτων δημιουργούμενα, αὐτοῦ δὲ τοῦ

d G.   In that case, you'll have a large, strange crowd of such people! All the lovers of sights seem to me to be like that, in the pleasure they take in learning; while the lovers of sounds are the strangest people to include in your category of philosophers, since they wouldn't choose to attend philosophical arguments and activities of that sort, but yet, behaving as though they've hired out their ears as an audience for every single choral performance, they race round the festivals of Dionysus, and don't miss any of them either in the cities or in the country villages! So are we going to give all of these people,

e   as well as others who are students of such things or those who learn some craft or other, the name of 'philosophers'?

S.   Certainly not – but we'll say they're like philosophers.

G.   Who are the ones you call *true* philosophers?

S.   Those whose 'love of sight' is for the truth.

G.   That's all very well; but just what do you mean by it?

S.   It wouldn't be easy for me to explain this to someone else; but I think that *you* will agree the following with me.

G.   What?

S.   That since 'beautiful' is contrary to 'ugly', these are two entities.

476a G.   Of course.

S.   So, since there are two of them, each of them is one?

G.   Also true.

S.   And the same argument holds for 'just' and 'unjust', 'good' and 'bad', and all such forms – each of them in itself is a single entity, but through being connected with actions, objects, and one another, each of them appears all over the place in a multiplicity of manifestations.

G.   Quite correct.

S.   Well then, on that principle draw a distinction between, on the one side, the lovers of sights and practical lovers of crafts, whom you

b   mentioned a moment ago, and, on the other, those who are the subject of our discussion – the ones whom alone one would be right to call philosophers.

G.   What do you mean?

S.   Surely the lovers of sounds and sights are devoted to beautiful voices, colours, shapes, and all the artefacts created from such

116

καλοῦ ἀδύνατος αὐτῶν ἡ διάνοια τὴν φύσιν ἰδεῖν τε καὶ ἀσπάσασθαι.

Ἔχει γὰρ οὖν δή, ἔφη, οὕτως.

Οἱ δὲ δὴ ἐπ’ αὐτὸ τὸ καλὸν δυνατοὶ ἰέναι τε καὶ ὁρᾶν 10 καθ’ αὑτὸ ἆρα οὐ σπάνιοι ἂν εἶεν;

Καὶ μάλα. c

Ὁ οὖν καλὰ μὲν πράγματα νομίζων, αὐτὸ δὲ κάλλος μήτε νομίζων μήτε, ἄν τις ἡγῆται ἐπὶ τὴν γνῶσιν αὐτοῦ, δυνάμενος ἕπεσθαι, ὄναρ ἢ ὕπαρ δοκεῖ σοι ζῆν; σκόπει δέ. τὸ ὀνειρώττειν ἆρα οὐ τόδε ἐστίν, ἐάντε ἐν ὕπνῳ τις ἐάντ’ 5 ἐγρηγορὼς τὸ ὅμοιόν τῳ μὴ ὅμοιον ἀλλ’ αὐτὸ ἡγῆται εἶναι ᾧ ἔοικεν;

Ἐγὼ γοῦν ἄν, ἦ δ’ ὅς, φαίην ὀνειρώττειν τὸν τοιοῦτον.

Τί δέ; ὁ τἀναντία τούτων ἡγούμενός τέ τι αὐτὸ καλὸν καὶ δυνάμενος καθορᾶν καὶ αὐτὸ καὶ τὰ ἐκείνου μετέ- d χοντα, καὶ οὔτε τὰ μετέχοντα αὐτὸ οὔτε αὐτὸ τὰ μετέχοντα ἡγούμενος, ὕπαρ ἢ ὄναρ αὖ καὶ οὗτος δοκεῖ σοι ζῆν;

Καὶ μάλα, ἔφη, ὕπαρ.

Οὐκοῦν τούτου μὲν τὴν διάνοιαν ὡς γιγνώσκοντος γνώμην 5 ἂν ὀρθῶς φαῖμεν εἶναι, τοῦ δὲ δόξαν ὡς δοξάζοντος;

Πάνυ μὲν οὖν.

Τί οὖν ἐὰν ἡμῖν χαλεπαίνῃ οὗτος, ὅν φαμεν δοξάζειν ἀλλ’ οὐ γιγνώσκειν, καὶ ἀμφισβητῇ ὡς οὐκ ἀληθῆ λέγομεν; ἕξομέν τι παραμυθεῖσθαι αὐτὸν καὶ πείθειν ἠρέμα, ἐπικρυ- e πτόμενοι ὅτι οὐχ ὑγιαίνει;

Δεῖ γέ τοι δή, ἔφη.

Ἴθι δή, σκόπει τί ἐροῦμεν πρὸς αὐτόν. ἢ βούλει ὧδε πυνθανώμεθα παρ’ αὐτοῦ, λέγοντες ὡς εἴ τι οἶδεν οὐδεὶς 5 αὐτῷ φθόνος, ἀλλ’ ἄσμενοι ἂν ἴδοιμεν εἰδότα τι. ἀλλ’ ἡμῖν εἰπὲ τόδε· ὁ γιγνώσκων γιγνώσκει τὶ ἢ οὐδέν; σὺ οὖν μοι ὑπὲρ ἐκείνου ἀποκρίνου.

Ἀποκρινοῦμαι, ἔφη, ὅτι γιγνώσκει τί.

Πότερον ὂν ἢ οὐκ ὄν; 10

things; but their mind is unable to see and love the nature of beauty in itself.

G. That's certainly right.

S. And isn't it the case that those who can approach and see beauty in and of itself, will be very few in number?

c G. Very much so.

S. Now, the person who believes in beautiful things, but doesn't believe in beauty itself and wouldn't be capable of following someone who tried to guide him to knowledge of it – do you think his life is one of dreaming or waking? Consider this: isn't dreaming a matter of thinking (whether asleep or awake) that something actually *is* the very thing which it merely resembles?

G. I would agree that someone who did this was 'dreaming'.

S. But what of the person who, by contrast, does believe in the reality

d of beauty itself, and is capable of observing both beauty itself and the objects which partake of it, and who never confuses these two things with one another – do you think that *he* leads a life of waking or dreaming?

G. He is awake in the highest degree.

S. So we would be right to describe this man's mental condition as one of knowledge, because it is knowledge that he exercises, but the other person's as one of belief, because that is all that he forms?

G. Absolutely.

S. Now, what if the person whom we describe as having beliefs but no knowledge becomes angry with us, and disputes the truth of our

e claim? Will we have any way of calming him down and persuading him gently, while dissembling the fact that he is not entirely in his right mind?

G. We certainly need one!

S. Come then, consider what we shall say to him. Would you like us to use the following line of questioning, with an assurance to him that we don't begrudge him any knowledge he may have, but would be glad to see it established? 'Do tell us this: does someone with knowledge know something or nothing?' *You* must answer me on his behalf.

G. I'll answer that 'he knows something'.

S. Something real or unreal?

Ὄν· πῶς γὰρ ἂν μὴ ὄν γέ τι γνωσθείη;

Ἱκανῶς οὖν τοῦτο ἔχομεν, κἂν εἰ πλεοναχῇ σκοποῖμεν, ὅτι τὸ μὲν παντελῶς ὂν παντελῶς γνωστόν, μὴ ὂν δὲ μηδαμῇ πάντη ἄγνωστον;

Ἱκανώτατα. 5

Εἶεν· εἰ δὲ δή τι οὕτως ἔχει ὡς εἶναί τε καὶ μὴ εἶναι, οὐ μεταξὺ ἂν κέοιτο τοῦ εἰλικρινῶς ὄντος καὶ τοῦ αὖ μηδαμῇ ὄντος;

Μεταξύ.

Οὐκοῦν ἐπὶ μὲν τῷ ὄντι γνῶσις ἦν, ἀγνωσία δ᾽ ἐξ ἀνάγκης ἐπὶ μὴ ὄντι, ἐπὶ δὲ τῷ μεταξὺ τούτῳ μεταξύ τι καὶ ζητητέον 10 ἀγνοίας τε καὶ ἐπιστήμης, εἴ τι τυγχάνει ὂν τοιοῦτον; b

Πάνυ μὲν οὖν.

Ἀρ᾽ οὖν λέγομέν τι δόξαν εἶναι;

Πῶς γὰρ οὔ;

Πότερον ἄλλην δύναμιν ἐπιστήμης ἢ τὴν αὐτήν; 5

Ἄλλην.

Ἐπ᾽ ἄλλῳ ἄρα τέτακται δόξα καὶ ἐπ᾽ ἄλλῳ ἐπιστήμη, κατὰ τὴν δύναμιν ἑκατέρα τὴν αὑτῆς.

Οὕτω.

Οὐκοῦν ἐπιστήμη μὲν ἐπὶ τῷ ὄντι πέφυκε, γνῶναι ὡς 10 ἔστι τὸ ὄν;—μᾶλλον δὲ ὧδέ μοι δοκεῖ πρότερον ἀναγκαῖον εἶναι διελέσθαι.

Πῶς;

Φήσομεν δυνάμεις εἶναι γένος τι τῶν ὄντων, αἷς δὴ καὶ c ἡμεῖς δυνάμεθα ἃ δυνάμεθα καὶ ἄλλο πᾶν ὅτι περ ἂν δύνηται, οἷον λέγω ὄψιν καὶ ἀκοὴν τῶν δυνάμεων εἶναι, εἰ ἄρα μανθάνεις ὃ βούλομαι λέγειν τὸ εἶδος.

Ἀλλὰ μανθάνω, ἔφη. 5

Ἄκουσον δὴ ὅ μοι φαίνεται περὶ αὐτῶν. δυνάμεως γὰρ ἐγὼ οὔτε τινὰ χρόαν ὁρῶ οὔτε σχῆμα οὔτε τι τῶν τοιούτων οἷον καὶ ἄλλων πολλῶν, πρὸς ἃ ἀποβλέπων ἔνια διορίζομαι παρ᾽ ἐμαυτῷ τὰ μὲν ἄλλα εἶναι, τὰ δὲ ἄλλα· δυνάμεως δ᾽ εἰς ἐκεῖνο μόνον βλέπω ἐφ᾽ ᾧ τε ἔστι καὶ ὃ ἀπεργάζεται, d

477a G. Real – how could something that wasn't real be known?

S. Do we have sufficient assurance (and would do, even after more extensive investigation) that the completely real is completely knowable, while that which is in no way real is altogether unknowable?

G. Complete assurance.

S. Right. But if, then, something is such as to be both real and unreal, wouldn't it lie somewhere between a state of pure reality and that of the completely unreal?

G. Yes, in between.

S. So knowledge, we agreed, covers what is real, ignorance must cover what is unreal, while something in between ignorance and knowl-
b   edge must be found to cover this in-between category (if there *is* any such thing)?

G. Yes indeed.

S. Do we agree that there is such a thing as belief?

G. Of course.

S. Do we think it a different capacity from knowledge, or the same?

G. A different one.

S. Belief and knowledge, therefore, have been assigned to cover different spheres, each according to its own capacity.

G. Yes.

S. Now, does knowledge naturally cover the real, and have an understanding of what is really the case? But, before that is answered, I think we must draw the following distinction.

G. What?

c S. We will agree that capacities form one class of entities, and it is these which enable us (and anything else which has an ability) to do the things that we can: vision and hearing are instances of what I mean by capacities – if you understand the class of things I mean.

G. I do understand.

S. Listen, then, to my view about them. A capacity has no colour for me to see, nor a shape, nor any such property which many other things have and which I consider in order to distinguish between different sets of objects in my sensory experience. With a capacity,
d   I can consider only its sphere and what it produces, and this is how

καὶ ταύτῃ ἑκάστην αὐτῶν δύναμιν ἐκάλεσα, καὶ τὴν μὲν
ἐπὶ τῷ αὐτῷ τεταγμένην καὶ τὸ αὐτὸ ἀπεργαζομένην τὴν
αὐτὴν καλῶ, τὴν δὲ ἐπὶ ἑτέρῳ καὶ ἕτερον ἀπεργαζομένην
ἄλλην. τί δὲ σύ; πῶς ποιεῖς;   5

Οὕτως, ἔφη.

Δεῦρο δὴ πάλιν, ἦν δ' ἐγώ, ὦ ἄριστε. ἐπιστήμην πότερον
δύναμίν τινα φῂς εἶναι αὐτήν, ἢ εἰς τί γένος τιθεῖς;

Εἰς τοῦτο, ἔφη, πασῶν γε δυνάμεων ἐρρωμενεστάτην.

Τί δέ, δόξαν εἰς δύναμιν ἢ εἰς ἄλλο εἶδος οἴσομεν;   e

Οὐδαμῶς, ἔφη· ᾧ γὰρ δοξάζειν δυνάμεθα, οὐκ ἄλλο τι
ἢ δόξα ἐστίν.

Ἀλλὰ μὲν δὴ ὀλίγον γε πρότερον ὡμολόγεις μὴ τὸ αὐτὸ
εἶναι ἐπιστήμην τε καὶ δόξαν.   5

Πῶς γὰρ ἄν, ἔφη, τό γε ἀναμάρτητον τῷ μὴ ἀναμαρτήτῳ
ταὐτόν τις νοῦν ἔχων τιθείη;

Καλῶς, ἦν δ' ἐγώ, καὶ δῆλον ὅτι ἕτερον ἐπιστήμης δόξα
ὁμολογεῖται ἡμῖν.   478

Ἕτερον.

Ἐφ' ἑτέρῳ ἄρα ἕτερόν τι δυναμένη ἑκατέρα αὐτῶν
πέφυκεν;

Ἀνάγκη.   5

Ἐπιστήμη μέν γέ που ἐπὶ τῷ ὄντι, τὸ ὂν γνῶναι ὡς ἔχει;
Ναί.

Δόξα δέ, φαμέν, δοξάζειν;
Ναί.

Ἦ ταὐτὸν ὅπερ ἐπιστήμη γιγνώσκει; καὶ ἔσται γνωστόν   10
τε καὶ δοξαστὸν τὸ αὐτό; ἢ ἀδύνατον;

Ἀδύνατον, ἔφη, ἐκ τῶν ὡμολογημένων· εἴπερ ἐπ' ἄλλῳ
ἄλλη δύναμις πέφυκεν, δυνάμεις δὲ ἀμφότεραί ἐστον, δόξα τε
καὶ ἐπιστήμη, ἄλλη δὲ ἑκατέρα, ὥς φαμεν, ἐκ τούτων δὴ οὐκ   b
ἐγχωρεῖ γνωστὸν καὶ δοξαστὸν ταὐτὸν εἶναι.

Οὐκοῦν εἰ τὸ ὂν γνωστόν, ἄλλο τι ἂν δοξαστὸν ἢ τὸ
ὂν εἴη;

I name each capacity, giving the same name to one which is assigned to the same sphere and produces the same thing, and different names to those with different spheres and products. Is this your practice too?

G.   Yes.

S.   To return to the main point again, my good friend: do you agree that knowledge is itself a capacity – otherwise, what class do you put it in?

G.   It *is* a capacity – the strongest of all capacities.

e S.   And shall we include belief as a capacity, or put it in another class?

G.   Not at all: belief is precisely the capacity by which we are able to form beliefs.

S.   Now, you agreed a little while ago that knowledge and belief are not the same thing.

G.   How could anyone with any sense think that something infallible was the same as something fallible!

478a S.   Well said; clearly we are in agreement that belief is different from knowledge.

G.   Yes, different.

S.   Then each of them, by difference of capacity, has by nature a different sphere?

G.   Necessarily so.

S.   Surely the sphere of knowledge covers the real, and involves an understanding of what is really the case?

G.   Yes.

S.   While belief, we agree, is for forming beliefs?

G.   Yes.

S.   Does belief believe the same thing as knowledge understands? Can the same thing be an object both of knowledge and of belief? Or is that impossible?

G.   It's impossible, according to what we've already agreed. Given that different capacities have, by nature, different spheres, and that both

b   belief and knowledge are capacities, yet, as we agree, different ones, it necessarily follows that the same thing cannot be an object of both knowledge and belief.

S.   So, if the real is the object of knowledge, the object of belief will have to be something other than the real?

Ἄλλο.

5

Ἆρ᾽ οὖν τὸ μὴ ὂν δοξάζει; ἢ ἀδύνατον καὶ δοξάσαι τό γε μὴ ὄν; ἐννόει δέ. οὐχ ὁ δοξάζων ἐπὶ τὶ φέρει τὴν δόξαν; ἢ οἷόν τε αὖ δοξάζειν μέν, δοξάζειν δὲ μηδέν;

Ἀδύνατον.

Ἀλλ᾽ ἕν γέ τι δοξάζει ὁ δοξάζων;

10

Ναί.

Ἀλλὰ μὴν μὴ ὄν γε οὐχ ἕν τι ἀλλὰ μηδὲν ὀρθότατ᾽ ἂν προσαγορεύοιτο;

c

Πάνυ γε.

Μὴ ὄντι μὴν ἄγνοιαν ἐξ ἀνάγκης ἀπέδομεν, ὄντι δὲ γνῶσιν;

Ὀρθῶς, ἔφη.

5

Οὐκ ἄρα ὂν οὐδὲ μὴ ὂν δοξάζει;

Οὐ γάρ.

Οὔτε ἄρα ἄγνοια οὔτε γνῶσις δόξα ἂν εἴη;

Οὐκ ἔοικεν.

Ἆρ᾽ οὖν ἐκτὸς τούτων ἐστίν, ὑπερβαίνουσα ἢ γνῶσιν 10 σαφηνείᾳ ἢ ἄγνοιαν ἀσαφείᾳ;

Οὐδέτερα.

Ἀλλ᾽ ἄρα, ἦν δ᾽ ἐγώ, γνώσεως μέν σοι φαίνεται δόξα σκοτωδέστερον, ἀγνοίας δὲ φανότερον;

Καὶ πολύ γε, ἔφη.

15

Ἐντὸς δ᾽ ἀμφοῖν κεῖται;

d

Ναί.

Μεταξὺ ἄρα ἂν εἴη τούτοιν δόξα.

Κομιδῇ μὲν οὖν.

Οὐκοῦν ἔφαμεν ἐν τοῖς πρόσθεν, εἴ τι φανείη οἷον ἅμα 5 ὄν τε καὶ μὴ ὄν, τὸ τοιοῦτον μεταξὺ κεῖσθαι τοῦ εἰλικρινῶς ὄντος τε καὶ τοῦ πάντως μὴ ὄντος, καὶ οὔτε ἐπιστήμην οὔτε ἄγνοιαν ἐπ᾽ αὐτῷ ἔσεσθαι, ἀλλὰ τὸ μεταξὺ αὖ φανὲν ἀγνοίας καὶ ἐπιστήμης;

Ὀρθῶς.

10

G. Yes.

S. Well now, can a belief be about something unreal? Or is it impossible even to have a belief about that which lacks any reality? Consider the point. Doesn't the believer direct his belief *towards* something? Or can one have a belief which is a belief about nothing?

G. It's impossible.

S. There must be *some* entity about which he holds his belief?

G. Yes.

c   S. But that which lacks any reality should properly be described not as some entity but as nothing?

G. Indeed.

S. And we posited a necessary match between ignorance and that which lacks any reality, and between knowledge and the real?

G. Correct.

S. So one does not have beliefs about the real *or* the unreal either?

G. One can't.

S. Belief, then, can't be either ignorance or knowledge?

G. It seems not.

S. Well, is there anything which lies beyond these two, surpassing knowledge in its clarity or ignorance in its obscurity?

G. No, neither.

S. Then, does belief seem to you a darker state than knowledge, but a clearer one than ignorance?

G. Very much so.

d   S. And it lies somewhere on the scale between them?

G. Yes.

S. So belief will be a mid-way state between the two?

G. Exactly.

S. Now, did we agree earlier that if anything turned out such as to be simultaneously both real and unreal, this would lie in between pure reality and complete unreality, and it would be covered by neither knowledge nor ignorance, but by whatever should turn out to lie between ignorance and knowledge?

G. Correct.

Νῦν δέ γε πέφανται μεταξὺ τούτοιν ὃ δὴ καλοῦμεν δόξαν;
Πέφανται.

Ἐκεῖνο δὴ λείποιτ' ἂν ἡμῖν εὑρεῖν, ὡς ἔοικε, τὸ ἀμφοτέ- e
ρων μετέχον, τοῦ εἶναί τε καὶ μὴ εἶναι, καὶ οὐδέτερον εἰλι-
κρινὲς ὀρθῶς ἂν προσαγορευόμενον, ἵνα, ἐὰν φανῇ, δοξαστὸν
αὐτὸ εἶναι ἐν δίκῃ προσαγορεύωμεν, τοῖς μὲν ἄκροις τὰ ἄκρα,
τοῖς δὲ μεταξὺ τὰ μεταξὺ ἀποδιδόντες. ἢ οὐχ οὕτως; 5
Οὕτω.

Τούτων δὴ ὑποκειμένων λεγέτω μοι, φήσω, καὶ ἀπο-
κρινέσθω ὁ χρηστὸς ὃς αὐτὸ μὲν καλὸν καὶ ἰδέαν τινὰ αὐτοῦ 479
κάλλους μηδεμίαν ἡγεῖται ἀεὶ μὲν κατὰ ταὐτὰ ὡσαύτως
ἔχουσαν, πολλὰ δὲ τὰ καλὰ νομίζει, ἐκεῖνος ὁ φιλοθεάμων
καὶ οὐδαμῇ ἀνεχόμενος ἄν τις ἓν τὸ καλὸν φῇ εἶναι καὶ
δίκαιον καὶ τἆλλα οὕτω. "Τούτων γὰρ δή, ὦ ἄριστε, φή- 5
σομεν, τῶν πολλῶν καλῶν μῶν τι ἔστιν ὃ οὐκ αἰσχρὸν
φανήσεται; καὶ τῶν δικαίων, ὃ οὐκ ἄδικον; καὶ τῶν ὁσίων,
ὃ οὐκ ἀνόσιον;"

Οὔκ, ἀλλ' ἀνάγκη, ἔφη, καὶ καλά πως αὐτὰ καὶ αἰσχρὰ b
φανῆναι, καὶ ὅσα ἄλλα ἐρωτᾷς.

Τί δὲ τὰ πολλὰ διπλάσια; ἧττόν τι ἡμίσεα ἢ διπλάσια
φαίνεται;

Οὐδέν. 5

Καὶ μεγάλα δὴ καὶ σμικρὰ καὶ κοῦφα καὶ βαρέα μή τι
μᾶλλον ἃ ἂν φήσωμεν, ταῦτα προσρηθήσεται ἢ τἀναντία;

Οὔκ, ἀλλ' ἀεί, ἔφη, ἕκαστον ἀμφοτέρων ἕξεται.

Πότερον οὖν ἔστι μᾶλλον ἢ οὐκ ἔστιν ἕκαστον τῶν
πολλῶν τοῦτο ὃ ἄν τις φῇ αὐτὸ εἶναι; 10

Τοῖς ἐν ταῖς ἑστιάσεσιν, ἔφη, ἐπαμφοτερίζουσιν ἔοικεν,
καὶ τῷ τῶν παίδων αἰνίγματι τῷ περὶ τοῦ εὐνούχου, τῆς c
βολῆς πέρι τῆς νυκτερίδος, ᾧ καὶ ἐφ' οὗ αὐτὸν αὐτὴν αἰνίτ-
τονται βαλεῖν· καὶ γὰρ ταῦτα ἐπαμφοτερίζειν, καὶ οὔτ'
εἶναι οὔτε μὴ εἶναι οὐδὲν αὐτῶν δυνατὸν παγίως νοῆσαι,
οὔτε ἀμφότερα οὔτε οὐδέτερον. 5

S. And now it is what we are calling 'belief' which has turned out to lie between these?

G. Yes it has.

e S. So it's now left for us to find out, it would seem, the thing which partakes of both reality and unreality but which could not properly be described as a pure case of either, so that, if it can be identified, we can justifiably describe it as the object of belief, and thus make the ends of our scales, as well as their middle sections, align with one another. Isn't that so?

G. Yes.

S. Given these premises, I shall request a further response from the
479a splendid person who does not believe in beauty itself and in a form of beauty which is always and invariably the same, but who acknowledges a multiplicity of beauties – I mean that lover of sights who would have no patience at all with anyone who asserted that beauty is a single entity, and likewise with justice and the rest. 'Of these many individual things of beauty, my good friend', we shall say to him, 'surely there isn't a single one which couldn't equally seem ugly? Or any piece of justice which couldn't seem unjust? Or any piece of piety which couldn't seem impious?'

b G. There is none: it's inevitable that these things should in some respect appear both beautiful and ugly; and likewise with the other properties you ask about.

S. And what about the many individual instances of doubleness: is there any less reason to regard them as cases of 'half' than of 'double'?

G. No.

S. And the same with instances of large and small, light and heavy: there will be no more reason to describe them in one of these ways than in the opposite?

G. No; each case will always be connected to both properties.

S. So, is there any more reason for saying of any individual instance that it 'is', rather than 'is not', whichever of these descriptions anyone may apply to it?

G. It's like the game of ambiguity played at parties, and like the
c children's riddle about the eunuch (about his hitting the bat, what he struck it with, and what the riddle says he was sitting on when he struck it). There is the same ambiguity with the properties we're talking about, and it's impossible to think of any of them as being, in a completely fixed sense, either real or unreal: they're neither both things at once, nor just either one of them.

Ἔχεις οὖν αὐτοῖς, ἦν δ' ἐγώ, ὅτι χρήσῃ, ἢ ὅποι θήσεις
καλλίω θέσιν τῆς μεταξὺ οὐσίας τε καὶ τοῦ μὴ εἶναι; οὔτε
γάρ που σκοτωδέστερα μὴ ὄντος πρὸς τὸ μᾶλλον μὴ εἶναι
φανήσεται, οὔτε φανότερα ὄντος πρὸς τὸ μᾶλλον εἶναι.   d
Ἀληθέστατα, ἔφη.

Ηὑρήκαμεν ἄρα, ὡς ἔοικεν, ὅτι τὰ τῶν πολλῶν πολλὰ
νόμιμα καλοῦ τε πέρι καὶ τῶν ἄλλων μεταξύ που κυλινδεῖται
τοῦ τε μὴ ὄντος καὶ τοῦ ὄντος εἰλικρινῶς.   5
Ηὑρήκαμεν.

Προωμολογήσαμεν δέ γε, εἴ τι τοιοῦτον φανείη, δοξαστὸν
αὐτὸ ἀλλ' οὐ γνωστὸν δεῖν λέγεσθαι, τῇ μεταξὺ δυνάμει τὸ
μεταξὺ πλανητὸν ἁλισκόμενον.
Ὡμολογήκαμεν.   10

Τοὺς ἄρα πολλὰ καλὰ θεωμένους, αὐτὸ δὲ τὸ καλὸν μὴ   e
ὁρῶντας μηδ' ἄλλῳ ἐπ' αὐτὸ ἄγοντι δυναμένους ἕπεσθαι,
καὶ πολλὰ δίκαια, αὐτὸ δὲ τὸ δίκαιον μή, καὶ πάντα οὕτω,
δοξάζειν φήσομεν ἅπαντα, γιγνώσκειν δὲ ὧν δοξάζουσιν
οὐδέν.   5
Ἀνάγκη, ἔφη.

Τί δὲ αὖ τοὺς αὐτὰ ἕκαστα θεωμένους καὶ ἀεὶ κατὰ ταὐτὰ
ὡσαύτως ὄντα; ἆρ' οὐ γιγνώσκειν ἀλλ' οὐ δοξάζειν;
Ἀνάγκη καὶ ταῦτα.

Οὐκοῦν καὶ ἀσπάζεσθαί τε καὶ φιλεῖν τούτους μὲν ταῦτα   10
φήσομεν ἐφ' οἷς γνῶσίς ἐστιν, ἐκείνους δὲ ἐφ' οἷς δόξα; ἢ   480
οὐ μνημονεύομεν ὅτι φωνάς τε καὶ χρόας καλὰς καὶ τὰ
τοιαῦτ' ἔφαμεν τούτους φιλεῖν τε καὶ θεᾶσθαι, αὐτὸ δὲ τὸ
καλὸν οὐδ' ἀνέχεσθαι ὥς τι ὄν;
Μεμνήμεθα.   5

Μὴ οὖν τι πλημμελήσομεν φιλοδόξους καλοῦντες αὐτοὺς
μᾶλλον ἢ φιλοσόφους; καὶ ἆρα ἡμῖν σφόδρα χαλεπανοῦσιν
ἂν οὕτω λέγωμεν;
Οὔκ, ἄν γέ μοι πείθωνται, ἔφη· τῷ γὰρ ἀληθεῖ χαλε-
παίνειν οὐ θέμις.   10

S. Do you have anything better to make of them, then, or anywhere better to place them, than a position midway between being and non-being? For they can't be regarded as darker than the unreal, in the

d sense of having even less reality than that, nor clearer than the real, in the sense of having a greater degree of reality.

G. That's entirely true.

S. We've discovered therefore, it seems, that the multifarious principles of beauty and all the rest to which most people subscribe, roll around in a no-man's-land between unreality and pure reality.

G. That's what we've discovered.

S. And we agreed earlier that if any such thing were to emerge, it ought to be called an object of belief but not of knowledge: an unstable, in-between object, matching the in-between capacity.

G. We did agree.

e S. So with those who contemplate many beautiful things, but neither see beauty itself nor are able to follow another who would guide them to it, and who recognise many instances of justice but not justice itself, and likewise with everything, we shall declare that their views are entirely matters of belief, and that they have no knowledge of the objects of their beliefs.

G. We must.

S. But what of those who contemplate each and all of these properties in themselves, in their permanent and unchanging form? Won't we declare that they have knowledge rather than beliefs?

G. Again, we must.

S. Well, shall we say that the latter embrace and love the things covered

480a by their knowledge, while the others have the same feelings for the things covered by their beliefs? Or don't we remember that we said this second group love and contemplate beautiful voices, colours, and things of this kind, but could not even tolerate the notion of beauty itself as a real entity?

G. Yes, we remember.

S. So we won't be making a mistake if we call them lovers of belief rather than lovers of knowledge? Will they be very angry with us if we use this description?

G. Not if they follow my advice, since it's wrong to be angry with the truth.

Τοὺς αὐτὸ ἄρα ἕκαστον τὸ ὂν ἀσπαζομένους φιλοσόφους ἀλλ᾽ οὐ φιλοδόξους κλητέον;

Παντάπασι μὲν οὖν.

S. Then we must call philosophers, but not lovers of belief, those who embrace each reality in itself?

G. Absolutely.

Apparatus Criticus

449c1 ὅτι N (Boter 232) ἔτι ADF

451b4 καὶ καθαρὸν A καθαρὸν DF

452a2 μὴν...γε Richards (111) μὲν...τε ADF

454b4 μὴ N (Boter 232) om. ADF

454d1 τὸ...τεῖνον τὰ... Galen, β (Boter 204) τὰ...τείνοντα ADF

454d2 ἰατρικὸν...ἰατρικὴν A²DF (-κῶν...-κὴν A¹) ἰατρικὸν...ἰατρικὸν β (Boter 212) ὄντα secl. Burnet ὄντας K. F. Hermann

456a1-2 καὶ D om. AF

456a11 ἡ δὲ Eusebius ἢ DF ἀσθενεστέρα ἰσχυροτέρα (-ας A²) A

457d9 ἂν F om. AD

460b9 μὲν γάρ A γάρ DF

462c12 τεταγμένη E

462e6 αὕτη β (Boter 204)

463c5 ἐντυχγάνῃ F -άνῃ τις AD

463e6 αὖ Stobaeus ἂν F om. AD

464e6 ἐπιμελείας Stobaeus, Par. 1810 (Boter 223-4)

467e3 διδαξαμένους Mon. 237 -ομένους ADF

468a4 ποῖ' αὖ Burnet ποῖ' ἂν A ποῖαν F ποίαν D ποῖα E

468a10 ἐλοῦσι van Leeuwen θέλουσι ADF

468b3 στρατείας ADF

472a2 στραγγευομένῳ Fᶜᵒʳʳ· (Boter 103-4) στρατευομένῳ AD

473a6 ἂν add. Bywater

473c6 ἐπ' αὐτῷ...εἶμι F ἐπ' αὐτὸ...εἶμι AD

474e2 μελιχλώρους A in marg. μελαγχλώρους ADF μελίχρουν Plut. *Mor.* 45a, 56d

477a9 εἰ ἐπὶ β

477a10 ἐπὶ δὲ τῷ F⁴ (Boter 209) ἐπὶ τῷ ADF

479a2 ἀεὶ μὲν A μὲν om. DF

Commentary

449a1-451b8

Having reached an understanding of justice as the harmonious unity of constituent elements in either a city (i.e. its classes) or the individual soul (its psychological 'parts'), Socrates is now proceeding to consider the four main types of injustice or evil. But he is interrupted by Adeimantus and the others present, who demand that he clarify what he had meant by his remark earlier in the conversation that justice requires some kind of 'sharing' (koinônia) of women and children. Socrates is reluctant to elaborate, both because of the scepticism which his ideas will encounter, and because he feels grave self-doubt about them.

The start of bk. 5 is one of the major transitions in the unfolding design of the *Republic*; it marks a turning-point which leads the conversation in the direction of new and startlingly radical proposals for the social structure of the just society. These proposals will eventually prompt the cardinal suggestion of the need for philosopher-rulers, and that suggestion will in turn generate the expression of a visionary metaphysics that occupies the whole of bks. 6-7. Only in bk. 8 will Soc. return to the discussion of defective cities and souls which is broken off at this point. The preliminary section of bk. 5 consequently takes on a dramatic character comparable to the openings of many Platonic works (including the *Rep.* itself); by referring to the larger group of listeners, it not only reminds us of the entire setting of the dialogue, but conveys a lively sense of the participants' personal engagement in the occasion: see nn. 449b2 (Adeimantus), 450b7 (Glaucon), 450a5, b3 (Thrasymachus), 449b1 (Polemarchus), b3, 6, 450a8 (parallelisms with the start of the work). P. uses this kind of detail to suggest that philosophical argument, however rarified it may sometimes become, grows from the commitment of, and the exchange of ideas between, particular individuals.

Above all, this scene both illustrates, and invites the reader to share, a fascination with the figure of Soc., who is even treated by some of his companions as a Proteus or Silenus-like figure (n. 449b6), capable of revealing, if only he could be made to, a special wisdom denied to ordinary men. But Soc. is at least as elusive as these mythological models, and shows deep reluctance to air ideas about which he feels extreme uncertainty (esp. 450d8 ff.). This poses a crucial question about P.'s use of the Socratic persona in the *Rep.* The hesitation and self-doubt of the present passage seem to belong with the Soc. of the *Apology* and the early dialogues, who disavows any knowledge of his own. Yet, once pressed by the others, Soc. will in fact proceed to elaborate suggestions of a far-reaching and apparently confident kind. It would be cynical to suppose that P. has merely preserved the empty shell of a Socratic manner and personality; the emphasis of the characterisation in these pages, as elsewhere in the middle books (e.g. 6.506b-e), must clearly carry more weight than that. But there is no way of *dissolving* the tension: better, and interpretatively more cogent, both to acknowledge it and to accept that it is something which P., as a consummate dramatist of philosophy, intends to be faced and reckoned with. On those premises, we can strive for a reading of the work which incorporates P.'s continuing, if increasingly complex, confrontation with the compelling yet mysterious person of Soc.: see the Introduction, §1.2-3.

449a1-2   **city and régime:** the social entity and its political organisation; P. often uses this virtual hendiadys (e.g. 7.536b3, 541a5, *Laws* 5.739b8).

449a1-2   **good and correct:** *orthos*, 'correct' or 'right', had, from its original sense of physical straightness, acquired common associations both with justice and with truth; here it perhaps also suggests stability of a kind conducive to political permanence. The term had some political currency before P. (see e.g. Thrasym. fr. 1 DK), but it is a particular, almost compulsive, favourite of his: in the present book cf. e.g. 449d5–6, 451c5, 459d4, and see 7.517c2 for 'all correct and fine things' as a compendious description of human values. The idea of the single 'correct' constitution occurs later at *Plt.* 293e1, 297a–d, etc., with 291c ff. Arist. *Pol.* 1297a17–20, etc., calls 'correct' those constitutions which embody a sense of common interest; he also calls the best constitution the 'most correct', ib. 1293b25. Note the enclosing Greek word-order of adjs. in a1–2, repeated in miniature in the δέ clause; cf. e.g. 459e5–6 (nouns).

449a3   **given that this kind:** the premise is not of a unique set of practical arrangements for a city/person, but of a single *ethical* ideal, i.e. a condition in which all four cardinal virtues are embodied, as bk. 4 argues.

449a3–4   **cities...individuals:** symmetry between the virtues of cities and persons was posited at the outset (2.368e-9a), and elaborately established in bk. 4 (esp. 434d ff., 441c ff.). The statement of it here is slightly oblique, since 'the others' (a2) refers grammatically to cities: the point is not that in a bad city individual lives will also necessarily be flawed (though that might be anyway entailed by the *Rep.*'s argument as a whole), but that there are four types of evil which can be discerned equally in societies and in persons (cf. 4.445c9-10). The nouns *dioikêsis* and *kataskeuê* both refer to a condition or state of organisation; they are here close to synonymous, as 455a2/b2 illustrates (cf. e.g. Isoc. 15.108, verb and noun). ψυχῆς τρόπου κατασκευήν, lit. 'the state of disposition of the soul', is slightly pleonastic: τρόπος is common in the sense of 'character', 'disposition', etc., but also means 'sort', 'variety'; cf. 473b7, 4.445c9 f.

449a5   **types of deficiency:** the phrase picks up 4.445c–d; the subject was originally promised at 4.420c4. *Eidos*, from a basic sense of physical form or appearance (e.g. 2.380d3, 3.402d2), develops two broadly related semantic ranges, which are straddled by the present use - (i) form, nature or character; (ii) kind, class, species, or variety: it is these meanings which P. adapts and extends for his so-called 'theory of Forms': cf. nn. 454a6, 476a4-5, with H. C. Baldry, *CQ* 31 (1937) 141-50, F. E. Peters, *Greek Philosophical Terms* (New York, 1967) 46-51.

449a7–b1   **going to describe these in turn:** for the compound future, ᾗα ... ἐρῶν, cf. e.g. 8.562c4, Herod. 4.82. As often with Greek, the two-part construction ('to describe these..., according to...) is equivalent to a single indirect question (i.e. 'to describe what I thought to be...'); cf. d2 below, and e.g. 6.484a1-3, 490e2-3. The adverb ἐφεξῆς, 'in turn', is here equivalent to an attributive adj.: sc. τὰς ἐφεξῆς ⟨πολιτείας⟩. The account of corrupt types of city/soul, and the sequence in which they naturally occur, will eventually be given in bks. 8–9: see the resumption of the topic at 8.543c4 ff.

449b1   **Polemarchus:** son of the Syracusan metic, Cephalus, and brother of the orator, Lysias; unlike the latter, he is said to be a devotee of philosophy at *Phdr.* 257b3-4. He was killed by the Thirty in 404 (Lys. 12.17). The *Rep.* is set in their family house in the Piraeus (1.328b). Pol. was last mentioned, in passing, at 4.427d; he has not spoken since 1.340a-b, where, as at 1.331d, his contribution was an intervention. The new juncture in the discussion is given the sort of circumstantial colour and detail that is most familiar at the openings of Platonic dialogues (cf. nn. b3, 6, 450a8). The *Rep.* contains other major points of transition, or changes of direction, of this kind: cf. esp. the starts of bks. 2, 4, 10, and 6.487b.

449b2   **Adeimantus:** older brother of P. and G. (n. 450b7), mentioned in court (with P.) at *Ap.* 34a1; cf. Davies 332. He has made more than one strong intervention in the conversation: see 2.362d ff., 4.449a; cf. 6.487b ff. Soc. admires him, with his brother, at 2.367e-8a; but overall he takes a lesser part than G. and is presented as a less lively character.

449b3   **gripped the...cloak:** the same phrase as 1.327b4; but there is no significant echo here, only a similarity in evocative narrative detail. In the same way, Pol.'s leaning over to whisper (b5) is matched by *Euthd*. 275e.

449b6   **let it pass:** since the verb will mean 'acquit' at 451b3, we should perhaps hear legal overtones here, as elsewhere in what follows (449c3, ?450a1–3, 451a–b). There is a parallelism, once again (cf. b3), to the opening of the whole work (the same verb at 1.327c11), where Soc. was humorously 'detained' by his friends (cf. 6.504e6). In both of these places (cf. also 472a8) we might catch a subtle allusion to the folk-motif of arresting a figure who has special knowledge which he will yield only under duress: see esp. Hom. *Od*. 4.383 ff. (Proteus), Herod. 1.138.3, Arist. fr.44 Rose (*apud* Plut. *Mor*. 115b–e). The last two cases involve Silenus, to whom Soc. is compared at *Symp*. 215a-b; while Soc. himself applies the Proteus motif to others at *Euthph*. 15d 3-4, *Euthd*. 288b-c, *Ion* 541e7. Soc. is someone both mysterious and entrancing; others experience a need to listen to him: cf. n. 453c7. The detention of Thrasymachus at 1.344d was somewhat different: there the point, as 344e indicates, was that staying in the discussion is a symbol of commitment to the search for truth.

       ἔφη (b6) is syntactically redundant; cf. 10.615d2-3.

449c1   **Why exactly?:** a combination of the form of question at b8 with the phrase ὅτι τί, lit. 'because why?' (see 1.343a10, *Chrm*. 161c10, and e.g. Ar. *Plutus* 136, Dem. 23.214). The lack of an answering ὅτι in c2 is not, *pace* Adam, a decisive argument against Burnet's text; Adam's alternative, 'because of what particular remark of mine?', construes the Greek awkwardly, and removes the parenthetic 'I said' which the exchange requires. ἔτι, found in the main mss., is hard but perhaps not impossible: 'Still <sc. I ask> ... why exactly?'

449c2   **shirking:** the word is (humorously) strong – apter, one might think, for one of Soc.'s own admonitions (cf. Xen. *Mem*. 3.7.9). The force of *rhathum*- terms is a mixture of idleness and softness: see esp. *Laws* 10.901c–e. Soc. is accused of varieties of the vice, somewhat ironically, at *Crito* 45d6, *Tht*. 166a6; yet it is a general feature of the Platonic Soc. that he is committed to the unflagging pursuit of truth and wisdom: see e.g. 1.336e8–9, 2.358d7–8, 374e10–11, 6.497d–e, 504b–e. There is, however, at least in P.'s development of the Socratic persona in his middle dialogues, a potential tension between this characteristic and that of self-deprecation; cf. nn. 450b5, 7.

449c2–3   **tricking...out of discussing:** lit. 'concealing ... in order not to discuss'. *Eidos* (n. a5), 'aspect', may perhaps mean 'section' (cf. Isoc. 15.74).

449c4   **making the remark casually:** at 4.423e–4a; 'casually', i.e. as though the matter itself were insignificant (*phaulon*). A. had used the term ironically at 423c5 (cf. d7), but Soc. himself seemed to think that the details of the subject really could be taken care of with relative ease: 423d8–e1.

449c4–5   **as though:** the ὡς clause expresses an alleged assumption of Soc.'s, and contains an accusative absolute (normal for impersonal verbs), with the participle of 'to be' omitted: ὡς ... δῆλον <ὄν>. See Weir Smyth §2086.

449c5   **'friends share everything':** the proverb occurs in ordinary applications at *Lys*. 207c10, *Phdr*. 279c6–7, Arist. *EN* 1159b31; at *Laws* 5.739c2–3 the point is the same communist scheme as in *Rep*.; Arist. *Pol*. 1263a30 quotes the phrase *à propos* the virtuous sharing of *private* property; and it is said to have been used by Diogenes the Cynic, D. Laert. 6.72 (cf. Introduction, n. 15). But the saying is also linked with early Pythagorean fraternities in south Italy: Timaeus *FGrH* 566 F13 (= scholia to P. *Phdr*. 279c [Greene 88] and D. Laert. 8.10), and e.g. Iambl. *Vita Pyth*. 168; cf. KRS 227–8. (*Grg*. 507e–8a may refer to *koinônia* as a link between Pythagorean ethics and cosmology: see Dodds' nn.) So we must reckon with the possibility that P. intends an allusion to their practices. But such an allusion would serve also to highlight P.'s distinctiveness, for even if women belonged to these groups (cf. Introduction n. 20), Pythagoreans practised no form of sexual communism.

449c6   **correct:** A. had said as much himself at 4.424a3, in a way which suggested that he did not take the point to be especially radical.

449c7   **the correctness:** A. quotes Soc.'s adverb, *orthôs*, in a nominalised form, as one might with inverted commas ('this "correctly" of yours'). Cf. 459d3–5.

449c8   **'sharing':** *koinônia* is a key concept for the entire *Rep.* It is a feature of any shared human enterprise (1.351c–2c), and thus the basis of a true society or city: see esp. 2.369c–71b; hence, for Arist. *Pol.* e.g. 1252a7, 1260b27, it is the subject-matter of politics. But the idea is also linked with marriage and the family: see esp. *Plt.* 310b2, *Laws* 6.771e1, 772d7, 773c6–7, with e.g. Eur. *Ph.* 16, Xen. *Oec.* 7.11–12, 10.3–5, Isoc. 3.40. P. is therefore using a well established concept, but giving it a radical interpretation which goes beyond Pythagorean ideas of friendship (n. c5), though not as far as the complete sexual promiscuity of Cynic and early Stoic *koinônia* (D. Laert. 7.131, with H.C. Baldry, *JHS* 79 [1959] 9–10). 'Sharing' of women and children will have several strands: (i) participation of women in the work of Guardians (457a7–8); (ii) the communal living of female with male Guardians (458c8–9); (iii) the holding of women and children in common (457c–61e). And this compound ideal will be the foundation for a larger, ideological *koinônia* in the citizen-body as a whole: esp. 464a–b. See the Introduction, pp. 7 ff., 19–22.

449d2–3   **procreation...rear:** the first topic, alluded to originally at 4.423e7, will be elaborated at 458e–61c; the second, which especially suggests, but need not be limited to, the earliest period of upbringing (cf. nn. 450c2, 451e4), has already been discussed in part (see the educational scheme of bks. 2–3), and is treated more diffusely throughout bk. 5, e.g. in the provisions for abolishing the family at 461d ff., or for taking the young to war at 466e ff.

449d3   **and the whole:** after μεμνῆσθαι περί (d2), we now get a direct object, ὅλην ... κοινωνίαν; the change of construction is helped by the fact that μεμνῆσθαι does sometimes take an accusative (cf. Weir Smyth §1358).

449d4   **fundamental difference:** lit. 'contributes a great amount and the whole'; perhaps a variation on the phrase '(διαφέρειν) ὅλῳ καὶ παντί' (469c3 n.); hence φέρειν εἰς may be influenced by διαφέρειν εἰς, e.g. *Laws* 6.780c1.

449d6   **this matter:** although the nouns in d2–4 were feminine, they are now treated as a compound phenomenon; hence the neuter participle (ctr. Richards 110).

449d7   **analysed:** this use of διαιρεῖσθαι (cf. e.g. 466d6) lacks any precise suggestion of 'division' as a dialectical technique (cf. n. 454a6).

450a3   **proposal:** lit. 'vote'; cf. the adj. *sumpsêphos*, 'in agreement' (e.g. 2.380c4, *Crat.* 398c6), to which P. is rather partial. G. (n. b7) speaks as though a member of a jury: he is perhaps meant to be picking up the judicial connotations of 'let go' (a1); cf. 451b, and n. 457e7.

450a5   **Thrasymachus:** sophist and rhetorician, from Chalcedon. He has not spoken since his aggressive defence of amoralism in bk. 1, and he will not speak again, though there is a jocular reference to him at 6.498c; but b3 (see n.) gives us a brief reminder of his manner. For the general wish of the group that the argument should be pursued, cf. 2.368c4.

450a7   **apprehending:** a mock-physical term here, with associations of suddenness and surprise; it reinforces the playful 'detention' of Soc. (449b8–9, 450a1).

450a8   **fresh start:** the transition at the start of bk. 5 is reminiscent of the opening of a dialogue in its own right (n. 449b1). The idea of effectively going back to the beginning (often a Socratic desideratum: cf. 6.502e2, and e.g. *Euthph.* 15c11, *Lch.* 189e2–3, *Prt.* 333d3, *Grg.* 488b2, *Tht.* 151d3, 164c1) is apt, since the proposals for female Guardians and the abolition of the family will have implications for a great deal of what has been discussed in bks. 2–4. Indeed, parts of the earlier argument seem (in retrospect) to show no preparation for bk. 5's suggestions: see n. 457d1–2. Why does P. structure his dialogue in this way, with a series of layers and fresh starts? Above all, surely, to convey the exploratory and open-ended nature of philosophical enquiry, and thus to maintain the intellectual challenge which he offers his readers. Nor should we assume that P. himself necessarily knew from the outset precisely what shape he would give to the discussion; philosophical exploration is part of his own relationship to the dialogue form, as well as of the effect he seeks to create by it.

'Provoking' (*kinein*) an argument, a7, perhaps anticipates the metaphor at b1: *kinein* is sometimes used of disturbing (e.g.) a wasps' nest (Hom. *Il.* 16. 264, Ar. *Wasps* 404, *?Clouds* 297). But elsewhere *kinein logon* seems rather to mean 'set an argument in motion' (e.g. *Phlb.* 15e2, *Plt.* 297c7).

450b1   **hornet's nest:** *hesmos*, lit. a collection of insects (or sometimes birds), in the form of either a swarm or a nest/hive; cf. *smênos*, which is often used similarly. It is a feature of P.'s writing that he characterises argument or dialectic by a large range of imagery, of which the following is only a selection: swimming, sailing, etc. (n. 453d5); hunting (e.g. 4.432b–e; cf. n. 476c3–4); journeying (n. 452c4); feasting (n. 458a1–2); warfare (n. 472a1–2); vision (n. 476b7–8); law-courts (n. 457e7); women (6.503a8). Fuller lists are given by D. Tarrant, *CQ* 40 (1946) 27–34.

450b3   **indulge our fancies:** for the proverbial metaphor, lit. 'make gold (by smelting)', see Eubulus fr. 19 *PCG*/20 K. It is surely too subtle to see an echo of Soc.'s analogy with prospecting for gold at 1.336e5, though A. D. Winspear, *CP* 30 (1935) 347-9, argues that this is Thrasymachus's rejoinder to that passage. We are certainly meant to be reminded of Thrasymachus's penchant for colourful language: see esp. 1.336b8 f., 338d3, 340d1, 343a7.

450b5   **within limits:** it is unlike Soc. to put limits on an enquiry; see e.g. 2.376d 6–7, with nn. 449c2, 450b7, d1 ('hesitation'). What we expect from him, and what is generally ascribed to him in P., is precisely the unflagging commitment which is here affirmed by G.: see e.g. 2.367d8, 374e10 f., 376d6–7, 6.498d, *Ap.* 38a, *Euthph.* 15c12. A popular image of philosophers as people who waste endless time arguing is reflected at Ar. *Frogs* 1496–9.

450b7   *our* **convenience:** G., brother of P. and Adeimantus (n. 449b2) – younger than A., but probably older than P.: Davies 332–3 – echoes the fullness of philosophical commitment normally associated with Soc. himself (n. b5); likewise with the frequently Socratic injunction not to 'tire' in enquiry (cf. 4.445b7, *Euthph.* 11e4, *Meno* 81d4, *Prt.* 333b7). G. represents the keen, cooperative spirit of an earnest disciple of Soc., who expresses admiration of him and Adeimantus at 2.367e6 ff., and who assumes him to have familiarity with philosophical ideas (n. 474c8). G. again shows qualities of liveliness, sometimes with humour (cf. 6.509c1–2), at 474a–b, and e.g. 2.357a2 ff. (an intervention which prompts the work's major argument), 372c2 ff. But he also occasionally displays, as here and at 4.432c, 10.596a2–4, a strong dependence on Soc.'s guidance. This characterisation is compatible with the portrayal of him as prematurely eager for a political career, and readily deflated by Soc.'s interrogation, at Xen. *Mem.* 3.6.1–18. Cf. also nn. 455d3–5, 474d3.

450c1   **Guardians' 'sharing':** the original hint of sexual communism at 4.423e–4a had directly concerned the Guardians; but as it spoke of them 'seeing to' (423e6) such arrangements, it was compatible with the establishment of a scheme for *all* citizens (as later understood by Plut. *Mor.* 140e). Bk. 5 clearly limits the idea to the Guardian class (comprising Rulers and Auxiliaries: cf. n. 458b9 f.), though there is some passing ambiguity at 462b5 (see n.). But *Laws* 5.739b–e, with a reminiscence of *Rep.* 5, speaks of the desirability of communism throughout a city (ib. c1–2), which helps to explain why Arist. *Pol.* 1264a11–40 found this aspect of P.'s intentions unclear.

450c2   **child-rearing:** though *trophê* here means the feeding and care of young children, it often has a wider scope (e.g. 458d2, 464c1, n. 451e4). G.'s focus on early nurture (cf. 449d3) indicates that he already suspects Soc.'s ideas to have radical implications for the family; it would be inapt to ask why he suspects this: the point serves to arouse certain expectations in P.'s readers. The 'heavy burden' to which G. alludes is one which he imagines as falling principally on mothers: see n. 460d6.

450c6   **good friend:** Soc. uses more such vocatives than his interlocutors, cf. d2, 5, and e.g. 1.344d6–345b2; the present one, which has a mildly exclamatory force (cf. 4.422e3), is unique in P. The mannerism is part of the personal attentiveness which marks Soc.'s style of conversation.

450c7   **scepticism:** the first mention of a point on which bk. 5 shows a sharp sensitivity. As 473e6 ff. especially (if humorously) suggests, P. is alert to how readers *outside* his philosophical school will react to the radical ideas advanced in this book. But the repeated anticipations of doubt or disbelief are not purely defensive: they are intended, in part, to warn interested but questioning readers of the need for an exceptionally open-minded attitude to what is to follow; cf. n. d3–4 below. The two focuses of scepticism will be used to structure virtually the entire development of the argument in bk. 5: for possibility or feasibility, see nn. 466d6–7, 471c6 ('put aside'); for the desirability of the proposals, 456c4 ff.

450c8   **even if...completely:** for εἰ ὅτι μάλιστα, lit. 'if however much', cf. e.g. *Euthph.* 9c3, *Meno* 80d7.

450d1   **hesitation:** this is sometimes treated as inimical to Soc.'s mode of dialectical earnestness; e.g. 1.349a4, 2.372a3–4, and cf. nn. b5, d5. But it is equally true that the Soc. of the *Rep.* shows great diffidence about some of his key claims and arguments: cf. esp. 3.414c–d, 6.506b–e. One (inadequate) explanation of this ostensible discrepancy is that it is the residue, in P.'s middle-period dialogues, of an authentically Socratic combination of indefatigable commitment to enquiry, with a personal disavowal of knowledge or wisdom (n. d9): the combination starts to look anomalous when, on this view, the second feature turns into a purely superficial dressing for the statement of large, ambitious philosophical theses. But the anomaly cannot be unwitting on P.'s part: it should be read as a dramatic means of indicating the provisional and exploratory character of his own writings; see Introduction, §1.3.

450d1   **utopian:** for this use of *euchê*, lit. 'prayer' (cf. Engl. 'wishful thinking', 'pious hopes'), see 7.540d2, *Laws* 8.841c7; at 456b12, 6.499c4, the phrase is '*like* prayers'. As the last passage shows, the idea of hopeless utopianism is connected by P. with fear of mockery (n. 451a1, 'incur laughter').

450d3–4   **hearers:** the dramatic comment, typical of the cooperative G. (n. b7), also serves as an implicit request to P.'s readers (cf. n. c7) for a similarly sympathetic and alert responsiveness. Socratic conversation requires a positive, cooperative attitude: cf. e.g. *Meno* 75d2–4, *Tht.* 146a6–8.

450d5   **encourage:** παραθαρρύνειν seems close to synonymous with the much commoner παραμυθεῖσθαι, as d9 and 451b1 indicate; the verbs occur together at *Critias* 108d1. Cf. παρακελεύεσθαι at 474a8. Encouragement is something which Soc. more typically gives than receives: see e.g. *Tht.* 151d4-6, 157d3-5.

450d9   **confident...that I know:** in Soc.'s uncertainty we can perhaps see traces of two features familiar from P.'s earlier works – one, Soc.'s personal disavowal of knowledge (*Ap.* 21b, etc., cf. Arist. *Soph. El.* 183b8); the other, Soc.'s view that argument should be built only on propositions to which the interlocutors can commit themselves (e.g. 1.346a3, 349a, *Prt.* 331c, *Meno* 75d6–7). The two features coalesce into a compound Socratic integrity in a passage such as *Hp. Mj.* 298b–c. Cf. n. d1 above ('hesitation').

καλῶς εἶχεν may look like the apodosis of a conditional, without the usual ἄν; but it should probably be taken to be a vivid alternative – i.e. 'your reassurance *was* all very well, <but...>' (Goodwin §431).

450d10   **greatest significance:** for this type of phrase see e.g. 2.377e6–7, 10.599c7, *Plt.* 302a8, *Laws* 7.801c3–4. The conjunction with *philôn*, 'dear to one's heart', is unusual, but there is balance with *philois* in the previous phrase.

451a1   **not because I might:** the idea of fearing in φοβερόν is followed first by an infinitive (ὀφλεῖν), then by μή + future indic. (μή ... κείσομαι, 2–3); for the latter construction, cf. *Phlb.* 13a4–5.

451a1   **incur laughter:** although no Socratic concern (cf. *Euthph.* 3c6–7), sensitivity to laughter seems to trouble P.; it will be further emphasised at 452a–e, and subsequently at 6.506d7–8. P. is likely to have known that ideas akin to those about to be broached had been exploited by Ar. *Eccl.* a few years earlier (see the Appendix), and some of them in other comedies too (n. 452a4–5). The idea of changes in the social roles of women was one which he realised to have particular potential for amusement (*Laws* 6.781c2–3). But his point is nonetheless wider; philosophers (incl. P. himself) were a well established target of humour, both popular and theatrical, and P. is very frequently aware of the fact: cf. e.g. 7.517a2, d6, 518a-b, 536b-c, 10.607b-c (with my nn.), *Ap.* 19c, *Tht.* 174a-5e, *Laws* 6.781c2 ff., 7.789e1, 790a5; such material, together with P.'s moral critique of humour, is discussed by M. Mader, *Das Problem des Lachens und der Komödie bei Platon* (Stuttgart, 1977). Yet P. is no mere puritan about laughter, and his nervousness about it partly reflects an active and extensive interest in the comic mode: see R. Brock, 'Plato and Comedy', in E. Craik (ed.) *'Owls to Athens': Essays on Classical Subjects Presented to Sir Kenneth Dover* (Oxford, 1990) 39-49.

451a2   **slip, miss the truth:** the genitive after *sphallesthai* marks that which one misses, or fails to attain, through error (LSJ s.v., III.2); it is of the same kind as the genitive taken by *hamartanein*. For the metaphor, cf. e.g. *Grg.* 461c7, d1; when the same verb is used of tripping up in argument, as at e.g. *Tht.* 165b1, 167e5, the image is taken from wrestling. Soc.'s fear of unwittingly misleading his companions will recur at 6.507a4–5.

451a4   **Adrasteia:** agent of divine vengefulness, who must be appeased by a disclaimer of offensive intention. She is sometimes associated with Nemesis (cf. Men. fr. 321 K); the scholia here (Greene 227) unreliably identify her with Atropos, one of the Fates (10.617c3). The range of comparable material suggests that Soc.'s expression is of a common type: see Aesch. *PV* 936, Eur. *Rh.* 342, 468, Dem. 25.37, Men. *Perik.* 304, *Sam.* 503. There is no significant link with *Phdr.* 248c2.

451a6   **lesser fault:** i.e. on the premise, which is Socratic in origin (cf. *Ap.* 29d–30b, *Crito* 47d–8a), that the soul is more valuable than the body. For involuntary homicide see n. b4.

451a7   **beauty, goodness and justice:** I take the trio of terms to stand as a defining or appositional genitive to *nomimôn*; cf. the inversion of the phrase at 479d 3–4, 6.484d2–3. Adam prefers to take the adjs. with *nomimôn*; Vretska 86–9 argues implausibly that they are masculine (referring to the company). The three terms form a standard set in P., delineating the essential sphere of ethical values (e.g. 6.484d2,

493b8f., 7.520c5–6, *Euthph*. 7d1–2, *Phdo* 65d, *Plt*. 295e4–5, *Laws* 7.801c8–9); *kalôn*, 'beauty', covers a wide range of aesthetic-cum-moral qualities (452e1, nn. 457b4–5, 476b5). Most importantly, these are the values central to the discussion of knowledge and 'forms' later in bk. 5: see n. 476a4–5. But that connection only heightens the paradox of Soc.'s doubts and hesitation in this passage (esp. 450d8–9): the figure who feels great uncertainty about his arguments will later present a case which suggests that there are some people, 'true philosophers', who have access to values that are ultimate and absolute.

451b4   **free from responsibility:** G. playfully maintains the criminal analogy. *Katharos*, lit. 'pure'/'clean', might suggest the absence of the pollution standardly incurred by homicide (e.g. *Laws* 9.864e, 865b, Herod. 1.35, Antiphon 5.11). But it can also denote guiltlessness (e.g. 6.496d9, Antiphon 2.4.11), and b6 seems to favour this sense here. In any case, guilt and pollution were closely correlated, though not always aligned, in cases of homicide; so *katharos* could here allude to both factors (cf. e.g. Andoc. 1.95): see P.'s own proposals at *Laws* 9.865–9, with D.M. MacDowell, *Athenian Homicide Law* (Manchester, 1963), for the legal background.

451b8   **that point is settled:** τούτου γ᾽ ἕνεκα, lit. 'as far as this point is concerned, at any rate'.

451b9–453e6

If the Guardians of the ideal state are its 'guard-dogs', women too should occupy this role alongside men, and thus will require the same education (set out in bks. 2-3) in music and gymnastics. Such a proposal, with its implications for women exercising in public, will elicit mirth from the facetious; but laughter of this kind grows not from a sense of true values, but only from the prejudices of narrow cultural experience. It will also, and more seriously, be objected that Socrates and Glaucon have contradicted their earlier principle that in the well-run city each person should perform only his own, 'natural' function: surely, an opponent will say, the idea of female Guardians flouts the fundamental difference between the natures of men and women. How can the argument escape from this difficulty?

The first of bk. 5's radical proposals (later called the first of three 'waves' to be surmounted: n. 457b7) posits female Guardians who will perform all the same duties as their male counterparts. This is the first application of the root principle of 'sharing', *koinônia* (Introduction p. 7), and it presupposes that, contrary to many deeply ingrained attitudes of Greek culture, women have the same basic potential for physical, intellectual and psychological development as men, and can be educated in the same way. It is, therefore, a deeply heterodox suggestion, though one which bears traces of a number of important influences on P.'s thinking (Introduction, pp. 10–12). The main philosophical considerations in support of the proposal are held back until the next phase of argument, and the present section bases its case, in a rhetorically provocative fashion, on an animal analogy - the same analogy between Guardians and dogs as was used earlier in the work (n. 451c8). The analogy raises many possible questions and objections, but it serves at least to give notice that the issues will be tackled in a way that undercuts existing social practice: however questionably, the animal analogy signals that the proposal of female Guardians will appeal to considerations of 'nature' that may be quite obscured by particular traditions, and which therefore need to be opened up by more indirect routes of thought.

Having stated the idea in this preliminary way, P. immediately addresses the inveterate and widespread resistance which he knows it will inevitably meet with. He does this in two stages. He starts by imagining the merely mocking response which the thought of female athletes and soldiers is likely to elicit from many people: like J. S. Mill, in 'The Subjection of Women' pt. IV, he confronts 'those who find it easier to draw a ludicrous picture of what they do not like, than to answer the arguments for it.' This allows him to convey the important principle that philosophy, if it is to have the courage of its convictions, must be prepared to withstand vulgar derision (452b6-7). But there is a further point at issue here, for P. treats such laughter as symptomatic of a mistaken attitude to the whole question of social change. In effect, P. is here emphasising a point which had been made familiar by intellectuals in the fifth century, namely the relativity of specific cultural practices (see e.g. Herod. 3.38, anon. *Dissoi Logoi* 2.9-18). Those who laugh at the idea of female athletes training naked alongside men, or of women taking part in military training, have failed to realise that what they take to be normal, because established in their own society, was in fact the product of earlier developments and innovations (452c6-d1). So the question of women's social roles cannot just be settled by appeal to local norms, for local norms vary and change; to treat them as a final arbiter is to fall into nothing more respectable than cultural prejudice.

Having dealt with unthinking prejudice, P. proceeds to confront the much greater threat of reasoned argument. Cultural practices may, after all, rest on natural necessities, and it is to nature that the articulate opponent of female Guardians will appeal. This opponent can, moreover, combine his claim that there are large natural differences between the sexes (an argument which G. is apparently happy to accept, 453b9) with a reminder to Soc. and G. of their earlier insistence that all citizens should perform the functions for which they are naturally fitted. We have here a good example of the constant process of philosophical reconsideration which P. uses his dialogue-form to express. P. is drawing to the reader's attention an apparent tension in the programme so far sketched for the just city. After the rigorous conception of fixed social roles which underpinned the city's class-system in bks. 2-4, we are now offered the proposition that within the Guardian class one of the most familiar of all social distinctions (that between the sexes) should be abolished. The ramifications of this aim could hardly be more far-reaching: they extend into the foundations of P.'s thinking about both individuals and human groups: see the Introduction, §§2-2.2.

451b9   **earlier:** 4.423e–4a. Soc.'s remark intensifies the question (n. 450a8) why P. constructs parts of the work in this 'revisionary' manner, with later sections qualifying earlier.

451c2   **male drama:** there is apparently a pun on two senses of *andreios*, (a) male, (b) courageous (alluding to the Auxiliaries' virtue, esp. 4.429a-30c). P. calls part of the argument a 'drama' at *Plt.* 303c8, and refers to his own dialogue as a 'tragedy' at *Laws* 7.817b. But the present passage alludes more specifically to two varieties, portraying male and female characters (though all acted by men), of the prose 'mimes', or popular character-sketches, of the Sicilian writer, Sophron (5th cent. B.C.): see Adam's n., with Sophron fr. 107 Kaibel. This passage therefore lends a little colour, if nothing else, to the ancient tradition (going back to Duris of Samos in the 4th cent. B.C.: *FGrH* 76 F 72) that P. had a particular liking for Sophron's work: cf. A. S. Riginos, *Platonica* (Leiden, 1976) 174-6.

The verb διαπεραίνω should here be connected with the semi-technical use of the simplex to mean recite or render a poem: see LSJ s.v. περαίνω, 4.

451c4   **earlier discussed:** at 2.376c–3.412b.

451c6   **possession:** this term, picking up 4.423e7 and repeated at 453d3, 6.502d4–5, seems to imply an imbalance in status, as though the female Guardians will be the property of the men. P. here employs language that was used of marriage and the family in contemporary society: e.g. Eur. *IA* 715, Pl. Com. fr. 105 *PCG*/98 K, for husband and wife; P. *Ap.* 20b6, Eur. *IT* 696, for father and children; cf. Dover (1974) 96 n. 2, with the Golden Age's lack of 'possession of wives and children', *Plt.* 271e8 f. But, *pace* Pomeroy (1974) 33, there is no question of the female Guardians officially belonging to the male Guardians: the Guardian class will have *no* property, 464c-e (including wives and children, ib. d1), and authority is in the hands of Rulers some of whom are women (n. 460b9 f.). Besides, the same nouns, 'use and possession', are applied to the practice of justice at 1.333a10, to friendship at Xen. *Mem.* 2.4.1, and to wisdom in Arist. fr. 52 Rose. So we should not draw strict inferences from P.'s terminology, which can be regarded as a lingering verbal habit or 'casual androcentrism' (Clark 8, cf. Vlastos [1989] 276). Cf. 464e 1-2, with e1 ff., *Laws* 7.805d8, Ar. *Eccl.* 212, for the 'use' of women.

451c6 **impetus:** Soc. talks, as often, as if the Guardians were under instructions from the participants in the discussion; the same noun is applied to the argument at 6.506e2, cf. *Prm.* 135d3. ὁρμάω, c7, is here transitive: αὐτούς is to be understood as object; ἥνπερ is internal accusative.

451c8 **guard-dogs:** the reference is to 2.375a ff.; for *phulax* of a sheep-dog cf. e.g. Xen. *Mem.* 2.7.14. Notice that the first argument for female Guardians (like that earlier passage, and cf. 459a2 ff.) depends purely on analogy, and is therefore implicitly hypothetical: *if* women are like bitches, they should be capable of all the same tasks as men (cf. Proclus 240–1 Kroll); the analogy was later used for a similar purpose by the 1st cent. A.D. Stoic, Musonius Rufus (p. 13 Hense). This suggestion serves a symbolic and thought-provoking function, but the idea it expresses will subsequently be tested by more rigorously dialectical considerations: see nn. 452a7, e4. Arist. *Pol.* 1264b4-6 faults this animal analogy, on the grounds that humans require *oikonomia*, domestic duties, while animals do not; but it will turn out to be part of Soc.'s argument that, within the Guardian class, women should be relieved of their current burden of such duties. Cf. the claim at *Critias* 110b-c that *all* social animals can share duties between the sexes.

Soc. here appeals to the ordinary fact that bitches were used both as hunting-dogs (e.g. Xen. *Cyneg.* 3.1–3, *Mem.* 3.11.8, 4.1.3) and as sheep-dogs (Xen. *Oec.* 5.6). The same dog might be used for more than one task: cf. Ar. *Wasps* 954–7. Given the detail of P.'s family home at 459a2, it is plausible that observation of dogs did influence P.'s thinking (cf. Wender 76); for criticism of the analogy see Annas (1976) 309–11. P. has, in any case, a penchant for animal imagery: see e.g. 3.401b–c (cattle); 3.413d8–9 (horses); 7.520b5–6 (bees); 8.552c, 564b–e (bees). Cf. the Introduction, p. 17.

The sheep-dog analogy can be regarded as a development from the old motif (Middle Eastern in origin, common in both the Bible and Homer), of the ruler as shepherd: see esp. 3.416a, 4.440d, where the Auxiliaries are sheep-dogs to the ruler-shepherds. The same image played some part in the political slogans of Athenian democracy (Ar. *Wasps* 954-5, Dem. 25.40), as did that of the domestic guard-dog (Ar. *Knights* 1018, 1023-4, *Wasps* 957, 970). Underlying P.'s own use of such imagery, which was foreshadowed in the argument with Thrasymachus (1.343b, 345c, cf. Xen. *Mem.* 3.2.1), are the twin principles that government is for the benefit not of the rulers but of the city as a whole, and that good rulers need to possess a superior knowledge of what constitutes this benefit. The notion of men as a 'flock' or 'herd' (*agelê*: n. 459e3), i.e. a social species (cf. Arist. *Pol.* 1253a8), and their relation to both divine and human shepherds or herdsmen, is treated intricately at *Plt.* 261d-68a, 271e, 275b ff., cf. *Critias* 109b-c.

451d6 **look after the house:** although part of the animal analogy, P.'s language alludes to the common social restrictions on human females in Greek society. The verb *oikourein* standardly applies to the domestic role of wives (e.g. ps. -Dem. 59.86, with LSJ s.v. and Fraenkel on Aesch. *Agam.* 809, 1626); the cognate adj. is used of a dog at Ar. *Wasps* 970, but with a pun on evasion of military service. 'Indoors' also alludes to the relative seclusion of respectable females in Athenian society; see 9.579b8, *Laws*

6.781c6, 7.805e4–7, and e.g. Ar. *Thesm.* 790–99, Xen. *Oec.* 7.20–30, with Gould 46–51, Just ch. 6. The confinement of such women to largely domestic lives seems to have been a general feature of Greek states in the classical period: despite the greater freedom of movement of Spartan women (Xen. *Lac.* 1.3–4, with Cartledge's article), it is notable that Herod. 2.35.2 can draw a sweeping contrast between Egyptians and other peoples in this respect. On aspects of this social limitation, see Pomeroy (1976) 71-3, and S. Walker, 'Women & Housing in Classical Greece', in Cameron & Kuhrt, 81-91.

451d7   **puppies:** cf. 2.375a2, 7.537a7 (other dog analogies for the Guardians); the puppies of 7.539b6 are adolescents fond of verbal point-scoring. The idea that child-rearing poses an obstacle to female participation in public life will be met in due course by special nursing arrangements (460c–d).

451d9   **flocks:** cf. 459e1, 3.415e3, 416a, with *agelê*, c8 above.

451e1   **weaker:** though a direct comment on dogs, this is assumed to be applicable to women, as 455e1, 457a10 will confirm; cf. Xen. *Symp.* 2.9 (with Introduction n. 14), ps.-Demades 37. At *Laws* 6.781a the 'weakness' of women is said to make them more cunning and secretive. Here, the point is purely physical, as the dog analogy indicates, and will make only a marginal difference to the functions of female Guardians (457a9–10, n. 471d3–5). Given the full range of the Guardians' duties, sheer physical strength is not of paramount importance: even their gymnastic education, though designed partly with warfare in mind (as often: e.g. Xen. *Lac.* 12.5, with Pritchett II 213-19), is really a training of the soul, 3.410b-12a; cf. n. 452a2. For the ellipse of ταῖς μέν in ὡς ἀσθενεστέραις, cf. e.g. 455e6-7, 456a11, with Denniston 166.

451e4   **nurture:** *trophê* may connote upbringing in general (e.g. 6.491d ff.), but here the main implication is surely that girls of the Guardian class will be fed the same diet as boys. This was no doubt unusual in most Greek societies, but P. may have been influenced here by Spartan ideas: cf. Xen. *Lac.* 1.3 (adolescent girls), with M. Golden, *Phoenix* 35 (1981) 326 n. 37. P. will probably have been aware of a range of contemporary ideas about diet and female fertility (cf. Preus 244–5); cf. the remarks on alcohol and procreation at *Laws* 2.674b5–6, 6.775b–c.

452a2   **music and gymnastics:** see, respectively, 2.376e–3.403c, 3.403c–412a. The suggestion of such an education for women goes beyond Athenian norms, but has affinities with what P. took to be Sparta's practices: as well as athletics (n. a11 below), P. ascribes to the Spartans the training of women in *mousikê*, i.e. the sister arts of music and poetry, at *Prt.* 342d4, *Laws* 7.806a2; but since classical Sparta was scarcely reputed for *mousikê* (cf. anon. *Dissoi Logoi* 2.10), this evidence is not above suspicion: cf. Cartledge 91–3.

In Athens, girls would not normally receive much physical training at all (the acceptance of moderate athletic exercise for women at Arist. *Pol.* 1335b 11–12 shows Platonic influence), and most would receive very little systematic education in *mousikê*, though *Laws* 2.658d3 refers to the taste of 'educated women' for tragedy; cf. *Grg.* 502d6, *Laws* 7.817c5, which imply that some women attended theatrical performances. Ar. *Lys.* 1126-7 indicates that some girls might receive informal 'tuition' within their families; cf. the idea that wives, typically much younger than their husbands (nn. 460e4-7), could be 'educated' by the latter (Xen. *Symp.* 2.9, *Oec.* 7.4). c1 below, reflecting Athenian attitudes, reveals that the idea of female education could easily be found comic: vase-paintings of women reading, dancing and playing music are not easy to interpret, but few of them need portray citizen women (cf. D. Williams in Cameron & Kuhrt, 99-100, and F. A. G. Beck, *An Album of Greek Education* [Sydney, 1975] ch. 10, with pls. 69-88). On the specific issue of female literacy, which need not be entailed by P.'s proposals, see S. G. Cole, 'Could Greek Women Read and Write?', in H. P. Foley (ed.) *Reflections of Women in Antiquity* (New York, 1981) 219-45, W. V. Harris, *Ancient Literacy* (Cambridge Mass., 1989) 106-8. Broader discussion of the upbringing of Athenian girls is provided by Golden 72-9.

P.'s plan for equality of (Guardian) education requires the premise that women are capable of developing the two attributes, 'spiritedness' and 'philosophy', earlier designated as crucial for the male Guardians (3.410-12); cf. 456a4. This will be confirmed by female participation both in warfare (next n.) and in the highest stages of Rulership (460b9-10).

452a4–5 **military training:** the point will be reiterated at c1–2, 453a3–4, 456a1, 457a7, 466c9, e4, 467a2, though also sometimes apparently overlooked (n. 467c2–3); P. sustains this proposal in the *Laws*, though more tentatively (6.785b7–9, cf. 8.829b5). To any ordinary Greek reader, the idea of female warriors would sound absurdly fanciful; hence the renewed sense of the mirth that the argument might cause (cf. n. 451a1): P. might here have in mind a comedy such as Theopompus's 'Women Soldiers', *Stratiôtides* (?early 4th cent.: *PCG* VII 733, Kock I 747). But Soc.'s suggestion might also bring to mind the legendary Amazons (note the old men's attitude at Ar. *Lys.* 678–9), or barbarian tribes sometimes associated with them: cf. Sarmatian women (Herod. 4.116–7), mentioned by P. himself, *Laws* 7.804e–5a, 806b5, in support of the idea of physical training of women (see the Introduction p. 11).

452a7 **tradition:** Soc. regards it as an incidental objection to his proposals that they are radically discrepant with current practice. Custom may itself be contrary to ideal standards (d–e below) and to 'nature' (456c1–2). Soc.'s condition, 'if they could be realised...', anticipates the later point that the truth of an argument may not be wholly realisable in practice (473a2).

452a11 **exercising naked:** P. knows that the women of Sparta, who did publicly engage in athletics (Ar. *Lys.* 82, Xen. *Lac.* 1.4, anon. *Dissoi Logoi* 2.9, Theoc. 18.22–3), were a subject of disapproval, even ridicule, in Athens (Eur. *Andr.* 595-600, Ar. *Lys.* 79-82). But he is not simply recommending the imitation of Spartan practices, which he later criticises, in their treatment of women, as no better than half-measures: *Laws* 6.780e–81b, 7.805e-6b. In Athens, there is evidence to suggest that young girls could engage in athletics within the cult of Artemis at Brauron: on a possible connection with P.'s ideas at *Laws* 8.833c ff., see P. Perlman, *GRBS* 24 (1983) 115-30. But it is not easy to regard this as more than a tangential influence on *Rep.* 5. The possibility of more extensive female gymnastics is mooted, somewhat sketchily, by Bérard 92-3. For other, rare evidence of female athletics, of little reliability for the classical period, see esp. Athen. 566e, Paus. 5.16.2-6, with H. A. Harris, *Greek Athletes & Athletics* (London, 1964) 179-86.

The adj. *gumnos*, 'naked', need not mean fully nude, but is relative to an implicit norm: cf. 474a1, 2.372a8, and e.g. Ar. *Clouds* 498, *Lys.* 1020, *Eccl.* 409, in all of which it means without a cloak; see L.M. Stone, *Costume in Aristophanic Poetry* (Salem, 1984) 144–54. It is arguable that here (as also, perhaps, at *Laws* 8.833c8) P. has in mind some limited dress – say, a short *chitôn* that would make free movement of arms and legs possible: cf. the idea of Spartan women showing their thighs when exercising (Ibycus fr. 339 PMG, Eur. *Andr.* 598, Soph. fr. 872 *TrGF*, cf. anon. *Dissoi Logoi* 2.9, Plut. *Lyc.* 14.2, 15.2, with Cartledge 91-2), and the curious proposal for adolescent dancing in scant clothing at *Laws* 6.771e-2a. This interpretation is perhaps favoured by 457a6-7, and is hardly impeded by the fact that c-d below refers to the established practice of nudity in male athletics: see nn. c6, 9. We might also note artistic depictions of the mythical athlete, Atalanta (cf. 10.620b6-7), wearing pants and (sometimes) breast-band: see Boardman (1975) pls. 62, 369, id. (1989) pls. 88, 143, with *LIMC* II.2 695-9 for a fuller range. P. nowhere else touches on the clothing of Guardians, male or female: would he have approved the practice of unisex dress which appealed to some Cynics and early Stoics (D. Laert. 6.93, 97, 7.33)?

452b1   **older ones:** female Auxiliaries might still be involved in military duties even after their child-bearing careers (from age 20 to 40: 460e4–5); cf. n. 459d7–8. Gymnastics would remain appropriate for such people. But 'old men' (b2) gives the impression that P. is also thinking of those, including the Rulers (?), who are past the age of soldiering: it is perhaps assumed that the Guardians' culture, with its emphasis on harmonious fitness of both mind and body, would always require a gymnastic component.

452b2   **old men:** like the 'late learner' of Thphr. *Char.* 27.6; cf. *Tht.* 162b2–3. It is quite wrong to infer from this passage any specific Platonic 'distaste for the unclothed female body' (Pomeroy [1974] 34, cf. Annas [1976] 308).

452b4   **by the standard:** ὥς γε ἐν τῷ παρεστῶτι ‹e.g. κρίνειν›, lit. '‹to judge› in the present situation, at any rate'; for the ellipse, see n. 453c7.

452c1-2   **not least:** first, because warfare and horse-riding (to be learnt in education, cf. 467e2– 3, 3.412b4) were not women's activities in Greek society (*Laws* 8.834d3–7 expresses some caution about female horse-riding); second, because both gave scope for *double entendre* and sexual innuendo: *hoplon*, 'weapon' or 'tool', also had the vulgar sense of 'genitals' (see Ar. *Ach.* 592, *Wasps* 27, LSJ s.v., V); and horse-riding was a common source of crude sexual imagery (e.g. Ar. *Wasps* 501–2, *Lys.* 677–8, with J. Henderson, *The Maculate Muse* [New Haven, 1975; rpr. Oxford, 1991] §§ 274–7). P. may also have in mind that *ochêsis*, 'riding', would allow risqué word-play on *ocheuein*, the sexual mounting of a female by a male (n. 454e1).

452c4   **rough ground:** hilly terrain (cf. 1.328e3, 2.364d3); P. has a liking for the imagery of dialectic as a journey (e.g. 4.435d3, 445c4–5, 6.504c9, *Lys.* 213e3–5, *Plt.* 265a–b). 8.568c9–d2 makes a different metaphor from hill-climbing.

452c5   **usual behaviour:** this sense must be carefully distinguished from other uses of τὰ αὑτῶν πράττειν, for which see n. 453b5.

452c6   **not so long:** similar phrases occur at e.g. Thuc. 1.6.3 (where c.50 years is meant: see Gomme *ad loc.*), 1.6.5. But such expressions are naturally flexible, and do not permit precise historical inferences. Athletic nudity, to judge from Athenian vases, was established by the late 6th cent., though perhaps not much earlier: cf. Boardman (1975) 220, with J.-P. Thuillier, 'La nudité athlétique', *Nikephoros* 1 (1988) 29-40, and S. Instone, 'The Naked Truth about Greek Athletics', *Omnibus* 20 (Sept. 1990) 1-3. P.'s observation of cultural change and relativity is not new: Herod. 1.10.3 draws the same Greek-barbarian contrast, while Thuc. 1.6.5 (next n.) makes related points; neither author is ever mentioned by P., but frequent Greek contacts with the Middle East must have made divergent attitudes to nudity a familiar topic. Although classical Greeks possessed, within limits (e.g. Aeschin. 1.26), a relatively shame-free view of male nudity, this point became idealistically exaggerated by Romantic Hellenists such as Winckelmann, *Gedanken über die Nachahmung der griechischen Werke* [1755]; cf. Wilkinson 92-3. Certainly, P.'s proposals for the extension of athletic nudity to women, if taken in the strongest sense (but see n. a11 above), would be remarkably bold. For female spectators of naked male athletes see Thuc. 3.104.3 (Delos and Ephesus), with S. B. Pomeroy, *Mnem.* 35 (1982) 118-9.

452c9   **first the Cretans:** Thuc. 1.6.5 says the Spartans were first (cf. Hornblower's n.); a different and anecdotal tradition cited an individual Megarian runner, Orsippus (? 720 B.C.), as an innovator (Paus. 1.44.1). Competing modern explanations of athletic nudity are discussed by D. Sansone, *Greek Athletics & the Genesis of Sport* (Berkeley,

1988) 107–14, who favours (improbably, in my view) a connection with primitive hunting. *Gumnasia* (c9), as perhaps at b 8 (?), must mean exercises (cf. 7.539d10), not places of training.

452d4–6 **what had struck the eyes:** i.e. a purely superficial, unreflective impression of absurdity. The compound phrases, τό ... γελοῖον, and τοῦ ... ἀρίστου, use a type of expression (article + [substantival] adj., with enclosed qualification) in which J.D. Denniston, *Greek Prose Style*, corr. rpr. (Oxford, 1960) 21, sees 'a sudden flash of parody' of writers such as Antiphon and Thucydides. I doubt this for two reasons: first, because τὸ γελοῖον and τὸ ἀριστον were both common as abstract nouns; secondly, parody is unlikely in a context where P. is making a morally serious point. Note that καί in d4 is an adverb, not a connective, and begins the main clause.

452d7 **as also...:** i.e. μάταιός ‹ἐστι› is to be understood with this clause too; cf. n. e1. '...as ridiculous...': sc. ὡς ‹ὄψιν› γελοίου.

452d8–e1 **ridiculous...stupid and bad:** P. enjoins a purely ethical conception of humour, though without the qualification (cf. *Phlb.* 49b–c) that only something *moderately* 'bad' is suitable for comic treatment. He assumes, not without reason, that much laughter expresses implicit values: relevant material is discussed by M. Mader (cited on 451a1). But P. was not alone in seeing that laughter raised moral issues: see my article, 'The Uses of Laughter in Greek Culture', *CQ* 41 (1991) 279-96. Cf. 10.606c, with my nn., for P.'s views on the psychological experience of comic drama: the link made there, between laughter and the lower part of the soul, helps to clarify the distinction drawn here (d4-6) between superficially laughable *appearances* and the rational establishment of genuine values.

452e1 **and likewise, moreover:** αὖ shows that a further person in meant; but μάταιός ‹ἐστι› ὅς... has to be understood from what precedes. Some editors follow ms. Sc. (Boter 220–1) in omitting καὶ καλοῦ αὖ; this leaves a clause running from καὶ ὁ γελωτοποιεῖν to the end of the sentence (i.e. 'the man who tries to raise laughter ... aims at a standard other than that of goodness.'). Adam construes a single clause here *without* emendation: the result is awkward, and founders on καὶ καλοῦ αὖ. See Adam 355–7 for a summary of views; cf. Vretska 89–91, whose own suggestions are textually too involved.

452e2 **takes for itself:** if στησάμενος is, as normally, transitive, its object must be implied by the preceding prepositional phrase; see Adam 356.

452e4 **first:** Soc. has so far made a proposal by analogy (n. 451c8), and suggested that *prima facie* objections to it exploit mere social prejudice. Now the argument will address the fundamental question whether human nature (n. 453a1) allows the kind of female role-equality (for Guardians) that is at issue.

452e5–6 **a humorist:** the adj. *philopaismôn* (lit. 'fond of play' [*paizein*]) is apparently the Attic equivalent of *philopaigmôn*; cf. *Crat.* 406c2, where it is applied to the gods. On the Greek association between laughter and play, see my article, cited in n. d8-e1 above, 280.

453a1 **nature of the human female:** the Greek phrasing, with a pair of attributive adjs. added separately to the noun (cf. e.g. Andoc. 1.16), nicely signals the issue to be faced – i.e. whether, as suggested by the appearance of a culture such as classical Athens (n. b7), men and women have different 'natures', or whether there is a *human* nature common to the sexes. P.'s own conception of human nature is broadly 'genetic': an individual's nature (cf. 2.370a–b) is inherited, as the later eugenic policies will make clear (esp. 459a–e), and as the whole class-structure of the city, justified by the myth of metals (3.415a–c), presupposes. But P. acknowledges an interplay between nature and nurture/education: cf. 3.395d2, 396c3, 4.424a–b, 431c7, *Laws* 2.655e, with

Bluestone 109–19. Soc. will argue against an opponent who appeals to the empirical evidence of existing (Greek) culture; but his own case will depend on at least semi-empirical criteria (nn. 454c7 ff.)

453a4–5   **starts...conclusions:** P. echoes a proverbial sentiment; cf. Soph. fr. 831 *TGrF*/Pearson (with the latter's n.), Antiphon fr. 60 DK.

453a7   **on behalf of:** an imaginary interlocutor is a common feature of Socratic conversations; cf. 455b ff., 476e4 ff. below, and e.g. 1.332c5 ff., *Prt.* 311d. But the device was used in oratory too, where it came technically to be known as either *schêma heteroprosôpon* or *hypophora*.

453a8–9   **go by default:** lit. 'so that the other side ... shouldn't be abandoned and besieged'; a combination of metaphors – (i) judicial, from an uncontested action (*dikê erêmê*: cf. *Ap.* 18c7–8), (ii) military, from an inadequately defended position. For metaphorical uses of πολιορκεῖν see LSJ s.v., 2.

453b4   **to found:** the image of Soc. and his interlocutors as founders of a city is a *leitmotiv* in the *Rep.*; in addn. to 456d8, 470e4, see e.g. 2.369c9, 3.403b4, 4.434e1, 7.519c8, 10.595a2. The fact that such an event, with the necessary drawing up of law-codes, property arrangements, etc., was not uncommon in the Greek world, gives the *Rep.*'s whole framework of discussion a less fanciful air than it strikes modern readers as having. P. exploits this idea more concretely in *Laws*, where the envisaged city is a blueprint for a Cretan colony to be founded by Cleinias and others (3.702b–e).

453b5   **natural principle:** Soc. introduced the idea of 'performing one's own function', which can also mean 'keeping to one's own affairs' (*to/ta hautou prattein*: cf. 452c5), at 2.369e–70c, as a principle of 'division of labour' among the city's farmers/artisans. It has since been laid down, together with the cognate notion of 'one person, one function', as the basis both of civic justice (4.433a–34c) and of the psychic integrity of the individual (4.443c–e). The idea thus represents what is 'natural', i.e. best, both for persons and for political classes (cf. 4.421c1–6). Soc.'s imaginary opponent now wishes to argue that women too form a distinct class, with a 'nature' of their own in the same sense as for farmers, soldiers, and Guardians. (4.433d3 might itself be held to hint at such a view.) The opponent is implicitly committed not just to a generally low estimate of female abilities, but to the premise that *all* women are *entirely* incapable of certain tasks; and it is this premise which will be specifically rejected at 455d3–4.

453b7   **differs utterly:** the opponent puts the view equivalent to 'none at all' at a2 above. It is a view which rests on the entrenched male assumptions of a society in which women were debarred from most forms of political, administrative and public activity. As G.'s agreement indicates, the view is taken as practically self-evident: for the Greek attitudes in question, see Dover (1974) 95–102, Just ch. 8. P.'s argument will challenge such attitudes, yet with slightly less than complete conviction (n. 455c6–7); and P.'s own writings not only sometimes accept the existence of a female 'nature' (*Tim.* 42a1–2, *Laws* 7.802e7), but also contain apparent endorsements of women's inferiority in mental, moral, as well as physical, capacities: e.g. 3.387e10, 4.431c2, 10.605e1 (with my n.), *Crat.* 392c–d, *Laws* 6.781b2–3, *Tim.* 42a–b, 90e8. For interpretations of this discrepancy, which was recognised by Proclus 247.27 ff., 255.28 ff. Kroll, and has also been a crux for modern readers, see e.g. Wender 80–83, Calvert 242–3, and Vlastos (1989).

453c7   **to find one:** the (epexegetic) infinitive is ellipsed in the Greek, as at 452b4; cf. e.g. Aesch. *PV* 46, Ar. *Ach.* 1151, and for such expressions with the infin., see e.g. 475d4, 3.414a6–7, 10.595b3. G.'s need for Soc.'s guidance is typical (see 470a8, with my nn. on 450b7 and 10.596a2–4), even though it is G. himself who will later produce the crucial consideration (n. 455d3–5).

453d1   **anxious and hesitant:** cf. 450a–51a. Soc. reiterates his uncertainty, though with humorous irony (d5–11), before embarking on the attempt to show that women do indeed share with men the range of natural abilities required for the city's Guardian class.

453d2–3   **possession and maintenance:** the phrasing has links with 450c1–2, 451c5–6 (see n.). *Trophê*, although sometimes limited to 'nurture' of children, can here encompass economic provision for the women as well (cf. 458d2, 463b3).

453d4   **No wonder:** the first οὐ in G.'s response is hard to explain; Adam records older suggestions. If the text is sound, G. is picking up the idea of negation (i.e. not wanting to discuss the subject) in what Soc. has just said. But it is worth considering the chance that the first οὐ has intruded from the following negatives: we would then have a plain oath, μὰ τὸν Δία (something like 'quite right!'), elaborated by the following γάρ clause.

453d5   **one falls:** cf. the Heracleiteans who, believing that 'everything is in flux', have 'fallen into a whirlpool', *Crat.* 439c5. Soc. anticipates the later imagery of 'three waves' (457b7–c5, 472a3–4, 473c6–8). Dialectic was previously described by a swimming metaphor at 4.441c4 (cf. *Phdr.* 264a5, *Prm.* 137a5–6), and by one from sailing at 3.394d8–9 (cf. *Prt.* 338a).

453d10   **dolphin:** P. probably has in mind not only the famous story of Arion's rescue (Herod. 1.24: note the same verb, *hupolabein*), but other similar tales. Cf. e.g. the statues of dolphin-riding Nereids at *Critias* 116e2, or the motif of the dolphin-rider on the coins of Tarentum (G.K. Jenkins, *Ancient Greek Coins* [London, 1972] 71, 197–8), a city which Plato may have visited on his travels in the west (cf. *Epist.* 7.338c ff., with Thesleff 27–37). Dolphins were probably not unfamiliar in the Mediterranean of P.'s day: Arist. *Hist. An.* 566b25–6 refers to fishermen's dealings with them.

     After the verbal nouns (gerunds) in d9, the sentence continues as though the idea of necessity had been expressed by δεῖ or χρή: hence the switch from the dative pronoun to the accusative; cf. n. 467e3.

454a1–457c5

The concept of 'different natures' needs more careful definition, particularly in relation to the practical tasks of which the sexes are capable. Considering the basic qualities, mental and bodily, which constitute natural ability, we can say that though women as a class are inferior to men at most things, and though they are physically weaker, they are still intrinsically capable of all the same practices, including warfare and philosophy: indeed, there are many women who are better than many men at many things. So the proposal of female Guardians must stand, and it is current social practice, with its sharp separation between the roles of the sexes, which is 'unnatural'. Moreover, the selection of the best women to serve as Guardians would be in the best interests of the state as a whole.

It is around this passage that the keenest modern debate about P.'s credentials as a 'feminist' has revolved. I believe that P.'s case reaches further than has been allowed by those who deny this description to him, but not as far as those who claim it for him have sometimes contended. In short, P. here explores and endorses some arguments which *could* be, indeed have been, deployed by feminists, but his reasons for doing so are very different from the values which have motivated social and political feminism in the modern world.

    P. constructs his positive argument for female Guardians in two main stages: first, by insisting that the concept of 'nature', whether men's or women's, must be broken down into specific components (so that reproductive differences are kept apart from other capacities); secondly, by observing that whatever statements might be made about women as a class, it remains an open question what is possible for any individual woman. In both these respects P. is counteracting an inclination, on the part of those who believe in the distinct and inferior nature of women, to rely on broad and imprecise generalisations about the female sex. (The fact that P. himself elsewhere succumbs to this habit [nn. 453b7, 469d7] does not, of course, lessen the force of his argument here.) Once the case is accepted both for a functional analysis of the concept of human nature, and for the need to separate judgements of particular women from beliefs about women in general, the ground is ready for facing the salient question: are there some women who would make good Guardians? The crucial premise for an affirmative answer is supplied by G.'s remark at 455d3-5: 'there are many women who are better at many things than many men'.

The implications of G.'s remark can be highlighted by comparison with a passage from one of the most eloquent of modern statements of feminism, J. S. Mill's 'The Subjection of Women' (1869). In Part III of his essay, Mill confronts the conviction that women are incapable of a large range of professional employments. To make this conviction at all consistent, he points out, 'it is not sufficient to maintain that women on the average are less gifted than men on the average....It is necessary to maintain that no women at all are fit for them...' This argument matches the shape of P.'s case at 455c-d: Soc. and G. do agree (unlike Mill) that 'women on the average are less gifted than men on the average', but they refuse to maintain that 'no women at all are fit' for the tasks and duties that would be placed on Guardians. Moreover, Mill comes extremely close to G.'s remark at 455d3-5 when he suggests that no-one will deny that 'women, and not a few merely, but many women, have proved themselves capable of everything, perhaps without a single exception, which is done by men, and of doing it successfully and creditably.' These, then, are much the same terms in which P. rejects the total exclusion of women from positions of social and political responsibility, and justifies his proposal that at least *some* Guardians, and perhaps a fair proportion of them (n. 455d8), will be women. We can add that if these principles were followed through, they would affect the roles of women at other levels of society too; but P. is not interested in pursuing that entailment in this context.

How, though, are we to characterise the thrust of P.'s argument? It certainly should not be regarded as foreshadowing what Mill, at the outset of his essay, called the 'principle of perfect equality'. And that is not only because P. suggests a situation of something less than perfect equality. It is, above all, because the kind of equality for which modern feminism strives presupposes an overall commitment to some form of liberalism, which attaches fundamental importance to the freedom of the individual. Such equality is utterly incompatible with P.'s political philosophy as a whole, and with his treatment of female Guardians in particular. The women who become Guardians in the ideal city will do so not because they are free to *choose* to do so, still less because they have a 'right' to do so. They will become Guardians because they are selected, and indeed obliged, to fulfil that function on behalf of the city. Any 'equality' they are granted, therefore, is at best a regimented role-equality, within a social framework which is completely collectivist in conception, and thus opposed to the value of individual autonomy. See the Introduction, p. 14.

454a1   **grand:** Soc.'s point is only semi-ironic. *gennaios*, lit. 'well-bred' or 'true-born' (n. 459a3), not only comes to be used of good character independently of aristocratic status (e.g. 2.361b7, 4.440c2, cf. Arist. *Rhet.* 1398a18–20, Dover [1974] 95), but acquires the general sense of 'good', or 'genuine', of its kind, in a very wide application: e.g. 2.372b4 (cakes), 8.544c6 (tyranny), *Plt.* 274e7 (a mistake); cf. LSJ s.v., II. It is the epithet in the phrase normally translated as the 'noble lie' (see n.459c8); at 6.488c4 it conveys something like 'honest but simple minded'. Soc. here means that clever debating skills make a superficial but unmerited impression.

454a1–2   **altercation:** a style of argument concerned with the pleasure of point-scoring and controverting one's opponent, rather than seeking the truth (cf. Arist. *Soph. El.*

171b22–34). It is described as a kind of adolescent 'sport' at 7.539b-c. The contrast between Socratic dialectic, and the contentious skill (known variously as eristic [a5, b5], agonistic, antilogical) of those who aim merely to win the argument, is a recurrent one: e.g. 6.499a, *Euthd.* 276-8 (and *passim*), *Grg.* 457c-8a, *Meno* 75c-d, *Tht.* 154d-5a, 167e, with Robinson 84-8. Yet the function of the contrast here, as also at *Phdo* 91a, *Tht.* 164c-d, is a Socratic *self*-reminder to avoid a shallow style of disputation.

454a6   **distinctions of kind:** the phrase anticipates the language of e.g. *Phdr.* 266e1, *Soph.* 253d1, *Plt.* 285a4–5, 286d9. This raises the question whether P. here presupposes the technical procedure of 'collection and division', or analysis by general concepts and their component elements (i.e., in many contexts, by genera and species): see esp. *Phdr.* 265d–6b, *Plt.* 285a–b, *Phlb.* 16c–18d, with Crombie II 368–74. It is hard to deny a connection altogether: both here and at *Phlb.* 17a3–5 the idea of 'division' is associated with the dialectic/eristic contrast. Yet the *Rep.* itself contains no statement of the collection-and-division method, despite its description of dialectic as the supreme technique of philosophical knowledge (cf. Robinson 162–5); so it is implausible that P. already has a fully developed concept of the method. We should therefore regard the technique as the crystallisation of ideas partially adumbrated in preceding works of P.'s, and indeed in the historical Socrates' interest in precise definitions (Arist. *Met.* 1078b27–9). The immediate point here is that generalisations about male and female natures need qualifying by specification of the 'kinds' or 'types' (*eidos*: n. 449a5) of difference which are alleged.

454a7   **a purely verbal level:** similar cautions are issued at *Tht.* 164c–d (linked to the dialectic/eristic contrast), *Soph.* 218c1-5. Here the pertinent difference is not between 'words' and 'things' (though that is in the background), but between the superficial manipulation of words and a use of them that is grounded in real (dialectically tested) understanding.

454b4   **the principle:** the definite article turns the whole of the following ὅτι clause (which includes everything from μή to τυχγάνειν) into the object of διώκομεν; for comparable examples see e.g. 457d9, 471c6, 1.327c10. μή, though missing from the main mss., is a required correction: μὴ τὴν αὐτήν = ἄλλην. τυγχάνειν + genitive (b4–5), to obtain or receive, is sometimes quasi-passive, hence 'be given'; cf. 455b8, 456d9.

454b5   **vigorously:** for the application of *andreios*, lit. 'manly'/'brave', to a style of arguing, cf. the description of G. ('indefatigable'?) at 2.357a3, and e.g. *Meno* 81d3 (where it is *contrasted* with eristic), *Crat.* 440d4, *Tht.* 151d5 (the verb, *andrizesthai*). At *Plt.* 306e the term is said to be used of many kinds of quickness and keenness; cf. n. 459c6 below.

454b8   **earlier:** both in the original context at 2.370a–c, and in bk. 5 itself. *Epitêdeumata*, 'activities', corresponds to *erga* in bk. 2 (e.g. 369e2, 370b2, 8): both terms refer to fixed social roles, duties, or habitual practices.

454c2   **bald people:** the example, as a rudimentary instance of physical variation, prepares for the contention that a physiological difference between the sexes need not entail distinctions at the level of social functions. *Phusis*, 'nature', here as quite often (LSJ s.v., II 2), refers to bodily form or appearance. But the example is both humorous and rhetorical; if pressed, it would be vulnerable to the objection that whereas sexual gender can impinge on many aspects of a life, baldness/hairiness is unlikely to do so.

454c9   **difference and sameness:** elsewhere in P., and usually in other authors too, *alloiôsis* and *homoiôsis*, as their formation from active verbal roots would suggest, mean 'alteration' and 'assimilation'. Their use here may involve a slightly playful pretentiousness; the attraction for assonance (-*ôseôs*) is not untypical of P.; see J.D.

Denniston, *Greek Prose Style*, corr. rpr. (Oxford, 1960) ch. VII (citing two instances from *Rep.* 5: 462b9, 480a6–7).

454d1   **activities themselves:** although a person's 'nature', *phusis*, involves, for P., a genetically given potential (n. 453a1), this must be tested by practical performance. The criteria of a sex's, or an individual's, *phusis* thus become substantially empirical, though the present argument stresses the need to look beyond the institutionalised traditions of existing society, which is all that the imaginary opponent was appealing to at 453b7–8. Yet P.'s argument supports the scenario of a city built upon strong class-divisions, with limited scope for individuals to move between classes (nn. 456a8, 468a6–7); and this scheme postulates the essentially inherited 'nature' of individuals (of either sex). There is thus no liberal motivation behind bk. 5's case as a whole: P. wishes to make a radical challenge to current social practices, but only in the name of an imagined political order that would deem most people's *phusis* to be fixed by their birth.

454d2–3   **a man and a woman with medical talents:** this is the apparent sense of Burnet's text, which follows the main mss. reading; it would be helped by Hermann's change of ὄντα to ὄντας, which is less drastic than Burnet's suggested excision of the participle. The obvious objection to this is that it inaptly anticipates the next, and crucial, step in the argument (from d7). This is true but not decisive: d2–5 makes the point that 'natures' need to be defined in terms of aptitudes (on *-ikos* cf. n. 456a7), and might emphasise this by the proleptic example of a woman capable of medical skills (cf. n. 455e6–7). To remove a reference to females at d2 favours the change of ἰατρικήν to ἰατρικόν, which yields a comparison between the natures of a practising doctor and a man with the mental capacity for the same practice: this may make a jejune example, but that (ctr. Adam, and Richards 113) does not rule it out. On balance, my own preference is for this latter reading. Cf. Pomeroy (1978), and Boter 212, 215.

454d8   **distinct capacity:** the verb *diapherein* can mean 'differ' (whether by degree or in kind), or 'excel'; its use here lends a certain tension to the sequence of thought, and the point, though crucial, has been widely misconstrued. Since it will be accepted, at 455c–d, that the male sex is generally superior to the female, we would introduce a fatal inconsistency into P.'s case if we took the issue here to be an average or overall difference between the sexes' capacity for any given activity. So we must understand a reference not to *degrees* of ability, but to an absolute difference of skills: i.e. any activity should be assigned exclusively to a single sex, *only* if that sex has an aptitude for it which the other sex altogether lacks. (Adam's 'plainly excels' presumably conveys this). Empirically, this condition will be satisfied only if there is *no* woman who possesses a greater capacity than *any* man engaging in the activity – and that is exactly what will be denied at 455d3–4: cf. the head-note to this section. P.'s argument can thus be kept consistent, despite the potential ambiguity of *diapherein*: cf. n. 455c5.

454e1   **begets:** the verb *ocheuein* is typically used of animals, e.g. 9.586a8, *Euthd.* 298e3. That association intimates that the *only* evident difference between the sexes is one of basic reproductive function, as in other mammals. The implicit analogy recalls the canine imagery earlier in the bk. (n. 451d4).

454e4   **their women:** for the phrasing cf. n. 456b9.

454e6   **our opponent:** the imaginary interlocutor who holds that the natures of men and women differ 'utterly' (453b7). The challenge to him now is to specify any skill/activity of civic and political importance for which women are intrinsically lacking in capability (cf. n. d8 above). One ostensibly strong answer, from the standpoint of existing Greek society, is 'warfare' (cf. 452a4-5, c1-2, 453a3-4). But even this example, which gains some plausibility from the relative physical weakness of women as a class (451e1, 455e1), can be blocked by the later consideration that many individual women can outstrip many men in their natural abilities (455d3-5, with n.). So even in military matters, we can expect some women to have a significant contribution to make.

455a5   **just as you did:** at 453c7.

455b1   **in the hope that:** for this use of ἐάν, see Weir Smyth §2354.

455b2   **peculiar to a woman:** i.e. to which women should be *restricted* – the negative phrasing recurs at d6-7 below, with the equivalent formulation for men.

455b5   **did you mean:** the opponent is expected to assent to a general definition of natural aptitudes or talents (for the broad scope of *euphuês*, see e.g. 3.410a1, 6.491e2). The qualities described are akin to the *eumathia* of *Chrm.* 159e, *Meno* 88a–b; they remind one of what Socrates finds lacking in the crass Strepsiades, Ar. *Clouds* 628-31. The generality of the terms promotes the goal of the argument, and hinders the sexist assumptions of the opponent, in two related ways: first, by emphasising capacities whose broadness of application militates against a special connection with the male sex; secondly, by subordinating physical to mental ability (n.b. 'adequately', b9, and cf. 3.403d), so as to minimise the significance of female 'weakness' (n. e1 below). Moreover, the passage delineates qualities particularly valuable for philosophers: the rare term *heurêtikos* (b7), lit. 'with an ability to find things out', is linked to dialectical skills at *Plt.* 286e2, 287a4; and there are resemblances to the philosophical attributes later stressed at 6.486c-d, 487a, 490a-c, 494b1-2, 503c2, 7.535b-c. The argument, after all, is concerned not with the treatment of *all* women, but with the selection of those capable of becoming female Guardians and even philosopher-rulers.

455b5   **whenever:** ἐν ᾧ, lit. 'in which thing...' – i.e. in any activity where such differences can be manifested.

455b9   **his mind...supported:** at *Prt.* 326b7, a similar phrase refers to the value of gymnastics, within traditional education, in providing a training conducive to courage; cf. Soc.'s remarks at Xen. *Mem.* 3.12.5–6. Likewise here, P. is alluding to the idea that the Guardians' physical discipline, though partly aimed at rendering them fit for military service (n. 451e1), is intended to foster qualities of *soul* and character (3.410b–c, 6.498b4–6).

455c3   **no-one:** the reply suggests that G. is not merely maintaining the role of imaginary interlocutor; he is answering on his own behalf, or indicating the answers he thinks an interlocutor *ought* to give. This is of some importance, since it is G. who will produce the crucial observation at d3-5 below. Cf. n. 476d8-9 for a related issue in P.'s dialogue technique.

455c4–6   **any practice:** having moved so far towards a case for women's possession of the same kinds of natural potential as men, Soc. now apparently takes a step backwards. He makes a concession to the male prejudice (cf. Dover [1974] 99) that women are generically inferior to men in intelligence as well as in physical strength; and the evidence to which he implicitly appeals is biased by just those inertly customary attitudes which the argument is intended to criticise (452c, 456c1–2). Given the evidence of P.'s work as a whole (n. 453b7), we might think this symptomatic of tensions in the philosopher's own views of women: see e.g. Okin 21–7 and ch. 3. But Soc.'s rhetorical question needs to be understood as a step in the argument; its effect is to prompt the crucial response from G. (n. d3–5), and thus to accentuate the need for judgements of individual women to be separated from generalisations about their sex. It is unclear, in any case, whether Soc. is citing a necessary state of affairs, or only the contingent facts of an existing culture. Cf. Calvert 239–41, who takes the point to have 'tactical' purpose within the argument. See the head-note to this section, and cf. nn. c6–7, d8, e1 below.

455c5   **superior:** as G.'s response indicates, the superiority meant by Soc. must be a matter of general or average difference; thus the force of διαφερόντως ἔχει cannot be the same as that of διαφέρειν at 454d8 (see n.).

455c6–7 **weaving...:** Soc. points to what, in context, are apparent and negligible exceptions such as clothes-making and cooking, two standard parts of the domestic economy of citizen wives in Athens (cf. e.g. Xen. *Oec.* 7.21, 36, and *passim*). It may be meant that even at these jobs men *could* be better (so Proclus 245.19–27 Kroll, and e.g. Pierce 1–3, Annas [1976] 309), though the point is moot: G.'s response ('virtually') implies acceptance of some exceptions. In any case, reference to the current roles of women inadvertently suggests a bias in Soc.'s preceding question: for it is only in those spheres which are allotted to them, and not in activities from which they are debarred, that Greek women can display the 'natural' abilities that are at issue in the argument. Soc.'s attitude, in other words, stands in uneasy relation to prejudices which underpin current social role-divisions.

455d2   **greatly surpassed:** G.'s remark accepts a clear *average* inferiority; but, in view of his next sentence, it is uncertain whether this implies that most women are inferior to most men. On any reading, room must be left for the inference that there are numerous women of substantial ability; nor can we even conclude, from the collective generalisation, that the best women must be inferior to the best men: cf. Calvert 234–7.

455d3–5 **there are many women:** G.'s additional observation is the vital element needed to reach the conclusion of the argument (d6–e1); it incorporates a recognition that 'nature' is *individual*, not generically fixed: the point is well taken by Proclus 249 Kroll; cf. Peirce 2-3, Lesser 113-15. This is dramatically striking, given that Soc. has guided the earlier parts of the argument and supplied all its key ideas. Without G.'s observation, the imaginary opponent (i.e. a Greek male with typical attitudes towards the relation of the sexes) is confronted with little to challenge his assumptions. G.'s point will not, and certainly should not, satisfy a modern feminist, as it leaves intact the idea of a collective female inferiority. But it is not as paltry as Annas (1981) 184 contends, since it *does* block the conservative expectation that 'men will still take all the front-rank positions': it is the whole thrust of G.'s triple 'many' to insist that, if it is the best individuals that the state needs for its Guardians, women will be *substantially* represented within this class, even at the highest level of philosopher-rulers (the best 5 per cent or less: n. 458b9f.); cf. 456a-b, 460b9-10, 7.540c. This thrust is reinforced by the conclusion Soc. now draws.

455d8   **distributed similarly:** but not 'equally' in the strict statistical sense (which would contradict c4–6, d2–3), nor 'randomly'. The essential implications are three: (i) *all* (d9) the same types of natural quality and aptitudes can be found among women as among men; (ii) these include some 'natures' that can be developed to the very highest level of politics and philosophy (n. d3–5); (iii) the distribution of valuable natural talents among women is a widespread phenomenon (G.'s 'many', d3). Despite the reservations which cling to the argument, this conclusion is one which commits its proponents to a radical critique of the prevailing restrictions on women's social roles, and to the conviction that such restrictions involve a great waste of human potential (cf. *Laws* 6.781a–b).

455d9   **creatures:** *zôion*, usually 'animal', is not a normal term for 'sex'/'gender' (ctr. *genos*, e.g. 455c5, d3); it may here add a further touch of quasi-biological neutrality to an argument which has tried (imperfectly) to treat human nature independently of social custom. Cf. 451e3, 466d7, n. 454e1.

455e1 **weaker:** there is no compelling reason to take this in anything more than a physical sense (as at 451e1), unlike e.g. 6.491e5; it represents much less of a rider than Soc.'s remark at Xen. *Symp.* 2.9 (cf. Introduction n. 14). The point has implications for the military duties of Guardians (n. 457a10), but not for the service of women in the highest role of philosopher-rulers (n. 460b9–10). b9 above implied that (some) women have sufficient bodily strength to engage in every kind of activity, and that passage anyway subordinated the physical to the mental. So the present sentence only marginally qualifies the scope for female Guardians. Besides, it does not rule out the possibility that, as in other respects (d3-4), some women could, with gymnastic training, become stronger than many men.

455e4 **assign:** the conclusion refers to the availability of women to serve as Guardians and Rulers, *not* to the general freedom of individual women. Indeed, P. considered such freedom to be, if anything, a mark of degenerate democracies: cf. esp. 8.563b7–8, with the Introduction p. 14.

455e6–7 **medicine...music:** the first provided an illustration at 454d2–5 (see n.), and 'music' is one of the two main components of the Guardians' education (452a2–5). But P. may also have selected these two fields because there were already women known to be active in them. Some forms of medicine were certainly practised by women in contemporary Greece. Medically skilled midwives existed (n. 460c8), as did gynaecological assistants to doctors (G.E.R. Lloyd, *Science Folklore & Ideology* [Cambridge, 1983] 70–73); and a 4th cent. gravestone from Athens, *CEG* (2) 569 iii (cf. Lefkowitz & Fant 27, no. 52), describes a woman called Phanostrate as 'midwife and doctor' (μαῖα καὶ ἰατρός): cf. Pomeroy (1978) 499–500. For women and 'music' see n. 452a2. The present argument *ought* to have implications for the whole society (incl. the wives of craftsmen etc.), but the discussion, here as elsewhere in bk. 5 (n. 450c1), is preoccupied with the Guardian class; cf. Reeve 219-20.

456a1 **isn't one woman gymnastic:** Soc. is effectively requesting an answer to the question originally posed at 453a3–4. He moves from general mental (455e6–7) to physical ability, and then (a4) to the key elements (intellectual, psychological and ethical) needed for Guardianship.

The text has caused much argument here, even though it is clear what the question as a whole must amount to. καί is certainly extraneous, and γυμναστική is put first for emphasis, displacing the interrogative οὐ (= *nonne*); οὐδέ repeats the interrogative before the second adj. Cf. Adam's n.; Boter 212–13 in unnecessarily sceptical about the explanation which I follow.

456a4 **philosophical...spirited:** the two essential qualities originally stipulated for the Guardian class (2.375a–6c, esp. c4–5). Spiritedness, a quasi-animal vigour, entails both courage and aggression (cf. nn. 457a10, 467e4–5). 'Philosophy' involves a combination of intellectual and ethical attributes (2.375e–6c); in both respects, it cuts against typical Greek views of women, which tended to see them as less rational and more emotional than men (Dover [1974] 98–102, Just ch. 8): the idea of 'clever' women could be a frightening one for some Greek males (cf. Eur. *Hipp.* 640–44). Implicit in the philosophical nature of certain women is the potential to reach the highest rank of philosopher-rulers (473c ff.); cf. n. 460b9 f. P. himself had at least two female students in the Academy, neither of them Athenian: D. Laert. 3.46, 4.2, Themist. *Or.* 23.295c; *P. Oxy.* LII 3656 may refer to one of these. Some women had probably been involved in earlier Pythagorean communities (Introduction nn. 20-2); in P.'s own time we know of Arete, daughter of Aristippus of Cyrene (D. Laert. 2.72, 86), and at least one female Cynic, Hipparchia (D. Laert. 6.96-8). *Tht.* 150b7-8 ignores female philosophers; but Soc. is there speaking in relation to Athenian norms.

456a7   **equipped to be a Guardian:** the form *phulakikos*, first used at 2.375e9, was almost certainly coined by P.; it is apparently peculiar to him, and occurs only in *Rep.* P. may have wished to avoid the form *phulaktikos*, which had the senses of 'preservative', 'defensive', etc. As throughout the preceding argument (454d2, 5, 455b7, e6–7, 456a1–2; cf. nn. 474c8, 475b4), the – *ikos* suffix marks a 'natural' capacity or disposition; but cf. n. c11 below.

456a8   **we selected:** originally at 2.374e7; cf. 458c7, 4.429e8. In the imagined city, the initial selection of Guardians will not be made afresh each generation; it will be built into the rigid class structure. But some scope for promotion, as well as demotion, between classes will remain (3.415a–c, 4.423c–d, *Tim.* 19a, and n. 468a6–7). And there will be constant observation and testing of Guardians, from early childhood, to identify the best of them for higher duties (3.412d-14a, with the sequence of levels at 7.537b-40c): all of this, we have to imagine (cf. 460b9-10, 7.540c5-9), will be equally true of the women of the class, even if P. does less than he might have done to keep the symmetry of the sexes in the reader's mind (cf. n. 460b9 f.).

456b2   **live with:** *sunoikein* would normally refer to individual marriages; cf. Harrison I 2, with n. 4, for formal usage. But we have already heard about the communal residences, *sussitia*, of the male Guardians (3.415d–17b), and 457d1 will stress the point; cf. the 'polite' use of *sunoikein*, for sexual unions, at 461e2–3. A system of common messes remains an element in *Laws*, esp. 6.780e–81d, but they are there no longer fully residential.

456b3   **equivalent and kindred:** the first adj. means 'competent' or 'adequate' (sc. to match the men); cf. 7.540c7. The second, *suggeneis*, perhaps plays on etymology, stressing that female and male Guardians are 'born with' the same abilities; in the more normal sense of kinship, the word could be applied to *all* citizens (3.415a7), though it will come to possess an intensified meaning for the inter-breeding members of the same class (cf. 463d8).

456b8   **earlier claim:** at 451e–2a.

456b9   **female Guardians:** in isolation, the phrase, like those at e.g. 454e4, 457a6, could mean either the 'women' or the 'wives' of the Guardians; this potential ambiguity lends a certain (untranslatable) piquancy to the idea of 'the sharing of women/wives and children' (449d4, 450c1–2), and the piquancy will become more acute from 457b10 ff. The status of the female Guardians is always formulated in relation to that of the males: see esp. 457c10 f., with the language of ownership or possession at 451c6. But as I noted on the latter passage, the import of these verbal points should not be exaggerated: they partly reflect P.'s need to use existing social norms as a foil for his own radical proposals. Cf. Calvert 242-3.

456b12 **utopian:** see n. 450d1.

456c4   **possible and for the best:** see the twin sources of Soc.'s concern at 450c8–9.

456c11 **equipped for Guardianship:** the adj. *phulakikos* (cf. n. a7) recalls the preceding discussion of natural aptitudes; but Soc. is now stressing that such aptitudes need to be drawn out and fostered by education: for this interplay see 451e–2a, 455b, with n. 453a1.

456d3   **what is your view:** lit. 'how are you in terms of opinion?' The same type of expression occurs at e.g. *Grg.* 451c4, Ar. *Lys.* 1125; cf. Weir Smyth §§1441–2.

456d6   **all equal:** the question is perfunctory, given G.'s statement at 455c3.

456d8   **founding:** see n. 453b4.

456d10 **cobblers:** who, like all farmers and artisans, will be trained in the single activity which defines their social role; music and gymnastics, i.e. 'education', is exclusively for the Guardians (7.520b6-7, and Arist. *Pol.* 1264a32). Cf. the similar contrast at

466a-b. But if the lowest class lacks all political education, how, we might ask, will it be capable of understanding the social order to which it belongs (nn. 463b1-3, 465b9-10)?

456d12   **best of the entire citizen body:** lit. 'best of the rest of the citizens'; on this Greek idiom cf. n. 472c2.

456e6   **better for a city:** the question is virtually rhetorical; it thus presupposes a uniform criterion of ethical and political goodness, applying equally to individuals and to a city. Later parts of bk. 5 will try to give some substance to this view. Cf. nn. 457b4–5, 458e4.

457a6   **strip off:** see n. 452a11. Cf. the term *apodutêrion* for a changing room in a gymnasium or palaestra (e.g. *Euthd.* 272e2, *Lys.* 206e6–7).

457a7   **clothe themselves:** though the future active of ἀμφιέννυμι in Attic is ἀμφιῶ (-έω), the middle form ἀμφιέσομαι appears also at Xen. *Cyr.* 4.3.20 (LSJ), and ἀμφιοῦμαι seems not to occur.

457a10   **weakness:** a reprise of 451e1, 455e1; the sense is again physical, cf. 'lighter' (a9). Note that P. does not question whether women have the same kind or degree of *aggression* as men; indeed, he explicitly accepts that they (can) have, by allowing for the same quality of 'spiritedness', *thumoeides*, in them (cf. 456a4–5). This view stems from the wider philosophical tenet that all human souls contain the same principal elements; but when P. sometimes refers to a different balance in women's souls (stressed by Annas [1976] 314), he shows the influence of current stereotypes: see n. 469d7 for references. As regards military service, it is unclear whether the present passage allows for adjustments necessitated by child-bearing (n. 460d6).

457b1   **who laughs:** the case for female Guardians is rounded off (a kind of ring-composition) by recalling the motif of ridicule from 452a–d.

457b2–3   **unripe fruit of humour's cleverness:** a distortion of Pindar fr. 209 Maehler (197 Bowra), where (presocratic) natural philosophers, *phusiologountes*, were described as 'plucking unripe fruit of wisdom/cleverness'. P. inserts 'of humour'. But Adam I 357 makes heavy weather of the sense, and supposes that P. has substituted 'humour' for Pindar's 'wisdom' (making *sophias* a scribal gloss insinuated into the text). Either way, P. is turning Pindar's expression, which was apparently derisive of philosophy, *against* those who mock philosophical ideas; the passage can thus be seen as an incidental allusion to the 'quarrel between philosophy and poetry' cited at 10.607b–c (see my nn.). There are thirteen passages in P. which quote Pindar – ten separate quotations, only three from surviving poems (Brandwood 1001–2) – and several other references, without quotation, to the poet. As with Homer, Pindar is both criticised (3.408b–c) and praised (*Meno* 81b1) by P.

457b4–5   **what brings benefit is beautiful:** beautiful/ugly correspond to fine/shameful (cf. n. 476b5); I prefer the former pair here, because P. has in mind not just the general issue of nudity, but also the appearance of individual bodies (cf. 452b1–3). The quotation was evidently a familiar saying; Arist. *EE* 1235a35 ('what is useful is loved' [*philon*]) may allude to a similar expression, and cf. the related proverb at *Lys.* 216c6–7, Eur. *Bacch.* 881. The equation of 'good' or 'beautiful' with 'beneficial' – i.e. what *is* good *does* good – is an invariable assumption and faith of P.'s: see, at different levels, 1.335d–e, 2.379b, 6.505a (the transcendent form of goodness), 10.608e4 (with my n.), *Euthph.* 13b8 ff.; for the views of the historical Soc. in this area, see Vlastos (1991) 6–10 and ch. 8. In *Rep.* the equation is closely associated, as here, with the political idea that what is good is good *for*, and embodies the happiness of, the whole city, not just one part of it: cf. nn. 458e4, 461a8 f., 465e–6b. This fulfils Soc.'s hint at 1.339b3–4 that justice is some kind of 'self-interest' (*sumpheron*): it turns out, on the civic plane, to be the common interests of all the classes (and individuals) in the harmoniously integrated city.

457b7   **one sort of 'wave':** the imagery echoes 453d; metaphors from difficulty at sea are common in Greek, whether in terms of swimmers (e.g. Eur. *Hipp.* 469–70, 822–4) or ships (Aesch. *Pers.* 433, *Suppl.* 470–1, *PV* 746). The present passage foreshadows the motif of a 'trio' of waves (i.e. female Guardians, abolition of marriage, and philosopher-rulers) at 472a3–4.

457b9   **for the suggestion:** τιθέντας – accusative after ὥστε, despite continuity of subject with the main clause. Such anomalies do occur: Richards 115 compares 8.547b8–c1; cf. the combined nominative and genitive at 458d1–3.

457c1   **female Guardians:** here, but only here, P. uses a special noun, *phulakis*, which must be a coinage. It is reminiscent of comic neologisms: cf. *stratêgis*, 'female general', at Ar. *Eccl.* 835, 870, and *stratiôtis*, 'female soldier', in the title of a play (?early 4th cent.) by Theopompus (*PCG* VII 733, Kock I 747), a poet who happens to have aimed at least one joke at P. (fr. 16 *PCG*/15 K).

457c1-2 **while our argument:** lit. 'but that the argument somehow agrees with itself that it is speaking of possible and beneficial things'. ὁμολογεῖσθαι should be taken after φῶμεν (b7) rather than ὥστε (b8).

457c4   **you won't say:** for similar phrases see 10.596c4 (with my n.), *Laws* 1.625c4.

457c6-461e4

The existence of female Guardians will be accompanied by the abolition of individual marriages and families. Instead, there will be a system of sexual sharing or communism, carefully organised for eugenic purposes: this will require breeding to be confined, so far as possible, to the best men and women. Only healthy children will be allowed to survive, and the women will be relieved of the practical burdens of child-rearing. Female Guardians will have child-bearing careers of up to twenty years (age 20-40); the men will beget between the ages of 25 and 55. With the removal of the family, biological parents and children will not be allowed to know each other's identities; all existing kinship terminology (father, mother, son, daughter, etc.) will be transferred from individuals to whole generational groups.

The argument now proceeds to the social consequences of having female Guardians who will be fully engaged in the 'professional' duties of their class: Soc. is here concerned with the 'how' (458b4), or the workings, of the Guardians' *koinônia*. The result is a programme whose revolutionary character centres on the removal of the most fundamental and widespread of all Greek social institutions, the *oikos*. What is original to P. in this passage, and what has caused his argument to be sometimes received with misgivings in more recent times, is the relentlessness with which he explores the ramifications of eugenics, sexual communism, and a revised system of kinship among the Guardians. Yet probably each of the main components of this programme can be connected to identifiable influences or precedents. The eugenics incorporates (while also transmuting) elements of aristocratic ideology, Spartan emphasis on breeding for the maintenance of a military caste, contemporary animal breeding techniques, and medical ideas about procreative fitness and the quality of offspring (Introduction §2.2). The sexual communism and extended kinship are themselves partly extrapolated from eugenic principles, but they must also have owed something to reflection upon quasi-anthropological claims about the lives of some non-Greek peoples (Introduction p. 10).

Everything P. has so far said about his city's Guardians, both in the earlier books and in bk. 5's own proposal for female Guardians, has emphasised that the class will comprise people with a certain kind of 'nature'. Since this nature is believed to be heritable, as the entire class-structure of the state presupposes (n. 456a8), a concern with how the Guardians will reproduce themselves, and how they will ensure the continuing excellence of their stock, assumes an essential place in the argument. The importance of these questions will receive confirmation much later in the work, when at 8.546a-b Soc. will trace the eventual dissolution of the ideal city (something that nature makes inevitable) to mistakes made by the Rulers in their eugenic policy. Such mistakes are perhaps only too easy to imagine, given the doubts that can be raised about the aim of perpetuating the Guardian class by special breeding (Introduction p. 17). Equally radical doubts adhere to the coherence and practicability of the collective kinship envisaged for the Guardians. Not only are there severe difficulties in seeing how this scheme could be put into action (nn. 461d4, e1-2); there are also conceptual problems about P.'s apparent assumption that the kinds of affection and loyalty manifested within present kinship relationships could be *transposed* onto a very different set of social structures (Introduction p. 20). At this point, P.'s thinking displays an element of paradox, and certainly of strain, that is perhaps unavoidable for even the boldest of social reformers. His ideas involve the attempt to construct and imagine a form of life that is sharply divergent from his own and his readers' experience; yet the understanding of human behaviour on which he necessarily draws is one that reflects the influence of precisely those institutions and practices which his proposals are intended to abolish.

457c7   **follows on:** the connection is logical (cf. e.g. 3.394e2–3), insofar as (i) if female Guardians are to live the same life as the men, that involves a radical communism which is incompatible with the existing family (cf. 3.416d–17b), (ii) the principle of producing the very best men and women for the city (456d–e) requires selective breeding that is, at any rate, hard to reconcile with marriage in its familiar form. Cf. Introduction, n. 44.

457c10f.   **That all these women:** the phrasing is redolent of a law or state regulation (*nomos*, c7); for this use of accusative and infin. in Athenian decrees, cf. e.g. ML no. 58.2, 4–5, no. 64. 16–20, with Weir Smyth §2013b.

457c11   **shared:** after the proposal that women should 'share' in the life of the Guardians (457a7, b9), Soc. adds two further layers to the central concept of communism, *koinônia*, within the Guardian class (449c5–8 etc.). The sexual status of the women is formulated from an ostensibly male point of view, but this does not show that women are still the property of men (ctr. Pomeroy [1974] 33). The phrasing reflects P.'s aim of challenging the customary attachment of women and children to individuals (cf. nn. 451c6 'possession', 456b9); cf. Ar. *Eccl.* 614, and the use of *epikoinos* at e.g. Herod. 1.216.1, 4.104 (sexual lives of non-Greek tribes: Introduction p. 10). See Eur. *Andr.* 124, with Stevens' n., for a possible use of *epikoinos* of a man.

457d1–2   **children:** earlier in the *Rep.* there was no anticipation of the abolition of the family; see the references to mothers (2.377c3, 381e2), fathers (2.378b3), parents (3.386a3, 4.425b2, 443a9), all of which look forward to conditions in the new city, and ostensibly presuppose normal familial relationships – hence, in part, Soc.'s feeling, 450a8, that bk. 5 is like a fresh start to the discussion. In the case of kinship, bk. 5 sets out not so much to erase existing patterns, as to transfer their energies and loyalties onto larger, collective networks: cf. the Introduction, p. 20.

457d2–3   **parent...offspring:** *goneus*, most frequently 'father', covers both parents. The measures to ensure ignorance of biological kinship are elaborated at 460c–d; for some modern analogues, see the Introduction, n. 43.

457d4–5   **doubt:** G. echoes Soc.'s original sense of uncertainty at 450c6–9.

457d6   **I don't think:** Soc.'s remark looks startling, but is probably somewhat wry; note the tone of G.'s reply (e1) and the humour of e2–6. However radical the proposals may look by current social norms, they are concordant with a uniform conception of the good of the city; cf. nn. 456e6, 457b4–5, 462b8.

457e2   **to escape:** Soc. harks back to his initial, ironic timidity at 450a–51a.

457e5–6   **provide your arguments:** *logon didonai* here probably combines a judicial (provide a defence or pay a penalty: cf. n. e7) with a philosophical sense (give a reasoned account or explanation).

457e7   **face the charge:** *dikên hupechein* can mean (i) provide a defence (cf. *logon hupechein*: Dem. 19.95 uses both objects), i.e. face a trial (e.g. *Laws* 6.754e4, 9.880b6); or (ii) suffer a penalty (e.g. *Phdo* 98e4, *Laws* 6.767e5); cf. LSJ s.v. ὑπέχειν, II 3, and n. e5–6 above. *Pace* Adam, (i) is here uppermost. Cf. the judicial imagery of e.g. 451a–b, 474a3–4.

458a1–2   **pamper...entertain:** 'pamper', *heortazein*, lit. 'hold a festival/holiday'; for 'entertain', lit. 'be feasted', cf. the metaphors applied to the discussion at 1.352b3–5, 354a–b, 9.571d8, *Lys.* 211c11.

458a5   **as available:** since τιθέναι can take either an infinitive or a participle construction, it is simplest to treat both ὡς ὑπάρχον and εἶναι as dependent on θέντες – 'taking it as given (ὡς ὑπάρχον) that what they want exists (εἶναι)'; cf. Adam. Boter 215 takes ὑπάρχον in the sense 'be possible'.

458b2   **later:** see 466d6 ff., though even then a final solution will be deferred until 471c4 ff., the argument for philosopher-rulers.

458b3–5   **now consider:** the two topics indicated occupy, respectively, 458c–61e and 462a–66d. As is made clear, the 'how' question is a matter of organisational detail, and is treated as quite distinct from the issue of possibility: the latter will be eventually construed as concerned with the ultimate conditions (the *sine qua non*: philosopher-rulers) needed to put such a scheme into practice. I have inserted an extra verb, 'argue', to cover the slightly different sense of σκέψομαι that applies, by zeugma, to the ὅτι clause at b5.

458b9f.   **Rulers...Auxiliaries:** the former, senior and trained to the highest philosophical level; the latter, younger and principally concerned with military and law-enforcing duties. Together, the two groups make up the Guardians in the wider sense of that term, though the Rulers are sometimes known as 'perfect' or 'true' Guardians: see esp. 3.412b–15a, 4.421b7f., 428d7, el; cf. 464c6–7. For reasons of age, it is the Auxiliaries who are most directly affected by the eugenic breeding policy: cf. 464b6. 4.423a8 gives a figure of 1,000 Auxiliaries: how many of these would be Rulers? *Plt.* 292e projects that not even 50 out of 1,000 people can attain to true political wisdom (cf. *Epist.* 7.337c); but the Auxiliaries are already an élite, so P.'s ideas may allow for a larger proportion as potential Rulers.

458c2   **carry out orders:** this subordination mirrors the subjection of the 'spirited' part of the soul to the rule of reason; cf. 4.440–41 (esp. 440d6, 441e5–6).

458c3–4   **heeding...emulating:** the city is endowed with a basic constitution and code of laws; the Rulers will adhere to this body of principles, but they will also possess an ability to discover and introduce many detailed, *ad hoc* regulations; cf. 4.425a–e. In the latter respect, they will be 'emulating', 'imitating', or 'modelling their behaviour on' (all possible senses of *mimeisthai*) the existing laws. At *Plt.* 300c5–6 (cf. d10f.) laws themselves are called 'imitations' or 'images' (*mimêmata*) of the truth (301a is a separate point), and *Plt.* 294a–c acknowledges that law can never be absolute or permanent, since human life is constantly changing. The fiction of Soc.'s and G.'s 'founding' of the city (cf. n. 453b4), and their 'selection' of the Guardians (456a8), allows Soc. to stress that the Rulers do not arrogate power to themselves, but are entrusted with it for the good of the city as a whole. They 'heed' the law, moreover, because they have philosophical understanding of the ultimate nature of all values (7.520a–e).

458c7   **selected:** cf. n. 456a8.

458c7–8   **hand them over:** G., as imaginary lawgiver, is responsible for the Guardians' education. Once more (cf. n. 456c11) it is assumed that 'nature', though inherited, needs to be actively shaped and brought out by training.

458c8–9   **dwellings and dining-halls:** i.e. communal barracks, as described at 3.415d–17b. P. had partial models for this arrangement in several parts of the Greek world, esp. the military messes of Sparta and Crete: see *Laws* 1.625c–e, 633a, 8.842b, Herod. 1.65.5, Xen. *Lac.* 5.1–7, Arist. *Pol.* 1272a1–4, 12–27, Plut. *Lyc.* 10–12, with Michell ch. 9, MacDowell (1986) 111–14, Powell 222–6, and (for Crete) Willetts 19–27. But P.'s scheme differs from these in at least two radical respects: first, participation of women was unheard of (cf. *Laws* 6.780e–81a); second, messes were not permanent residences, but were attended, like clubs, by individuals who also possessed homes. In any case, Doric cities fall well below P.'s ideal: they are, in his terms, timocracies (8.544c2–3, 547c ff.), which show an unbalanced interest in honour, wealth, purely physical training, and warfare (cf. *Laws* 2.666e–7b). It is possible that Pythagorean communities provided a partial model for the shared life of a philosophical group: for their 'communism', *koinônia*, see n. 449c5; Iambl. *Vita Pyth.* 98, for what it is worth, refers to *sussitia*. But this comparison too is limited; Pythagorean groups had neither a military nor a sexual dimension. In the comic scheme of Ar. *Eccl.*, communism of life-style will apply to *all* citizens (590 ff.), but P.'s proposals restrict it to the Guardian class: for the rest, justice will involve reference to private property (4.433e6-8). But cf. n. 450c1.

458d1   **lives together:** P. posits a total lack of segregation (all the more remarkable, given strict regulation of sexual activity: d8 ff.), though practical details about sleeping, washing, etc., are left unstated. Comparable communal arrangements would have to be made not only for adult Guardians, but also for the younger and adolescent members of the class; yet apart from the reference to babies at 460c–d, P. is wholly silent about how this aspect of social communism would work. The present passage shows how mistaken it is to say that 'in the gymnasiums... there must... be an absence of erotic desire' (Saxonhouse 41).

458d2–3   **natural necessity:** *emphutos*, lit. 'inborn', which stresses the force of instinct, is used of sexual desire at *Phdr.* 237d7, *Symp.* 191d1, and of other desires at *Laws* 6.782e3. In a prescriptive and puritanical context, at 8.559c6, sexual desires will be called 'unnecessary'. But 9.571b ff., elaborating this judgement, makes it clear that 'unnecessary' is not a denial of their natural or instinctive character (even the good man can be smitten by passion: 3.396d1–2), only a recognition of the extent to which, as products of the lowest part of the soul (4.436a10–11, 439d6), they have a 'lawless' tendency which ought to be controlled by reason – especially in the case of Guardians, who have a particular need for sexual self-control, *sôphrosunê* (3.389e1–2, cf. 390b–c, 402d–3c). Uncontrolled erotic desire is a feature of 'tyranny', actual or psychological: 9.572e ff., 587a13 f. The present passage leaves it unclear whether the 'necessity' of sexual instinct, which might be connected with desire to procreate (4.436a11, *Laws* 1.636c3–5), is distinct from erotic love for specific individuals; but since P. knows that the two things often go together, there is a radical difficulty lurking here for his attempt to erase individualism from the life of the Guardians: see nn. 460b3, 461a-b, 464d9, 468c1-3 (incl. homosexual desire). There is no indication here that women have weaker sexual urges than men; likewise at 461b9-c4. *Laws* 8.836a7 f. and *Tim.* 91a-d posit symmetry between the sexes in this respect, but cf. 460b1-3 for a more one-sided male view.

458d6   **keener:** *drimus* has an association with things that can sting or bite (e.g. bees, 8.564d9), as is indeed said of erotic passion at 474d5–6 (cf. 9.573a7); cf. the similar adj., *oxus*, applied to sexual desire at 3.403a4.

458d7   **draw:** or even 'drag'; used of the psychological power of desires at e.g. 4.439d1, 10.604b1, Xen. *Mem.* 4.5.6. Such internal tensions in the mind are a major entailment of the tripartite soul of the *Rep.*, but they had been denied by the historical Soc., who refused at any rate to believe that knowledge could be 'dragged about like a slave' (Arist. *EN* 1145b24, cf. P. *Prt.* 352c2).

458d9   **unregulated:** it is an important Platonic principle that there should be regulation or order, *taxis*, in everything (cf. e.g. *Laws* 6.780d5–8); but the point would be stretched by the acute difficulty of 'policing' sexual behaviour; see, for precisely this, *Laws* 8.836a6-b4. Xen. *Lac.* 1.5 ascribes to Sparta some regulation of sex within marriage: this is, as always, a possible source of influence on P.'s thinking.

458e1   **pious:** a concept usually associated in the *Rep.* with justice (cf. 461a4, 463d5, and e.g. 2.368b8, 4.427e1, 10.615b7), and never discussed as an independent virtue. This is compatible with the idea that piety is a part of justice (esp. *Euthph.* 12c–d), and also with the *Euthyphro*'s insight that piety needs a moral justification, rather than a theological explanation: i.e that it is *because* they are good that certain actions are pleasing to the gods, not vice versa. In the present context, where 'sacred' is translated into 'beneficial' (e4), the religious implications of the point are anyway left obscure (but cf. n. 459e5): we can say only that the justice of the ideal city is intended, *ipso facto*, to conform to divine standards; cf. n. e3, and e.g. *Phlb.* 39e10 f., with Dover (1974) 252–3 for the weakened force of the term *hosios* in general usage. The juxtaposition of 'pious' with 'happy' draws attention to the literal sense of *eudaimôn*, 'favoured by the gods'; on the city's happiness cf. 465e–6a.

458e3   **marriages...sacred:** for *gamos* of non-matrimonial liaisons, cf. e.g. Dem. 18.129; 'sacred' anticipates the practice of organising the Guardians' breeding within the framework of religious festivals, 459e–60a. Although the city will, in this as in other respects, contain religious institutions, their justification is always assumed rather than explained: cf. n. 469a4. I doubt (ctr. Adam) that the concept of a *hieros gamos* as a marriage between gods, or gods and humans (Burkert [1985] 108–9), is at all pertinent here; it is ordinary marriage to which the same phrase is applied at *Laws* 8.841d7.

458e4   **most beneficial:** the only criterion of the quality of sexual and procreative activity among the Guardians will be its contribution to the common good; cf. nn. 456e6, 457b4–5. This criterion, which entails the control of desire by reason, will be applied to the behaviour of the Auxiliaries by the Rulers. But can the power of erotic impulses be so confidently restricted by political regulations? Cf. nn. d2–3, 9.

459a2   **in your house:** probably not the original family house of Ariston, father of G., P. and Adeimantus (nn. 449b2, 450b7), but that of Pyrilampes, who is known to have kept an aviary (incl. peacocks): Antiphon fr. 57 (= Athen. 397c–d), Plut. *Per.* 13; cf. *Chrm.* 158a–b for its luxury. Pyrilampes (c.480–c.420) had become the stepfather of P. and his brothers when he married Ariston's widow, Perictione, who was also his niece; cf. Davies 329–30. For other references to aviaries see *Tht.* 197c–e, Ar. *Birds* 1084–5, Thphr. *Char.* 21.6. Hunting dogs were a common possession of rich families: cf. Xen. *Cyneg.* 3–4. Soc.'s choice of remark has, of course, a facetious edge; G. seemed less than interested in dogs at 2.376a9–10, and it cannot be right, with Rankin (1965) 417, to infer that G. was himself an animal-breeder. But the point may intimate something about P.'s own experience: cf. n. 451c8.

459a2–3   **dogs...birds:** as at 451c8, Soc. begins an argument from an animal analogy; cf. n. 466d7, Introduction p. 17, and for the same two comparisons see Iambl. *Vita Pyth.* 212

(DK I 476: influenced by P.?). Here the point is purely illustrative, and does not strictly compare human with animal behaviour, since it is the breeding of animals by men that is cited. The comparison is redolent of the Socratic use of example/comparison (*parabolê*), which is so familiar in the early dialogues and seems to have been a feature of the historical Soc. (6.487e6, Arist. *Rhet.* 1393b3–4). As a broad principle, one might say that Socratic analogy appeals, for purely clarificatory purposes, to readily recognisable facts, while Platonic analogy tends to serve more rhetorical, persuasive, or intimatory functions: cf. Robinson 204–8.

459a3   **well-bred:** *gennaios* (n. 454a1) was, like *eugenês* (LSJ s.v., 3), commonly applied to pedigree animals, esp. birds and horses; cf. 2.375a2, e2, Xen. *Cyr.* 1.4.15, Ar. *Birds* 285, Arist. *Hist. An.* 558b15, 631a2, *Gen. An.* 730a10, Men. fr. 223.12 K.

459a10f.   **breed...from the best:** Soc.'s appeal to the principles of animal breeding (cf. 4.424b1) underscores the assumption that individuals carry an inherited 'nature' (n. 453a1). Yet, as a8 re-emphasises, nature needs to be tested and drawn out by appropriate training: cf. Xen. *Mem.* 4.1.3–4.

459b7   **about horses:** ἵππων is best understood as a genitive of connection without the usual περί; for comparable cases see e.g. 470a5, 9.576d7, with Weir Smyth §§1380–1. A possible alternative is to understand γένος from b5.

459b10   **Good heavens:** the exclamatory noise, *babai*, familiar in comic language, is both colloquial and humorous; of its eleven occurrences in P., only one (*Soph.* 249d9) is not in the mouth of Soc. It usually expresses surprise or astonishment, sometimes, as here, at the formidable nature of a task (cf. *Phlb.* 23b5). For its combination with a vocative (another Socratic mannerism: n. 450c6) cf. 2.361d3.

459b10f.   **need our Rulers to be:** the construction is a cross between δεῖ + genitive, 'there is a need of', and δεῖ + accus. and infin., 'it is necessary that'; cf. e.g. Herod. 5.38.2.

459c3–5   **doctor...good enough:** for the contrast between drugs and regimen cf. 1.332c9f., 3.406d. 2.372d1–3, 373d1–2, 4.425e–6b express the view that a controlled way of life would reduce the need for medical drugs, and 3.405a ff. takes doctors to be an index of the decadence of a society (for good doctors cf. 408c ff.). *Laws* 4.720a–e, 9.857c–d contrast superior doctors, who discuss the patient's condition, with others, usually slaves, who prescribe hurriedly; cf. E. D. Phillips, *Greek Medicine* (London, 1973) 188-9.

    The subject of ἐθελόντων, c4 (genitive absol.), is best understood as the patients, not their bodies (ctr. Adam); there is thus no anacolouthon after σώμασι, c3. εἶναι, c5, is awkward, but can be explained as accus. and infin.: 'we regard it as sufficient that <the doctor> be rather inferior.'

459c6   **acute:** lit. 'more manly/brave'. But this use should be connected with the sense of 'keen'/'vigorous' (n. 454b5); less likely is a direct reference to courage (cf. *Lch.* 192e–3a, 195b5–6). Adam offers a different view.

459c8   **falsehood and deception:** perhaps one of the most disturbing (and unSocratic) sentiments in P., and a major flaw in the scheme of the ideal city. We are told elsewhere that the true philosopher shuns and hates all falsehood (6.485c–d, 490a–c, 494b1–2), and indeed that it is something that *no-one* could willingly take into his soul (2.382a–c, cf. 3.413a6–7). Yet it is here suggested that truth would often be inadequate to persuade even the Auxiliaries. This represents a crack in the feasibility of the city's unity. If the sense of common interest were strong, and selfish individualism absent (462–4), why should political deceit be needed? If the breeding of 'the best' is for the benefit of the whole class, why cannot this class be trusted to recognise and accept the value of the eugenic arrangements? Such doubts about the possibility of forging a feeling of shared interest apply even more sharply to relations between the Guardians and the rest of the citizens (cf. n. 465b9–10). At moments such as this, P. argues from a calculated view of political manipulation, rather than from the higher ideals on which the whole discussion is supposed to rest. It may not be coincidental that deception was perceived as playing a structural role in Spartan life (Powell 214-18). A defence of P.'s concept of 'verbal lies' is attempted by Reeve 208-13.

459d1   **we...agreed:** at 2.382c–d, 3.389b–d, and 3.414b8 ff. (the so-called 'noble lie', or perhaps 'beautiful fiction', introducing the myth of the metals). In two of these passages, the stress falls on the avoidance of evil (cf. 1.331c5–9). The 'evil' which the present proposal addresses can only be the resentment of Auxiliaries at the greater sexual opportunities of certain individuals (cf. 460a8–10). But such resentments indicate a more intractable human mentality than the one implied by later parts of the book, where the psychological unity of the Guardian class is described: this tension points to a fundamental weakness in the entire scheme. See the Introduction, p. 18.

459d1   **as a sort of drug:** ἐν φαρμάκου εἴδει (cf. 3.389b4), lit. 'in the class/category of a drug', = ὡς φάρμακον (2.382c10).

459d7–8   **the best...with the best:** in the first instance, the Auxiliaries who have proved outstanding during their education in music and gymnastics (the latter being designed partly for procreative fitness: cf. Xen. Lac. 1.4); at later stages, those who perform best in warfare and other duties (460b1-2). The eugenic policy thus involves selecting individuals with a view to biological transmission of the attributes, both physical and mental (cf. 455b), which they display in action. It is assumed that both parents contribute equally to the quality of offspring (cf. the implications of 10.603b4, Symp. 203c-e, Laws 8.839a1-3), and P. apparently believes in the possibility, though not the actuality, of constant 'genetic' improvement: see n. 461a8 f.

'In as many cases as possible' (d8), or 'as often as possible', should be understood in relative terms. Lefkowitz (1989) 497 supposes that some female Guardians would be regularly pregnant, a fact that would evidently limit their participation in other duties; but P. may not intend this, given his aim of a stable population (460a3–4). Laws 6.785b7–9 proposes military service for women only after their child-bearing careers (which would mean between the ages of 40 and 50, if one combined that passage with 460e below). The general point is, however, unquantifiable, since P.'s account lacks any statistical specificity (cf. n. 460a3–4). The remarks of Lucas 225, about the Guardians' chance to 'sleep around', grotesquely misconstrue P.'s aims.

459d8–9   **the worst:** relative, of course, to the standards of the Guardian class (cf. a 7–8 above); for phaulos of low breeding quality, cf. 10.603b4. (The city's farmers/artisans are presumably allowed to breed in less regulated ways: see n. 460c2.) P.'s underlying concern here may be with avoidance of transmissible defects and diseases: cf. 3.407d7–8. el and 460c3–5 imply that some sexual relations between inferior Auxiliaries will be allowed; this is confirmed by the summary at Tim. 18d-19a. P.'s focus is upon procreation; but he would have other reasons for excluding such things as prostitution or expensive courtesans, hetairai (cf. 4.420a4, with 2.373a3).

459e1   **not of the latter:** the phrase is intrinsically vague; cf. Rankin (1965) 410. It is therefore compatible with the removal of these infants to the artisan class, as indeed Tim. 19a1–2 proposes (though the reference back is principally to 3.415b–c: Adam I 359). But if, as I believe, 460c3–5 (see n.) encompasses infanticide, that gives us information about P.'s thinking which we cannot ignore in reading the present passage.

459e1   **our flock:** the same term was applied to the entire population at 451d9.

459e2   **the Rulers:** since they will be over 50 years of age (7.540a), they will be mostly too old for 'official' breeding (460e7: till age 55), but not necessarily past sexual desire

(461b9–c1). The myth at 3.415b1–2 might seem to suggest that Rulers and Auxiliaries would breed separately, but this is incompatible (where women are concerned, and in other respects) with the scheme envisaged in bk. 5.

459e3   **herd...free from faction:** *agelê*, 'herd', like 'flock' (el), was previously applied to the whole citizen body (n. 451c8); its appearance here echoes the use of the term for bands of young boys and girls in various Doric states; see *Laws* 2.666e2–3 (in a context of criticism), Plut. *Lyc.* 17.2 with MacDowell (1986) 54–5 on Sparta, Willetts 13–26 on Crete. Cf. 6.498c1 for a further image of Guardians as grazing animals.

'Faction', *stasis*, epitomises everything that threatens to cause disunity in a social group (and, by extension, within the individual soul): see esp. 4.440b3, e5, 442d1, 444b1. As well as being a symptom of injustice (1.351d4), it is the reverse of the *koinônia*, the 'sharing' or 'communism', which forms bk. 5's root principle: nn. 449c8, 465b8. The present passage intimates that, after the abolition of private property, sexuality would be the main source of fragmentation within the Guardian class: the *body*, if nothing else, would remain a locus of intensely individual feelings (cf. n. 464d9) – hence P.'s resort to the idea of systematic political deception.

459e5   **festivals:** *Laws* 6.775a (cf. 784b1) envisages small-scale wedding festivities, but that is in a context of permanent marriages, not sexual communism. Here P. thinks of occasions in which the entire class would participate; their religious nature lends solemn authority to the sexual unions arranged within them. Cf. the 'sacred marriages' at 458e3–4, and note the argument of *Laws* 8.838b–9c that sexual mores can be strongly shaped by religious convictions.

459e6f.   **hymns:** probably to the gods, though praise-poems to the Guardians themselves is a possibility, in view of 468d9 (see n.). After the major critique of existing Greek poetry, from Homer onwards, in bks. 2-3, 'our' is here emphatic: *these* are poets who will know how to use their art to laud the virtues of both gods and good men (cf. 10.607a3-5). Yet, somewhat anomalously, these same poets will presumably not themselves be Guardians, but will, *qua* 'artisans', belong to the third class of citizens (cf. 3.401b-c, 6.493d4). Or are we to imagine some of the Rulers themselves composing the hymns, along the (deeply unpromising) lines of *Laws* 8.829c-e?

460a3–4   **number of males:** the salience of this factor is presumably attributable to military considerations. P.'s account does not quantify such details, though it assumes that a demographic policy, aimed at overall stability of population (a5-6), could be worked out by the Rulers (helped by 'births and deaths' records, *Laws* 6.785a-b): cf. *Laws* 5.740b–41a for the same aim; on techniques of population control, see Preus's article. Such questions may have been touched on by earlier political theorists such as Hippodamus of Miletus (flor. c. 450), the first Greek 'town planner' (J.B. Ward Perkins, *Cities of Ancient Greece & Italy* [London, 1974] ch. 3), who proposed a hypothetical citizen body of 10,000, divided into three classes: see Arist. *Pol.* 1267b22 ff.; for the figure 10,000, which seems to have been a standard model, cf. P. *Epist.* 7.337c, with H. Schaefer, *Historia* 10 (1961) 292-317. For some demographic ideas which reflect P.'s own influence, see Arist. *Pol.* 1326a5-b25. In the discussion of population at 4.423a-c, a possible figure of 1,000 was suggested for the Auxiliaries, while 4.428d11-9a1 indicates that the artisan class would be the largest, and the Rulers (the 'true Guardians') the smallest (cf. n. 458b9 f.). *Laws* 5.737e1-2, 746d, for what it is worth, propose 5,040 families as the citizen-body of the city envisaged there.

These scanty details point towards a citizen population comparable to many modest Greek city-states, probably no greater than Hippodamus's 10,000, and certainly much smaller than that of P.'s own Athens, which may have had c. 25,000 adult males, and perhaps a roughly similar number of women, in the early 4th cent. Since P.'s

Guardians will not engage in economic activity, but will be supported by the city's farmers (n. 463b3), the latter will need ample land allotments (cf. Arist. *Pol.* 1265a13 ff., on *Laws*). Yet P. seems confident that such an arrangement could be maintained without recourse to territorial acquisitiveness, which is said to be the main cause of war at 2.373d–e (cf. Introduction p. 22).

460a5–6　**in order that our city:** a2–4 clearly concerned the numbers of Guardians, yet the present clause seems to refer to the entire population. It is simplest to infer that P. intends the Rulers to pay special attention to the size of the Guardian class, but as part of a larger demographic policy (last n.).

460a8　**specious lotteries:** the idea of this mechanism, part of the Rulers' 'falsehood and deception' (459c8), may conceivably betray P.'s familiarity with, or suspicion of, the misuse of the 'lot' in many appointment procedures in classical Athens. *kompsos*, 'specious', has connotations of cleverness and ingenuity (see e.g. 7.525d1 for the positive sense of 'subtle'), but also, sometimes, of false or exaggerated appearances (6.499a6, *Laws* 1.634a3). P.'s use of the word is more often than not derogatory; yet Arist. *Pol.* 1265a12 applies it to P.'s own dialogues (see Introduction p. 2).

460a9　**pairing:** *sunerxis*, an act of joining together, is a rare term, found elsewhere in P. only at *Tim.* 18d9 (a summary of this passage); cf. the cognate verb at 461b5. It may be meant to give a tone of official gravity to the (potentially absurd) political control of sexual behaviour (Adam, on 460c1, suspects an association with animals). Much the same is true of *sunkoimêsis*, b3 (cf. *Phdr.* 255e5). Note the implication that there will be no standard concept of adultery among the Guardians; contrast 4.443a9, where it was cited as a category of immorality.

460b1　**young men:** *neos* is here used loosely; it should correspond to *akmazontôn*, 'in their prime', at 459b2–3, and to the age-brackets given in e below.

460b1　**any other context:** presumably including athletic competition and other physical tests. But, given the nature of the Guardian class, and especially the need to find Auxiliaries who can progress to the level of Rulers, identification of 'the best' should take full account of intellectual as well as physical qualities (cf. 455b, 7.535a–c, with n. 461a8 f.). So Annas (1981) 175 is reductive in stating that the eugenic programme selects only for physique and courage (a Spartan one-sidedness, which P. would reject as such: cf. n. 458c8–9). It remains an open question, of course, whether it is realistic of P. to imagine that physical and intellectual excellence could be consistently bred for in a particular group.

460b2　**must...give:** we would expect δοτέον to be a verbal noun (gerund), and γέρα ... καὶ ἆθλα its object (precisely as at 6.503a6–7); but the sentence continues as though the latter nouns were nominatives (which should have required the plural verbal adj., δοτέα). Either (i) δοτέον is passive, on the analogy of singular indicatives with neuter pl. subjs. (cf. Adam, and note 3.403b1); or (ii) there is anacolouthon, i.e. 'we must give...rewards, and among them <must be given> a more generous chance...'

460b2　**among them:** others would be praise-songs, and special portions of food, on official occasions (468c–e, cf. *Laws* 8.829c–e); for 'privileges' cf. 465d9.

460b3　**with the women:** Soc. speaks as though only males could be sexually rewarded; but why not women themselves, given their service as Auxiliaries (and their equal experience of sexual desire, so 458d1–3 implied)? The same point recurs at 468b–c. It is hard in this instance (cf. n. b9–10) to suppose that we are meant to supply a corresponding point for female Guardians; much likelier is an inhibition on P.'s part about treating citizen women as the active partners in sexual relationships. We need also to remind ourselves that P. is envisaging a situation in which the Auxiliaries would regard sex purely as a gratification, and would be ignorant of the concealed eugenic policy: this could surely only exacerbate the status of sexual activity as a locus of potential resentment and rivalry (see nn. 458d2-3, 459e3).

460b7 **be taken:** with no allowance for maternal feelings; the system aims to block such feelings, as well as other forms of individual sentiment. A biological parent-child bond is acknowledged at *Symp.* 208b4–5; cf. n. c9 f. below.

460b9 **for surely:** the μέν, if correct, is purely emphatic, since there is no antithesis implied; cf. Denniston 365, who compares e.g. 3.403e8.

460b9f. **shared by women:** a clear, if passing, statement that women will be able to rise to the highest political ranks. The point is reiterated at 7.540c5–9, in a passage which perhaps indicates that P. would want his readers to supply, at every mention of male Guardians, equivalent propositions for the females of the class: it is therefore misleading, as well as wrong, to speak of 'only one reference to women officials' (Annas [1976] 311). Some allowance certainly needs to be made for P.'s need to avoid saying '...and women' at every relevant stage in the argument. Even so, some aspects of the discussion do not comport well with the principle of 'female equivalence'; these mostly involve matters of sexuality and warfare: see nn. b3, 467c2-3.

460c1 **compound:** *sêkos* has two main senses (LSJ s.v.) – (i) a compound for animals (cf. *Tht.* 174e1; (ii) a sacred enclosure. The former best chimes with the other animal imagery in bk. 5 (451d4–9, 454e1, 455d9, 459a2 ff., e1–3).

460c2 **nurses:** who are probably to be imagined as belonging to the third, i.e. artisan, class (cf. 2.373c2–3); the alternative is to suppose them slaves (cf. nn. 465c3, 469c6–7, with *Laws* 7.790a6). Wet-nurses were a familiar element in well-to-do Greek society of all periods: e.g. *Prt.* 325c7, Hom. *Od.* 19.354–5, 482–3, Aesch. *Cho.* 749–60, Ar. *Knights* 716, *Lys.* 958, *Thesm.* 609, Thphr. *Char.* 16.12, 20.5, with Garner 113–18, 317–18. Both free and servile examples are known from classical Athens: cf. Dem. 47.55–6, 57.35–45, with Lacey 171–2, Lefkowitz & Fant 29 (cf. 110–11, 164–8); *Laws* 7.789e–90a assumes large numbers of them.

460c3–5 **dispose of:** i.e. expose, with the intention of allowing to die; cf. 459e1, and see Adam I 357–60 for detailed argument. P.'s language is oblique and solemnly euphemistic (cf. Rankin [1964] 46–9, [1965] 410–16), but the verb *katakruptein*, unique in P., denotes physical concealment: cf. the pit used for infanticide at Sparta, Plut. *Lyc.* 16.1–2 (a passage which suggests P. may have had a Spartan model in mind), with MacDowell (1986) 52–4. If what was meant were mere demotion to the artisan class (cf. n. 456a8), as Viljoen 63-6 contends (citing *Tim.* 19a), why not just say so? (For the third class itself, 2.372b8 f. may imply use of exposure. Cf. also 10.615c1-2?)

Infanticide by exposure was a far from rare practice in classical Greece, and one against which there was no legal bar (Harrison I 71, for Athens): *Tht.* 160e8 (cf. 151c4–5) – a crucial piece of evidence – shows that a decision whether to rear a neonate was commonly faced, sometimes on medical grounds; and an extensive vocabulary for exposure existed in Greek (M. Golden, *Phoenix* 35 [1981] 316–31, at 330–1). Cf. Arist. *Pol.* 1335b19–23, which mentions the possibility of exposure on grounds of physical defect or population control, and the Gortyn law-code, cols. 3–4 (R.F. Willetts, *The Law Code of Gortyn* [Berlin, 1967] 41–2, with 29). For general discussion see e.g. Lacey 164–7, Garner 84–93, 311–13, and the discerning critique of recent arguments by C. Patterson, *TAPA* 115 (1985) 103–23. R. Sallares, *The Ecology of the Ancient Greek World* (London, 1991) 129–60, offers a new demographic approach, but his statement that there is 'no evidence' (151) for infanticide in classical Athens is false. Taken as a whole, Greek exposure of infants encompassed both effective infanticide and abandonment of the kind intended to allow the baby's rescue (cf. Ar. *Clouds* 531); both practices have been widespread in other societies: see, respectively, W. Langer, 'Infanticide: A Historical Survey', *Hist. of Childhood Quarterly* 1 (1974) 353-74; and J. Boswell, *The Kindness of Strangers* (New York, 1988).

460c6 **pure:** the term as such is not remarkable (cf. e.g. Arist. *Ath. Pol.* 13.5), but it is applied not to lineage or legitimacy, but to the eugenically desired qualities, both intellectual and physical, required for the Guardians. Cf. 6.495b–6a.

460c8 **for feeding:** τροφῆς is genitive sing. of τροφή (object of ἐπιμελεῖσθαι), not (ctr. Grube's translation) nominative pl. of τροφεύς. ἐπιμελεῖσθαι is here a technical term for an official sphere of control: see e.g. 6.499b6, *Laws* 11.929e10, and LSJ s.v., 2. οὗτοι are the magistrates, both male and female, of b–c; they are the equivalent of the 'nursing supervisors' of *Laws* 6.784a, 7.794a (does Plut. *Lyc.* 3.3 attest the existence of some such group of women in Sparta?). P. may assume that such people possess the knowledge of midwives: at *Tht.* 149b–50a the latter are said to possess eugenic principles; on the profession, cf. Garner 61–4, 307, and n. 455e6.

460c9f. **taking every precaution:** the phrase tacitly acknowledges the biological existence of a 'maternal bond', whose operation is to be counteracted. Such bonding would be a force for 'individualism', of the kind which P. associates with separate families (cf. 464d1–2); it would thus cut against the collectivist ethos of the Guardians' lives. Cf. nn. b7 above, and 467a10 f.

460d4 **broken nights:** in Athens, even mothers in households with slaves would sometimes get up to breast-feed; cf. Lys. 1.9-14. But presumably, given the familiarity of wet-nurses (n. c2), P. is proposing an advantage that was already customarily enjoyed in rich families.

460d4–5 **wet-nurses:** P. uses two virtually synonymous terms (cf. c2); in so far as they can be distinguished (cf. 2.373c2–3), *trophos* probably has a wider scope, covering women who look after children beyond the stage of weaning. P. clearly has in mind a situation in which child-care as a whole, not just feeding of infants, would be taken away from the female Guardians. This would put nurses in a position of potential influence over children's early development, a point alluded to at 2.377c2–3, *Laws* 10.887d3. It would be a function of the nursing magistrates (b8, c8) to control such influence.

460d6 **relief:** from the burdens to which G. referred at 450c4; the women will thus be freed, so far as possible, for the same training and duties as male Guardians. Lefkowitz (1989) 497 objects that limitation of breast-feeding would allow the women to bear *more* children (cf. Arist. *Gen. An.* 777a12–15 for recognition of the physiological facts), and Huby 22 that large numbers of women would be simultaneously pregnant. But it is unclear whether P. himself, given his aim of stable population (a2-6 above), recognises these implications (cf. n. e4-5 below). *Laws* 6.785b8 cites child-bearing, not just pregnancy, as an obstacle to military service for women, but the present passage gives the impression (without addressing details) that this difficulty is susceptible to an administrative solution. For 'female Guardians', lit. 'Guardians' women/wives', see n. 456b9.

460d9 **we said:** at 459b1–3.

460e1–2 **twenty...thirty:** the discrepancy reflects the one biological difference between the sexes accepted at 454d10 f. Arist. *Pol.* 1335a7–10 suggests upper limits of 70 and 50, respectively, to the procreative careers of men and women, but clearly thinks that these are extremes; cf. ib. b26–37, proposing a more realistic limit of 50 for most males. As the next nn. show, there is nothing radical about P.'s figures in the present passage.

460e4–5 **twenty to...forty:** it was not unusual in Greek societies for brides to be appreciably younger than 20; cf. Hes. *WD* 698 (?c.16: see West *ad loc.*), Xen. *Oec.* 7.5 (14), Arist. *Pol.* 1335a28 (18), with Lacey 106–7, 162–3, 212, and Wyse on Isaeus 3.31.2. P., given his dominant concern with eugenics, presumably has reasons (Arist. *Pol.* 1335a11–24 gives several) for doubting the wisdom of child-bearing by younger girls (though *Laws* 6.785b suggests marriage between the ages of 16 and 20; cf. 8.833d): Spartan practice, where girls married later than at Athens (Xen. *Lac.* 1.6–7), is a possible influence here; see Cartledge 94, MacDowell (1986) 72–4. One need not follow Lefkowitz (1989) 497 in inferring that Guardians will bear children *throughout* this twenty-year period; the point depends on demographic factors about which P. is simply vague: cf. nn. 459d7–8, 460a3–4.

460e5–7 **from the age...:** i.e. 25–55. In the *Laws*, P.'s suggestions for the age of males at marriage are: 30–35 (4.721a–d, 6.785b), 25–35 (6.772d); cf. Hes. *WD* 695–7 (c.30), Solon 27.9 West (28–35), Arist. *Pol.* 1335a29 (37 or slightly less), and see M. Golden, *Phoenix* 35 (1981) 322 n. 21, Garner 210–13, 332. The identification of 25 as the end of a man's 'sharpest fitness for running' (perhaps a poetic phrase referring to horses: see Adam) probably reflects the belief that extreme athletic exercise is not a good accompaniment to procreation: this idea occurs at Arist. *Pol.* 1335b5–7, in a passage which seems to betray Platonic influence; also related are the Pythagorean principles in Aristoxenus fr. 39 Wehrli, Iambl. *Vita Pyth.* 209–13 (DK I 475–6), on which see the Introduction n. 36.

461a1–2 **physical and intellectual:** the eugenic policy presupposes that both types of quality are genetically transmitted (cf. 455b with nn. 460b1, 461a8 f.). Despite the ostensible suggestion that a person's intellectual prime is over by 55, bk. 7 will describe a scheme of philosophical training that culminates at the age of 50 (7.540a4). But P. is thinking here only of mental acuteness, strength of memory, etc.; older philosophers may grow weaker in these respects, but they will have attained a depth of knowledge that makes them more advanced in the pursuit of (metaphysical) truth.

461a3 **anyone:** the subject of the sentence, though qualified by masculine adjs., presumably encompasses women as well as men; on the other hand, P. may assume that illicit sexual relations would be more likely to be instigated by men (cf. n. 460b3). Here, and at b4–7, P. again acknowledges that sex poses acute problems for the desired unity of the Guardian class; cf. n. 458d2–3. The whole sentence, a3–b2, is composed in somewhat formal language (cf. n. a5), including a long series of paired and balanced phrases: the effect is meant to be redolent of a written law (b4). Cf. Rankin (1965) 413.

461a4 **impious:** see n. 458e1.

461a5 **propagating:** the verb *phituein* occurs mostly in poetry (cf. Friis Johansen & Whittle on Aesch. *Suppl.* 313); its tone here is solemn, perhaps legalistic: cf. *Critias* 116c6 (myth of Atlantis), *Laws* 9.879d1 (text of a law).

461a5–6 **goes undetected:** the implication is that *were* an illicit pregnancy of this kind discovered, it would be officially dealt with by abortion (n. c5 below).

461a7 **priestesses, priests:** who will be in charge of the city's temples, shrines, etc. (and would presumably be members of the Guardian class); the combination is common in the *Laws* (e.g. 6.759a2, 7.800b1, 8.828b4). P. says very little about this aspect of the state in the *Rep.*; for the kind of detail he might have supplied, cf. e.g. *Laws* 6.759a–d, with Morrow 411–34. But in both works it is clear that a strong link would exist with Apollo's shrine at Delphi: see n. 469a4. It is also evident, given bk. 5's general rejection of individualism and the family, that the condemnation of *private* religion at *Laws* 10.909d–10e would fit the lives of the *Rep.*'s Guardians too.

461a8f. **good and beneficial:** see n. 457b4–5. The prayer that parents should be better than their children may have heroic overtones: cf. Hom. *Il.* 6.479, Soph. *Aj.* 550–1. It is assumed both that moral qualities are heritable, and that eugenic breeding *could* produce progressive improvement: cf. 4.424a, where it is not quite clear whether P. propounds Lamarckianism, i.e. the idea that acquired features can be genetically transmitted (see Arist. *Gen. An.* 721b29–34 for an explicit formulation of this view); 8.546a2–7 (inevitable human deterioration, because of incorrect breeding); *Plt.* 310c–e (moral character is partly inherited).

461b2 **irresponsibility:** the only occurrence of *akrateia* in the *Rep.*; it signifies the contrary of 'self-control', *sôphrosunê*, which is one of the prime virtues required of Auxiliaries (cf. n. 458d2–3). Irresponsibility implies surrender to excessive or inappropriate pleasures: see esp. *Laws* 5.733e-4b. The Guardian class would be trained and expected to resist sexual desire, except when its indulgence received the endorsement of the Rulers; but P. is too realistic to imagine that this would be an easy thing to maintain (n. 459e3).

461b5 **pairing them:** the verb *sunergein* is cognate with *sunerxis* at 460a9 (see n.).

461b6 **uncertified:** *anegguon* is a rare term, literally denoting a child of parents whose union lacked an *egguê*, 'betrothal' or contract to marry (Harrison I 3–9). Although P.'s whole scheme depends on the abolition of individual marriages, he retains for the Guardians' sexual relations, and the offspring which they produce for the state, the social force of a distinction between legitimate and illegitimate unions. For 'unholy' cf. 458e3–4.

461b9f. **pass the age of breeding:** why, after the rigorous control of younger Auxiliaries, does P. allow sexual freedom to women over 40 and men over 55? Probably because, first, he supposes that the chances of reproduction are greatly diminished by this stage (but cf. c5–6), and, secondly, he believes that sexual desire will take more moderate and controllable form at this age.

461c1–4 **except for daughter, mother...:** because of the freedom indicated at b10 f., P. mentions incest first in connection with sexual relations beyond the age of official breeding. But what is said here must apply to the reproductive pairings of Auxiliaries too (see e1–3). Given the use of standard kinship terms before the explanation of their new application (d2 ff.), we might detect signs that P. is working out details in the process of writing. He here mentions only incest between direct ascendants and descendants, omitting the other standard Greek incest taboo, on marriage between full siblings (cf. *Laws* 8.838a-b, anon. *Dissoi Logoi* 2.15, with Harrison I 22-3), though e1 then seems to imply that brothers/sisters *were* covered by the present passage: this prepares the way for the ambivalent provisions made at e2-3 below (see n.). Incest as a consequence of sexual communism is mentioned at Ar. *Eccl.* 1040-42. About the risk of homosexual incest, raised at Arist. *Pol.* 1262a32-7 (cf. Xen. *Lac.* 2.13), P. seems unconcerned.

461c4 **And we shall allow all this...:** my translation breaks the Greek sentence into two. With ταῦτά γ' ἤδη πάντα we must assume ἀφήσομεν (or the like) from b10.

461c5 **not...reach birth:** a euphemistic reference to abortion (cf. Rankin [1965] 414–16), which is here contemplated neither for medical reasons (*Tht.* 149d3), nor on demographic grounds (*Laws* 5.740d5–6, Arist. *Pol.* 1335b24–6), but because P. considers it eugenically out of the question that older Guardians (b9–10) could produce offspring worth keeping for the class. The Hippocratic Oath contains a clause refusing to provide abortifacient drugs, but it is contentious how far this reflects general medical practice: for a possible Pythagorean connection see L. Edelstein, *The Hippocratic Oath* (Baltimore, 1943) 10-18, a view questioned by Burkert (1972) 294. A massive treatment of abortion in antiquity is supplied by E. Nardi, *Procurato aborto nel mondo greco romano* (Milan, 1971): see 116-22, 502-3, 561-3, for the present and other passages of P. Nardi's book is summarised and reviewed by S. K. Dickison,

Arethusa 6 (1973) 159-66; cf. also Garner 52-5, 305-6, Lefkowitz & Fant 222-4, Preus 251-6.

461c5–6   **no nurture is available:** cf. 459d9 f.; both these passages, in view of the tellingly ominous language of 460c3–5 (see n.), are best taken as implying exposure. If P. had demotion to the lower class in mind, it is hard to see why he should not say so; but exposure has a gravity which will explain the use of euphemism in all these passages. See Rankin (1965) 410, 414.

461c8f.   **how will they recognise:** the question stems, of course, from Soc.'s earlier suggestion that the Guardians will not live in families (457d1–3, 460c9 f.).

461d2   **They won't:** Arist. *Pol.* 1262a14–24 objected that facial resemblance might reveal biological kinship; given the small numbers of the Auxiliaries (n. 460a3–4), this has some pertinence. Aristotle also wondered about the possible sexual consequences of transferring children between classes (n. 456a8), ib. 1262b24–35: such practical details are ignored by P.

461d3   **tenth...seventh:** the figures refer to lunar months, and correspond to around $8^3/_4$–$9^3/_4$ and $5^3/_4$–$6^3/_4$modern calendar months. The provision for premature births is probably based on the assumption that 'seventh-month' offspring are the earliest to be viable: cf. Arist. *Hist. Anim.* 584a35–b3, with Garner 43–4, 77–8 on the allegedly special perils of the eighth month of pregnancy. Greek medicine in P.'s time paid much attention to calculating gestation periods for humans, and to correlating its variations with viability: see e.g. Hippoc. *Alim.* 42 (270 and 300 days as alternative norms for the full term), with G.E.R. Lloyd, *The Revolutions of Wisdom* (Berkeley, 1987) 259–64. A congeries of ideas on the subject is preserved by Aulus Gellius, *Noct. Att.* 3.16.

461d4   **he will call:** though the spirit of P.'s proposals is evident, his scheme could not be operated for long without the addition of complex qualifications for whose need he seems unaware. The major problem is that Auxiliaries have breeding careers of 20/30 years (460e), and would apparently stand in a 'parental' relation to *all* the children born at marriage festivals throughout that period (cf. n. d7–8). This would in turn make into 'siblings' whole groups of people who, in some cases, effectively belonged to different generations. The resulting overlaps, once the scheme had run for some time, would become confusing to the point of eventual incoherence. E.g. I could be precisely contemporary with some of the offspring of my brothers/sisters (who had been born at the start of a male parent's breeding career, while I had been born at the end): these offspring would be *my* brothers/sisters (because conceived at the same festivals), but the sons/daughters of those other brothers/sisters of mine. Such generational criss-crossings would become increasingly tangled with time, esp. at the grandparent/-child level. There are also apparent gaps in what is envisaged: what, for instance, would children call the non-breeding contemporaries of their 'parents'? how would children promoted from the lowest class (n. 456a8) be integrated? This points to greater tensions in a system which, while applying to intricately inter-related groups, is designed to use only the existing range of kinship terms; cf. nn. e1-2, 463c5-7, and Richards 116-9.

It is not merely pedantic to criticise P.'s proposals in such practical terms (as Aristotle already did), since they must lose in validity, even as a 'sketch' (cf. 3.412b2), if they are intrinsically unworkable. Nor is it sufficient to fall back on a merely approximate application of kinship terms according to broad age-groups, even though this is what the summary at *Tim.* 18d evokes, and perhaps 467a2 also (cf. the comic equivalent at Ar. *Eccl.* 636–7). Even this, though feasible, could not avoid the objection that *all* marriages would then by definition involve siblings: cf. nn. d7–8, e1–2.

461d7–8 **in the period:** this must mean for the entire duration of their 20/30 year breeding careers, as indicated by the imperfect, *egennôn*, 'were breeding' (cf. Richards 117–8); *Tim.* 18d, summarising this passage, confirms this. But, if so, P. restricts relations between members of the same generation to those of quasi-siblings, and this makes untenable his conviction (e1–3) that brother-sister liaisons would be generally avoidable. An alternative, urged by Grube 97–9, is to suppose that only those born at the same marriage festivals will count as brothers/sisters (thus dividing the class into a series of enlarged families). But though d2-4 above might seem to fit with this, it would introduce the kinship category of 'cousins' or collaterals for contemporaries born at different festivals (with corresponding variations in cross-generational relationships). Not only is there is no hint of this anywhere in bk. 5 (cf. n. 463c5-7); it would contradict the statement of *koinônia* at e.g. 457c-d, it is evidently not discerned by Arist. *Pol.* 1261b38 ff., and it would in any case seriously weaken the ethos of tight bonding to which the whole plan aspires (462a-e).

461e1–2 **'sisters' and 'brothers':** P.'s design here comes under acute, probably insupportable, strain. If all members of the Guardian class stand in a basic kinship relation to one another, as 463c5–7 states, then members of the same generation will inevitably be siblings, and *all* 'marriages' will be between 'sister' and 'brother'. Since P. evidently does not accept this, his consistency can be saved only (i) by treating that later passage (spoken by G.) as an over-simplification which omits relationships between 'cousins' and others (see n. d7-8 above); or (ii) by taking 'brothers'/'sisters' at e2 to mean *natural* siblings (see Grube 97-8); or (iii) by positing an implicit limitation to certain peculiar patterns of Guardian marriage (see Adam *ad loc.*). (i) brings with it difficulties of its own (n. 463c5-7). (ii) is hard to credit, first because it would involve an abrupt switch from the *new* denotation of 'brother'/'sister' at e1, and secondly because it would require the Rulers to keep meticulous records of the biological kinship of all the Auxiliaries (something P. has certainly not signalled). (iii) entails a far-fetched upshot, and would anyway entail either remote or no kinship at all between certain Guardians (ctr. 463c5-7). It is hard to avoid the inference that, in arguing boldly for the abolition of the family from the Guardian class, P. has not anticipated the complications of the sexual communism which he imagines as replacing it.

461e2–3 **the law *will* allow:** marriage between siblings was not normally permitted in the Greek world of P.'s day; the rule did not always apply to half-siblings, though the criteria varied (cf. Harrison I 22–3, and n. c1–4 above). The radicalism of P.'s position depends partly on interpretation of his use of 'brother'/'sister' here (n. e1–2). It seems clear enough that the terms do not denote strict biological kinship; P. is merely indicating that their new extension would not need to carry an invariable taboo on sexual relations. This is supported by the reference to 'the lottery', which can only allude to the concealed decisions of the Rulers (460a8–10); for the role of Delphi cf. n. 469a4. *Laws* 8.838a9 treats incest between siblings as something rightly abhorrent to most people. But if P. did not wish to make a major change to standard Greek incest regulations, other philosophers were ready to go much further: the early Stoics Zeno and Chrysippus, perhaps under the influence of the Cynics (Philodemus, *P. Herc.* 339 col. 11), challenged incest taboos altogether (D. Laert. 7.188, Sext. Emp. *Pyr.* 3.246, *SVF* 3.743, 753); and such attitudes may have had earlier antecedents (cf. Xen. *Mem.* 4.4.20-3: the sophist Hippias). Other Greeks are likely to have regarded both parent-child and sibling incest as barbarian practices: see Eur. *Andr.* 173-6, with Stevens' n. On *sunoikein*, 'form unions', cf. n. 456b2.

461e5-466d5

The greatest good for a city is its unity. This will be achieved, in the case of the Guardians, by the effects of the proposed 'sharing', which will erase all sense of personal distance or individual selfishness, and create a social cohesion of consciousness and values which comes as close as possible to the integration of an individual's body and soul. In addition, the Guardians and the rest of the citizens will have a clear awareness of mutual dependence. The Guardian class will treat each other as members of a large family: for this reason, and because of their lack of private property, there will be little or no conflict in their lives. And if they are united, so will be the people as a whole: in this way, the Guardians' 'sharing of women and children' will ensure the preservation and happiness of the entire city.

Having explained the sexual implications of the Guardians' 'sharing' or 'communism', Soc. now turns to the demonstration that such a system is in the best interests of the city. The demonstration hinges entirely on the value of civic unity, and the corresponding evil of divisiveness. In its general formulation at 462a9-b2, the principle of unity is meant to have something like the force of the self-evident: how could any argument for the well-being of a society deny the basic necessity for unity? What remains contentious, of course, is the translation of unity into particular political practices and regulations. P. intends his emphasis on unity to be the complement and fulfilment of the theme of *koinônia* (community, sharing, partnership, etc.) which runs through the entire work (n. 449c8). But *koinônia*, like unity, is a concept which admits, in a human context, both of variations and of degrees of realisation. Any community or social structure must, by definition, involve some degree of cooperation and inter-dependence (i.e. *koinônia*); as Arist. *Pol.* 1260b39-40 puts it, 'it is impossible that citizens should share (*koinônein*) *nothing*, since the state is a kind of partnership (*koinônia*)...' Yet what is so remarkable about this aspect of bk. 5's programme is a paradoxical combination of facts: first, it pushes the idea of *koinônia* to an extreme in the case of the Guardians, by creating for them a collectivist way of life that reaches down as far as their sexual and personal relations; secondly, it hypothesises that this collectivism will not only bind together the Guardians themselves, but guarantee the unity of the city as a whole.

It is a commonplace observation that the collectivism of P.'s city shows the influence of Spartan ideology (an ideology for which the bee simile of Plut. *Lyc.* 25 is especially suggestive), reinforced, perhaps, by more general reflections on militaristic organisation (as the ruthlessly corporate ethic of *Laws* 12.942a-d indicates). Admiration of Sparta (as also of Dorian Crete) is a factor which probably goes back to the historical Socrates (cf. *Crito* 52e6, *Prt.* 342e-3a, Ar. *Birds* 1281-2). At any rate, the traces of Spartan precedents, though almost always qualified and adjusted, are not hard to discern in many details of the *Rep.* (cf. Introduction p. 10 with n. 11). Yet P.'s hypothetical city has to be understood in terms of its own philosophical dynamics: in its abolition of marriage and the *oikos*, as in much else besides, it goes well beyond the Spartan model. It would indeed be surprising if it were otherwise, since the intensity of social unity proposed for the Guardian class is such as to press against the limits of what can even be imagined. Inevitably, therefore, P.'s thesis raises a whole series of acute problems. It posits a degree of unity which, in Aristotle's terms, would turn the social entity into something *other* than a city (n. 462b4). P. himself practically acknowledges this, since he requires of his Guardians a sense of mutual closeness for which his paradigm is the psycho-physical integration of an individual (462c-d). This gives an ironic twist to the argument, for it is precisely 'individualism', *idiôsis* (462b8), which the communism of the Guardian class is meant to eliminate. Something comparable takes place in P.'s treatment of the family and kinship. These institutions are perceived as forces for fragmentation and division within existing cities, yet the cohesion of the Guardians revolves around a sense of kinship which represents an enlarged version of the current system: here P.'s largest difficulty is that he is trying to use for purely integrative purposes a network of relations which, in practice, combine inclusive with *exclusive* functions. See the Introduction p. 19.

But even if the unity of the Guardians could be realised as proposed, we are left, as already indicated, with the difficulty of understanding how, as P. so cursorily states, the unity of the entire city would follow from it (n. 465b9-10). The issues raised by this depend partly on interpretation of 'citizenship' in this context (nn. 462b5, 463c3); but they also take us down to the roots of P.'s thinking about the relationship between individuals and a society. All that can be said here is that beneath bk. 5's conception of the unity of the city, there lies the tenet that the rule of reason must always be for the best (9.590d), and P. is sometimes encouraged by this principle into a paternalist faith that *all* the inhabitants of a just city could be persuaded of the benefits of good government (nn. 463b1, 466b1).

461e7   **by far the best:** the second of the aims which Soc. set himself at 458b4–6.

461e8   **securely established:** such language is sometimes associated in P. with the conditions of full knowledge; cf. n. 479c4. But it is hard to see that implication here, since the agreement which Soc. and G. go on to reach depends on a series of assumptions, many of which can readily be questioned.

462a3   **greatest good:** 456e6–7 gave one implicit answer to this question – i.e. that the city should contain the best people possible. But that condition, though necessary, is not sufficient for the city's happiness, which also requires a political organisation to ensure that 'the best' have control of the city.

462a6   **pattern:** lit. 'track' or 'footprint'; but the image is not, as commonly, that of following tracks (e.g. 2.365d2, 4.432d3), but one of matching something up with its print (cf. *Tht.* 193c3–4). Cf. the idea of testing things by reference to a *paradeigma* or ideal model at 472c.

462a9   **can we name:** ἔχομεν picks up ἔχομεν εἰπεῖν from a3.

462b1   **many...rather than one:** this harks back to bk. 4's thesis that happiness, whether in city or individual, involves a condition of complete unity. For the 'many vs. one' motif cf. esp. 4.422e8 ff., 8.551d5 (cities); 4.423d5, 443e1, 8.554d9–10 (individuals). P. associates states of internal conflict particularly with the rich/poor divisions of oligarchy, but it is a fine question, already raised by Arist. *Pol.* 1264a22-6, how far his own class-divisions contain a potential for political antagonism: cf. n. 463b1.

462b4   **sharing:** a further appearance of *koinônia* (nn. 449c5, 8), an ideology of shared interests; cf. 3.412d–e, and the echo at *Laws* 5.739d1–3. But this idea involves multiple tensions. P. has already acknowledged the possibility of sexual jealousy and resentment among Auxiliaries (n. 459e3), and, as the subsequent nn. will indicate, there are conceptual difficulties in the way in which the nature of political unity is elaborated. The most subtle objection of all was stated by Arist. *Pol.* 1261a16–61b15, where he argues that if civic unity were carried to an extreme, the result would be no longer a *city* at all, but some kind of quasi-individual (precisely, of course, what P. aspires to, 462c10 ff.): complete unity, Aristotle contends, would 'destroy' the very thing whose 'greatest good' it is supposed to be. Cf. Simpson 103–6.

462b5   **all the citizens:** this ought to mean all three classes (Rulers, Auxiliaries, artisans/farmers); cf. d8, 463a, and 'the greatest majority' (c7 below). Yet at 463b10 ff. the sense of kinship involves only the Guardians (Rulers and Auxiliaries combined). This instability extends more widely within the present section, and it stems from the fact that P.'s scheme takes little cognizance of the Guardians' dealings with the labouring class, or of the latter's own view of the city. But communism of all citizens may nonetheless have been P.'s ultimate ideal: see *Laws* 5.739c1–2, d1–3, with n. 450c1 above.

462b8 **individualism:** *idiôsis*, an extremely rare term, is almost certainly a coinage of P.'s (in whom it appears only here); formed as a noun of action from the verb *idiousthai* (also rare: see 8.547c1, *Laws* 5.742b7), its *prima facie* sense is 'making one's own', i.e. appropriation (cf. *oikeiousthai*, 466c1). But the context requires it to embrace all the ways in which individuals can conceive of themselves as independent agents, with interests and needs ('pleasures'/ 'pains') of their own: it would arise, in other words, wherever something might be spoken of as 'personal', 'private', or 'individual'. This means that P.'s argument is aimed not merely at selfishness (cf. *Laws* 5.731d-2b), but at the psychological basis of individuality: cf. Lucas 228-30, who suggests that P. elides the distinction between selfishness and selflessness. It is possible to object not only that feelings of individuality are a vital spring of much behaviour, and cannot simply be erased (cf. Arist. *Pol.* 1261b32-62a1, 1262b22-4, 1263a40-b1), but also that P. himself seems to admit this fact, first by allowing for individual achievements, rewards, etc., among the Guardians (e.g. 460b1-3, 468b2 ff.), secondly, by using the very notion of individuality as a model of an integrated entity (c10 ff.).

462c4–8 **'mine'...'not mine':** an inescapably paradoxical formulation (cf. n. c10), since application of 'mine' is necessarily singular. If *all* citizens applied 'mine' to *all* the same things, the word would no longer serve any purpose: the situation would be exactly as if all citizens had the same name (cf. n. 463d1). It would therefore have been apter to stress the desirability of reducing the use of 'mine' to a minimum (which is how Plut. *Mor.* 140d-e, 484b, paraphrases the passage), and making the use of 'our(s)' the norm: so that, e.g., Auxiliaries would speak of 'our fathers/mothers' etc., not of 'my father/mother' (cf. Lucas 225). Why then, here and again at 463e5, does P. phrase the point in this way? His contention has to be understood in symbolic rather than literal terms (for in practice, of course, even the Guardians would still have many contexts in which to use 'mine' in its normal sense). 'Mine' is a token of the values, desires and principles of individual possessiveness, which P. wishes to see replaced by the citizens', or at least the Guardians', feelings of communal identity. The passage is criticised at Arist. *Pol.* 1261b16-62a14, 1262b14-17; cf. Simpson 107-11. Iambl. *Vita Pyth.* 167 alleges a Pythagorean influence on P. here.

462c7 **the greatest majority:** cf. n. b5 above.

462c7 **apply...to the same things:** a precise parallel for the mss. reading, ἐπὶ τὸ αὐτό, is lacking, but passages such as *Soph.* 237c2–3 do, *pace* Adam, lend some support for the accusative. ἐπί + accus. is more appropriate to deliberate application of an expression, while ἐπί + dative (cf. 470b7, with LSJ s.v. ἐπί, B III 5) better suits the usual application of a term (though *Soph.* 218c2–3 somewhat blurs this distinction).

462c10 **closest to...a single individual:** the suggestion heightens the paradox inherent in the preceding remarks on '(not) mine'; P.'s paradigm of unity is that very thing - the individual - which the argument takes as naturally inimical to civic unity. *Pace* Adam, the point is distinct from the basic analogy between city and individual which runs through the *Rep.* (e.g. 2.368e-9a, 4.435e, 8.544d-e): that analogy is essentially ethical, and asserts that the same virtues, arising from the same underlying forces, can be predicated both of souls and of political states. But the present argument advances the much more challenging proposition that a city, or its ruling class, should aspire to something like the unity of *experience* which characterises persons. Cf. the religious use of similar imagery by St Paul, *Ep. Cor.* I 12.12-26.

There are both conceptual and ethical difficulties in this new comparison. (i) The idea is, in a strict sense, inconceivable. Individuality has a biological basis; it involves, as Soc. goes on to explain, a psycho-physical integration and continuity. It is intractably obscure how any social entity, no matter how closely bonded by common beliefs or shared values, could approximate to this aspect of the nature of a person. (ii) Precisely because of the biological basis of individuality, it is not easy to see how human behaviour could be culturally moulded so as to subordinate all personal drives, as P. advocates, to the interests of the group, especially since P.'s own scheme requires significant achievements by individuals (see n. b8). At the most, then, the present passage functions as rhetorical symbolism in the service of the larger argument for ideological unity.

462c11   **shared awareness:** the same term, *koinônia*, as is used repeatedly of the state's social and political arrangements (nn. 449c5, 8). Here it refers to the interrelation of body and soul as a unified field of sensation (or, in one use, consciousness). The language of c11–d1 is somewhat convoluted and open to slightly different construals. A fuller explication might run: 'the entire partnership which extends through the body to [i.e. as far as] the soul, <joining them> into the single organisation of [i.e. under the control of] the ruling element within it...' This final 'it' could in principle refer to the partnership or the soul (or even, though less likely, the organisation). The point is not readily decided, but anyway makes little difference to the idea that the psycho-physical combination involves a centre (the ruling element) of sensation or awareness.

    Adam (cf. I 360–1), citing *Laws* 10.903d3–4 (where, however, the emphasis falls on the soul's temporary association with a body), accepts the reading of Ven. 184, τεταγμένη, 'organised', in c12, and punctuates accordingly. But we should keep the dominant mss. reading, τεταμένη: the corporeally 'extended' capacity for perception, with its link between body and soul, is described in very similar language at 9.584c4–5 and *Tht.* 186c1–2; it may be instructive to compare the description of veins at *Tim.* 65d1. Note that P.'s point is stressed by the use of συν– compounds (c12, d1), which become a motif in what follows (e2, 463b7, 9, e3, 464a2); interaction of body and soul is one variety of *sumpaschein* (e.g. ps.-Arist. *Physiogn.* 808b11-14). It is tempting to see the passage as partially anticipating the Aristotelian doctrine of a 'common sense' or unitary faculty of perception (esp. *De somno et vig.* 455a12-b2: n.b. the use of συντείνει at a34). It can also be read in a perspective of ideas leading to the Greek discovery of the nervous system in the Hellenistic period: see F. Solmsen, 'Greek Philosophy & the Discovery of the Nerves', *Kleine Schriften* I (Hildesheim, 1968) 536-82.

462d1   **feels...sensation:** treating P.'s two verbs, ἤσθετο and συνήλγησεν, as a compound idea (hendiadys). The aorists mark the instantaneous nature of the experience, but also express a generalisation about a regular occurrence. The term 'gnomic' is sometimes applied to such aorists, which belong to a family of usage rather than a narrow type. Notice also the change from the aorist participle, d2, to the present, d4: although such variation is not always significant, the aorist here probably represents the onset of pain, while the present indicates a physical process or condition.

462d8–e1   **when an individual...:** thus the unity of the city will entail a highly developed psychological capacity for sympathy or identification between its citizens. (It is curious that P. here appears to justify a kind of human fellow-feeling which he will later dismiss in his critique of poetry, 10.605c–6b). But this is something which can only be culturally and ideologically maintained (n. 463d6–7), and whose operation is bound to be provisional and fragile (cf. 466b); here again, the comparison with the nature of individual awareness appears unrealistic (n. c10).

462e3   **well-governed:** for the concept of *eunomia*, which had particular associations with Spartan ideology (e.g. Xen. *Mem.* 4.4.15 ff.), see my n. on 10.605b3.

462e4–5   **to return...to see:** this corresponds to the earlier suggestion of checking whether the city fits a certain pattern of good or evil (462a5–7).

463a1   **there exists:** the singular verb, ἔστι, before plural subjs. is paralleled at e.g. 2.363a3 (but is to be distinguished from a series of singular subjs., e.g. Arist. *EE* 1231b27); its use is eased both by its initial position, and by the sense that 'magistrates and people' form a political compound: cf. LSJ s.v. εἰμί (*sum*) A. V, and Dodds on *Grg.* 500d2. 'Magistrates', *archontes*, although the same word as P. uses for his 'Rulers', is here equivalent to the wider use of 'Guardians': as b1 shows, it includes Auxiliaries (n. 458b9 f.).

463a8   **most:** i.e. cities with régimes which P. would classify as oligarchic, timocratic, or despotic/tyrannic (bks. 8–9 *passim*). In all such cities, the magistrates/rulers are permanently distinguishable from the 'people', and thus merit the appellation 'masters'; only in democracies such as Athens, where most magistracies are open (typically for annual service) to all the people, is the dichotomy of rulers and ruled blurred.

463b1   **'saviours'...'helpers':** for the former see 465d8, and e.g. 3.417a5–6, 6.497a5, 502d1. It is the primary task of good rulers to 'preserve' or 'safeguard' (*sôzein*) the state (*Plt.* 297b2), a function built into the very concept of 'Guardians' as protectors (cf. esp. 4.414b1–3, with 6.484d3 for synonymity of *sôzein* and *phulattein*); *sôtêria* was a slogan in contemporary Athenian politics (cf. Ar. *Eccl.* 202, 209, 396 ff., with David 23–5). 'Helpers', *epikouroi*, is the normal denotation for 'Auxiliaries' within the Guardian class: but that title refers to their subservience to the rulers (see 458c1, 414b5), whereas here the description embraces *all* Guardians (cf. n. a1).

P. posits a sense of mutual dependence between the Guardians and the rest, recalling the original idea that all citizens will be regarded as 'brothers' and 'kinsmen' (3.414e–15a). This, however, points to potential strain within the city's design, for bk. 5 has so far elaborated a system of communism which stresses the special 'kinship' of the Guardians. Thus the general bonds between all citizens must coexist with a heightened form of 'class-consciousness' on the part of the Guardians. Could this be prevented from becoming divisive? P. thinks so, since the Rulers will be ruling for the benefit of all, while the people will recognise the justice of this: there will be agreement and concord between the classes (esp. 4.431d-e, 432a8, 433c6-7), even *philia* or friendship (Introduction n. 50). In particular, the workers will not experience the kind of resentment normally felt by the poor towards the rich, since the city will not be torn by this economic rift (cf. 3.417a-b, 4.422e-3a, 8.551d). As later passages make clear, P. believes that the masses are capable of responding to persuasion from the Rulers: cf. 6.499e-500a (where Adam's n. is too dismissive), 500d-e, 502.

463b3   **'paymasters' and 'providers':** a virtual hendiadys, since the Guardians will be recompensed by the people not with money, but only with subsistence (cf. 465d6–9, 8.543c1–2, 547c2); this was earlier called *misthos*, pay or remuneration, at 3.416e2, a point at which Adeimantus jibbed (4.419a) and which Soc. duly qualified (420a). It is striking that P. should use the word *misthos* at all (again at 464c2), since it was associated not only with the socially 'low' status of hired labourers, but also with the democratic payment of stipends to some office-holders. Yet is is precisely these associations which give P.'s point an ironic edge: the Guardians, for all the preeminence of their natures, will be the political servants of the city. (Compare the idea that the Guardians are also 'craftsmen', *dêmiourgoi*: 3.395c1, 4.421c2, cf. *Laws* 8.829d2). This means that the Rulers will satisfy Soc.'s original principle, in bk. 1, that government is a 'craft' to be exercised for the benefit not of the rulers but of the ruled, and that 'wage-earning' is distinct from the performance of political duties (esp. 1.346b-e). On the workers' possession of monetary wealth see 2.371b.

463b5   **'slaves':** this attitude to the people is a feature of timocracy (8.547c2–3); yet 9.590c–d suggests that, even in the ideal state, the inferior are in a sense 'slaves' to the rational rulers. But, understood more precisely, 9.590c8 refers *only* (cf. c3) to the banausic character who cannot control his desires: the working class of the ideal city need not be of this kind, since it is taken to recognise, and assent to, the justice of the régime (n. b1 above). Annas (1981) 172–4 is therefore unfair to P. in portraying the relation of Guardians and producers as entirely fitting that later model, though it remains true that P. gives only the sketchiest reasons why his farmers and craftsmen should be satisfied with their political status.

463b7 **'fellow-magistrates':** this term was commonly used in Athenian democracy; see the multiple occurrences in state decrees such as ML nos. 72, 76–7, 84.

463c3 **Guardians:** after the earlier reference to 'all the citizens' (n. 462b5), P. now switches back to the Guardians alone, thus causing ambiguity between the unity of a class and the unity of the city. Contrast, in particular, the use of 'brother' at c5 below, with its application to all citizens at 3.414e–15a; and note the ostensible return to 'all citizens' at d6, 464a4. Moreover, since P. gives no reason to suppose that the family would be abolished for the farmers/artisans, there would remain a salient difference between *their* conception of kinship and the Guardians'.

463c5–7 **everyone that he meets:** the *prima facie* implication is that relations between Guardians will be limited to those stipulated; cf. 465b2–3, 471d1–3. But if this were so, it would be impossible for Guardian marriages to avoid 'incest' in relation to the newly extended kinship categories; yet 461e1–3 (see n.) apparently reckoned otherwise. If, however, we take G. to be speaking approximately, and omitting lesser degrees of affinity, two difficulties present themselves: (i) no further relationships (e.g. uncles and cousins) are mentioned elsewhere in the bk.; (ii) if such relationships did exist, they would surely represent a dilution of the *uniform* sense of kinship at which the abolition of individual families is aimed. Cf. n. 461d4. Grube 99 cannot be right to explain this sentence by reference to unknown *blood*-relations: the context clearly evokes a positive sense of shared kinship, not a cautious allowance for concealed affinities.

463d1 **the *terms* of kinship:** for the words/actions contrast cf. e.g. Dem. 9.15. Does P. envisage a situation where people are called *only* by kinship terms, not by individual names? It is impossible to say; but bk. 5 contains no hint of how, if at all, personal names would be given to Guardians: cf. n. 464d9.

463d1 **the case of fathers:** the τε in this phrase creates an expectation that the explanation will be extended to further kinsmen, but the complementary καί is never reached (or, at least, not till the next sentence, d8). The repetition of περὶ πατέρας in d2 seems stylistically casual rather than emphatic.

463d2 **custom requires:** P. here carries over a traditional ethic into the new, extended kinship; for this aspect of behaviour, cf. 4.425b2–3, 443a9, with the anxieties about poetic myth at 2.377e–8e, the view that family discipline particularly deteriorates under democracy at 8.562e8–9, and the evidence for popular attitudes collected by Dover (1974) 273–5.

463d3 **obedience:** the adj. ὑπήκοος derives from ἀκούειν; hence the fact that it can, as here, be followed by a genitive (γονέων).

463d3 **or that otherwise:** ἄμεινον ἔσεσθαι is loosely parallel to πράττειν (d1) and dependent on νομοθετήσεις (c9) – 'will you legislate that they should behave in accordance... or <sc. if they fail to> that things will not be well...' P. compounds the rather straggling effect by switching from αὐτοῖς, c9, to a hypothetical individual (d3–5): cf. Adam on 1.347a6 for numerous parallels.

463d4 **gods:** the apparent implication is that the Guardians will believe in gods who reward and punish men; see 10.612c–13b (with the following myth of Er) for similar ideas. On 'pious', d5, cf. n. 458e1.

463d6 **all your citizens...reiterate:** see n. c3 above for the fluctuating references to 'citizens'; here the point can hardly be taken literally, since it would mean that the Guardians' sense of collective kinship would be reinforced by the attitudes of farmers and artisans. The form of ideology advocated is evidently limited to the milieu of the Guardian class. *Humnein* is common in the sense of 'repeat regularly', see e.g. 1.329b2, 2.364a1, 8.549e1; but in P.'s Greek, the statements themselves are made the subject of the verb, which is thus intransitive ('resound in the ears of').

463d7 **from their earliest days:** for the emphasis of this phrase cf. e.g. 3.386a2, 395c4, 401d1, 413c8. No conviction emerges more consistently from all P.'s works than the importance of education, which he takes to be the indispensable cement of any social order (4.423e–425c); it is likely that the conviction grew from a Socratic root (cf. esp. *Euthph.* 2c–d, on the young as a prime subject of politics). Childhood is a period when the soul is 'soft' and malleable; hence the crucial significance of beliefs imprinted, or ideas absorbed, at that age: see esp. 2.377a12–b3 (at the start of P.'s great critique of poetry in education), and cf. 6.485d3–4, 486b10 f., 7.519a9, for the relevance of childhood even to philosophy. Given 7.540e5, P. may have regarded the years before the age of ten as particularly vital. P. supposes that a sufficiently intensive environment could mould behaviour to conform with the extended kinship that was earlier described, just as it is moulded, in existing societies, into conformity with the structure of the domestic family: there is a latent premise that conceptions of kinship are not biologically given, but formed by nurture and culture.

463e2 **to mouth:** διὰ τῶν στομάτων e.g. Xen. *Cyr.* 1.4.25) and διὰ στόμα (e.g. Eur. *Or.* 103, Ar. *Lys.* 855) elsewhere stress frequency of utterance; cf. English, 'on (their) lips'. But P.'s concern is with possible insincerity.

463e4 **earlier:** see 462c. P.'s belief that his new system of kinship would engender strong mutual concern is challenged by Arist. *Pol.* 1262a1–14, b14–24, who thinks the result would be a *dilution* of attachment; cf. Cic. *De rep.* 4.5.5. Adam contends that Aristotle missed P.'s 'deeper truth'; but Aristotle argues from a biologically realistic position that has its own kind of depth.

464a9 **Guardians' sharing:** for the male-centred formulation cf. nn. 450c1, 457c11.

464b1 **we agreed:** at 462a–d.

464b2–3 **to the way...a body relates:** lit. 'to a body in relation to one of its parts, what its condition is as regards pain and pleasure'; a characteristic Greek way of phrasing an indirect question in two parts.

464b5 **the city's greatest good:** the frame of reference since 462a; but the emphatic conclusion alerts us again to attendant paradoxes. The abolition of the family, and its replacement by an integrated kinship group using familial terminology, is not for the immediate benefit of the Guardians themselves, but for the sake of the entire city's unity. How, we must wonder, can this really be so? Soc.'s hesitation at the outset of the bk., and his expectation of disbelief (450c), is by now easy to understand; P.'s proposals are meant to be nothing if not challenging. At their base is the conviction that *disinterested* rulers are indispensable to a good political order: thus, if the sexual and social communism of the Guardians can succeed in removing divisiveness from their ranks, then Rulers and Auxiliaries will be unimpeded in maintaining the cohesion of the entire city; cf. n. 465b9–10.

464b6   **Auxiliaries:** the term is used loosely, since it corresponds to Guardians at a 9. The usage is helped by the fact that sexual communism mostly concerns Guardians of breeding age, who will largely be Auxiliaries; cf. n. 466a8.

464b8   **we said:** at 3.416d–17b.

464c2   **wages...resources:** on 'wages', *misthos*, see n. 463b3; it is followed by a verb, *analiskein*, which standardly means 'spend' (cf. esp. 4.420a2–6, with *misthos*) but is here given a figurative force. The Guardians will have no money as such; their economic activity (apart from ultimate control of the population) will be limited to the direct use of food, buildings, clothing, and other basic resources provided by the farmers/artisans. Cf. n. c8 ff.

464c6–7   **true Guardians:** at 4.428e1 the same phrase denoted Rulers as opposed to Auxiliaries; here it covers the whole class, and 'true' means 'conforming to the essential definition of their function'. P. is fond of this use of *alêthinos*; cf. 475e3, with e.g. 6.486b3, 489a5, 499c1-2.

464c7   **pulling...apart:** cf. 462b1.

464c8–d3   **each individual...private affairs:** money and wealth were a preliminary theme in the conversation with Cephalus, esp. 1.329e–331b; they were subsequently marked out as a cause of evil, 3.416e–17b, 4.421d–e, including war between cities, 2.373d–e; and they will later be presented as, in particular, the root-vice of oligarchy (political or psychological), 8.550c–555a. Yet the city will nonetheless contain a 'money-making' class (e.g. 3.417a2–3, 4.437c7, 441a1), on whose produce the Guardians will depend for their own subsistence; the generalisations at 4.422a5–6, d2–3, play down this fact, as though, *per impossibile*, the city as a whole shared the Guardians' economic status. There is a danger of tension here, but P.'s idea is that, once confined to the city's 'third' class, money-making will have an acceptable place, since it will be subject to the control of the Rulers.

464d1–2   **wife and children:** it is preferable to take these as further objects of ὀνομάζοντας (c7–8), rather than of ἕλκοντα; but the latter construal too is defensible (*pace* Adam), if we allow a zeugma, and the implication is the same either way: families too, in existing cities, are effectively 'private possessions' (cf. e1–2), and tend, through their narrow emotional ties, to promote social divisions (cf. 1.330c4 for children). For Soc.'s earlier reference to 'possession' of women and children, see n. 451c6.

464d2   **who create:** ἐμποιοῦντας agrees with γυναῖκά τε καὶ παῖδας, not the Guardians themselves, since the verb means to produce an effect *in* someone/something else. The long sentence, c5–d5, illustrates an additive use of participles (cf. e.g. 465c4–6); but my translation makes a convenient break at ἀλλά, d3.

464d7   **legal charges and accusations:** P. sometimes regards litigation and law-courts less as a necessary instrument of justice than a symptom of a flawed social order; see esp. 3.405a–c. Yet elsewhere the *Rep.* seems to accept that even the ideal state would require a judicial system, presumably for the money-making class of farmers/artisans (cf. 4.425c–d, 433e, with *Tim.* 17d4, and Arist. *Pol.* 1264a27–9), though crime among these too will be reduced by the policing of the Guardians (3.414b2–4), as well as by the removal of economic beggary (cf. 8.552c–e). The notion that money is the main source of litigation is attributed to the Spartan Lycurgus at Plut. *Lyc.* 24.4. Law-suits are also expected to disappear under the comic version of communism at Ar. *Eccl.* 657 ff.: this idea shows the influence of the same kind of 'utopian' thinking as is reflected at Ar. *Birds* 39–45.

464d9   **their bodies:** the exception might be thought more of a threat to the envisaged sense of unity than is here acknowledged. The body is the locus of the individualism which P. seeks to eradicate; cf. the emphasis on the physical basis of individuality in the analogy at 462c-d, with *Phdo* 66c-d (the body as the source of desire for property, and hence of war). Even if all inclination towards material possessions could be blocked (and 466b-c will admit the perpetual risk of a relapse), the body would remain a spring of powerful and inescapably individual sexual needs: not only does P. not recommend any way in which this biological fact could be overcome; he actually provides for sexual desire as a mechanism of competition among the Guardians (460b1-3, 468b-c). Yet in his later thoughts on the nature of an ideal communism, P. goes so far as to suggest that even parts of the body would in a sense become common property (*Laws* 5.739c-d).

One detail of personal identity left unmentioned, here and elsewhere in bk. 5, is *names*. Since Greek nomenclature was typically the responsibility of families, the Guardians would need an alternative custom – or perhaps would emulate the Libyan tribe, Atarantes, who, according to Herod. 4.184.1, dispensed with individual names altogether. Cf. n. 463d1.

464e1-2 **faction:** cf. nn. 459e3, 465b8.

464e4 **violence or assault:** two criminal categories in Athenian law. The first, *biaia*, covered acts against either property or person, including rape and other sexual violence; P. elsewhere refers to both types: see *Laws* 9.879b6, 10.884a2, 11.914e9, with Harrison I 34, MacDowell (1978) 124–5. The second (whose Attic form may have been αἰκεία, though mss. usually give αἰκία) was mentioned at 4.425d2, and is elaborately legislated for at *Laws* 9.879b–882c; cf. MacDowell (1978) 123, T. Saunders, *Plato's Penal Code* (Oxford, 1991) 268–79 (who remarks, 272, that the present passage is 'provocatively casual').

464e6 **declare:** i.e. the principle will be built into the city's ideology, and inculcated in the Guardians from an early age; cf. 463d6. The need for the Guardians to 'look after their bodies' (cf. 6.498b4–5), lit. 'placing compulsion upon care of their bodies', is merely an extra incentive for strenuous physical exercise, additional to the already substantial element of gymnastics and military training in their way of life.

465a1-3 **angry...faction:** P. seems to picture something like the Spartan practice reported at Xen. *Lac.* 4.6, whereby young Spartiates settle their quarrels by street-fights. But the idea looks optimistic: if Guardians had an inclination to express anger through physical force, why should they not equally harbour lasting grudges? One answer is that the younger Auxiliaries, who typify the force of *thumos* ('spirit', incl. 'anger': n. 456a4), are under the general control of the Rulers. But this solution presupposes, as does so much else in the bk., that the mechanisms of authority can prevail over individual sources of disorder and insubordination: cf. n. 466b5.

465a5-6 **older...younger:** the age-difference is broadly correlated with the status of Rulers and Auxiliaries (cf. 3.412c2-3). The effect would be psychologically reinforced, if P.'s intentions were realised, by the fact that the older generation are collectively 'fathers'/'mothers' (women must not be forgotten: cf. *Laws* 9.882c2-4) to the younger; cf. a11-b3. Once more (cf. n. a1-3), P. may have Spartan custom in mind: for the general authority of the old over the young see Xen. *Lac.* 2.10, 6.1-2, with MacDowell (1986) 54–8.

465a8 **also clear:** δῆλόν ‹ἐστι› is understood from a7.

465a8 **Rulers...older men:** not all older Guardians will become Rulers, only those capable of higher philosophical training (7.540a-b).

465a8–10 **force against an older man:** cf. the greater detail of *Laws* 9.879b–882c.

465a11 **'guardians' – fear and respect:** P., playing on the term for the Guardian class itself, personifies fear and respect as a pair of sentinels or protectors. The coupling of these feelings is as old as Hom. *Il.* 15.657-8 (cf. *Euthph.* 12b–c), and P. attaches considerable importance to it (e.g. *Laws* 1.646e-50, *Epist.* 7.337a). But there is an objection to be put: since these ethical restraints operate imperfectly within existing societies (cf. n. 463d2), why should they be any more effective where kinship terms are extended to larger groups? (The question is anticipated, with comic cynicism, at Ar. *Eccl.* 638-40.) P.'s answer might be that the ideological education and habituation of the Guardians would be much more rigorously sustained than the ethics of kinship in ordinary societies, especially democracies (cf. 8.562e).

465b1 **and fear that:** τό can be parsed either (i) after δέος, which has then to be supplied again after βοηθεῖν: δέος δὲ τό...δέος ('and fear, namely the fear...'), with the accusative and infin., τοὺς ἄλλους...βοηθεῖν, indicating the content of the fear; or (ii) with βοηθεῖν, so that the whole phrase τό...βοηθεῖν is in apposition to δέος ('and fear being the fact that...').

465b2–3 **sons...brothers...fathers:** for the possibility that these relationships (with their female equivalents, and extended to grandparents/-children) are exhaustive, see n. 463c5–7. Because P. posits a situation in which Guardians would treat no affairs as properly private or personal, he can suppose that any act of force would cause the intervention of those who were aware of it. But he is thinking only of overt or identifiable actions; covert behaviour (of the kind he *did* allow for in the sexual realm, 461b2) is not considered. On this point, Ar. *Eccl.* 641–3 furnishes a striking parallelism of thought.

465b8 **free from...faction:** P.'s conviction that a philosophical politics would have to guarantee the elimination of faction or civil discord, *stasis* (n. 459e3), was perhaps generated by his upbringing in strife-torn Athens of the late 5th cent. 7.520c8–d3 explains *stasis* as arising from competition for power; *Plt.* 303c2 implies that *all* actual cities (as opp. to the one perfect constitution) are in an inherent condition of *stasis*.

465b9–10 **either with them or with one another:** the claim rests on the notable premise that the concord of the ruling class (cf. 464e1) is both a necessary and a sufficient condition for the unity of the entire city: cf. 8.545d1–3 (with 545d–7c on the breakdown of unity), and Arends 199. Why should this be so? A united ruling class may have the organised *force* to maintain the social order; P. allows for force (e.g. 414b2–4), though he also intends his Guardians to be 'gentle' where appropriate (2.375b–6c, *Tim.* 17d4, cf. n. 470e3). But while force may maintain the status quo of 'ruling and being ruled' (4.430e–432a), it cannot create the political 'harmony' needed for true unity, which calls for the *agreement* of the 'ruled' (n. 463b1): P.'s argument leaves it obscure how such agreement could be achieved, especially since the farmers etc. will have no political education as such (cf. n. 456d10). Moreover, we have been given no grounds for believing that many normal kinds of conflict could be erased from the life of the third class, since for them there will remain the divisive experience of family and property; cf. n. 464d7 on their need for law-courts. At best, therefore, the Guardians will be able to prevent major unrest, but not to ensure positive amity or concord, among the workers. All these problems can be traced back, in fact, to difficulties that arise from the parallelism between social classes and parts of the soul: cf. n. 466b1.

The verb διχοστατεῖν (b10) is rare in prose; here it may indicate that P. had in mind Solon's great reflections on *stasis*: see fr. 4 W (esp. 19, 37), with *Laws* 1.630a6 (quoting Theog. 78).

465c1ff. **flatterings...:** the list is stylistically impromptu and casual (n. c4) – hence the resumptive formula at c6. Its tone expresses distaste for the 'bourgeois' concerns of family life (the mention of slaves, debts and children strongly reminds one of Strepsiades' grumbling prologue in Ar. *Clouds*). Cf. the female Guardians' relief from child-care duties, 460d4–7.

465c3   **household slaves:** although it is clear that the Guardians cannot *own* individual slaves, who would constitute private property (464d8–9), and while the Guardians' main economic needs are provided by the farmers and workers (464c1), it remains uncertain whether P. assumes the existence of some communal slaves available to Auxiliaries and Rulers. See n. 469c6–7.

465c2   **by the poor:** the Greek text is awkward; if πένητες is authentic, it should probably be understood as depending on a nominative carried over from the preceding clause – i.e. κολακείας τε πλουσίων ‹ὧν ἀπηλλαγμένοι ἂν εἶεν› πένητες, 'flatterings of the rich ‹from which they would escape› as poor men'. Adam provides a conspectus of older suggestions.

465c4   **so that they borrow:** the Greek of c4–6 strings together participles (cf. n. 464d2), conveying the impression of an extendable catalogue of economic difficulties ('borrowing here, avoiding debts there...').

465d2–3   **Olympic victors:** cf. the athletic imagery for the lives of the just at 9.583b1–2 (with Adam), 10.613b–c (with my nn.), 621c7 f. The life of the Guardians will *be* happy (on philosophical criteria); that of Olympic victors is merely *makaristos*, 'fêted' or 'celebrated', i.e. publicly *deemed* (and envied) as happy by the material standards of ordinary people (cf. *Phdr.* 256c4). P. may well be remembering the contrast between the worth of philosophers and athletes in Xenophanes fr. 2 DK; cf. Eur. fr. 282 N². (Iambl. *Vita Pyth.* 44 contrasts only their numbers). P. is also attracted by the idea of Guardians themselves as 'athletes (of war)' (3.416d8, 4.422b4, c8, 7.521d5, 8.543b8, cf. *Laws* 8.830a1), whose training is meant to foster a combination of athleticism with virtue (cf. *Laws* 7.807c). For athletic imagery in *Rep.*, including the last sentence of the work, see my nn. on 10.608b4, c2.

465d6–7   **at public expense:** i.e. the provision of all the Guardians' subsistence by the city's farmers (n. 463b3). Olympic victors often received life-long privileges, including free meals, from their cities: for Athens, see *Ap.* 36d5–9, *IG* I² 77.11 ff. (with S. Dow, *Classical Weekly* 37 [1943–4] 130-2, W. Thompson, *AJP* 92 [1971] 226-37); cf. e.g. Xenophanes fr. 2.14-15 DK, Plut. *Aristid.* 27.2.

465d8   **salvation:** for the Guardians are the city's 'saviours', n. 463b1.

465d8–9   **the crowns...wreathed:** lit. 'they are wreathed/crowned with maintenance...'. The metaphor comes from the award of olive wreaths to Olympic victors.

465d9–e1   **privileges...death:** cf. the honorific awards to those preeminent in military and other duties, 460b1–3, 468b–e. Treatment after death, anticipated at 3.414a3, is discussed in more detail at 468e–9b. The τε in e1 connects the whole of γέρα...ζῶντες with the following clause, but its placing is unusual: the effect is to accentuate the living/dead contrast, as well as the chiasmus of verbs (δέχονται/ζῶντες/τελευτήσαντες/μετέχουσιν.)

465e4   **I forget whose:** Adeimantus's, at 4.419a ff.; cf. 7.519d–e.

466a1   **although they were in a position:** ἐξόν is accusative absolute; the relative pronoun, οἷς, has been attracted from nominative into dative (i.e. for οἳ ἐξὸν αὐτοῖς...: 'who, although it was possible for them...'); cf. *Grg.* 492b5.

466a4–5   **the *city*...one particular group:** the contrast makes obvious sense as either a distinction between total and partial happiness, or a statement of priorities; for something like the latter, cf. Pericles' remark at Thuc. 2.60.2–3 (whose Socratic/Platonic affinities are discussed by S. Hornblower, *Thucydides* [London, 1987] 123–6). But a suspicion lingers that P.'s position depends on a more 'disembodied' concept of happiness altogether. This is because the *Rep.* argues for a happiness (which it identifies with a state of justice), whether individual or collective, which arises from the relationship between component parts. But while this is intelligible for an individual, since the resulting happiness will still belong to the person, it may yield a political 'happiness' which is not directly experienced by any element in the city: this is a point strongly urged by Arist. *Pol.* 1264b15-24 (employing a principle which P. himself uses in the case of ethical qualities, at 4.435e3). In fact, contrary to Aristotle's assertion, it is clear that the Guardians *are* taken to be in some sense 'happy'; but nothing is said to convince us that the rest of the city can be so (n. b1).

466a6   **fashioning:** the verb *plattein* can be used of sculpture (4.420c2) or other modelling (*Laws* 11.933b2), of imaginative pretence or make-believe (*Laws* 4.712b2), or of fictional story-telling (2.377b6). All three associations are pertinent, and help to accentuate Soc.'s sense that the discussion involves its own mode of (philosophical) fiction and imagination; cf. n. 472d4.

466a8   **Auxiliaries:** since *most* of the Guardians are Auxiliaries, P. can sometimes treat the terms as loosely synonymous; cf. nn. 458b9 f., 463b1, 464b6.

466b1   **cobblers:** a deliberately mundane choice of example; cf. 456d10, and e.g. 2.374b, 4.443c5. But the general contrast between the classes inadvertently highlights a weakness of P.'s whole political programme, since it apparently concedes that the lives of the city's workers have little claim to be thought happy (cf. 456d8–11). This suggests that *qua* 'ruled' part the working class must participate in the city's totality of happiness (a4–5), while the individual lives of its members need not be truly happy at all. And this reflects a larger tension in the soul-city analogy which is threaded through the *Rep.* (cf. n. 462c10). Within the city, the third class represents the lowest element, whose portion of happiness will be secured by subordination to the Rulers (as with the desires' subordination to reason in the soul). But each farmer/artisan has a soul of his/her own, and happiness for each *individual* requires, on P.'s own premises, an internal harmony of the psyche, which cannot be guaranteed by political subjection. It is in the best interests of such people, even as individuals, that they should be controlled by their betters (see esp. 9.590d). But this is, at best, a paternalist view which calls for much fuller justification; at worst, it leaves P.'s psychology and his politics badly unintegrated. The risk that the city's happiness will not be fully shared by all seems to be intimated at 4.421c4–6.

466b5   **if a Guardian tries:** P. acknowledges the permanent possibility of individual insubordination, even among those whose entire upbringing has inculcated a collectivist ethic of communal identity (and who are carefully 'watched' and tested for adherence to this ethic, 3.412d–e, 413c). It is P.'s own psychological views, with their stress on the potentially disruptive forces in 'the city in the soul', which commit him to recognising this threat to any system of social order and ideology. If we distinguish two major senses of political idealism - one, a belief in the possibility of rationally prescribing the necessary conditions for a good society; the other, a conviction that such a society could be realistically maintained - P. is much more consistently idealist in the first than in the second of these respects.

466b8   **immature:** lit. 'adolescent'. The noun *meirakion* is somewhat flexible in denotation (cf. Gomme-Sandbach on Men. *Dysc.* 27), but P. typically uses it of the years between childhood and adulthood, i.e. 14–21: see 468b3–4, 6.497e9–98b6 (dangerous years for would-be philosophers), *Ap.* 18c6–7, *Chrm.* 154b4–5, *Symp.* 192a1–2; Lacey 294 n. 28 suggests, a shade too narrowly, that it is always P.'s word for what were later called 'ephebes' (i.e. 18–20 year olds). So the adj. here marks the mentality of those on the verge of becoming Auxiliaries, at a vulnerable age when the values and beliefs inculcated by their education have not been translated into stable adult habits.

466c1   **take private possession:** i.e. relapse into the acquisitive individualism prohibited to the Guardians; cf. 6.485e, and note the resemblance to Thrasymachus's brutal 'realism' (1.343–4c). P. will later identify the love of money in the ruling class as a prime feature of degeneration from the ideal state to timocracy (8.547b, 548a6, 549a–b), *en route* to the rampant greed of oligarchy (ib. 550c ff.). Cf. n. 469d6. In passages such as this, P. evokes traditional Greek moral scruples about the dangers of excessive wealth (e.g. Solon fr. 6 W, Theog. 153–4; Dover [1974] 110–11).

466c2   **Hesiod:** at *WD* 40 (a smaller amount honestly obtained is preferable to larger but unfair acquisitions); cf. *Laws* 3.690e for the same point and quotation. P. has in mind, and expects his readers to remember, the larger Hesiodic context, where the poet is criticising the 'bribe-eating kings' for their disregard of justice. Hesiod is quoted again at 469a1–2 below, and with fair frequency elsewhere: see Brandwood 996–7. There are important respects in which P. can be seen to have been influenced by him; cf. n. 469a1–2.

466c8f.   **that the women:** the accusative and infin. beginning at κατά τε πόλιν... is in explanatory apposition to κοινωνίαν (c6), the direct object of συγχωρεῖς.

466c9f.   **'go hunting'...as dogs do:** a résumé, with the virtual status of self-quotation, of the opening of the argument for female Guardians, 451d4–6.

466d1   **in every way possible:** subject to allowances for the relative physical weakness of women; see nn. 457a10, 471d3–5. Nowhere in bk. 5 does P. explicitly consider the possible impact of pregnancy and child-birth on the careers of female Guardians: cf. n. 460d6.

466d6–471c3

The female Guardians will participate fully in military campaigns, and special arrangements will be made to give the children of this class opportunities to watch the activities of war from an early age. Martial prowess will be rewarded with sexual prizes, thus furthering the state's eugenic policy. After their deaths, eminent Guardians will receive the religious attention due to heroes. Conflict between the city and other Greeks, which should be regarded as 'faction' (stasis) between kinsmen, rather than true 'war', must be conducted in awareness of the natural unity of the Greek race: in particular, fellow-Greeks should not be enslaved, and their property should not be destroyed. But Greeks and barbarians are natural enemies, and war between them is therefore appropriate.

This section begins as though it will address the fundamental question of 'whether and how it is possible' for the proposed communism of the Guardians to be realised in a human society. But the point is postponed almost at once, and we move instead into a general discussion of how the city will organise certain aspects of warfare: this all helps, it is true, to explain the details of the scheme whose feasibility is at issue, but it would do little to convince those whose scepticism about female Guardians (and the rest) P. has had in view throughout (cf. 450c).

Warfare was a regular fact of life for most Greek city-states. It is an important part of P.'s conception of his ideal city that it would coexist, and have dealings, with other Greek cities: cf. Introduction p. 21. About the causes of war, or the types of war in which the city would be prepared to engage, *Rep.* 5 is wholly unexplicit. In a much earlier context, at 2.373d, the interlocutors had apparently countenanced the possibility of the city fighting to acquire extra territory. But that context concerned a preliminary scenario of population growth; bk. 5, by contrast, has posited a policy of stable population (460a). Presumably, however, we can contemplate the city deciding to go to war for either of the reasons mentioned at *Laws* 5.737d3–5: first, to defend itself against belligerent states; secondly, to give assistance to its neighbours when these are themselves exposed to unjustified attack. Finally, it is evidently implicit at 469c1-2 and

470c that the city would be prepared to contribute to combined or panhellenic campaigns against non-Greeks - above all, we must assume, against Persia (cf. n. 470c1–3). But in all these situations we have to imagine that the city's Auxiliaries would fight only in the cause of justice, never for the sake of aggrandisement or mere self-interest.

Even after allowing for qualifications (n. 471d3-5), P.'s hypothesis of the equal involvement of female Guardians in the tasks of warfare is utterly radical. It contradicts a standard view of women as unfitted for such tasks (e.g. Xen. *Oec.* 7.23), and it transcends the normal social fact that Greek women were either passive victims of war, or, at most, a last line of civil defence (D. Schaps, 'The Women of Greece in Wartime', *CP* 77 [1982] 193-213). Equally far-reaching is the envisaged introduction (the 'apprenticeship') of the Auxiliaries' offspring, from an early age (n. 466e5), to the experience of war. What is most remarkable about this last detail is that it appears to suit the ethos of a wholly militaristic class with an exclusive dedication to a life of war (cf. head-note to 461e-6d). Yet such militarism is something that P. himself elsewhere criticises in Sparta (n. 458c8-9), and it is discrepant in various ways with the larger conception of the Guardian class, Auxiliaries included. For these are people whose education will be principally in music and gymnastics (452a2), and whose natures will ideally involve a harmonious balance of 'spirit' and 'philosophy' (n. 456a4). Warfare, therefore, cannot be the centre of the Guardians' existence or of their aspirations. But it remains something that they must be equipped to engage in with success, since without the capacity to defend itself the city cannot be confident of protecting the structure and the ideals which give it its *raison d'être*. And where wars are fought only in the cause of justice, the Guardians need have no qualms about preparing their young to participate in it.

466d6–7 *whether* **it is...possible:** a question raised at the outset (450c8). It was apparently answered by the general argument for women's possession of the 'same nature' as men (see 456b12–c7), but was raised again in connection with sexual communism and extended kinship (457d–8b). Yet the present passage seems to have the original question of female Guardianship still in mind (c8–d2), as though the entire issue of feasibility were being reopened. Moreover, the discussion does not proceed directly to offer an explicit answer, and G. has to remind Soc. of this fundamental concern at 471c4 ff.

466d7 **other creatures:** this seems to pick up and generalise the preceding reference to dogs, d1; cf. 2.375d10/e2. If so, P. is repeating an 'ethological' consideration already mentioned in favour of his proposal of equality of duties between male and female Guardians: cf. nn. 451c8, 459a2-3, with 467a10 f. for a further development. Perhaps surprisingly, the animal parallel does not encompass the idea of sexual communism: although dogs, birds and horses were mentioned at 459a–b, P. was there thinking of animal breeding, and no allusion was made to natural mating patterns. P. either is unaware, or is disinclined to exploit, the fact that monogamous mating is exceptional among mammal species; birds (459a3), of course, are another matter. For a later appeal to animal behaviour as a way of challenging human sexual mores, see Plut. *De Sto. rep.* 1044F–5A (Chrysippus).

466e1 **warfare:** Soc. moves first to what might be thought the most difficult application of the 'shared duties' principle; the special status of this topic was anticipated at 452c1-2, 453a3-4. But although the immediate point (e3) emphasises that female Guardians would be expected to serve as soldiers, the conversation then broadens out to cover other aspects of military organisation. That war is only part of an answer to the larger question (d6-8) is intimated by μέν solitarium: hence 'first' in the translation.

466e5 **robust:** P. uses the adj. *hadros* nowhere else (the cognate verb is a doubtful reading at 6.498b5); it gives only an oblique idea of age. At Herod. 4.180.6 it refers to young children, *paidia* (old enough to have their facial features compared with possible fathers), but at Hippoc. *Genit.* 2.3 it indicates puberty. The term *paides* must here, as at 467c2, 5, have its regular sense of children under c.14, and perhaps, given 467d12–e2, as young as 7 or 8; the fact that the term can elsewhere stretch as far as adulthood (e.g. Dem. 21.154; cf. Dover [1978] 85–6) is a separate matter, though it may be relevant to 468b4 (see n.). The point of taking the young to watch war is, in part at least, to test their mettle: cf. 3.413d–e for this basic principle. It also conforms with the broader rule that individuals should be initiated from an early age into the 'single occupation' which they will perform in the community: cf. e5–6, with 2.374b–e (esp. c6–7), *Laws* 1.643b–d, and n. 463d7 on the general importance of upbringing. Some affinity with military training of the young in Sparta (cf. Powell 227-31) may perhaps be suspected, but P.'s present proposal seems independent of any known model.

466e6   **other craftsmen:** the Guardians too are, at least metaphorically, 'craftsmen' (n. 463b3); in particular, the military aspect of Guardianship is treated as a *technê*, a professional craft, at 2.374b–e.

467a1   **give help and assistance:** such assistance would naturally bring at least limited contact with the weapons and physical realities of warfare; 7.537a4–7, referring back to this passage, speaks (chillingly) of the young 'tasting blood, like puppies'. The terms 'fathers and mothers' (a2) must of course be understood in the newly extended sense of all kinship terms (461d).

     The Greek infinitives in a1 are perhaps influenced by the preceding δεῖν, but their function is to continue the sense of the purpose clause (e5). In *therapeuein*, 'attend', P. may be playing on the Homeric use of *therapôn* for a military squire, though such figures fight as well as preparing armour etc.

467a3   **crafts:** for apprenticeship to a family craft cf. 4.421e1, *Prt.* 328a, with A. Burford, *Craftsmen in Greek & Roman Society* (London, 1972) 82–7.

467a7–8   **less care than potters:** the Greek, a little illogically, formulates the point in reverse ('should potters show more care than the Guardians?'). For the comparison, cf. 456d8–10, 2.374b4; the implication is that the Guardians are the most important people in the city (2.374d8–e2), since it is above all on them that the city's unity and happiness depend (n. 465b9–10).

467a10f.   **every creature:** similar claims occur at *Symp.* 207b (Diotima positing a universal force of *erôs* throughout animal life), *Laws* 7.814b2–4 (female birds). Although the present proposition is an exaggeration, it is clear enough as an allusion to protective parental, especially maternal, behaviour of a kind broadly typical of both mammals and birds, and familiar to Greeks from ordinary observation of e.g. dogs, goats and domestic fowl. But the point also inadvertently raises a difficulty about P.'s treatment of kinship among the Guardians, since the type of animal behaviour in question arises from close *biological* kinship, as b1 intimates (where the verb is properly applicable to females). But parental instincts, above all the mother-child bond, is something which P.'s plans for the Guardians are meant to override: see 460b–d (esp. c9 f.), 461c–e. So it transpires that P. wishes the *affective* forces of biological kinship to be carried over to the extended kinship in which the Guardians will live: cf. the Introduction p. 20.

467b3   **as tends to happen:** οἷα δή ‹sc. γίγνεσθαι› φιλεῖ. οἷα δή, lit. 'which sort of things', is common in this adverbial usage: cf. e.g. 8.565e5, *Ap.* 32c7, *Phdo* 60a4, with LSJ s.v. οἷος V.2, and Denniston 221.

467b4   **recovery:** ἀναλαβεῖν is an intransitive use of a normally transitive verb.

467c2–3   **military men:** the phrase recurs at 7.521d11; on the Auxiliaries as soldiers see Introduction p. 21. The hold of male habits of thought (nn. 451c6, 456b9) is evidently strongest where warfare is concerned, since residual doubts remain about female warriors (n. 471d3–5): hence the masculine nouns here and at c9, 468b3 (*meirakion*) below. This should be distinguished from the use of masculine adjs. and participles throughout the passage, since these can serve as a 'common' gender in generalisations. There are reminders of female Guardians at 468c3, e2, and the same adj. *polemikos* was applied to women at 456a1.

467c5   **means must be found:** lit. 'this, then, must be the case, that <we> make the children...' ὑπαρκτέον is equivalent to δεῖ τοῦτο ὑπάρχειν; cf. n. e3 below.

467c10   **within human limits:** lit. 'so far as human beings <can know>'; ὅσα is adverbial accusative of 'extent': cf. e.g. 456a11, 458c4, *Crito* 46e3 (with Burnet), and LSJ s.v. ὅσος, IV. 1.

467d5   **the worst:** relative to the standards of the Guardian class, as at 459d8.

467d5–7   **leaders and tutors:** as e7 probably indicates, these will be Guardians who are themselves past the prime age for fighting. The children will form an organised appendage to the army, and are presumably to be imagined as involved in their own kinds of military training, as at *Laws* 8.829b6.

467d10   **happen:** the Greek has a gnomic aorist, expressing an aphorism.

467e2   **on horses:** the beginning of a skill which will be encouraged by other aspects of Guardian education; cf. 3.412b3–4 (hunting; riding contests). In most Greek cities, including Athens, educational horse-riding was associated with the 'aristocratic' rich, and with subsequent service in the cavalry; but P., who gives no hint of any military divisions within the Guardians, wishes it to be integral to the training of all Auxiliaries.

467e3   **after training them:** the accusative of the agent, διδαξαμένους, with verbal nouns is by analogy to δεῖ or χρή; cf. Weir Smyth §2152a and n. 453d10.

467e4–5   **spirited:** a standard epithet for certain animals; cf. 2.375a11–12 (horses, dogs), with e.g. Xen. *Mem.* 4.1.3, *Symp.* 2.10 (LSJ), as well as the reference to wild beasts at 4.441b2–3, and the symbolic lion in the soul, 9.588d ff. As 2.375a–b shows, it is because of its animal connotations that P. applies the word to a key quality of the Guardians' character, and to the equivalent part of the soul; cf. n. 456a4.

467e5   **most amenable:** lit. (of a horse) 'responsive to reins'; it is used of the chariots of the gods at *Phdr.* 247b2, but the other three occurrences in P. are metaphorical (*Soph.* 217d1, *Laws* 5.730b6, 9.880a7).

468a4   **what they are:** the αὖ read by Burnet, in place of ἄν, presumably means 'in this case too' (sc. as previously), though αὖ is sometimes used just to add urgency to a question. Keeping ἄν would require a far-fetched ellipse.

468a5–6   **anything of that sort:** P. assumes something close to the distinctions found, with some overlap, within Athenian law – between desertion, discarding weapons (in flight from battle), and evasion of military service; cf. Pritchett II 233–5, and MacDowell (1978) 160, with the latter's nn. on Andoc. 1.74. These matters receive extensive consideration at *Laws* 12.943a–5b; cf. T. Saunders, *Plato's Penal Code* (Oxford, 1991) 324–8. Cowardice counts as such a basic denial of the duties of the Guardians that it is later described as antithetical to the character of a philosopher (6.486b3). P. may have been influenced in this area by the particular reputation of Spartans for preferring death in battle to cowardice: cf. Xen. *Lac.* 9.1–6, with Powell 232–4. Heroic models are also pertinent: see c–d below.

468a6–7   **demoted:** the equivalent of *atimia*, disfranchisement, as the penalty for military offences under Athenian law (Andoc. 1.74, Aeschin. 3.175–6), or of the corresponding practice in Sparta (MacDowell [1986] 42–6). The principle of demotion (and promotion) was set out at 3.415b–c; cf. *Tim.* 19a, and n. 456a8. Arist. *Pol.* 1262b29–35 raises the possibility of unwitting incest and other undesirable acts between biological kin who found their way into separate classes; but this seems an academic point: P. simply does not allow for free social mixing between the Guardians and the rest.

468a9–10   **make a gift of him:** i.e. refuse to ransom him back; slavery would otherwise be a likely fate for such prisoners (cf. 469b8–c2, 3.386b6, 387b5–6). It was a normal ancient assumption that military victors had unconditional rights over captured property, including humans: see Y. Garlan, *War in the Ancient World* (London, 1975) 68–9. The implication here is that Guardians should always be prepared to fight to the death, since they have no hope of being recovered from captivity. Indeed, captured Auxiliaries merit no higher an estimate than lost animals: hence the animal metaphor, 'catch' (a10), which, though in keeping with some of the imagery used earlier in the bk. (n. 460c 1), intimates that those who have allowed themselves to be captured, rather than fighting to the death, have betrayed the corporate ethic of their class. We are perhaps also to sense an allusion to the need to avoid the corrosive effects of grief for individuals: cf. n. e5-6 below.

468b3–4   **first place...still on campaign:** the complementary point (civic honours) occurs at c10 ff. The verb *sustrateuesthai* would normally refer to fellow-soldiers (cf. 471d3). But the 'children' at any rate are not precisely that (n. 466e5), and even the *meirakia*, 'adolescents' or 'youths' (n. 466b8), probably include no more than the very youngest among the adult troops, perhaps just overlapping with the age-group indicated at d3 below; on relevant conceptions of the stages of childhood, cf. Golden 12–22. One purpose, therefore, of this ritual of congratulation, is to set up the successful Auxiliary as a role-model for his juniors, though b11 ff. introduces the further dimension of affective/sexual desire on the part of the older figures.

468b4–5   **crowned:** P. follows an existing Greek practice (e.g. Isoc. 16.29) which belongs to the bestowal of *aristeia*, 'military prizes'; cf. n. c4 below.

468b11   **kiss:** given the male reference at b3, as well as the relationship between older and younger Auxiliaries, we think most immediately of male homosexual kissing, specifically allowed for, with a prohibition on full physical gratification, at 3.403b5 (contrast Xen. *Mem.* 1.3.8–13). c3 makes it clear that male-female relations are also covered, but not comprehensively (see n.); and it is not easy to believe that P. intended female homosexuality to be tacitly supplied (though the phenomenon is acknowledged at *Symp.* 191e2–5, *Laws* 1.636c5: cf. Dover [1978] 171–84; 'once only' on p.172 is incorrect). The fact remains that the whole passage is male-centred in outlook (n. 467c2), and does not consistently apply the principle of female role-equality (esp. 466d1–2), despite the reference to women at e2.

468c1   **while...on campaign:** the qualification is needed, since, within the collectivist ethos of the Guardians' lives, no 'pair-bonding', whether hetero- or homosexual, can be permitted. But this gives the passage an equivocal status, since it simultaneously allows some pursuit of particular sexual desires (c2–3), while prescribing an exchange of kisses between successful Auxiliaries and the entire band of juniors. This reminds us of the earlier treatment of erotic feelings, where a similar tension was discernible between individuality and communal interests: see n. 458d2–3.

468c3   **male or female:** but, as at 460b1–3, P. here seems to think of women as the objects of sexual desire, and men as its agents; at any rate, it is more plausible to take the phrase this way, as stressing both hetero- and homosexual desires of men, than as covering the desires of men and women symmetrically. It is worth remembering that, extrapolating from 458c8–d1, we are presumably meant to imagine a complete absence of segregation between the sexes on campaign. On the homosexual side, P. is adapting the idea that lovers would fight for one another with special ardour; cf. *Symp.* 178e–9a, and (with reservations) Xen. *Symp.* 32–5, with Dover (1978) 190 ff.

468c4   **military prizes:** *aristeia*, a long-standing Greek tradition (already alluded to at b2–5 above), marking public recognition of heroic or otherwise distinguished feats of valour; see Pritchett II 276–90. Despite the collectivist ideology of the Guardians, P. is keen to acknowledge the space for particular acts of courage by individuals: indeed, the passage links two areas of behaviour (warfare and sexuality) where P. seems to realise the severe limitations on his project of eliminating individuality from the life of the Guardians. A philosophy of competition as a spur to excellence is ascribed to Sparta at Xen. *Lac.* 4.2-6.

468c6–7   **chosen:** by the Rulers, for eugenic breeding. So the braver Auxiliaries will be given more sexual opportunities, and they will exercise freedom within the limits of c1–3; but they will not necessarily or always be allowed to select their partners for sexual intercourse. Even so, it is to this type of context that the concerns of Arist. *Pol.* 1262a32–40, about unwitting sexual contact between biological kin, have particular relevance: for the problems of incest, under P.'s scheme, see nn. 461c1–4, e1–2.

468c8   **earlier:** at 460b1–5; cf. 459d7–8.

468c10   **Homer:** beyond the immediate topic of rewards, it is implicit that the bravest Guardians would challenge comparison with Homeric heroes; this confirms, in retrospect, how important it was for the Guardians' education in poetry to be censored of elements (allegedly) unfavourable to such heroes (3.386a ff.).

468d2–3   **Ajax:** at *Il.* 7.321–2. P. previously showed interest in the roast-meat diet of Homeric heroes (a diet not normal for ordinary Greeks) at 3.404b–c.

468d3   **young man:** the verb *hêban* commonly refers to the onset of adulthood; cf. *Ap.* 41e2, *Prt.* 309b1 (Alcibiades, c.18–19?), *Laws* 11.928c2, and e.g. Thuc. 3.36.2, 4.132.3, with Garland 166, 323–4. Here it marks the young warrior's physical prime; for relevant Homeric usage see e.g. *Il.* 7.133, 157, 12.382.

468d7   **follow Homer:** for this attitude to poetry, which stems from a cultural assumption that poets are teachers of wisdom, cf. e8, with e.g. 1.331d5, 3.408c2. Despite the trenchant strictures on the Homeric epics in bks. 2–3 (e.g. 378d5, 379c9, 387b1–2), P. continues to cite Homer, as 2.383a7 anticipated, for points which can be made consistent with his own arguments (e.g. 3.404b10, 405e–6a, 408a). But he does so in a spirit which leaves no doubt that the philosopher's judgement is higher than the poet's.

468d8   **sacrifices:** cf. 459e6, 461a6, 3.415e3, with n. 469a4 for the city's religion.

468d9   **hymns:** the term was at this date still applied fluidly to several kinds of poetry and song. P. uses it of praise-poems to humans at *Laws* 7.802a1–2 (deprecating such things for the living, but cf. 8.829c) and 12.947b7; more often, it denotes poetic addresses to the gods (cf. n. 459e6, and e.g. 10.607a4, *Symp.* 177a6, *Laws* 3.700b1–2, 7.801e1). Praise-poems are here conceived both as honorific rewards, and as celebrations of the virtues to which the city's ideology expects all Guardians to aspire.

468d9   **a moment ago:** i.e. the sexual rewards of c1–7.

468d10f.   **'first seats...wine':** P. recalls the repeated line, Hom. *Il.* 8.162, 12.311, but he adjusts the wording to keep the metrical shape only of the last two words. This is a way of partially 'absorbing' the poetic text into his own sentence; longer quotations, as at 469a1–2, can be left fully metrical: P.'s methods of quoting are discussed by D. Tarrant, *CQ* 45 (1951) 59-67. Honorific (front) seats were a standard element of many kinds of Greek ceremonial; cf. *Laws* 12.947a1, with e.g. Xenophanes fr. 2.13 DK (athletes).

468e1   **train:** *askein*, which can signify any form of methodical practice or educational exercise (cf. *Prt.* 323d7, *Laws* 7.804e1), is applied to military activity at *Laws* 7.805a3, 8.832b2; for its common association with athletic discipline, which is highly pertinent to the militarism of the Guardians (4.422b4, c8, with n. 465d2–3), see e.g. 3.389c3,

7.536b3 (noun), *Laws* 7.795b6. But since P. here pictures a training that is at least as much ethical as physical, the idea of 'cultivating [*askein*] virtue' (which leads to later notions of spiritual 'asceticism') is also relevant: see 3.407a8, c3, 7.518e1–2, *Grg.* 527d–e, and e.g. Eur. fr. 853 N², with H. Dressler, *The Usage of 'Ἀσκέω and its Cognates in Greek Documents to 100 A.D.* (Washington D.C., 1947). Compare the 'gymnastics of the soul' at 6.498b7–8.

468e2   **women:** is the reminder of female Guardians sufficient to convince us that P. wants every detail of the passage to be applied equally to them? It is hard to give an unqualified affirmative: cf. nn. 460b9 f., 467c2–3, 468c3.

468e5–6   **belongs to the Golden Race:** in the terms of the 'myth of metals' (3.415a–c), an ideological fiction intended to convince the city of the 'naturalness' of its class-divisions, this amounts to posthumous 'promotion' from the Auxiliaries to the rank of Rulers. Strictly speaking, a valiant death in battle could not guarantee *all* the qualities (especially philosophical ones) required for ruling; but the declaration, like the myth of metals itself, serves a propaganda purpose in relation to the rest of the Auxiliaries.

We ought to notice, throughout this passage, the absence of any mark of mourning for the dead; the principles used to criticise normal behaviour in this respect, at 3.387d–8e and 10.603e–4d, are here implicitly put into practice. But given the existence of affective elements in the Guardians' sense of kinship (n. 467a10 f.), we might wonder how easy the avoidance of grief would be for such people: P.'s case requires the assumption that the Guardians' entire upbringing will endow them with sufficient self-discipline.

469a1–2   **'Some become...':** Hesiod *WD* 122–3, referring to the destiny of inhabitants of the 'golden race' of men, but at the end of the entire golden age; for the text of the quotation (which occurs with differences at *Crat.* 397e–8a), see West *ad loc.* On P.'s attitude to Hesiodic *daimones*, see F. Solmsen, 'Hesiodic Motifs in Plato', in *Hésiode et son Influence* (Fondation Hardt, Entretiens VII: Geneva, 1960) 173–96, at 183 ff. Cf. n. 466c2.

469a4   **the god:** Delphic Apollo, whose religious authority for the city was emphatically asserted at 4.427b–c (incl. special mention of the dead) and is cited for particular points at 461e3, 470a3, 7.540c1. The same holds for the *Laws* (e.g. 6.759c6-7, 8.828a); cf. Morrow 402-11, Reverdin 89-95, 163-7. But in comparison to that later work, which devotes extensive attention to the subject (incl. the whole of bk. 10), the *Rep.* contains only occasional references to the city's religion. No doubt P. takes ' ' granted that the city would possess appropriate temples, priests, etc.: cf. esp. 461a7, 469e7, n. 468d8, 4.427b6-7; note the participation in panhellenic festivals such as that at Delphi (470e10 f.). It is also a sure inference, necessitated by the whole ideology of the class, that there should be no *private* religion (household shrines etc.) among the Guardians, though such things would presumably be possible among the city's workers: cf. the derogatory allusion at 4.419a7, with the later statement of principle at *Laws* 10.909d-10e.

469a4–5   **akin to spirits and god-like:** the adj. *daimonios* must here, though not always, be understood as directly suggestive of *daimôn* (a1, 8); likewise *theios*, though commonly used as a more general term of approbation, needs its properly religious sense. Passages such as 7.540b–c, *Symp.* 202d–e, offer a view of *daimones* as intermediate between divine and human; for other Platonic uses of *daimôn* cf. my n. on 10.617e1. P. is effectively proposing that the deceased Auxiliaries (women as well as men: *Laws* 7.802a3–5) should receive 'hero cult', as figures who can continue even after death to exercise influence on the living: cf. Sparta's treatment of its dead kings (Xen. *Lac.* 15.9), and see Burkert (1985) 203–8 (but n. 50 overstates the scope of P.'s proposal: cf.

468e4–5). The same is suggested for deceased Rulers at 7.540b–c, but with some hesitation; and later, at *Laws* 7.801e, '*daimones* and heroes' (cf. *Rep.* 3.392a5) are distinguished from dead citizens: see Reverdin 149–67, Morrow 457–68, for somewhat different views of relevant passages in *Laws*. It has to be said, however, that the tenor of the present context seems more cultural than theological. It is a continuation of the discussion of honours for outstanding Auxiliaries, and emphasises the status of the dead within the community that memorialises them, rather than offering clear religious doctrine about their destiny: not till bk. 10 will the idea of the soul's immortality become explicit, though there will be passing hints at 6.496e2, 497c4. It may therefore be pertinent that at *Crat.* 397e–8c we are given an allegorical reading of Hesiod's reference to once-human *daimones*.

469b2–3   **anyone else:** lit. 'anyone of those who...'; τῶν serves as a virtual pronoun.

469b8   **for Greek cities:** πόλεις, not Ἕλληνας, should be taken as the subject of the infinitive, as μηδ' ἄλλη shows; the Greek word-order places an emphasis on the object, Ἕλληνας: see Adam for fuller arguments. P. uses the plural, 'cities', because he is invoking a general principle, but it is of course the ideal city of the dialogue whose conduct is being prescribed.

469b10f.   **the Greek race:** cf. n. 470c1–3.

469c3   **supreme importance:** lit. 'it makes a difference by whole and all'; for the latter phrase see e.g. 6.486a5, 7.527c7, *Laws* 12.944c3; cf. n. 449d4–5.

469c5   **urge:** how such persuasion might be attempted, or why it should prove effective, is left unsaid; but P. assumes normal types of diplomacy (cf. 4.422d), and that his city will strive to promote the virtue of other Greeks (n. 471a6). The passage may also posit widespread preference for barbarian over Greek slaves, and a tendency to believe that it was barbarians, not Greeks, who were most fit to be slaves (cf. Eur. *IA* 1400–1 for one reflection of this idea). Yet enslavement of fellow-Greeks was certainly practised by Greek cities: P. himself has posited it as a standard risk of warfare (n. 468a9–10), and we know of cases where Athens enslaved entire populations of women and children, as at Scione in 421 (Thuc. 5.32.1) and Melos in 416/15 (Thuc. 5.116.4); cf. Pritchett I 81. But there can be no doubt that barbarian slaves greatly outnumbered Greek: for Athens, see e.g. the details of slaves among the confiscated property of the Hermocopidae in 414 (ML p.247); and for arguments against regarding intra-Greek warfare as a major source of slaves, see Y. Garlan, 'War, Piracy and Slavery in the Greek World', in M.I. Finley (ed.) *Classical Slavery* (London, 1987) 7–21, who comments (13–15) on a 4th cent. trend of feeling against enslaving Greeks (see Xen. *Ages.* 7.6. *Hell.* 1.6.14). At *Plt.* 309a5–6, however, P. appears to envisage enslavement of individuals purely on grounds of low intelligence.

469c6–7   **against non-Greeks:** the whole context suggests that G. has warfare in mind, even though, in existing fact, many barbarian slaves were obtained by trade (M.I. Finley, *Economy & Society in Ancient Greece* [London, 1981] ch. 10). It is, in any case, a clear enough implication of G.'s remark, as of Soc.'s preceding statements, that the acquisition of barbarian slaves *will* be acceptable and actually practised. If so, P. accepts that his ideal state will still be, in some degree, a slave-owning society, even though he has made very little mention of slaves at any previous point. The one explicit, though incidental, mention of slaves is 4.433d3: that this, in conjunction with the present passage, is enough to show that P. assumed the availability of slaves, is argued by Vlastos (1981) ch. 6 (with ch. 7 for P.'s work as a whole). The most obvious place for slaves is in the ownership of the third class (farmers/artisans); if they are to be available to the Guardians, they cannot be their formal 'property': cf. nn.

460c2, 465c3. B. Calvert, *CQ* 37 (1987) 367-72, stresses that there is no strict role for slaves in this city; but that cannot show that P. has ceased to think of their existence.

469c8   **stripping the corpses:** taking booty from the bodies of enemy dead was a standard Greek practice (Pritchett I 53–84, III 277). P.'s objections to it may look unremarkable, since (i) the exception of armour covers what was anyway the major object of the exercise (though clothing too was sometimes removed), (ii) his observations on possible military risks (d3-4) amount to no more than a rudimentary point of discipline: prudent officers would naturally prohibit booty-taking in inappropriate circumstances (cf. the parody of military orders at Ar. *Lys.* 461). But P.'s chief point, as d6 shows, is more far-reaching: the Auxiliaries, living as they do without material wealth, can have no interest in booty as *property*. The removal of weapons, therefore, is not really in line with normal practice, since its purpose is merely defensive (to prevent re-use of the arms) not acquisitive.

Plut. *Mor.* 224B, F, prompts the question whether P. had a Spartan precedent for his prohibition. But other evidence (e.g. Thuc. 5.74.2) suggests that the Spartans scarcely diverged from common practice: cf. A.H. Jackson, in V.D. Hanson (ed.) *Hoplites: the Classical Greek Battle Experience* (London, 1991) 241.

469c9   **is this...acceptable:** on the delayed interrogative cf. Denniston 283–4. But it would perhaps be possible to repunctuate c8–9 so as to make τί δέ ... νικήσωσιν a single question: cf. 470a5–6 (with Adam).

469d6   **base and greedy:** or, 'illiberal and acquisitive'; for the combination, see 3.391c5, 6.486b6. The first feature, *aneleutheria*, is associated with cowardice (d1, cf. 6.486b3) and meanness of spirit (6.486a), but connotes a general taint of corrupt character (3.395c6, 401b5, 4.422a2–3). The second is a kind of 'commercial' vice, attributed to Phoenicians and Aegyptians at 4.436a1–3, and ascribed more generally to the 'oligarchic' character, 8.551a7–8; it is something we could believe of no hero, 3.390d–e, and is utterly antithetical to the Guardians' (philosophical) lack of concern for wealth: see 464c9, 466c1, and e.g. *Phdo* 68c1-2.

469d7   **womanly:** the epithet seems inapt, given the existence of female Auxiliaries. But P.'s lapse into conventional prejudice is induced by verbal habits, and does not detract from the earlier arguments for women's possession of the 'same nature' as men: cf. nn. 451c6 ('possession'), 453b7, 456b9.

469d9   **the means:** lit. '<that> with which...', i.e. his body (not his weapons). The notion of the life-soul that escapes at death is here purely traditional; as Adam observes, poetic form ἀποπταμένου, 'flown away', is a reminiscence of a Homeric phrase (*Il.* 16.469, *Od.* 10.163): cf. the occurrence of similar language in funerary epigrams (R. Lattimore, *Themes in Greek & Latin Epitaphs* [Urbana, 1962] 33, 36, 56), and the old idea of the soul as a bird (E. Vermeule, *Aspects of Death in Early Greek Poetry & Art* [Berkeley, 1979] 18).

469e1–2   **bitches...:** the image was memorable enough to be quoted, with admiration, by Arist. *Rhet.* 1406b32–4. It is revealing that P. can cite dogs as a symbol of shabby, craven behaviour, after earlier using them as a model for his Guardians: see 451c8 (with n.), d4, 459a2, 466d1.

469e4–5   **refusals:** the right to bury one's dead was not normally refused even to the vanquished; where necessary, a truce might be arranged for that purpose (e.g. Thuc. 3.109.1–2, 4.114.2). But, as P. implies, departures from this code did occur: see Thuc. 4.98.7–99, with Eur. *Suppl.* 16–19 for a mythological case.

469e7   **weapons into our temples:** an extremely common Greek practice, exemplified by the Athenians' behaviour after the capture of Spartans on Sphacteria in 425 (Ar. *Knights* 846–9); other instances: Thuc. 3.114.1, Aeschin. 3.116, and many temple inscriptions

(Pritchett III 277–95). The dedication of weapons would serve both as a thank-offering to the god, and as a memorial of victory; cf. Burkert (1985) 93–4. But a sense of *triumph* over fellow-Greeks is incompatible, P. implies, with the strong concept of Greek kinship which he wishes his Guardians to possess (hence, too, the suppression of the common practice of battle-field trophies: cf. Pritchett II 246–75). *Laws* 12.955e–6a proposes that all temple offerings should be simple and modest.

470a2   **pollution:** attaching both to persons and to objects associated with kin-killing. But P.'s application of this principle to the spoils of normal warfare between Greek states is highly unorthodox; cf. *Laws* 12.956a1–3. The reference to Apollo, a3 (cf. n. 469a4), seems almost ironic, in view of the fact that Delphi was a major centre for dedications of just this kind.

470a5   **What about...:** a verb (e.g.) of thinking can easily be supplied in Greek as in English; for the genitive of connection, τμήσεως, cf. n. 459b7. Some editors punctuate after τί δέ, turning what follows into a single question.

470a5   **ravaging...burning:** the former refers (as a9 f., d7–e1 confirm) not to the mere destruction of grain-crops, but to attempts to inflict more lasting damage by cutting down fruit-trees and vines: cf. Hanson 6-7, 17-18, 45, 51-7, with 58-63 on the burning of farmhouses.

470a8   *your* **view:** on G.'s need for Soc.'s guidance see n. 453c7.

470b4–6   **two names...two distinct things...two elements:** lit. 'It seems to me that just as they are called by these two names, 'war' and 'faction', so they actually are two things, which exist in the case of disagreements of [i.e. within and between] two elements.' ταῦτα ὀνόματα is the usual cognate (or internal) accusative of naming (e.g. 471d2). δυοῖν τινοιν is neuter dual, and is explained by the following sentence. (Adam's note is too stringent, and wrongly equates ἐπί at b5 and b7.)

470b5   **'war'...'faction':** at *Laws* 1.629c–d the distinction is reformulated as one between 'two species of war'.

470b6–7   **affinity...the alien:** the categories are essentially the same as those invoked, at 463b10 ff., to analyse the special unity of 'kinship' among the city's Guardians. Hence we have already met the concept of 'faction', *stasis*, in connection with (hypothetical) discord within the city, either among the Guardians themselves or between them and the third class (459e3, 464e1, 465b8–10). But this overlapping of categories and values might place a strain upon the loyalties of the city's inhabitants, especially its soldiers (Auxiliaries): cf. the Introduction p. 19.

470c1–3   **Greek race...barbarian race:** P. here draws on two pre-existing elements – 'panhellenic' sentiment, and anti-barbarian chauvinism – and combines them into an uncompromising doctrine of 'natural' race; cf. *Menex.* 245c–d. Evidence elsewhere for a sense of Greek nationhood is intermittent and partial: see esp. Herod. 8.144.2 (common blood, language, religion and culture), Thuc. 1.3 (gradual diffusion of the terms 'Hellas' and 'Hellenes'; cf. West on Hesiod *WD* 528), Ar. *Lys.* 1128–34 (religion, and common interests against Persia; n.b. 'kin', *suggeneis*, 1130), Isoc. 4.50 (alternative conceptions of Hellenism – cultural and racial). The notion of a single Greek race had to compete with the existence of perceived ethnic divisions between (above all) Dorians and Ionians: see e.g. the Spartan view of the Athenians as 'of alien stock' (*allophulous*) at Thuc. 1.102.3, with J. Alty, 'Dorians & Ionians', *JHS* 102 (1982) 1–14; for this interplay of categories cf. Dover (1974) 83–5, and, on the limitations of Greek nationhood, M.I. Finley, *The Use & Abuse of History* (London, 1975) ch. 7. But P., possibly influenced by the contemporary panhellenism of Isocrates (whose *Panegyricus* dates from c. 380), ignores all such limitations, and stretches the idea of a natural or racial Hellenism to the extreme point of regarding inter-Greek conflict as *stasis*, 'faction' or civil strife, not true war.

In a later work, at *Plt*. 262c–d, we find criticism of the simple division of the human 'race' (itself a *genos*: cf. 473d6) into Greek and barbarian, as though the multiplicity of the latter constituted a single *genos*: the objection appears to be that, contrary to the implication of c6, 8 here, 'barbarian' is not a *natural* unit. Elsewhere, P. sometimes acknowledges wide variation among barbarians (e.g. 4.435e-6a), and, more significantly, he is prepared to appeal to non-Greek practices as support for his own contentions: see e.g. the approval of Egyptian art at *Laws* 2.656d-7b, the references to women in non-Greek societies at *Laws* 7.804e-6b, and the incidental though remarkable speculation, at *Rep*. 6.499c9 f., that the philosophical state may already exist somewhere in the barbarian world. Nor can there be any doubt, despite the obscurity of exact lines of contact, that P.'s thought was variously influenced by ideas which he knew to be of non-Greek origin: cf. the ascription of the myth of Er in bk. 10 to a Pamphylian source (with my edn., p. 169, for possible middle-eastern and other connections), and the vexed issue of putatively Egyptian elements in P. (for contrasting views see Thesleff 28, 105-6, and M. Bernal, *Black Athena*, vol. I [London, 1987] 105-8). There is a general reference to barbarian sources of wisdom at *Phdo* 78a 4-5, and to barbarian 'great deeds', incl. law-givers, at *Symp*. 209d-e. Such considerations make the present passage seem disappointingly crude in its assertion of a 'natural enmity' between Greeks and barbarians: the only obvious mitigation is that P.'s positive aim is to assert a far-reaching principle of kinship among all Greek states, and this leads him into a rhetorically convenient appeal to anti-barbarian feeling. For one appraisal of P.'s views on barbarians see Baldry 76-84.

470c6 **natural enemies:** P. invokes nature here without any scrutiny, though the context (c2) indicates that nature *qua* kinship is the relevant conception. But *Menex*. 245c–d, claiming that only the Athenians are 'pure' Greeks, while others have an ancestry mixed with barbarian blood, shows that even in this respect P. would have grounds to qualify his clear-cut assertion. And if the idea of 'nature' were to be subjected to the same kind of critical interrogation as it received in the discussion of women (esp. 454a ff.), the natural enmity of Greeks and barbarians might be reduced to a purely contingent historical situation. P. is not interested in pursuing that line of enquiry, though at least one earlier thinker had flatly denied the naturalness of the Greek/barbarian dichotomy (Antiphon, *On Truth, P. Oxy*. LII 3647, cols. ii–iii, giving a fuller text of fr. 44B DK); for other challenges to the distinction, see Baldry 24–51.

470d1 **'faction' is the name:** but at 7.521a7–8 conflict between Greeks will still be called 'internal war (*polemos*)'; cf. n. e1–2 below.

470d5 **regarded as heinous:** ὡς duplicates the ὅτι of d3; cf. *Hp. Mj*. 281c4–7, with LSJ s.v. ὡς, B I 1. ἀλιτηριώδης, 'heinous', is associated with pollution or inherited 'guilt' in its three other occurrences in P. (*Laws* 9.854b4, 881e4, *Epist*. 7.351c3); it thus appeals to a similar religious sentiment as 470a2-3.

470d7–8 **nurse and mother:** see the same phrase and attitude at 3.414e2–3, but within a mythical account of the birth of the city's first inhabitants. Cf. the Cretan practice of calling their country 'motherland' (*matris*), 8.575d7. At *Laws* 5.740a5–7 the idea of the earth as 'mother' is given a religious setting. The same imagery occurs at e.g. Isoc. 4.25, Dem. 60.5.

470d9f. **deprive...of their crops:** purely to induce surrender, as 471b3–5 specifies. The strategy was widely used in Greek warfare; Athens had experienced it, at the hands of Spartan armies, several times during P.'s childhood; cf. Hanson ch. 8. The present participles in e1 sometimes mean 'victors' and 'vanquished', but the context requires them to signify provisional positions.

470e1–2   **not...forever:** P. alludes to, and reinterprets, a proverb ascribed to the sage, Bias of Priene (mid-6th cent.), that one should love in the expectation of hating, and hate in that of loving (Arist. *Rhet.* 1389b23-4, with Jebb's edn. of Soph. *Ajax*, pp. 231-2). *polemein*, 'fighting', needs to be logically independent of the new definition of 'war', *polemos*, presented at b-c.

470e3   **more civilised:** lit. 'this attitude belongs to people who are much more civilised than that <attitude>'; alternative comparative formulations are run together. *hêmeros*, 'civilised', has connotations of gentleness; it represents a complex quality sometimes overlooked in assessment of P.'s political psychology. The antithesis of 'wild' or 'beast-like' character, it is a primary requisite for the Guardians, 3.416c2–3, nurtured in them by the balanced combination of music and gymnastics in their education, 3.410c–e (where the difference from 'softness', *malakia*, is stressed), and connected both with reason (9.571c4) and with social justice (6.486b11, 10.620d4–5). It amounts to a humaneness that is informed by strong ethical values.

470e4   **founding:** n. 453b4.

470e10   **festivals:** *hiera* denotes both shrines or temples, and the festivals located at them; the reference is to great panhellenic events such as those held at Olympia and Delphi: P. appeals to a factor which had figured in other conceptions of Greek 'nationhood', e.g. Herod. 8.144.2, Ar. *Lys.* 1129–32 (with n. c1–3 above). P. accepts that his city should have regular peace-time contacts, incl. trade (2.370e5 ff.), with other Greeks: this highlights his conviction that such a city could have a feasible place within the Greek world of his own day. Yet, surprisingly, he sees in inter-state contacts no threat to the order or ideology of the city: cf. the Introduction p. 21, with n. 46.

471a6   **control...'controllers':** the cognate verb and noun stress the idea of corrective punishment or coercion, aimed at establishing/restoring virtue, esp. *sôphrosunê*, self-control or temperance; cf. *Grg.* 478d6, *Critias* 121c1, *Laws* 9.854d5. (P. may intend *sôphronistês* to have a quasi-official ring: it became an Athenian title for superintendents of ephebes [18-20 year olds], though we cannot be sure that this usage predates the reformed system of the mid-330s: see Arist. *Ath. Pol.* 42.2, with Rhodes' n., and ps.-P. *Ax.* 367a2.) The sentiment lends a notable dimension to the activities of the ideal city's Rulers: they will have, it seems, a genuine interest in the condition of *other* Greek cities, and will help to spread certain political and moral values through the Greek world; cf. the 'advice' regarding slavery, 469c5, and see n. b4-5 below. For the distinction between two aims in war, cf. *Menex.* 242d1-3 (fighting for victory *vs.* fighting to destroy).

471a11   **the entire population:** implicit criticism of the mentality which allowed a power such as Athens to kill all adult males, and enslave all the women and children, of cities rebelling from its empire (cf. n. 469c5). We find the issue of restricted *vs.* collective 'guilt' being debated in a case of this kind at Thuc. 3.36.2, 4, 39.6, 47-8, 50.1 (Athens' recapture of Mytilene, 427 B.C.). It would be particularly important for the Rulers of P.'s city to draw this distinction, since they would be dealing with cities that, unlike their own, were not socially harmonious but riven by divisions: 4.422e-3a.

471b1   **all these reasons:** i.e. because (i) the city does not aim to 'triumph' in war, or to destroy its opponents; (ii) these opponents are fellow-Greeks, and therefore 'kin'; (iii) the Guardians will be 'civilised', and will have 'affection for all Greeks'; (iv) only some of one's opponents can be considered responsible for the conflict.

471b2   **raze:** Greek armies sometimes ransacked dwellings to the point of smashing their building stones and foundations; cf. Hanson 62.

471b4–5   **pay for their offence:** following the general pattern of Greek inter-state politics, this might involve imposing a change of government upon the city concerned; for a case of this kind involving Athens, see Thuc. 1.115.3 (Samos, 441). If this is what P. has in mind, then it increases the extent to which the Guardians would be expected to influence the political and moral arrangements of other cities; cf. n. a6 above.

471b7   **our citizens:** here, effectively, the Guardians, since the city's third class would take no part in warfare. For a related point cf. n. 462b5.

471c4-474b2

But now, insists Glaucon, however desirable all these proposals may be, the question whether they are really feasible must be faced once more. Socrates maintains that the point of the discussion has been to establish a 'paradigm' or ideal depiction of the just city, by which the lives of individuals could be measured. It will always be impossible to make practical arrangements fully match the truth that can be formulated in words, but there is one crucial change which could be made to existing societies in order to create the optimum conditions for justice on earth: that is, the combination of political power with philosophy, or the establishment of 'philosopher-rulers'. Without this, neither social nor individual happiness will ever be achieved

This section marks perhaps the most important transition in the entire *Republic*. It is a juncture which harks back to the outset of bk. 5 (for it is a final attempt to answer the question of 'possibility' which has hung over the discussion since 450c8), yet simultaneously begins a progression into what will turn out to be the great centrepiece of the dialogue, occupying the whole of bks. 6-7: an account of the 'true philosopher' in terms which involve an extensive and ambitious scheme of metaphysical ideas. The introduction of the theme of philosopher-rulers is thus both a completion of all the political and social proposals so far made for the just city, and at the same time the basis for a new and larger perspective on the ultimate nature of reality. But it would not be correct to say that this amounts to a transition *from* the practical to the metaphysical. Rather, it is the start of an extremely complex thesis that the rulers of the ideal city would have to be men and women (for there can be no doubt that the philosopher-rulers are not all men: 7.540c) who combined the practical, i.e. politics, and the metaphysical, i.e. knowledge of absolute truths, in a single, fused form of life. Philosopher-rulers would themselves be both theorists and people of practical wisdom: they are the solution to a political question (how could a human society be organised in full accordance with justice?), but a solution which transforms the question by subordinating the interpretation of all human concerns to a hypothesis of immutable reality.

The conception of philosopher-rulers is one of the great nodal points in Platonic philosophy: it represents an effort to resolve strains and tensions (between the contingent and the necessary, the temporal and the eternal, the practical and the abstract) which run deeply through P.'s life and thought. If the 7th *Epistle*, whatever its authorship, contains reliable information, one of the roots of P.'s philosophy lay in the combination of a strong impulse towards political activity, with a despairing withdrawal from the actual politics of contemporary Athens (7.324b-6b). Another, as we can see from P.'s own dialogues, developed from the Socratic conviction that good government ought to be a knowledge-based art or *technê*. Philosopher-rulers are thus intended to satisfy needs, and confront problems, that had grown in P.'s mind through his personal and intellectual experiences. But because those needs and problems relate to perennial human dilemmas (about power and morality, order and freedom, self-interest and the common good), and because P. expresses his response to them in such evocative style (n. 473c11 f.), the idea of philosopher-rulers has had repeated resonance in the subsequent history of political thought. It has exercised fascination not only upon idealists (in medieval Islam, fifteenth-century humanism, and elsewhere), but also upon many who have been troubled by the gap between the practice and theory of politics (see e.g. the sombre close to Hobbes, *Leviathan*, part II). Equally, it has repelled those who believe that political judgement cannot be the preserve of a select few (e.g. M. I. Finley, *Aspects of Antiquity* [London, 1986] ch. 6).

471c5   **never recall:** G.'s new challenge echoes the opening of the bk. (cf. nn. 472a 6, 8). Like that earlier juncture, the present stage is a major transition in the growth of the whole dialogue: its ramifications could not have been predicted from an acquaintance with the earlier sections of the work.

471c6   **put aside:** G. refers in particular to 458a–b (cf. the similar verb at 458a4). But the question of possibility or feasibility has hung over the entire discussion, since 450c8–d2. It was taken up initially, *à propos* of female Guardians, at 452e4 ff., and given an affirmative answer (using the principle that what is 'natural' must be possible) in the demonstration that women have substantially 'the same nature' as men: see 456b12-c7, 457a3, c2. It was faced once more, *à propos* the proposals for sexual communism, at 457d4-58b7, where Soc., as G. here reminds him, put it aside in order to concentrate on the principles of eugenics and kinship. The return to the issue of feasibility at 466d6-9 was short-lived, and was overtaken by further (military) details of Soc.'s scheme. Soc.'s final answer to the challenge will involve (i) a conceptual reorientation of the issue (appealing to the notion of a paradigm or model: 472c), (ii) an attempt to stipulate the one necessary and sufficient condition for the realisation of the ideal city (473c11 ff.). But the question of possibility will resurface yet again in later bks.: see esp. 6.499c-d, 501e-2b, 7.540-41a.

471c6   **to show that:** for the use of the definite article, making the whole of ὡς ... ποτὲ δυνατή into the object of μνησθήσεσθαι, see n. 454b4.

471c8   **I agree that:** no such verb appears in the Greek, but needs to be supplied (cf. e1) to cover the ὅτι clause; such an ellipse is not uncommon, and easily understood (Adam compares 1.352b6 ff.), even though it creates a break of construction (anacolouthon) at καὶ ... λέγω. A less preferable alternative is to take ὅτι (c8) to mean 'to support the claim that...': 'to support your claim that the city would enjoy..., I would also add that...'

471c8   **advantageous for the city:** G. talks as though convinced on the second of the two sources of scepticism (is it possible? and would it be for the best?) originally stated at 450c8–9. The question of benefit was directly addressed, in relation to female Guardians, at 456c–7c, and incorporated into the discussion of sexual communism at 457d ff., 461e ff.; cf. 464b4–5.
          The subject of the second γένοιτο is the same as that of the first (ctr. Boter 215), i.e. πολιτεία (c7). ᾗ is possessive dative, not locative.

471d2–3   **'brothers'...:** G. again speaks as if these relationships (with female equivalents, and generational extensions) were exhaustive; cf. n. 463c5–7.

471d3–5   **if women too...:** G. shows a lingering reservation on this point, in contrast to the clarity of Soc.'s earlier proposal that the female Guardians would participate fully in warfare (esp. 457a7, b9 f., 466e4, 468e2, and cf. 8.543a3–4); but see nn. 457a10, 466d1, 467c2–3, for some other uncertainties on this matter. The passing suggestion that women Auxiliaries might form a separate rear-division has not been anticipated in the earlier conversation, but it reflects earlier references to their relative physical weakness (451e2, 455e1). The idea that female soldiers could produce a special 'shock-effect' recurs at *Laws* 7.806b4–5, where the context betrays the influence of a mythical prototype, the Amazons: cf. the Introduction, p. 11.

472a1–2   **assault:** the cognate verb (*katatrechein*) is used with similar metaphorical force at *Laws* 7.806c9; for the application of military imagery to dialectical discussion cf. 474a3-b7, 1.335e7, *Tht.* 153a1-3, and my n. on 10.610c6. This aspect of the context helps to explain the reading of most mss. at a2, στρατευομένῳ, 'campaigning', instead of στραγγευομένῳ, 'hesitating'; but it is hard to make sense of the former: why, in military terms, should Soc. expect any 'sympathy' from G.? It is characteristic of P. to juxtapose metaphors from different sources (here, he switches again at a3). The corruption of στραγγεύομαι is not uncommon (LSJ s.v. give several cases).

472a3–4   **of the three:** the three being female Guardians, sexual communism, and now philosopher-rulers; the image echoes 457b7–c5 and prepares for 473c6–8. *trikumia*, a triple or huge wave, had proverbial status: cf. *Euthd.* 293a3, Aesch. *PV* 1015 (with Griffith's n.), Eur. *Hipp.* 1213 (literal). I am unconvinced by the arguments of Z. Planinc, *Plato's Political Philosophy* (London, 1991) 277–84, that P. is echoing Odysseus's shipwreck in Hom. *Od.* 5.

472a6   **right after all:** Soc. is reminding G. of his original hesitation about the entire subject of 'sharing of women and children'; see esp. 450c–51a, 453d1–3. Part of the explanation for that nervousness, he now reveals, was his awareness of where the whole discussion would eventually lead them – to the most crucial of all his political proposals, 'philosopher-rulers'.

472a8   **let you get away:** the same verb as at 449b6, 8 (and, differently, at 451b3, 6); cf. 450a1. G., like Soc., is reverting to the (playful) attitude which the interlocutors struck at the start of bk. 5; cf. n. 471c5.

472b4   **the nature of justice:** lit. 'justice, what sort <of thing> it is' (cf. n. 464b2–3 on the divided indirect question). The conjunction of predicative neuter adj. with feminine noun can be explained by an ellipse of χρῆμα: it is repeated several times in the following passage, and is common (e.g. 477e8, 1.332e13 f., 2.368e5, *Symp.* 176d1); cf. n. c4 ('justice itself') below. For the idea of dialectic as a metaphorical journey, see n. 452c4.

472b7   **nothing:** the same ironic understatement as *Chrm.* 164a9, *Grg.* 498a1, and (in milder form) *Tht.* 146d6.

472b7   **if we discover:** in fact, a definition of justice was reached at 4.432b–34a, and was tested by reference to the individual and the city, 434d–44a; n.b. the claim to have 'discovered' justice, 444a6. Soc. now implies that the earlier account, built on the principle of each person to his own function (n. 453b5), was incomplete. We can see that this was so in two main ways: first, because the ramifications of the definition had still to be fully explored (bk. 5's social reforms are themselves part of this process, and bks. 8–9 will take it further by elucidation of types of injustice); second, because the argument is about to move onto the plane of metaphysics, and it will emerge that justice is truly comprehensible only as part of an ultimate scheme of values which was not included in the earlier definition.

472c2   **much greater share:** the Greek, lit. 'most of the others', involves an idiomatic coalescence of a comparative, 'more than the others', with a superlative, 'most of all;' cf. 456d12 f., and Weir Smyth §1434.

472c4   **ideal:** it is important to specify the sense of *paradeigma* with some care. The parallel with a painter (d4 ff.) makes it clear that an ideal need not be known to exist, but requires a conception of what the thing – justice, physical beauty, etc. – would be like at its best: for a *paradeigma* (of a different sort) in the mind cf. e.g. 3.409b1, c7, d2. P. sometimes speaks of ultimate truth or reality being used as a *paradeigma* by philosophers: see esp. 6.484c8, 500e3, 7.540a9. But this does not mean that it is part of the nature of a *paradeigma*, as such, to be true or real. At 7.529d7, for example, P. suggests that the movements of actual heavenly bodies, because they fall short of the (transcendent) astronomical truth, should be used as *paradeigmata* for knowledge of astronomy only in the way that fine (artistic) diagrams can serve the study of true geometry, i.e. as guides or models. At *Euthph.* 6e3–6, it is a definition of a virtue which supplies a *paradeigma*.

So the account of justice that Soc. and G. have been constructing, in the form of a hypothetical social order, is the equivalent to a model, a picture, or a definition, against which particular people and cities can be tested. Whether or not this ideal is realisable in practice, remains an open question: cf. 9.592b, *Laws* 5.739e (communism as *paradeigma* of a constitution). But Soc. now proceeds to transform this into a further question – what is the source of the values which a model of justice is designed to capture? This in turn opens up the metaphysics of bks. 6–7.

472c4   **justice itself:** the feminine noun has a neuter adj., implying *chrêma* in apposition – i.e. 'justice, <the thing> itself' (cf. 2.363a1, 6.505c2, *Prt.* 360e8, *Crat.* 411d8, *Tht.* 146e9); cf. the predicative use at b4 above. The force of *auto*, 'itself', is something like 'pure and simple', or 'without qualification'. The phrase anticipates the later reference to uniform, invariable values, as opposed to their imperfect realisation in particular instances; see n. 476b6–7. But while it here implies objectivity of values, it need not entail the metaphysics developed in that later context.

472c5–6   **if he *could* exist:** the syntax of ἄνδρα...εἰ γένοιτο could in principle be treated as a divided indirect question (cf. n. 464b2–3), i.e. '...searching to discover whether the perfectly just man could exist'. But that would introduce a blatant anomaly into Soc.'s notion of constructing a *paradeigma*. Doubts have been raised about the text (see Adam), but it can stand as a loosely phrased emphasis on the hypothetical nature of the whole discussion.

472c7   **looking to see:** i.e. treating them as a standard of reference. Such expressions, of which P. is fond, occur in conjunction with the idea of a *paradeigma* (c4) at 3.409c7, 6.484c8-d1, 500e-1b, 7.529d-30a, 540a8-9, *Euthph.* 6d-e, *Tim.* 28a-9a, *Laws* 7.811b8. Several of these passages mention or allude to an artist's or craftsman's model/template (cf. n. d5), and the same is true of some other uses of 'look to/at' (e.g. 10.596b6-7, *Grg.* 503e, *Crat.* 389a-b, 390e). Ironic though it may seem, P.'s conception of philosophical 'paradigms' has been influenced by the terminology and activity of manual crafts. So he may here have in mind not just the painter's ideal *paradeigma* (d5), but the templates etc. used in other areas of artistic design: cf. the craftsman's drawings at 7.529e1-3, and see J. J. Coulton, *Greek Architects at Work* (London, 1977) 55-8, for architects' specimen capitals etc.

472c8   **happiness or its contrary:** for this type of phrase, avoiding a specific noun for 'unhappiness', cf. Arist. *EN* 1100b10–11, *Poet.* 1450a20.

472d1   **the fortune most like theirs:** lit. 'a fortune/destiny most like that one' (i.e. happiness/unhappiness, c8); the genitive is possible after *homoios* (LSJ s.v., B2), and need not be emended. *moira* traditionally denotes an allotted 'portion' of life; P. employs it here without any implication of forces outside the individual's own psychological and ethical responsibility: in that sense, the passage is in keeping with the idea, found in the myth of Er, that souls choose their own 'destiny' (esp. 10.620e3–4).

472d4   **paint an ideal:** for other recognition of this type of art cf. e.g. Arist. *Poet.* 1448a5–6, 1461b13 (*paradeigma*), Xen. *Mem.* 3.10.2. But P. himself will take no account of it in his attack on painting as mirror-like copying in bk. 10 (cf. my edn., p. 8). The motif of philosophers as painters in a different medium – namely the ethical and political fabric of men's lives – recurs at 6.500e-1c; for other analogies between philosophy and visual art, see 4.420c–d (with n. 466a6), 8.548c–d, *Plt.* 277a–c, *Tim.* 19b–c.

472e4   **to be organised:** *oikein* is here, as at e.g. 462d7, 473a8, intransitive with a quasi-passive sense; cf. LSJ s.v., B II 2. The passive form at 473b6 below, and e.g. 2.371c6, 7.521b9, is identical in sense.

473a2   **less contact with the truth:** contrasts between word and deed (cf. 463c9 f.), *logos* and *ergon* (a5–6), are common in Greek; but P.'s contention here is a source of difficulty. The most direct interpretation is that truth can be defined precisely in relation to language, but less reliably in relation to states of affairs. Some such sentiment might appear 'natural' (a1), and will explain Soc.'s anxiety not to be compelled to show *exactly* how his proposals could be realised. But why does he add, 'whether or not anyone thinks this', and appeal to G. for his personal agreement? One view is that P. is here preparing the ground for the metaphysical doctrines which will shortly be explored: Soc. is thus alluding to the idea that words can be used to denote 'forms' (476a5) of pure and absolute values, while objects in the world have mixed and even conflicting attributes (cf. White [1979] 152-3). On this reading, the passage points forward to the special interpretation of 'truth' that will be used in the subsequent argument (n. 475e4). But these are metaphysical implications which, it has to be said, P. has scarcely signalled here, and it remains possible to read Soc.'s question without discerning them at all; cf. *Laws* 1.636a4-5 for a comparable sentiment.

473a2–3   **whether or not...:** this clause recurs identically at 9.579d9, where P. is similarly proposing something contrary to common beliefs. For κἄν εἰ = καὶ εἰ, with a redundant ἄν, see e.g. 10.612c8 (with my n.), *Prt.* 328a8, *Phdo* 71b7, and Weir Smyth §1766b; 477a2 below is a slightly different case.

473a5–6   **don't compel me to show:** lit. 'don't place this compulsion on me', τοῦτο and με forming a double accusative after ἀνάγκαζε. Although ἀποφαίνειν, a7, is dependent on ἀνάγκαζε, there is a redundant δεῖν at a6, as if the sentence ran (e.g.) 'don't say that I need to show...' For other cases of a superfluous δεῖν in P., see e.g. 6.486d2, 7.535a10, with R. Renehan, *Studies in Greek Texts* (Göttingen, 1976) 127–9, who suggests that it is a colloquial idiom. Without the insertion of ἄν in a6, the mss. reading would mean: 'to show that they *do* come about in practice': Adam defends this.

473a8   **be prepared...:** φάναι, infinitive, serves ... 2nd person imperative, a usage commoner in poetry than prose. Adam compares 6.508b12, 509b7; add e.g. *Crat.* 426b8.

473b6   **the smallest change:** the presupposition is not, of course, that existing cities get most political arrangements right, but that if such a change can be identified, it will make the possible realisation of the ideal city all the more credible. Unfortunately, as Soc. concedes almost at once (c3), the necessary condition for the just city is no small matter at all!

473b7   **type:** *tropos* combines the senses of 'kind' and 'character'; cf. n. 449a3–4.

473c3   **it isn't...small:** Soc. at once abandons the hope of b6, 9; the qualification is oddly overlooked by the summary of White (1979) 153. The idea of difficulty will be reiterated at 6.501a3–4, 7.540d2–3.

473c4   **possible:** the argument seems in danger of being caught in a kind of regress at this point. The aim is to show that something like the city hypothesised in bks. 2–5, and particularly the communistic scheme of bk. 5 itself, is a practical possibility. The present contention is that this possibility depends on the (prior) existence of philosopher–rulers; but rulers who are also philosophers are already an integral feature of the city in question: the solution to this apparent circularity lies in the new and fuller meaning to be given to 'philosopher' in the following argument (Introduction p. 26). Yet the feasibility of philosopher-rulers is at least as vulnerable to scepticism as, say, the proposal for sexual communism. P. is aware of this difficulty, as we can see from his later insistence on the necessity of philosopher-rulers at 6.499b-502c: note

especially the defensiveness of 499c-d. But P. does not undertake to show that the just
city is ever *likely* to come into existence, only that it requires conditions which are
conceivable within the limitations of human life. Cf. n. c11 f. below.

473c6 **we compared:** at 472a4.

473c7 **cannot be evaded:** lit. 'nonetheless (δ' οὖν), it will be said'. εἰρήσεται expresses a
sense of obligation; cf. e.g. Isoc. 7.76, 12.225.

473c7–8 **wave of...laughter:** Soc. blends two earlier motifs – the laughter anticipated from the
outset of bk. 5, 452a–d; and the marine imagery of waves/drowning at 453d, 457b7–9.
One might well expect the idea of philosopher-rulers to be greeted with mirth or
derision, since there was a general Greek stereotype of the philosopher as utterly
remote from the 'real world' of politics etc., and the *last* person capable of running a
city. Cf. Adeimantus's objection at 6.487b ff., esp. 487d5, with the ensuing discussion
of the apparent 'uselessness' of the philosopher (to 489c).
  Trans. lit. 'even if it [the topic] is likely to deluge <me>, just like a 'laughing' wave,
with laughter and contempt'; ἀτεχνῶς goes with ὥσπερ: cf. e.g. *Phdo* 90c4. The text
has been needlessly doubted (cf. Adam I 361–2). κῦμα ἐκγελῶν, 'laughing wave',
nicely plays on use of the γέλως word-group for the shimmering of the sea: cf. e.g.
Hom. Hymn Dem. 14, Aesch. *PV* 90.

473c11f. **unless...philosophers come to power:** a grandiloquent statement (reiterated in similar
terms at 6.499b–c), projecting a deliberately portentous and oracular tone (n. d5); the
twin aorist subjunctives, c11/d2, are 'ingressive', marking the decisive onset of a new
political order: cf. Weir Smyth §§1924-5. The passage, whose tone should be
compared with *Plt.* 301e-2b, became one of the most renowned in P.: Boter 324-5
collects ancient references to it. Although its subject is traditionally labelled as
'philosopher kings', it is important to grasp that P. means this to cover rule by any
number of philosophers, and that these philosophers are to include women alongside
men (n. 460b9-10). P. sometimes distinguishes between kingship of one person, and
'aristocracy' of a group (e.g. 4.445d5-6); but he also wishes *basileus*, 'king', *basileuein*,
'rule as king', and their cognates, to symbolise true and just political leadership by one
or more philosophers: see esp. the description of the Guardians as 'kings' at 7.520b6,
8.543a4-6, with the use of the verb, referring back to earlier bks., at 9.576d2, e4; cf.
the general application of such terminology to the just man at 9.580c1-2, 587b-e (n.b.
587d1, the equation of 'aristocratic' and 'royal'); and compare the ideal politician, the
'royal ruler' (*basilikos*), of *Plt. passim*. So the ideal philosophical ruler could, in
principle, be either an individual or a member of a group (cf. 7.540d4); but P.'s belief
that genuine philosophers are scarce (n. d4-5) makes the chances of a philosophical
city higher if just one such person is enough: this is a consideration stressed at 6.502a-
b, and P. continued to think along such lines, as *Laws* 4.709-12 (with many
modifications) shows.
  Yet a deep difficulty remains. The just city requires philosophical government for
its maintenance, but the only kind of city conducive to the *production* of true
philosophers is the just city itself: see esp. 6.497a–d. This looks like inescapable
circularity, which is no doubt why P. later introduces the idea of special, perhaps
divine, fortune helping to create the rule of philosophers (6.499b5, c1; cf. *Laws*
4.709b7-8). The circularity, however, concerns only the question of *how* such a city
might be created; it does not affect the *Rep.*'s use of the city as a model of justice
(472b–c). For the (unjustified) suspicion of a further circularity, see n. c4 above.

473d1–2 **kings and princes:** the combination recurs at 6.499b7, 502a6; although *dunastês* and
its cognates are sometimes associated with unjust or lawless forms of power (cf.
8.544d1, *Grg.* 526b3, with Dodds on *Grg.* 492b3, Gomme on Thuc. 4.78.3), they can

also readily be used as neutral terms for (members of) ruling groups, and that is P.'s intention here, as also at 7.540d4.

473d4–5 **compulsorily barred:** notice the drastic implications for philosophy itself, as well as for politics. Detachment from the world, something that might be only too congenial to a philosophical mind (cf. e.g. 6.486a8–10, 500b–c), would be forbidden to all philosophers in the just city. Adam understands P. only to be prohibiting one-sided lives, not to be excluding the individuals who now lead them. But I think that the strength of language, taken together with 474c2–3, favours *both* inferences. Much of bk. 6, esp. 484–500, will be taken up explaining why genuine philosophical natures are extremely rare (cf. *Tim.* 51e5-6), and how they can easily be corrupted by the pressures of current societies; but P.'s whole thesis is averse to a philosophical life that is cocooned from the pursuit of justice in the human world. We must not, of course, draw direct inferences from this about the right way for philosophers to behave in existing cities (cf. 9.592a-b).

473d5 **there will be no respite from evil:** the Greek has a present tense, whose force is quasi-prophetic. The same tense, with the same phrase, *paula kakôn* (cf. Soph. *Trach.* 1255), occurs in the mock-oracle at Ar. *Lys.* 772; for the 'oracular present', cf. Fraenkel on Aesch. *Agam.* 126. With the spirit of this remark compare *Epist.* 7.337a-b (societies will never eradicate evil without fear and shame); but *Phdo* 66b5-7 (philosophers will never attain real truth while embodied) and *Tht.* 176a (evil is the necessary counterpart of good in the human world) put a more pessimistic, or realistic, point of view.

473d6 **the entire human race:** Popper 279–81, n. 50, followed by Cross & Woozley 137–8, denies any general humanitarianism in this phrase, and takes it to mean individual souls, as opposed to whole cities; for a different view see Adam on 470e. But there remain passages in which P.'s perspective on the reform of human societies transcends a purely Greek perspective: see 6.499c9 (about which Popper 280–1 is too dismissive), with nn. 470c1–3, 6.

473e3 **originally:** at 450a–51a; see n. 450d1 ('hesitation'), and cf. 472a5–7.

473e5 **private or...social life:** what is said here about happiness depends on what was previously said about justice, though the mutual entailment of justice and happiness will not be finally asserted until 9.580–92b, 10.612 ff. The conception of justice put forward in bks. 2–5 regards the individual and the social as fully interdependent: it is right both for individuals and for the city that each person should fulfil his own appropriate function within the social order (esp. 4.433a–b). It is also true that the picture which has been built up of civic justice is meant to provide a model for the understanding of individual psychology: see esp. 4.434d–e, 443c–e. Both these considerations are relevant to the present passage.

473e7ff. **a great throng:** G. builds up a droll, graphic image of physical and verbal aggression, in order to accentuate the controversial status of the proposal for philosopher-rulers. The image is taken from vulgar street-fights and public abuse (cf. e.g. Lys. 3.7–18, Dem. 54.3–10, 17–20); but G.'s language also has associations with both military and forensic conflict (cf. nn. 457e7, 472a1–2). It is a revealing fact about P.'s control and variation of dramatic tone that he juxtaposes Soc.'s sombre, somewhat vatic, pronouncement (n. d5) with this entertaining exclamation of astonishment from young G.

474a4 **mockery:** the verb *tôthazein* denotes strong, jeering language, as *Hp. Mj.* 290a 4–5 confirms; although it was sometimes associated with ritual abuse in religious settings (Herod. 2.60.2, Arist. *Rhet.* 1336b16, and probably Ar. *Wasps* 1362/8), there seem to be no special overtones here. G.'s point recalls, of course, the motif of anti-

philosophical laughter which has been sounded several times in bk. 5: see 452a–e,
457b, 473c7–8.

474a6   **And I'm glad...too:** a colloquial expression; cf. e.g. *Lys.* 204a4, *Prt.* 352d4, *Crat.*
431a7, with LSJ s.v. καλός, C II 5–6, for exclamatory uses of καλῶς.

474a6   **I...won't desert you:** G. is always portrayed as a close and affectionate, if sometimes
rather innocent, disciple of Soc.'s; cf. n. 450b7. It is not inconceivable, though
speculative, that P. projects onto the persona of his brother some of what, in retrospect,
he saw in his own youthful feelings about Soc.: Xen. *Mem.* 3.6.1, for what it is worth,
implies that P. was closer than his brother to Soc. The 'good will', *eunoia*, of which G.
gives a promise is not something that can always be counted on in dialectic: see the
contrasting attitude of Thrasymachus, 1.336b ff. (esp. 336c1–2). G.'s 'encouragement',
parakeleuesthai (a8), may here have military connotations: cf. e.g. Thuc. 4.25.9,
7.70.7; compare 450d5, 9 (*paratharrunein, paramuthia*).

474b2   **disbelievers:** the opponents who have been in view since 450c; see n. 450c7.

474b3-476d7

*It is necessary, then, to define the true philosopher (the 'lover of wisdom'). As with other 'lovers',
his desires embrace an entire class of objects - in this case, all learning and knowledge. There
may be other people, such as lovers of sights and sounds, who desire to experience as many
particular instances of a given quality (such as beauty) as they can. But such people refuse to
believe in, and their minds are incapable of grasping, the single, real form of 'beauty itself' (and
likewise with other qualities): they are like dreamers, who mistake mere images for the truth. The
philosopher, the only person who can apprehend 'beauty itself' etc., has genuine knowledge,
whereas the others have only belief or opinion (doxa).*

The solemn pronouncement that only philosopher-rulers can bring happiness to human societies,
creates the need for a fuller, deeper account of what is meant by a 'philosopher'. The origins of the
words *philosophos* and *philosophia* are uncertain; one tradition ascribed their distinctive use to
Pythagoras (Heraclides Pont. frs. 87-8 Wehrli; DK I 454 §15; Iambl. *Vita Pyth.* 44), but the
reliability of this is debatable: compare Morrison 207-9, W. Burkert, *Hermes* 88 (1960) 159-77,
and H. B. Gottschalk, *Heraclides of Pontus* (Oxford, 1980) 23-33. We can in any case see from
passages such as Isoc. 12.263, 15.50, 270 ff., 285, that these terms, and the concepts they
expressed, were still highly contestable in the fourth century (cf. Morrison 216-18 on the contrast
between Isoc. and P.); and, as Burkert *op. cit.* maintains, P.'s own contribution to their definition,
after a period in which they were current in somewhat freer senses, was of major historical
significance. It is an implicit aim of all P.'s works to give meaning to the idea of philosophy, but
the final section of bk. 5 (with its sequel in bks. 6-7) faces the issue directly: it does so by equating
the wisdom, *sophia*, that is the object of the philosopher's love, with a special kind of knowledge.
The combination of an emphasis on the 'true philosopher' with a metaphysical account of
knowledge is particularly reminiscent of *Phaedo* (n. 475e3), a work which, perhaps relevantly, has
strong Pythagorean associations; but *Rep.* 5 and *Phaedo* diverge in other respects (see below).

The argument of the present section begins in what might appear a light-hearted and oblique
manner. The use of a model of 'lover of *x*', such that the title belongs only to the person who
loves the entire class of '*x*', certainly involves touches of humour (esp. 474d-e, 475d), as well as
some rather fluid reasoning (nn. 475a5, b2, 4, 8-9). Nor, perhaps, do boys, wine, honour and food
immediately seem the aptest analogies for the philosopher's love of wisdom or knowledge. But
the analogies do in fact serve a rhetorically significant purpose - namely to suggest that
philosophy, though pursued through the exercise of reason and intellect, nevertheless involves an
element that P. wishes us to think of as a strong *passion* or appetite. The erotic aspect of this
suggestion, later picked up at e.g. 6.485c6-7, 490b, is the same as that which is fully developed in

Diotima's speech in *Symp.* (esp. 209-12); and it is corroborated by many other passages in which P. applies erotic imagery to philosophy (e.g. *Euthph.* 14c 3-4, *Prt.* 309a-c, 317c7, *Grg.* 481d-2b, *Meno* 70b, *Phdo* 66e3, 68a).

But what is the philosopher's passion *for*? Soc.'s initial answer – all 'learning' or 'studies', *mathêmata* (475b-c) - elicits G.'s obvious objection that one can learn or understand (*manthanein*) many different things. G. suggests a contrast between philosophers and 'lovers of sights and sounds' (i.e. devotees of poetry, music and related cultural arts). This in turn allows Soc. to construct the crucial distinction, whose special status is acknowledged (475e6-7), between (e.g.) beauty as a property of particular things, and 'beauty itself'. The latter is the object of a philosophical experience which is evoked in terms that have visionary overtones (nn. 475e4, 476b7-8, 10); in his passionate love of knowledge, the philosopher is depicted as a kind of mystic. This knowledge is of unchanging entities which 476a5 (see n.) refers to as 'forms', since they correspond to collections or 'classes' of particulars in the sensible world. There is one such entity for each kind of property mentioned by the argument, and these properties belong to two groups: (i) those, such as beauty and justice, which define central human values (n. 476a4-5); (ii) relational properties, such as doubleness, largeness or heaviness (n. 479b3). All properties in both groups are such as to possess contraries or opposites (n. 475e9), and it may also be that P. takes them *all* to be somehow relational (n. 479a6-7). The following statements can be made about forms *vis-à-vis* particular instances of the corresponding properties (see individual nn.):

forms are each 'one entity', particulars are 'many things' (475e-6a);
forms become 'connected with', or are 'common to', particulars (476a6-7);
particular properties are 'like', i.e. resemble, forms (476c6-7);
particulars 'participate in' forms (476d1-2).

Although the argument undoubtedly has wider implications, it is the properties marked by value-terms which provide its centre of interest, for it is knowledge of these, and only of these, which can support the case for philosopher-rulers. Thus, while the passage provides one version of P.'s so-called 'theory of Forms' (see e.g. Woodruff [1982] 162-3 for a summary), it is important to focus on the special emphases and concerns of its context. In *Phaedo*, for example, knowledge of 'forms' is said to be attainable only after death (66d-67b), a claim which is integral to the work's theme of immortality. In *Rep.* 5-7, that claim does not figure, since it would be of no use in justifying the need for philosopher-rulers: cf. the Introduction §4.

474b5   **define for them:** *autous* is separate from the following accusative.

474b7   **clear:** the force of *dia-* in *diadêlos* is the same as in *diapherein*, 'differ'; the adj. thus means 'clear' in the sense of distinguishable from related/confusable entities: cf. e.g. Thuc. 4.68.5, Arist. *De an.* 421a14.

474c1   **naturally:** i.e. they possess the 'nature' requisite for philosophy; cf. the kinds of mental quality sketched at 455b, with nn. 455b5, 476b11.

474c8   **remind you:** a dramatic hint that G. has familiarity with special philosophical arguments; cf. n. 475e6, and compare e.g. 6.504e7-8, 507a7-9, *Phdo* 100b. It might be supposed (see White [1979] 154) that Soc. refers back to 4.437d-8a, where he argued that desires do not, in their pure form, specify a particular object, but can be satisfied by *any* object in the relevant class: e.g. thirst, as such, is simply a desire for 'drink'; if one has desire for a specific drink, then this is no longer a simple, but a qualified, case of thirst. But the point in the present passage is not really the same (n.b. G.'s uncertainty, d1-2): Soc. is now talking only about those desires (embraced by the verb *philein*, n. c9-11) which form *dispositions* – a point reinforced by the use of adjs. in *-ikos* at d5, 475b4, e1 (cf. n. 456a7). One may, on some occasion, desire (e.g.) 'honour'; but one will count as a 'lover of honour' (475a9 ff.) only if one has a dispositional tendency to desire or value honour. So it is doubtful whether there is any reference to bk. 4; the allusion is to (imaginary) discussion on other occasions: cf. e.g. 10.596a6 ('our usual method').

474c9–11   **a 'lover'...to love the whole:** the Greek verb *philein* has a usage broadly coextensive with that of the English 'love'. Likewise its partial synonyms, *stergein* (c11), *aspazesthai* (d7), *agapan* (475b2), and *eran* (implied by *erôtikos*, 474d4-5), to which P. adds words of the *epithum-* group (475b2 ff.): whatever may be true elsewhere (cf. D. Hyland, *Phronesis* 13 [1968] 32-46), P. does not here rely on careful distinctions among these various terms.

     Soc.'s equation of love with love of a whole class, reiterated at 6.485b5–8, seems initially implausible: it is obvious that someone may 'love' a boy, a wine or an honour, without loving *all* members of the same class or type. But Soc. is not talking about everything that can be described by this verb, only about behaviour of a dispositional character (n. c8) which makes one a 'lover of *x*', where *x* is indeed a class not an individual: in this respect, the plain Greek and English verbs are equally capable of ambiguity, and Soc.'s usage of *philein* must be normative – i.e. it asserts the conditions which will make one a 'lover of *x*' in the specified sense. P.'s reason for developing the argument in this way is to construct a model of 'love of *x*' to which *philosophia*, 'love of wisdom', will precisely conform, and of which it will be the supreme example: cf. the head-note to this section.

474d3   **not something one expected...:** Soc. playfully treats G. as someone addicted to homosexual attachments to adolescents; although G. seems to disclaim the description (475a3–4), Soc. had earlier referred to a young but less than ideally beautiful 'beloved', *paidika*, of G.'s (3.402e2–3). Perhaps that passage too was teasing; we lack the relevant information about G.'s life.

474d4–5   **of the right age:** lit. 'in their <adolescent> stage/season of life'; cf. e4–5, 475a2. For the equivalent adj., *hôraios*, see 10.601b6–7, a passage which complements this one by suggesting that adolescence may carry an attraction which is not identical to obvious beauty; cf. *Chrm.* 154b9–10.

474d5   **passionate lover of boys:** in Greek, a hendiadys – lit. 'boy-loving and passionate'. The first adj., *philopais* (first occurring here, since Simon. 66.6 *EG* is Hellenistic), reflects the fact that a younger homosexual partner could always, regardless of precise age, be called *pais*, 'child' or 'boy' (cf. n. 466e5), and hence *paidika*: Dover (1978) 16, 85–6. The second, *erôtikos*, repeated from d4, is applicable to any form of sexual desire (cf. 458d5), but it is accepted by Aeschines (1.136) as a description of his own behaviour as a lover of many boys. It is notable that, humour apart, Soc. supposes there to be men who possess a consistent, though not necessarily exclusive, sexual orientation (a disposition: nn. c8, 9–11) towards younger males: cf. Cratinus fr. 163 *PCG*/152 K, Eur. *Cycl.* 582–4.

474d6   **bite and sting:** cf. n. 458d6.

474d7   **your favourites:** I avoid translating *kalos* here in the strict sense of 'beautiful', since that would make Soc.'s point illogical. Clearly the term is applied generically, by a principle of association, to all male adolescents who are the object of sexual attention from older men: cf. *Chrm.* 154b9–10, with Dover (1978) 15–16, 111–24. Soc.'s point is complicated by the fact that he cites *individual* features which detract (except in the lover's eyes) from beauty, while presupposing that such boys are found physically attractive in other respects. This passage finds later echoes, perhaps mediated by a Hellenistic text (see Bailey *ad loc.*), at Lucretius *DRN* 4.1155 ff., Ovid *Ars Am.* 2.641 ff., 657 ff.; the point is wittily inverted (imagining non-existent faults, to counteract love) at Ovid *Rem. Am.* 315 ff.

474d8   **snub-nosed:** a feature typically thought ugly (Ar. *Eccl.* 617, 705); here there is a piquant allusion to Soc.'s own appearance (*Tht.* 143e8, 209c1–5). But there are degrees of snubness, not all of which are entirely unappealing (Arist. *Pol.* 1309b23–5, cf. *Rhet.* 1360a27–30)!

474e1–4   **dark-skinned...pallor:** the passage presupposes a general interest, on the part of homosexual 'lovers', in the complexions of their favourites; on this and related matters cf. Dover (1978) 73–81.

'Dark-skinned' (e1): not 'black' (a standard sense of *melas*) but swarthy or heavily tanned. The Greeks tended to connect such skin-colour with the outdoor work of the less affluent: cf. the contrast between the 'sunburnt' poor and the rich man 'reared in the shade' at 8.556d2-4; and see e.g. Ar. *Thesm.* 31, Arist. *EE* 1220a20, ps.-Arist. *Physiogn.* 812a12, Theoc. 10.27 (a country girl). Nice discrimination would be needed to distinguish acceptable from unacceptable darkness of complexion, since many wealthy males must also have been well tanned: Soc.'s 'manly' may allude to an association between sun-tan and the bodies of young athletes. But the eye's discrimination may be guided by social prejudice or other kinds of favouritism - that, of course, is part of Soc.'s point about the behaviour of lovers.

'Fair-skinned' (e2): i.e. having the 'whiteness' of complexion thought characteristic of women (Eur. *Bacch.* 453–9; Ar. *Thesm.* 191, *Eccl.* 387, 428, 699, 878, with 63–4; ps. -Arist. *Physiogn.* 812a13–14). Dover (1978) 80, n. 33, takes 'children of the gods' to reflect a general association between gods and light/purity; cf. my n. on 10.617c2, with *Laws* 12.956a6.

'Honey-fresh' (e2): a term capable of more than one nuance, since at Theoc. 10.27 it describes a dark-skinned girl (cf. Gow *ad loc.*), while at ps. -Arist. *Physiogn.* 812a19 it appears to mean a special shade of pallor (distinct from both *leukos* and *ôchros*). This is not surprising, since there is honey of more than one colour: for both 'golden' and 'white' varieties see e.g. Arist. *Hist. An.* 554b16 (honeydew), 626b30, 627a2–3. That said, many Greek compounds in *meli-* ('honey-') are affective rather than neutrally descriptive, so *melichlôros* should not be treated as a strict colour-term. The second part of the compound, *chlôros*, 'fresh', which sometimes signifies a shade of yellow, was itself applied to honey as early as Hom. *Il.* 11.631, *Od.* 10.234. Cf. E. Irwin, *Colour Terms in Greek Poetry* (Toronto, 1974) ch. 2 (*chlôros* in general), 56-60 (*melichlôros*).

'Pallor' (e4): *ôchros*, said at *Tim.* 68c4 to be a mixture of white and yellow, mark the reputed sallowness of reclusive philosophers who avoid the sunlight (Ar. *Clouds* 103, 1017, 1112, Theoc. 14.6), or the bloodless look produced by great fear (e.g. Ar. *Frogs* 307, Arist. *EN* 1128b13–14). Technical surveys of *ôchros, leukos*, and *chlôros* are provided by H. Dürbeck, *Zur Charakteristik der griechischen Farbenbezeichnungen* (Bonn, 1977).

475a1   **utter every kind of language:** *Laws* 10.890d3–4 indicates that the phrase φωνὴν/ας πᾶσαν/ας ἀφιέναι was a recognised expression; to judge by other occurrences, at *Euthd.* 293a1, Dem. 18.195, 218, it can apparently cover many situations in which speech is strained for a special purpose.

475a5   **lovers of wine:** at Herod. 3.34.2 and Theopompus com. fr. 78 K, *philoinos* is a 'wine-bibber' rather than a connoisseur of wine, and that is the sense required by Soc.'s argument too, in order to exemplify a dispositional desire for all and every kind of wine. But that also turns the example into one of compulsive behaviour, and does little to illuminate what it might mean elsewhere to 'love' a whole class of objects (474c8-11); cf. n. b2.

475a10   **minor military offices:** lit. 'they command a *trittus*'; the latter was a 'third' of each of the ten Athenian tribes, and comprised a group of districts or 'demes': see Arist. *Ath. Pol.* 21.3–4, with Rhodes *ad loc.* Soc.'s remark echoes well-established cynicism about 'office-seekers' in democracy: cf. Ar. *Ach.* 595, Eupolis fr. 248 *PCG*/234 K, Xen. *Symp.* 1.4.

475b2   *every* **kind of honour:** once again (n. a5) Soc. illustrates a petty and vulgar species of compulsiveness. The points seems all the more rhetorical for being offered as a definition of *philotimia*, 'love of honour', since *philotimia* need not reduce itself to an obsessive desire for *any* honour: in contemporary usage, the idea was often positively interpreted as a striving to gain public recognition for service done to one's community; Dover (1974) 230–33. P. treats the term as intrinsically derogatory (cf. 1.347b2–3), and he will later analyse it as the vice of the city/man of 'timocracy' (synon. with *philotimia*: 8.545b5–7): see 8.545c–550b. Such a city is one ruled by the 'spirited' part of the soul, typified by the soldier-class (550b6–7, 9.581a–b). This reminds us that honour is a legitimate aim even for the Auxiliaries (esp. 468c10–e2): the timocratic city is one in which desire for such honour has broken away from the control of reason.

475b4   **constant desire:** such is the emphasis of the *-ikos* adjectival suffix, making it equivalent to the adjs. in *philo-* in the preceding passage (474d5, 475a5, a9); cf. n. 474c8. Soc. reformulates his prescriptive definition of what it means to be a 'lover of *x*', from 474c8–11. The intervening examples have been playful in tone, miscellaneous in character, and remote from *philosophia*, 'love of wisdom': yet G. now happily agrees to a generalisation which had originally puzzled him. The whole passage, from 474d, is a somewhat rhetorical and humorous treatment of the 'love of *x*' model, where *x* is a whole class (*eidos*, b5) of objects. It is rhetorical partly in the sense that it makes no conceptual or logical difference to the ensuing definition of philosophy: philosophy can count as the love of all wisdom, *regardless* of how we construe such ideas as 'love of wine' or 'love of honour'; equally, even if all other phenomena of the 'love of *x*' type followed the pattern suggested by Soc., it would still need to be asked whether this is the right model for philosophy.

475b8–9   **desire for...*all* wisdom:** cf. Heraclitus fr. 35 DK, 'philosophers must be enquirers into very many things'. But given the semantic scope of *sophia* in contemporary Greek (embracing skill or expertise in a wide range of areas: Dover [1974] 119–21), Soc.'s contention is not self-evident. The difficulty is increased by the even wider senses of 'studies', 'learning', etc., in what follows - hence G.'s frank exclamation at d1 ff. When the argument is later recalled, at 6.485a4 ff., Soc. will stipulate (ib. b1-3) that it is the wisdom of *eternal, immutable* things that the philosopher 'loves', and he will go on (6.502 ff., 7.521c ff.) to design a curriculum of specifically philosophical 'studies'. But the carefully defined terms of those later passages - turning 'love of wisdom' into a highly intensive, discriminating disposition - make it even more curious that P. should here dwell on compulsive love of boys, wine, and honour (plus food, c3-4) as analogies (cf. 6.485b7-8 for a reminder of the point). P.'s motive, perhaps, is a wish to draw attention, by means of a rhetorically pointed juxtaposition, to the idea that philosophy is a passion in its own right, an all-consuming 'love' that bears a structural, though not of course a substantive, similarity to many ordinary types of appetitive behaviour; cf. n. c6 below.

475b11   **studies:** *mathêma* could be used of anything one might study, learn, know (cf. 4.438c7) or understand; it here refers broadly to the intellectual contents of education. But P. is preparing for a redefinition of what it means to 'know' something, and this will eventually produce the notion that the only true *mathêmata* are the philosopher's studies of eternal, unchanging reality (6.485b1–3; cf. *Symp.* 211c6–d1). The person who has a 'strong dislike for studies' is, in this context, much the same as the person lacking aptitude (*aphuês*) at 455b – i.e. someone 'naturally' unequipped for philosophy: in both passages, P. treats intellectual ability as essentially innate, and its possession/lack as discernible from an early age (cf. 6.485d3–4).

475c2   **lover of learning:** the adj. *philomathês* does not occur before P.; LSJ also give exx. from Isoc. and Xen. with philosophical overtones. In P. the word is often virtually synonymous with *philosophos*: e.g. 2.376b8–10, 6.485c12/d3, 490a9, 9.581b9, *Phdo* 82c1, with the noun at 6.499e2; cf. Arist. *EN* 1175a14. It is pertinent that *manthanein*, 'understand' (c7 etc.), can be equivalent to *eidenai*, 'know': see e.g. Xen. *Cyr.* 5.2.23.

475c6   **taste...study:** the same metaphor as at 3.411d2, 7.539b2–3; but it is here prompted by the preceding reference to food, and thus sustains the larger analogy, as does 'insatiable' (c7). P. seems to intimate that the true philosopher's appetites are sublimated forms of ordinary human desires.

475c8   *this is the one:* the δέ in τοῦτον δ' is repeated from the start of the sentence, c6, to sustain the contrast being drawn; cf. Denniston 184–5.

475d1   **you'll have...a strange crowd:** G.'s humour is directed against the *ostensible* looseness of Soc.'s definition. It is inappropriate to speak of a mistake or misinterpretation on G.'s part (White [1979] 154–5, Annas [1986] 4–5).

475d2–3 **lovers of sights...lovers of sounds:** sight and sound might be thought to constitute particular realms of beauty (cf. *Hp. Mj.* 297e–8a); Arist. *EN* 1118a 3-9 refers to those who take special pleasure in such things. The sights and sounds meant here are not of an abstract or 'pure' variety; they are the materials of art-forms: the visual arts of painting and sculpture, and the musico-poetic arts which the Greeks classed together as *mousikê* (n. 452a2). There is no reason, *pace* Woodruff (1982) 120 n. 6 (referring to 476b), to discern any allusion to sophists in this passage; cf. n. 476c2. With the comparison/contrast between philosophers and lovers of artistic beauty, cf. Philoxenus fr. 40 Wehrli, which opposes 'true' love of beauty (*philokalia*: cf. *Phdr.* 248d3), i.e. Pythagorean philosophy, to vulgar conceptions of the trait. Note, in a more liberal vein, Pericles' boast at Thuc. 2.40.1, that Athenian culture embraces both love of beauty (*philokalein*) and philosophy.

   Neither of P.'s adjs. appears in any earlier author: the first, *philotheamôn*, which does not occur in P. himself outside this bk., is almost certainly a coinage (its later appearances, see LSJ s.v., are largely in authors influenced by P.); *philêkoos* is likely to be one. The latter refers, at *Lys.* 206c10, *Euthd.* 274c3, 304c6, to fondness for listening to (philosophical) conversation (cf. Isoc. 1.18), but G. here patently applies it to lovers of music and poetry, as at 8.548e5, and, probably, 7.535d5; for poetry as something 'heard', i.e. recited or performed, see my n. on 10.595b5, with G.L. Hendrikson, 'Ancient Reading', *CJ* 25 (1929–30) 182–90. Cf. the 'poet-lovers', *philopoiêtai* (another coinage), of 10.607d7.

475d4   **to include:** ὡς...τιθέναι is epexegetic (cf. nn. 452b4, 453c7), explaining and limiting the preceding adj. - 'such people are very strange, that is to say (γε) as regards inclusion in the category of philosophers.'

475d5   **activities of that sort:** the noun *diatribê* can refer to practically any 'pastime', but seems to have acquired an association with philosophical conversation or argument; cf. 10.597a9 (verb), *Ap.* 41b, *Lys.* 204a2–3, *Grg.* 484c, *Tht.* 172d1, *Plt.* 285c, with e.g. Isoc. 15.50, 175, and LSJ s.v., 2c–d, for later philosophical meanings. The quality which many people are here said to lack is elsewhere in P. sometimes known as *philologia*, 'love of discourse' (9.582e8, *Tht.* 146a6, 161a7; cf. *Lch.* 188c6, e1, *Phdr.* 236e5).

475d7–8 **festivals of Dionysus:** those, that is, at which choral and dramatic performances were organised – in Attica, principally the Lenaea (c. late Jan.) and the City Dionysia (March) in Athens itself, and the Rural Dionysia (Dec.) in the villages: see A. Pickard-Cambridge, *The Dramatic Festivals of Athens*[2] (Oxford, 1968, rpr. 1988), with the more recent discussion of the Rural Dionysia in D. Whitehead, *The Demes of Attica 508/7-c. 250 B.C.* (Princeton, 1986) 212–22. Though G. speaks as an Athenian, and it is no doubt Athens which P. chiefly pictures, the plural, 'cities', makes wider reference to other parts of the Greek world (cf. Pickard-Cambridge *op. cit.* 36–7 for skimpy evidence on the Lenaea outside Athens). The remark implies that Greeks travelled as visitors to dramatic festivals outside their own city (cf. the cultural tourists of *Laws* 12.953a). In Athens itself, no great amount of 'running around' would be needed to attend all the relevant festivals (except for the Rural Dionysia in various demes: Whitehead *op. cit.* 212); but G. is, in any case, caricaturing a certain kind of keenness: cf. the young man crazy about tragedy at Ar. *Birds* 1444–5.

475e1 **some craft or other:** G. uses a diminutive, *technudrion*, which is attested nowhere else by LSJ, and whose suffix is itself fairly rare (cf. e.g. *helkudrion, klepsudrion, meludrion*). Diminutives need not be derogatory (cf. e.g. 'our little city', *polichnion*, at 2.370d6), but G.'s point is that there are countless specific crafts/techniques which people can 'study' or 'learn', without thereby becoming philosophers: cf. the contrast between crafts and philosophy at 6.495d (with another diminutive, *technion*, at d4).

475e2 **like philosophers:** presumably because they manifest, in however limited or attenuated a way, the desire for learning and knowledge which P. takes to be, in its truest form, the hallmark of the philosopher. This kind of thought underlies the more general Aristotelian observation that 'all humans have a natural desire for knowledge' (*Met.* 980a21; cf. the comparison between philosophers and others at *Poet.* 1448b12–15). Moreover, G.'s objection had focussed on lovers of *mousikê*, and a kinship between this and philosophy was already implicit in the role assigned to music and poetry in the education of the Guardians (2.376e ff., with n. 452a2).

Note μέν solitarium; the implicit antithesis (οὐ δὲ φιλοσόφους) has preceded; cf. Denniston 377–8.

475e3 *true* **philosophers:** for the adj. *alêthinos* see n. 464c6–7; cf. the stress on true or genuine philosophers at *Phdo* 64a–b, e2, 66b2, 67b4.

475e4 **'love of sight'...for the truth:** Soc. takes G.'s term from d2, and reapplies it as a metaphor which suggests that philosophy involves, or leads to, a 'visionary' experience; the suggestion will be reinforced at 476b10, d1. Cf. the 'philosopher or lover of beauty' of *Phdr.* 248d3. This is the first appearance in the *Rep.* of a motif which will recur several times in bks. 6 and 7's account of philosophical knowledge, above all in the mystical imagery of the simile of the Cave (7.514a ff.). The context thus requires 'truth' too to take on a special charge of significance, by denoting the realm of unchanging reality: cf. e.g. 6.485c4, d3, 486d8, 9.585c12, and e.g. *Phdo* 67b1 ('truth' as ultimate object of 'pure thought'); 'truth' in any plain sense would not help to distinguish philosophers from others. Arist. *EN* 1098a31, the philosopher as 'spectator of the truth', adapts P.'s phrase, but only as a fleeting image: unlike here, the overtones are not sustained.

475e6 **someone else...*you*:** the remark signals that the dialogue is about to enter difficult (metaphysical) territory which may require both heightened attention and a degree of sympathy with the line of argument. It also functions dramatically as a reminder of the unusually cooperative character of G. as interlocutor of Soc.'s; cf. n. 450b7, with n. 474c8 for passages where Soc. expects G. to be familiar with special philosophical doctrines.

475e9 **two entities:** for the pattern of inference, from 'contraries' to 'two', cf. 10.604b3–4. Unlike that later passage, however, 'contrary' here implies that we are dealing with what, in later terminology, would be called attributes rather than substances (but cf. n. 476a4–5): this is also true at 7.523–4. The point is in preparation for 479a5–8, where it will be claimed that material particulars, unlike unchanging 'forms', can simultaneously possess contrary attributes. On this 'argument from opposites', see R.E. Allen, *Review of Metaphysics* 15 (1961) 325–35.

476a2 **each...is one:** the claim initiates a far-reaching line of thought. It is not simply that 'beautiful' and 'ugly' (or what is 'noble' and 'shameful': n. b5 below) cannot mean the same, but that each of them refers to 'one thing', i.e. (as will emerge) a distinct and invariable entity. But since it will later be contended that such qualities cannot be consistently identified in the material world (479a), P. is working towards the thesis that to each such value-term there corresponds an immaterial reality, beyond the plurality of objects to which the term (e.g. 'beautiful') might be applied.

476a4 **'just' and 'unjust':** the inclusion of negative qualities shows that not all 'forms' can provide positive standards or paradigms; cf. *Tht.* 186a5–8, *Prm.* 129a1–2, *Soph.* 257e, with Vlastos (1981) 64.

476a4–5 **all such forms:** lit. 'all the forms/classes'; on the noun *eidos*, which seems here to denote both each 'class' of predicate (beautiful, just, etc.) and the corresponding entities ('beauty itself' etc.), see n. 449a5 and below. Similar phrasing occurs at 479d4, e3 below, and in a number of related contexts: see 6.501b2–3, 507b5–6 (recapitulation of the present passage), *Phdo* 100b6–7, and *Prm.* 135c9–d1, in every case with reference to terms such as 'beautiful'/'noble' (n. b5), 'just' and 'good'. What 'classes' or 'forms' does Soc. have in mind, and how many of them are there? The main examples given in the following discussion are the properties marked by the value-terms 'good', 'just', 'beautiful' (with their respective contraries): these terms form a common triad in P. (n. 451a7), and mark out fundamental parts of the framework of Greek ethical evaluation, though 'good' will later be declared the source of the others (6.505a ff.). To these are obviously to be added other ethical terms, such as 'holy' (479a7–8); cf. 6.501b2–3, 'the just, the noble, the self-controlled (*sôphron*), and all such things'. But the argument will later encompass predicates such as double/half, large/ small, heavy/light (n. 479b3); cf. *Phdo* 65d12 f. (largeness, health, strength), 100b6-7 ('good, large and all the rest').

So P.'s 'forms' include two main groups of properties – (i) ethical and kindred values, (ii) relational attributes. This means that *eidos* is being used here differently from its recent appearance at 475b5, where it signified a class or variety of *objects* ('substances', in philosophical terminology), concrete or abstract: boys, wine, honour, food, studies. Nothing in the following section commits P. to the view that there is a single, invariable entity matching any 'class' in that broader sense of the word, although some such argument will in fact be (surprisingly) developed much later in the work: see 10.596a6 ff., with my nn. there. White (1978b) 148–52, however, argues that 'forms' of substances are not here excluded.

476a5 **each in itself is a single entity:** 'in itself', *auto*, marks two key implications, (i) a universal/abstract(ed) form, as opposed to particular instances, and (ii) a unitary entity, as opposed to the multiplicity (a7) of many separate cases described by the predicates in question; cf. n. b6–7. For 'a single entity', *hen hekaston*, cf. 6.507b6–7, 7.524b7–10, 10.596a6, and *Crat.* 439c8, 440b6 (in a context which exempts 'beauty', 'goodness', etc., from the instability of the 'flux' posited by Heracleitean philosophers); other references in Penner 373 n. 29. P. understood the idea of flux in the sensible world to be incompatible with *anything* being 'one thing': see *Tht.* 152d–e, 153e4–5, 157a8.

Parmenides, on the other hand, had talked of the totality of reality as being 'one thing' (fr. 8.6 DK). P.'s thinking here can be interpreted as an attempt to take account of both of these positions, by accepting the instability of *certain aspects* of the material world, and accordingly projecting features like those of Parmenidean reality onto a metaphysical plane of pure, eternal verities; cf. n. 479c4.

476a6–7 **being connected with:** lit. 'through partnership/association with', or 'by being common to'. The point seems to be equivalent to the idea (d1–2) that individual things 'partake of' the qualities predicated of them. In both cases, P.'s language implies that qualitative properties 'in themselves' – i.e. in their unitary, unchanging 'form' – are distinct from the particulars which are judged to manifest them. If we compare an earlier passage such as *Euthph.* 5c–d, where Soc. posits unitary ethical concepts that are wholly realised in particular cases ('holiness is self-consistent in every <holy> action', d1–2), we can see that the present context bears out the contrast drawn at Arist. *Met.* 987b1–10 between Soc.'s interest in moral definitions, and P.'s development of this into a metaphysical doctrine that 'forms' are entities independent of, and '*separate*' from (e.g. *Met.* 1040b27-8), the flux of the material world. (On 'separation' see Vlastos [1991] 256-65.)

The connection of forms 'with one another' has been the source of much technical argument. Does this mean only (i) that forms become associated *qua* properties of particulars (as when, say, a man is both large and beautiful), or (ii) that there is some further, perhaps logical level of inter-relationships between forms; for a variety of views see Adam I 362–4, Owen 174 n. 33, Penner 374, Vlastos (1991) 75 n. 139.

476a7 **appears all over the place...multiplicity:** *phantazesthai*, 'appear', often has connotations of illusion; cf. e.g. 2.380d2 (apparitions), 9.572b1 (dreams), and my n. on *phantasma*, 10.598b3; it is similarly used at *Symp.* 211a5 of the imperfect manifestation of transcendent beauty in particular cases. It is an illusion that (e.g.) beauty *is* many things, as opposed to a single, invariable entity. P.'s contrast between the 'single' value and its multiple appearances undoubtedly evokes, without simply reproducing, a larger contrast, drawn by Eleatic philosophers, between reality as 'one' and false impressions of it as 'many': the connection is confirmed in *Prm.*, where the discussion of Eleatic ideas (127d ff.) leads into a critical reconsideration of the metaphysics of 'forms' as propounded in P.'s own dialogues.

'All over the place', *pantachou*, might remind one of the occurrence of the adverb at 3.401c4, where Soc. spoke of the need to be able to recognise the 'forms' (*eidê*) of the virtues in all their manifestations: but the use of *eidos* there was different again from here, and there is no need to see metaphysical implications in that passage. On 'multiplicity' see n. 479a3.

476a10 **practical lovers of crafts:** lit. 'lovers of crafts and practical people', a hendiadys, referring back to 475e1; these are people whose interest in 'beauty' is not abstract or general, but linked to certain kinds of objects.

476b5 **beautiful voices:** of singers, actors or reciters of poetry, the defining interest of the 'lover of sounds' (n. 475d2–3). Part of the emphasis here falls on the beauty discerned in particular objects; cf. c2, 'beautiful things', and *Symp.* 211d3–4 ('beauty itself' *vs.* gold, clothes, boys). But 'colours, shapes...and all the artefacts...' also leaves room for lovers of beauty to believe in certain *types* or characteristic features of beauty. So the important contrast is not simply between universals and particulars, but between philosophical knowledge of single, changeless 'forms' (which can provide universals), and views (whether judgements of particulars, or general concepts) that are not informed by such knowledge. Cf. n. 479a3.

Although 'beautiful' is the fittest translation of *kalos* here, it is implicit in P.'s contrast that 'beauty itself' must be something non-sensual. Given this, we should bear in mind the wider semantic scope of *kalos* as a more or less ethical term of value, 'noble', 'fine', 'good', etc.: for its Platonic conjunction with *agathos*, 'good', see 451a7, 452e1-2, with e.g. 6. 505b3, 508e-9a; cf. Woodruff (1982) 110, with Dover (1974) 69-73 for ordinary usage. It is part of P.'s purpose, which cannot be conveyed by any single English translation of *kalos*, to intimate that the beauty desired by lovers of poetry, painting, etc., is an imperfect apprehension of a much grander (transcendent and mystical) value: his argument here, in other words, is moving in the same direction as Diotima's speech in *Symp.* (esp. 208-12).

476b6–7   **beauty in itself:** or 'beauty as such', i.e. without embodiment in, or reference to, any particular object; cf. n. a5 above. This use of the adj. *autos* is a signal instance of the way in which terminology capable of carrying metaphysical significance can be created by P. from extremely ordinary and common components of the Greek language. In its use as an intensifying adj. and pronoun, *autos* ('him/her/itself') often lends an emphasis either of actuality (cf. c6, 'the very thing', *auto*, as opposed to a likeness of it), or of independence/self-sufficiency in relation to some given criterion: see e.g. 2.366e5, 10.612c10 (justice/injustice 'itself', i.e. independently of its *consequences*), 4.437e4–5 (simple or pure thirst, i.e. thirst without any qualification), *Tht.* 152b5, 160b10 (physical objects, independently of how they are experienced). P. adapts such usage into a philosophical formula which combines both the emphases just indicated: he employs phrases of the type, *auto* + noun (esp., as here, a nominalised adj.), in order to represent values (beauty, justice, goodness) which have a reality independent of the collections of particulars of which they are predicated.

But precisely because of the closeness to ordinary Greek, such phraseology always calls for delicate analysis. Thus, the present section of argument will give us grounds to infer a metaphysics of immutable entities (a 'theory of Forms', to use the standard label), but as recently as 472c4–5 the phrase 'justice itself' did not require such major assumptions. At *Phdo* 65e3 the phrase 'each thing in itself' involves reference to transcendent forms, but 'by thought itself' (65e7; i.e. without sense-experience) has no such implication: thus P. can closely juxtapose varying uses of the adj. *autos*. *Hp. Mj.* may be one of the earliest dialogues in which P. endows the '*auto x*' formula (see 288a9, 289c3) with philosophical significance: for the place of this work in P.'s output see Woodruff (1982) 175–9.

476b7–8   **see and love:** the language carries quasi-mystical and erotic overtones. The motif of philosophical 'vision', as experience of unchanging reality, was broached at 475e4 (see n.); it will be developed in the coming books, e.g. 6.500c3, d4, 511a1, 7.519c10–d2: cf. *Symp.* 210e4, 211b6, 211d–12a. *Aspazesthai*, 'love', is often synonymous with other verbs of loving, esp. *philein* (n. 474c9-11), *agapan* (1.330c1-4), and *eran* (*Symp.* 205e6/206a1); but it has additional connotations of welcoming or embracing something that one recognises (e.g. 1.328c5, 2.376a6): compare the philosopher's experience of 'touching' the ultimate form of goodness, e.g. 6.511b4-7. The 'nature of beauty' is equivalent to P.'s use elsewhere of phrases such as 'that which is by nature just' (6.501b2, with my n. on 10.597b5-6).

476b10   **approach:** the metaphor, which occurs also at e.g. 6.490b2, 7.537d6–7, here probably evokes progression towards a moment of visionary enlightenment; *Symp.* 210a4–6 lends strong support to this suggestion, and cf. the upward and outward journey from the Cave (esp. 7.521c7, 532b–c), with n. c3–4 below. P.'s use of the language of mystery religion, above all in *Symp.* and *Phdr.*, has been analysed by C. Riedweg,

Mysterienterminologie bei Platon, Philon, und Klemens von Alexandrien (Berlin, 1987) 1–69.

476b11 **in and of itself:** *kat' hauto* intensifies the emphasis of *autos*, b6; in the fuller form, *auto kat' hauto*, 'alone by/in itself', the phrase occurs in other passages which posit immutable forms: see esp. *Phdo* 65d1–2, 66a2, 78d5–6, 100b6, *Symp.* 211b1, *Prm.* 128e6 f., 129d7–8, 130b8; but *Tht.* 152d3, 153e4, 156e8–9, may imply a weaker form of 'realism'. Cf. Vlastos (1991) 72–6, 256–64, who explains the function of the phrase within P.'s doctrine of 'an eternal, self-existent world, transcending everything in ours' (76). It is no accident that comparable phraseology occurs at Parmen. fr. 8.29 DK.

476b11 **very few:** the true philosophers (474c1–2) whom the argument seeks to define, and whose selection and training will be described at length in bk. 7; on their scarcity see n. 473d4-5. If we ask whether Soc. himself is one of the few, it is hard to give an unequivocal answer: he certainly does not *claim* to be, and expressions of doubt such as 450d8-9, or the disavowal of ultimate philosophical knowledge at 6.505a5-7 (cf. 506b ff., 507a, 509c), would seem to disqualify him; yet why should his metaphysical arguments, or his account of what it is that true philosophers would need to know, carry any persuasive weight at all, unless P. intends him to be understood as in some way an authoritative voice in the discussion? The tension points to a larger paradox about P.'s attempts to convey, by dramatic dialogue, ideas which he does not believe to be properly expressible in language: cf. esp. *Phdr.* 277d-e, *Epist.* 7.341c-4d.

476c2 **believes in beautiful things:** i.e. judges certain things (whose *existence* is not at issue: n. 479b9–10) to be beautiful. These judgements entail a belief in beauty *qua* property of particular objects; but the person who holds this belief can refuse to accept that 'beauty as such/in itself' has any *independent* reality. Such a refusal might suggest the position of (in later philosophical terms) the 'nominalist', who takes universals such as beauty, justice, etc., to exist only in the individual things of which they are predicated: cf. Penner 62-6 for a reading along these lines. But there are varieties of nominalism, and the character of P.'s imaginary figure remains only sketchily stated: cf. nn. 476b5, 479a3. It has sometimes been thought that P. here has in mind a specific philosophical opponent, Antisthenes (c. 445-360): see Adam on 476d8 for older views. But quite apart from the obscurity of relations between these two followers of Soc. (cf. Thesleff 35), this is a dubious reading: the current contrast still refers to G.'s lovers of sights and sounds, who are principally devotees of poetry and art (n. 475d 2-3). So the point is aimed not at rival philosophers, but at the mentality of cultured people who cannot grasp, or are uninterested in, arguments for the independent existence of the values which they pursue. Note that when the point is repeated at 6.493e-4a, the contrast is between philosophers and the 'mass' (*plêthos*) of people. Cf. White (1978a) 130-1, Cooper 230.

476c3–4 **following...guide:** although such terms have many ordinary uses, including 'following' an argument (e.g. *Euthph.* 12a3, c8), P. may here mean them to signify a process of intellectual 'initiation' (cf. n. b10 above); similar language occurs in Diotima's overtly mystical account of the lover's progression through rising stages of enlightenment, esp. *Symp.* 210a4–7. For superimposition of such religious associations onto a more mundane image, cf. 4.432c (hunting), 445c (climbing a hill, to obtain a panorama).

476c4 **dreaming or waking:** this anticipates bk. 7's parable of the Cave, whose inhabitants (i.e. everyone, except true philosophers) live among dream-like illusions (esp. 7.520c6–7). All human existence, in so far as it falls short of the highest dialectic, is a kind of dream (7.534c6-7, with 533b-c, applying the point even to philosophical geometry); similarly, life is a dream by comparison to the 'waking' state of knowledge possessed in our pre-existence, *Plt.* 277d. *Tht.* 157e-8d uses the idea of dreaming to pose a general epistemological puzzle. Yet at *Crat.* 439c7 Soc. describes a concept of permanent, non-relative values (i.e. something suggestive of P.'s eventual 'theory of Forms') as a dream; and the *Rep.*'s ideal city is itself a dream (4.443b7): in these last two passages, there is a different, quasi-mystical sense of dreaming as something that permits glimpses of a superior reality. Cf. S. S. Tigner, 'Plato's Philosophical Uses of the Dream Metaphor', *AJP* 91 (1970) 204-12, D. Gallop, 'Dreaming and Waking in Plato', in J. P. Anton & G. L. Kustas, *Essays in Ancient Greek Philosophy* (Albany, 1971) 187-201.

476c6–7   **resembles:** this implies that though 'beauty in itself' is distinct and separate from particular 'beautiful things', the latter are at any rate 'like' the former in some respect. The point thus recalls P.'s tendency to construe the 'forms'/particulars relation as that between models and copies/images: cf. 10.597a4-5, *Phdo* 73d-5a (linked with recollection of pre-existence), *Phdr.* 250a-b, *Prm.* 132d-3a (criticism of the idea), *Tim.* 52a (generalising the point to *everything* in the visible world); for one philosophical analysis, see R. Patterson, *Image & Reality in Plato's Metaphysics* (Indianapolis, 1985). The (alleged) mistake of the imaginary opponent here is to take his beliefs to be the whole truth about (e.g.) beauty: he denies that there is any more to beauty than either beautiful things or the features which some of them share (cf. nn. 476b5, 479a3).

476d1–2   **partake of it:** P.'s use of the verb *metechein* in metaphysical contexts, to describe the 'forms'/particulars relation, has long been a source of concern, at least since Aristotle's blunt dismissal of it as 'empty talk and poetic metaphor' (*Met.* 991a20–22, 1079b24–6) and his suggestion that it matched the Pythagorean notion of the world's 'imitation', *mimesis*, of numbers (*Met.* 987b9–14). In general Greek usage, if *x metechei y*, *x* 'shares in' or 'has a portion of' *y*, where the necessary implication is that *y* is more extensive than *x*'s share of it. But there are many cases which do not precisely fit this model: cf. e.g. *Symp.* 211a7, where a human body *metechei* (?'comprises') its limbs and parts. Moreover, where *y* is a quality such as a virtue, to 'partake in' it will be to possess (some) real *y*: that seemed to be true even at 472c2; and cf. e.g. *Prt.* 322d5, 325a3 (though *Symp.* 208b3, 'the mortal *metechei* immortality', is certainly not a case of a genuine property). For pre-platonic philosophical usage, cf. H.C. Baldry, *CQ* 31 (1937) 145–6.

But if ordinary possession of an attribute were meant here, it would be obscure why so clear-cut a distinction should be drawn between '*y* itself' and things that 'partake in *y*', still less why the latter should be only 'like' the former (c6-7). The point cannot be limited to, though it may include, a logical observation about universals and particulars. As is intimated by the imagery of dreaming and waking, P.'s case is ontological. The 'lover of sights/sounds' is unable to see that particular beauties are dependent upon, and somehow derivative from, something more *real* than they are - 'beauty itself'. P. sometimes hedges his use of the language of 'sharing' and 'participation' with some caution (*Symp.* 211b2, *Phdo* 100d5-6); like the entire metaphysics of this passage, it was eventually subjected by him to searching criticism (*Prm.* 129-31).

476d5–6   **knowledge:** *gnômê* is here (unusually) synonymous with both *gnôsis* (c3, 477a9, cf. e.g. 6.484c7) and *epistêmê* (477b1, 5, etc.); likewise, *gignôskein*, 'understand', is effectively synonymous with *eidenai*, 'know' (e5–6 etc.). Words from the root *gnô-* (to which the English 'know' is etymologically related) can broadly denote the active use of understanding and intelligence, rather than the static possession of items of knowledge; on *gnômê* cf. Dover (1974) 123-4. P.'s purpose here is to contend that the highest knowledge involves intellectual grasp of the nature of reality - a grasp which brings with it *ethical* insight (cf. 10.599d4, 600c5, for *gignôskein* and ethics). It may also be relevant, given the quasi-mystical imagery of approaching, seeing and embracing ultimate reality (b7-11), that *gignôskein* sometimes implies a kind of recognition; but the pertinence of this is arguable: cf. Gosling (1973) 124-5. For *gignôskein* and *gnôsis* combined cf. esp. *Crat.* 440a-b.

476d6   **belief:** alternatively, 'judgement' or 'opinion'. *Doxa* can encompass any belief or conviction; but it can also, especially in conjunction with the verb *doxazein* (d8 etc.), suggest the result of conscious appraisal or reflection: see e.g. *Tht.* 170d4–5, 187a4–8, with Crombie II 33–4. It is firm beliefs of this kind that are in target throughout the present argument: P. is not contrasting philosophers with *unreflective* people, but with those who may well hold their views on (e.g.) beauty with great confidence, and who would not readily be shaken by philosophical argument (as c2–3 and d8 ff. indicate). Nor is P. condemning such beliefs or judgements as false, only as insufficient and falling short of knowledge of 'the real'. The lover of sights and sounds is not simply wrong about which things (in the material world) should be called 'beautiful'; his mistake is about the reality of 'beauty itself'. In other words, 'belief', here and in what follows, needs principally to be understood as belief that is *right so far as it goes*: if that were not so, the tripartite scheme of knowledge/belief/ignorance would be greatly weakened. Cf. nn. 477a9, e6–7.

476d8-480a13

Knowledge is of that which is completely, perfectly or 'purely' real; ignorance or error, correspondingly, is concerned with that which has no reality at all. Knowledge and belief are different capacities with different spheres and different products. Belief must therefore have objects which lie somewhere between perfect reality and complete unreality: these objects can be identified with the various and entirely relative properties, including the fundamental values of ethics, which are ascribed to things in the material world. The objects of true knowledge, on the other hand, are the absolute and invariant 'forms' of justice, beauty and all other relevant attributes.

In this final section of the book, the distinction between single 'forms' and multiple particulars is expanded and incorporated into a tripartite scheme of mental states and their correlates, as follows:

KNOWLEDGE	BELIEF	IGNORANCE
(*epistêmê, gnôsis*)	(*doxa*)	(*agnoia, agnôsia*)
complete reality	between reality and non-reality	non-reality
'forms'	particular properties	nothing

On one standard view, this part of the argument, because addressed directly to the 'lover of sights/sounds', is intended to utilise only uncontroversial, commonsense premises. But we need to be highly cautious about this assumption (nn. 476d8-9, e10, 477a2, 3, 9). The argument contains numerous points of detail which involve difficulty or uncertainty - among them: crucial but contentious uses of the verb 'to be' (nn. 476e10, 477a3); the treatment of knowledge and belief as different 'capacities' with different 'objects' (nn. 477b5, d1); the meaning of the 'many' beauties in which the lover of sights believes (n. 479a3); the type(s) of relativity implied at 479a5-8; and even the concepts of knowledge and belief themselves (nn. 476d6, 477b1). It would be hard to explain this number of interpretative problems, if P.'s purpose were to set out a sequence of contentions to which a real lover of sights or sounds could be imagined as happily assenting.

Besides, from a *reader's* point of view it is inevitable, and part of P.'s design, that the terms and premises used in this section should be coloured by the immediately preceding passage. The effect of this is that the ontological language of 'being' is slanted, so to speak, towards the metaphysical perspective already adumbrated at 476a-d. As a result, the dialogue can be read as having a double significance which is not apparent to the imaginary interlocutor (nn. 476e2, 477a2). Over and above this issue, however, it is vital to bear in mind the intricate question of how far it is legitimate for us to translate P.'s terminology into, or analyse it by means of, later philosophical concepts and concerns: cf. I. M. Crombie, *Philosophy* 51 [1976] 361-2, and my Introduction p. 28.

The relationship between knowledge and belief had long been of interest to Greek philosophers (e.g. Parmen. fr. 1.29-30, Xenophanes fr. 34 DK), and it is one which came to hold major significance for P. But his treatments of it vary considerably in scope and aim. In *Rep.* 10.601d-e, for example, the contrast between knowledge and belief (there called *pistis*) is linked to the difference between activities of using and making. In *Meno* 85c-6a, 96d-9a, it is suggested that true belief may be just as useful as knowledge for many practical purposes, including politics. In *Tht.*, the nature of knowledge is investigated in extensive and subtle detail, and two of the three definitions of it which are considered involve the issue of its relation to true belief. In all these texts, allowance is made for things that are *ordinarily* called knowledge, such as knowing a route (*Meno* 97a9) or eye-witness knowledge of an event (*Tht.* 201b8). But that is not true of *Rep.* 5, which concentrates purely on one particular variety of knowledge: knowledge of the single, invariable 'forms' of attributes which include beauty, justice, goodness, on the one hand, and doubleness, largeness, and heaviness, on the other. Cf. 'true knowledge', *Phdr.* 247c8, as the special vision of metaphysical reality.

In this context, the separation of knowledge from belief is meant to underpin a trio of interlocking theses: one, that the objects of knowledge (especially of values) must be unchanging and absolute; two, that certain beliefs or judgements which apply to the material world are subject to basic, inevitable relativism (479a); three, that philosophers, who are lovers of knowledge, must have access to standards of value that are independent of the sensible world. Although it is not directly invoked in this section, there lurks behind this argument the distinction, long established in Greek philosophy, between 'being' and 'becoming': for its use in the later stages of the definition of the true philosopher, see esp. 6.485b2-3, 508d7-8, 7.518c8-9, 521d4. This distinction could be, and had been, employed to throw doubt on the reliability of *all* sense-experience. Bks. 6-7 will develop a wider argument of that kind, but that is not the overt scope of this final portion of bk. 5 (n. 479b9-10). What is at issue here is the kind of knowledge which is required to give substance and justification to the concept of philosopher-rulers: and that can only be ethical knowledge of how men ought to live, and thus how they can best be governed.

476d8-9   **what if the person...disputes:** for an exchange with a hypothetical opponent, cf. 453a7 ff.; for the opponent's anger cf. 480a7, 6.500e1. It is commonly held that the present section draws only on uncontroversial premises that an ordinary person might accept (e.g. Gosling [1973] 130, Annas [1981] 196). Three qualifications should be placed on this: first, several key terms and premises are difficult, obscure or ambiguous (see head-note), and an interlocutor without philosophical leanings (475d4-5) would scarcely pass them with equanimity; second, the positing of a hypothetical opponent is an artificial exercise, as often, and we might well think that G.'s answers are really those which he (or P.) would *like* such a person to give; third, it is not clear how far beyond 479a the imaginary conversation is sustained (n. 479b1-2): no end to it is marked, yet by 479e the opponents are back in the third person; for this point cf. 455b ff. (with n. 455c3). Moreover, when Fine (1990) 87 suggests that the exchange should match the model of (Socratic) dialectic given at *Meno* 75d (truth plus personal commitment to the premises), she ignores the ironic disingenuousness of e1-2, which hardly prepares us for the friendly cooperation of which the *Meno* passage speaks.

476e2   **not...in his right mind:** the phrase has crude, colloquial force, and is associated with 'talking nonsense' (cf. *Lys.* 205a7–8, and e.g. Ar. *Clouds* 1273–5). Despite a touch of humour, Soc.'s attitude is superior and disingenuous: his remark signals that the significance of the following exchange is not wholly on the surface, but has an esoteric dimension. Compare 475e6-7.

476e10   **real or unreal:** lit. 'being or not being'. There are three main senses of the verb 'to be' which might be applicable to the participle here, and to other uses of the verb throughout the following argument (nn. 477a3–4, 478b6–7, 479b9–10): (i) existential (= 'exist'); (ii) predicative (= 'be + complement [e.g. beautiful]'); (iii) veridical (= 'be true'). P. himself was to investigate such distinctions in *Tht.* 188d ff., *Soph.* 236e ff., but he does not apply them here; much modern interpretation has centred on trying to provide them for him: cf. the Introduction, p. 27. Cases have been made for understanding each of the given three senses here, with varying ramifications for all of what follows: see e.g. Cross & Woozley 145–65, Vlastos (1981) ch. 3, Fine (1990) 87–90. But it remains severely doubtful whether P. is operating with such clear discriminations here, especially since there is a tendency for veridical and existential uses of 'be' to coalesce in Greek (Kahn 453–7, with 349–55). Moreover, *gignôskein* (e9), 'know' (but also 'recognise' and 'understand'), could embrace both knowledge by acquaintance (e.g. knowing a person) and propositional knowledge (knowing that). If, therefore, a plain interlocutor *could* give a straight answer to Soc.'s question, it would have to be inclusive and imply: if *x* is known, there must be either some actual state of affairs or some true proposition (or both) corresponding to the knowledge of *x*.

477a1   **how could something that wasn't real be known:** cf. *Crat.* 439e7–40a2; G.'s reply comes, in its wording, very close to Parmen. fr. 2.7 DK.

477a2   **and would do...:** 'more extensive investigation' is a hint that much fuller philosophical arguments could be given: it seems more appropriate between Soc. and G. than between Soc. and the supposedly unphilosophical interlocutor. In any case, it is difficult for a reader to make allowances here: P.'s written arguments must be judged on their own merits, as they often were, indeed, even by his own pupil Aristotle.

     κἂν εἰ here (unlike 473a2–3: see n.) involves an ellipse, for καὶ ἱκανῶς ἔχοιμεν ἄν, εἰ καὶ πλεοναχῇ..., 'and would have sufficient assurance, even if we examined it in multiple ways.'

477a3   **the completely real:** 'the real', *to on*, is a noun formed from the neuter participle of 'be' (n. 476e10); cf. the plural, *ta onta* (n. c1 below). Both forms occur in many kinds of Greek, without special philosophical implications, to denote truth, facts, or actuality (e.g. Herod. 1.97.1, 4.32, Xen. *Cyr.* 5.4.7, with Kahn 453–7). But *to on* had also been intensified by some philosophers into a highly charged term: see esp. Parmenides' employment of it for the single, changeless reality posited by his system (frs. 4.2, 8.19, 32, 35, 37 DK). P. himself, though he sometimes retains ordinary usage (e.g. 10.613b10, *Tht.* 152c5), also employs the term to denote immutable reality (e.g. 7.518c8-9, *Tim.* 27d-8a, *Phdo* 78d4, 83b2, *Phdr.* 247d3); on this variation, see Gallop 93 and my nn. on 10.597a4, 598b2. A metaphysical meaning will certainly be in play by the conclusion of the present argument (479d5); but *if* we wished to make Soc.'s question unproblematic for an interlocutor (cf. nn. 476d8-9, e10), we would have to assume a plainer sense for the noun, perhaps most readily that of 'the truth'. Even so, we would be left with the qualification, 'completely' (cf. *Soph.* 248e7-8), which must imply some notion of 'degrees of being' - a highly problematic notion, whether we think in terms of truth or of existence. For the adverb *pantelôs* with adjs. which admit of degrees, see e.g. 9.573b5 (tyrannical), *Meno* 80a4 (similar), *Phdo* 82b10 (pure); cf. the similar use of 'perfectly', *teleôs*, at 10.597a3, and for one interpretation of 'degrees of reality' see Vlastos (1973) ch. 3. P.'s phrase might be taken to echo Parmen. fr. 8.11 DK (the real must either 'be completely' or not at all).

Throughout this passage, up to 478d, P. is thinking in quasi-diagrammatic terms: note the schematic emphasis of 478d–e, and cf. nn. b7, 478c3. He thus posits a scale that runs from complete reality to complete unreality, with a less determinate area of being-and-not-being in between; and all the other distinctions drawn in this argument match the divisions of this scale.

477a3–4 **in no way real:** lit. 'not being in any way at all'. The same question about the sense(s) of 'be' arises with the negative as with the positive phrases just preceding (nn. 476e10, 477a3). At 478b12, the unreal is equated with 'nothing', which entails an existential sense of 'be' (cf. Owen 106). But it does not follow that the existential sense is applicable throughout, for it remains at issue whether P. has built the passage upon a clear sense of such distinctions. Not until *Soph.* 237b-41a, 257b-9b, does P. offer detailed analysis of the logic of 'not being'.

477a6–7 **lie...between:** cf. *Symp.* 201e–2a, where the position of correct belief between knowledge (*epistêmê, sophia, phronêsis*) and ignorance (*amathia*) is taken as a model of an intermediate state between two contraries.

477a7 **pure reality:** this use of *eilikrinês* recurs at 478d6, e2, 479d5; the adj. is close to synonymous with *katharos* (cf. 7.520d8, 9.585b12, with e.g. *Phlb.* 52d6–7, 53a5–8, *Symp.* 211e1): P. applies it to thought (*Phdo* 66a2), transcendent reality (ib. 2–3), truth (ib. 67b1), soul (ib. 81c1), and non-sensible beauty (*Symp.* 211e1). On one interpretation, this phrase refers to forms as unqualified bearers of the appropriate predicate, e.g. 'beauty itself' as that which is 'purely beautiful': this would raise the highly controversial issue of how Platonic forms involve 'self-predication' (e.g. Woodruff [1982] 153-6, 172-5). But the context gives no direct clue as to how the phrase is to be understood, though its obscurity goes unchallenged by the interlocutor (cf. Cooper 234).

477a9 **knowledge...covers:** *epi*, used repeatedly in what follows, combines extension ('over') with supervision ('in control of', e.g. 1.345d2); cf. e.g. 2.376e2–3 (gymnastics 'covers' the body in the sense both of applying to it and being responsible for its condition). But when the concept of 'capacities' is introduced at c1 ff., the preposition takes on a nuance of function: cf. n. 477d1. 'We agreed' translates the so-called 'philosophical imperfect', ἦν, which marks a point previously mentioned; cf. e.g. 7.522a3.

477a9 **ignorance:** the Greek term (*agnôsia* or *agnoia*, b1 etc., as well as their cognates), like the English, can cover both (i) the 'empty' or purely negative state of not-knowing (e.g. 1.331e8, Arist. *Met.* 982b18–21), and (ii) the positive state of being in error (e.g. 2.382b8; but elsewhere often called *amathia*: e.g. 4.444a1–2); for the distinction cf. *Laws* 9.863c. Since 'the unreal' is equated with 'nothing' (478b12 f.), it is sense (i) which seems aptest here. If we take sense (ii) to be also pertinent, then we face the problem of how ignorance *qua* error could be distinguished from false *doxa*, as the argument's tripartite scheme requires. To answer this, we would need to invoke degrees of falsehood, and take ignorance in sense (ii) to involve beliefs so false as to have no contact whatsoever with actuality. The correlative of this would be that P. intends *doxa*, in the present context, to represent beliefs or judgements with some *prima facie* reasonableness – i.e. beliefs about some actual entity (cf. 478b10). But on any reading, the relation between false belief and ignorance calls for clarification, and augments the reasons for inferring that the imaginary exchange with the 'lover' is not conducted from entirely lucid premises (n. 476d8-9). For various views of 'ignorance', see Cross & Woozley 145-6, Gosling (1968) 125, Annas (1981) 201.

477b1 **knowledge:** *epistêmê*, now brought into the argument for the first time, is evidently synonymous here with *gnôsis* (a9). We can distinguish several senses in which *epistêmê* is employed in P. (cf. Woodruff [1990]): knowledge of individual facts (e.g. *Tht.* 201c1); command of a body/subject of knowledge (*Tht.* 145e: synon. *sophia*); knowledge 'how', of the kind possessed by the expert *user* of something (2.374d5, 10.602a1); political wisdom, or knowledge of how a city should be governed (e.g. 4.428b–9a); a synonym of *technê*, i.e. a systematic craft or body of practical knowledge (e.g. 4.428b10, with 438c–e; *Plt.* 258b ff., *Tht.* 146d1–2); 'pure' or 'true' *epistêmê*, which is knowledge of immaterial, transcendent being (e.g. *Phdr.* 247c–e). The present context slants the word towards the last of these senses, though the larger purpose of the argument (since 474b) is to explain how philosopher-rulers will also possess political wisdom. But if the current conversation involves a non-philosopher (n. 476d8-9), why should he make allowance for any types of knowledge other than those commonly accepted?

477b3 **Do we agree...:** lit. 'do we say that 'belief' is something?'; for this form of question cf. my n. on 10.608d13.

477b5 **capacity:** Soc. uses the term *dunamis* – whose senses include 'power', 'ability', 'force', 'faculty', as well as more technical meanings – before narrowing down its application at c1 ff. If the subject of discussion were knowledge and belief as ordinarily understood, it would be obscure why they should be said to differ in their *dunamis* – something that might apply, for example, to different skills or crafts (1.346a3). But for a reader, with the warning at 476e1–2 in mind, the question is hard to dissociate from the conclusion drawn about knowledge and belief at 476d5–6. So while it is possible to construe Soc.'s question in a way that could appear innocent to the interlocutor (cf. Gosling [1968] 122–9), this deals only with the dramatic surface and not with the underlying motive of the argument. For 'a different *dunamis*' as a way of expressing total difference, cf. *Tht.* 158e–9a (involving an imaginary opponent).

477b7 **assigned to cover:** the same phrase as at 7.524a1–2 (senses and their objects), 10.610e7–8 (evils and the things affected by them); for the preposition *epi*, 'to cover' (i.e. 'in control of') see n. a9 ('knowledge... covers'). The verb *tattein* is predominantly used of military appointments and assignations, though it is common in other applications. Here it reinforces the sense of a sharply drawn demarcation (perhaps with diagrammatic overtones: cf. 6.511e2–5, with n. a3 above) between knowledge and belief, as well as an element of unalterable fixity (*Tht.* 153e1–2); cf. the idea of metaphysical 'forms' as themselves 'organised', *tetagmena*, in an immutable order (6.500c2). The point might be paraphrased by saying that belief and knowledge are 'responsible for' different kinds of experience: but, once more (n. b5), a reader is invited to interpret this in the light of the special significance already outlined for 'knowledge'.

477b10 **naturally cover:** the same type of phrase occurs at e.g. 1.341d7. γνῶναι is dependent on πέφυκε (cf. LSJ s.v. φύω, B II 2); P.'s sentence merges two formulations: 'knowledge by nature covers the real', and 'knowledge is by nature such as to understand...'; cf. 478a6.

477b10f. **what is really the case:** the Greek is even more emphatically pleonastic, since the noun, *to on* (from a3, 7, 9), is formed from the participle of the same verb; lit. '...understanding that that which is *is*'.

477c1 **one class of entities:** cf. *Phdo* 79a6–7, 'two classes (*eidê*) of entities' (visible/invisible); *Crat.* 386e7-8, actions are 'one class (*eidos*) of entities'. In these passages, a 'class of entities' amounts to a basic division of reality (something akin to an Aristotelian 'category'). *Genos*, 'class', is synonymous with *eidos*, 'class' (c4), as at d8/e1 below, and often elsewhere (e.g. 4.435b7/c1, 6.509d2/4, *Crat.* 411a1/5, *Soph* 227d13/228e2): P. does not distinguish the terms, as 'genus' and 'species' respectively in the way standard in Aristotle (e.g. *Met.* 999a4). 'Entities', *ta onta*, is the plural of the phrase which P. has just used for 'the real'; but he now allows it to function in it ordinary, non-metaphysical sense, as a general term for whatever exists, or is the case in the world: this juxtaposition highlights the way in which P. prefers to explo ordinary Greek for his own philosophical ends, rather than creating a distinc vocabulary of technical terms. For plain uses of *ta onta* cf. e.g. 1.353d4, 3.413a7, *Tht* 152a3, 160d2, with Heraclit. fr. 7 DK.

477c8   **consider:** for this use of *apoblepein* cf. n. 472c7.

477d1   **sphere...produces:** the first phrase, lit. 'what it is responsible for', maintains the use o *epi* started at 477a9; the second refers to the performance of an *ergon*, 'effect' or 'function' (cf. e.g. 1.353a–e; n.b. 353b3 for *apergazesthai* with *tattein*, as here). As regards the former, much hinges on whether we think the argument implies tha knowledge and belief have distinct 'objects', or only distinct 'contents': for differin views see Cross & Woozley 150–1, 170–8, Crombie II 57–8, Fine (1990) 90–1. O the 'objects' reading, P. is usually taken to be committed to a 'two worlds' doctrine whereby knowledge is of entities which are eternally real and altogether separate fron the material world: for contrasting views see Vlastos (1991) 66–76, and Fine (1990) N.D. Smith, *Philos. Studies* 30 (1976) 427-9, construes 'objects' in this context not as distinct entities but as things apprehended under a given description. I have already contended that the whole argument is designed to be significant on more than one leve (nn. 476e2, 477b5); if so, it will necessarily be open to divergent interpretations.

477d2–3   **same name...same sphere...same product:** 'same' is here idiomatic, not strictl logical; the point becomes clearer in English if 'the same' is replaced by 'a single' Does the passage offer independent or linked criteria for sameness/difference o capacity? Proclus 239.1–4 thought them alternatives; Gosling (1973) 132 thinks a single criterion is involved. At 478a3 it is assumed that the distinctness of knowledge and belief necessarily entails a difference of 'sphere': this apparently rules out the possibility that knowledge and belief might have different 'products' (i.e. mental states) but the same 'sphere' (or 'objects', n. d1), and thus suggests that P. is working with a pair of mutually entailing criteria. The issues raised by this passage are pursued in detail by J. Hintikka and G. Santas, in J. M. E. Moravcsik, *Patterns in Plato's Thought* (Dordrecht, 1973), 7-16, 31-51.

477d7   **my good friend:** Soc. addresses the imaginary interlocutor (cf. 479a5), using a characteristic vocative (n. 450c6).

477e2   **by which:** alternatively, 'with/through which'; P. wishes *doxa*, 'belief', to denote both a capacity and its use or functioning, in the same way that e.g. *opsis*, 'vision', or *akoê*, 'hearing', can do (c3). This is philosophically problematic only if taken as an attempt to suggest that in cases of belief the mind operates in a way quite distinct from its capacity for knowledge.

477e4   **you agreed:** at b5–6.

477e6–7   **infallible...fallible:** if the remark is one which would make sense for an unphilosophical interlocutor to give, the point should be restricted to a logical observation (in short, that knowledge necessarily entails truth). But some interpreters have detected an implicit allusion to the Platonic doctrine that philosophical knowledge, i.e. knowledge of 'forms', is knowledge of that which in itself is necessarily, timelessly true. As regards the fallibility of belief, this might appear to jeopardise the distinction between *doxa* and *agnoia* (ignorance). The difficulty disappears if *agnoia* is confined to 'empty' ignorance, or if a difference of degree can be placed between false belief and ignorance: see n. 477a9 ('ignorance').

478a3–4   **each...has by nature:** for the inference cf. n. 477d2–3. The formulation combines the terms of 477b7–8, b10; a6 does likewise for 477a9, b10–11.

478a6   **involves an understanding:** γνῶναι depends on the verb πέφυκε, which is to be supplied in the preceding clause (from a3); for the construction, which carries over to δοξάζειν, a8, cf. n. 477b10. The equivalence of understanding and knowledge is effectively carried over from 476d–7a.

478a10   **belief believe:** the words δόξα δοξάζει must be supplied from a8.

478a10f.   **an object both of knowledge and of belief:** verbal adjs., lit. 'to be known/believed', terms that will later be given heavy metaphysical meaning (6.510a9, 7.517b8, 534a6–7). The sense of the question is highly contentious; it is hard to imagine an unphilosophical interlocutor giving a ready reply to it; as elsewhere, G. gives an answer that he thinks such a person *ought* to give (cf. n. 476d8–9). In Greek just as in English, the question *could* admit the answer 'yes' – if by 'object' were meant either a state of affairs, or the content of a proposition which expresses it: it can equally be known or believed, e.g., that Alcibiades loves Socrates. This point is borne out by *Tht.* 202b7, where it is allowed that the same thing *can* be objects of both knowledge and (true) opinion (with the same verbal adjs. as here); cf. *Epist.* 7.342a–c. Why, then, is the imaginary interlocutor made to reply as he does? Not, I think, because there is any unequivocal ordinary way of construing the propositions he accepts, but rather because the whole argument proceeds under the pressure of metaphysical assumptions already intimated in the exchange between Soc. and G. at 475e–6d. Soc. now steers the dialogue relentlessly towards a conclusion that will be in keeping with that earlier passage: from b3, the interlocutor's assent is utterly mechanical; his cause is lost.

478b6–7   **something unreal:** the same term as 477a3, 9, where it denoted the sphere of *agnoia*, 'ignorance'. The equation of 'not being' with 'nothing' (b12) requires the existential sense of 'be' (n. 476e10). It also suggests that ignorance is the entirely empty or negative state of not-knowing, unless (n. 477a9, 'ignorance') we take it also to embrace total falsehoods which make no meaningful contact at all with the world: in that case, the difference between ignorance and false belief will be one of degree. In later works, P. refines his logical analysis to the point where it can be regarded as possible, in a specifiable sense, 'to believe something unreal' (*Soph.* 240d–41a, 260c, 263b–d, cf. *Phlb.* 40c9–10).

478b7–8   **direct his belief *towards* something:** belief must refer to some identifiable element of the world; cf. *Phlb.* 37a7, *Tht.* 189a6–b5.

478b12   **nothing:** that of which only 'nothing' can be said, *Prm.* 142a.

478c3–4   **posited a...match:** at 477a9–10. *apodidonai* implies quasi-diagrammatic connections (n. 477a3); cf. e5, 6.511e1 (the Divided Line), *Phlb.* 40d4.

478c6   **one does not have beliefs about the real:** a startlingly counter-intuitive statement; taken in isolation, Soc.'s words could easily be translated 'no-one has true or false beliefs'. We can highlight the acuteness of the paradox by noticing that P. himself elsewhere uses, without difficulty, such ordinary Greek expressions as *ta onta doxazein*: see e.g. 3.413a7, with context. But ordinary meanings are now largely irrelevant to the momentum of the argument, built up since talk of 'the completely real' at 477a. The notional interlocutor has become a tenuous, unresisting fiction.

478c10   **is there anything:** Burnet's text misprints ἆρα for ἄρα.

478c11   **clarity...obscurity:** these terms hark back to the language of vision used at 476b7, 10, and help to prepare for the elaborate development of such ideas in bk. 6's analogy of the Sun, and bk. 7's simile of the Cave; cf. also the distinctions of 'clarity', corresponding to truth, in the Divided Line, 6.509d9, 511e3. The association of clarity with philosophical truth occurs also in Xenophanes fr. 34.1 DK.

478d5   **did we agree:** at 477a10 f.

478d5–6   **such as to be:** Adam, pointing out that this sense of οἷος requires an infinitive (of result), takes οἷον adverbially ('so to speak'). This could be right, but the first interpretation can be saved if we understand ὄν/μὴ ὄν in d6 to be quasi-adjectival (cf. 10.597a5, 611a1) and εἶναι to be implied.

478e2   **partakes:** cf. n. 476d1–2.

479a1   **splendid:** the term may have a touch of irony, as it certainly does at *Tht.* 166a2; cf. the somewhat wry 'my good friend', at a5 (with 450d5). But there is no need to see pointed sarcasm, since Soc. has in mind not an identifiable opponent (Adam; cf. n. 476c2) but a hypothetical 'lover of sights/sounds' (cf. a3 with 475d). Such people were described as '*like* philosophers' (475e2), i.e. as trying in their own (limited) way to appreciate things of value: it is not P.'s purpose to scorn them, but to suggest that they are unable to grasp the nature of non-sensible and changeless reality.

479a1   **and in a form of beauty:** the phrase is epexegetic, i.e. explanatory of 'beauty itself'. *Idea* here is synonymous with *eidos* in the original statement at 476a5; the equivalence is common elsewhere too (e.g. 2.380d2–3, 10.596a6/b3, *Euthph.* 5d4/6d11). For *auto*, 'itself/as such', see n. 476a5.

479a2–3   **always and invariably the same:** for this characteristic Platonic phrasing, see e7–8 below, and e.g. 6.484b4, 500c2–3, *Crat.* 439e3, *Phlb.* 59c4, 61e3, *Phdo* 78c–d, 79d–e, 80b2–3, *Plt.* 269d5. These and other passages link changelessness with the idea of an immaterial, non-composite, but intelligible realm of being, as opposed to the shifting, temporary appearances of 'becoming' (e.g. 6.485b2–3, 508d7, *Symp.* 211a1); immutability is also, for P., a property of the divine (*Symp.* 208a8 f.). P. thus projects onto a metaphysical plane something which Parmenides had predicated of all reality (esp. fr. 8.29–30, 57, DK). (These points are unaffected by P.'s occasional use of similar language for merely human kinds of stability: see *Laws* 7.797b1-2.) It follows from the possession of eternal permanence that the entities posited at 476a ff. are entirely distinct from the properties of the material and human world, even though 476a6-7 indicates some kind of dependence of the latter upon the former.

479a3   **acknowledges a multiplicity of beauties:** lit. 'thinks that beauties [or beautiful things] <are> many'; cf. 476a–c, esp. a7. The emphasis of 'many' conveys both (i) numerical plurality of objects (cf. 476c2, 6.507b2–3, *Phdo* 78d10, and n. b3 be') and (ii) variety of *standards* (hence the impossibility of a unitary definition: cf. *Euthph.* 6d6–11, *Tht.* 148d6). It is much clearer what the imaginary opponent *denies* than what he believes. In particular, it must be uncertain how far he adopts the position of a 'nominalist' (n. 476c2), by asserting that there is nothing more to beauty than the collection of particulars which are called beautiful; or to what extent he is prepared, while rejecting any single concept of beauty, to identify certain general criteria of beauty. 476b5 (see n.) is compatible with some degree of generalisation about types of beautiful colour, shape, etc. But the ramifications of the point remain vexed: for various views, see Gosling (1960), White (1978a), Vlastos (1981) 67 n. 41, and Crombie II 55-6.

479a4–5   **a single entity:** without division or variation (n. 476a5); the point is related to immutability (a2–3). For 'justice and the rest', see n. 476a4–5.

479a6–7   **equally seem ugly:** *phainesthai*, 'seem', also covers the meaning, 'be thought' (cf. *Hp. Mj.* 291d1–3), and applies to all cases of belief about the attributes of sensible objects, actions etc. (including, perhaps, *types* of such attributes: n. a3). The argument here states, without specifying, the necessary relativism of all beliefs of this kind. But beliefs can be 'relative' in many different ways, some of which are listed at *Symp.* 211a1–5 (relativity of material change, aspect, time, standards, place, persons), but not all of which look wholly relevant here. The relativity of time or place, for example, has no bearing on the use of 'double' or 'half' (b3); and the 'simultaneously' of 478d5 would in any case lead us to think in terms of co-presence, not mere succession, of opposite attributes (but cf. Jordan 61–2). Nor does P. have in mind the extreme doctrine of subjectivism, despite the fact that we find very similar language in the account of Protagoras's views at *Tht.* 152d ff.: subjectivism would, for one thing, rule out a distinction between belief and ignorance (n. 477a9, 'ignorance'). The question probably rests, therefore, on the assumption of relativism in the most flexible sense. Its point is to emphasise that any human belief about either moral (476a) or relational attributes (b3–6 below) will always be non-absolute in at least *some* respect, and therefore cannot meet the conditions indicated at a1–3 above. On difficulties in P.'s treatment of relativism here, see Cross & Woozley 151-61; cf. the related passage at *Phdo* 74b7-9 (with Gallop 121-3).

479b1-2   **it's inevitable:** in view of the ambiguity of the question (n. a6–7), we might wonder once more whether an unphilosophical interlocutor would give so obliging an answer (cf. n. 476d8–9); why, for example, should the lover of sounds suppose that a beautiful piece of music *must* 'in some respect' seem ugly? And what precisely does he concede by 'inevitable' (cf. White [1978b] 145)? Even if explanations can be supplied for his answer, the argument here takes a great deal for granted: its progress, as a result, is not such as to convince non-platonist readers. Cf. n. b8 below.

479b3   **doubleness:** the terms 'double'/'half', 'large'/'small', 'light'/'heavy' are now added to those originally cited at 475e–6a. The two sets of predicates have in common the fact that they form pairs of opposites (n. 475e9). P. also implies that they are comparable by virtue of all being somehow relative (n. a6–7); cf. Owen 174–5 on their status as 'incomplete' predicates (i.e. in need of some qualifying specification). If we combine this passage with 7.523a–5a, which distinguishes properties that can be adequately judged by sense-perception from those (including 'large' and 'light') which cannot, we can say that all those mentioned here fall into the latter category: this means, at the least, that they involve judgements not of 'substance' (e.g. this is a finger) but of quality or relation (e.g. this finger is large/soft etc.). Yet elsewhere, at *Euthph.* 7b-e, P. contrasts the disputability of moral values (cf. *Phdr.* 263a-c) with the quantifiable, and thus non-disputable, nature of (e.g.) 'large' and 'small'.

479b8   **be connected to:** the verb should be compared with *metechein* at 476d1–2, 478e1–2. But if so, that poses a double problem: what does the imaginary opponent mean by such language, and why does he acquiesce in a movement from things 'appearing' (a7) to have contrary properties, to their actually having them? As previous nn. have stressed, I do not think that the opponent's part in the argument is couched in plausibly independent terms; his answers are designed to do no more than assist progress to the desired conclusion.

479b9–10   **'is'...'is not':** the formulation anticipates the language of later Greek scepticism, e.g. Pyrrho at D. Laert. 9.61, 74–6 (we can no more say of anything that 'it is' than 'it is not'). But the argument does not have the scope of general scepticism (which would apply to the content of any and every belief). It applies only to predication of qualities or relations of the kinds mentioned in a–b, *not* to the subjects of which they are predicated (ctr. Cross & Woozley 162–3); cf. *Hp. Mj.* 289c4–5, with Vlastos (1981) 65–6. Thus the verb 'be', here at least, requires its predicative not its existential sense (n. 476e10). White (1978b) 151 puts a different view.

479b11   **game of ambiguity:** lit. 'the ambiguities'; the Greek participle is neuter, though the verb does sometimes have a personal subject.

479c1–3   **riddle:** the scholia (Greene 235) give two versions, both in iambic trimeters. The longer runs: 'a man, who was not a man, saw and did not see a bird, which was not a bird, sitting on wood, which was not wood, and hit it with a stone, which was not stone'; the solution is: a eunuch, with imperfect sight, hit a bat on a reed with a pumice-stone. Riddles were a familiar source of amusement among Greeks: see Athen. 10.448b–459b for the largest collection (with the present one cited at 452c–d), and *OCD*[2] 924 for further information. With ἐφ' οὗ (c2) we must supply a participle, καθημένην, agreeing with αὐτήν.

479c3   **ambiguity...properties:** lit. 'these things too <seem> to be ambiguous...'; ταῦτα must refer to all the attributes exemplified in a–b. ἐπαμφοτερίζειν is dependent on ἔοικεν, still understood from b11.

479c4   **to think:** *noein* cannot here embrace all kinds of thought; it implies, at the least, clear and coherent reasoning, and will later be used for the highest philosophical exercise of intellect (e.g. 6.507b9–10, 508d6). *pagiôs*, 'in a fixed sense', suggests that knowledge, as opposed to *doxa*, is sure, stable and immovable: cf. 434d2, with *Euthph.* 11b-d, *Meno* 97d-8a, *Grg.* 508e, *Plt.* 309c5-8, Parmen. fr. 4.1, and n. d4 below for the corollary. Arist. *Met.* 1078b16 refers to the Platonist assumption that, given the (Heracleitean) flux of the sensible world, there must be other, immaterial entities which are static and permanent (*menousas*); cf. ib. 987a29-b7. See *Tht.* 157a3-4 on the impossibility of fixity (*pagiôs* once more) in perceptions of the flux. The present argument is related to P.'s view of the flux by Jordan ch. 3.

479c7   **being:** the noun *ousia* is used by P. in two main ways, to denote (i) existence in a broad and compendious sense (e.g. *Tht.* 185c9, 186a–c), (ii) unchanging metaphysical reality, as opposed to the world of 'becoming' (e.g. 6.485b2, 7.525b5, c6, *Phdr.* 247c7, *Tim.* 29c3). The word therefore reflects something of the variation in the senses of 'be' itself, especially the nominalised participle, *to on* (n. 477a3). For further discussion of *ousia* see Kahn 457–62, Vlastos (1991) 254–5.

479c8f.   **darker...clearer:** see 478c13–14. Both adjs. are followed by defining phrases: lit. 'darker/clearer in relation to...'

479d3–4   **multifarious principles:** lit. 'the many conventional <values> of the many', generalising the motif of plural instances/standards of value from the preceding argument (476a7, 479a3, 6, b3, 10). The substantival use of *nomima* encompasses the principles embodied both in a society's laws, and in its unwritten traditions, attitudes and *mores*; cf. 451a7, 457a3 (= *nomos*, b8), and e.g. 6.484d1–2, *Grg.* 488d9, *Laws* 7.793a10 ('unwritten'). The whole sentence bears out two points: first, that P. is arguing not against a specific opponent but against the cultural relativity of values which are not underpinned by philosophical knowledge (nn. 476c2, 479a1 'splendid'); second, that his concern is chiefly with values that are, either directly or indirectly, ethical (cf. n. 476b5 on the meaning of *kalos*). Cf. the description of prevalent values as 'the beliefs (*dogmata*) of the many' at 6. 493a-d.

479d4   **roll around:** the opposite of being apprehensible 'in a fixed sense', *pagiôs* (c4); cf. n. d9, and e.g. *Euthph.* 11c-d, *Phdr.* 275e1, *Tim.* 52a6.

479d5   **pure reality:** cf. n. 477a7.

479d8   **capacity:** see n. 477b5, with 477c–8a.

479d9   **unstable:** lit. 'wandering'; cf. 6.485b2, where the term is linked with 'becoming and degeneration', and n. d4 above. The verb is applied to non-philosophers, in their dependence on fluid values, at 6.484b6; cf. the 'wandering' souls at *Phdo* 79c7, d5.

The same word-group is associated with mental or perceptual confusion at e.g. 4.444b7, 6.505c7, 10.602c12.

479e1–3   **beautiful things...many instances:** the point continues to cover both particulars and types/standards of beauty, justice etc.; cf. n. 479a3.

479e2   **see:** cf. 476b7, 10. For the idea of being 'guided' to knowledge of true values, see 476c3.

479e7   **each and all...in themselves:** this is the generic plural which represents all the separate entities, 'beauty/justice (etc.) in itself'; 480a11 (cf. 476a5–6) gives the equivalent singular. The same plural occurred much earlier, at 4.438b2, but it referred there to 'unqualified' properties (e.g. thirst pure and simple), and lacked the metaphysical implications of the present context.

479e10   **embrace and love:** the terms take us back to the discussion of various species of 'lovers' at 474c ff., which led to the attempt to distinguish *philosophoi*, lovers of wisdom/knowledge, from others such as lovers of sights and sounds (475d ff.).

480a1   **covered by:** a reversion to the formula earlier used to mark the spheres or realms of knowledge, belief, and ignorance: n. 477a9 ('knowledge...covers').

480a3   **we said:** at 476b.

480a6   **lovers of belief:** elsewhere, *philodoxos* and its cognates usually refer to desire for a reputation (another sense of *doxa*). P. uses the adj. only here (with a12), and has created a setting for its special meaning; but he may intend its more usual sense to provide a kind of satirical overtone: 'opinionated' could perhaps capture something of this play on the two senses of *doxa*. 'Philodox(ical)' has made occasional appearances in English.

480a7   **be angry:** cf. 476d8.

Appendix

Republic 5 & Aristophanes' *Ecclesiazusae*

This appendix attempts only a concise summary of an old, vexed controversy. The fuller treatment of Adam (I 345-55) remains judicious; I dissent from it largely on points of emphasis. Cf. Ussher xiv-xx, David 20-29, who both cite further literature on the subject.

(A)   *Eccl.* is a play which dramatises a women's revolution in Athens, masterminded by Praxagora as female 'general' (246, 727 etc.), whereby: (i) women are to occupy all magistracies, and control all political functions (455 ff., 555 ff.); (ii) private property is to be abolished, and the city organised as a communist economy (esp. 590 ff.), with the citizens dining in common 'messes', *sussitia* (676 ff., 715); (iii) a system of sexual communism too is to be instituted (614 ff.), which will entail the abolition of the domestic family (635 ff., 673–5) and the diffusion of a new sense of common kinship (esp. 641–3); (iv) society will become a blissful utopia from which social problems and divisions will disappear (558 ff., 657 ff.).

(B)   In all four respects noted in (A), there are interesting similarities between *Eccl.* and *Rep.* 5; for further details cf. Adam I 350–1 (where items 2 and 7, at least, are immaterial; on others cf. (D) below). But the following features of *Eccl.* are notably different from P.'s proposals: (i) Praxagora's scheme is democratic (631): it involves all citizens, not just a particular class (but cf. my n. 450c1); (ii) although in charge of the city, the women will continue to perform certain traditional roles (599 f., cooking; 654, clothes-making); (iii) women will not, it seems, participate in the common dining-halls or messes (676, 693); (iv) despite Praxagora's title (above), it is not envisaged that women will serve as soldiers (cf. 233-5), nor is anything said of female gymnastics; (v) the sexual communism of *Eccl.* is both populist and hedonistic; unlike P.'s eugenic scheme, it is designed only to spread sexual pleasure round the city.

(C)   *Eccl.* was staged in either 393 or 392 B.C. (Ussher xx–xxv). For *Rep.* 5, as for the whole dialogue, we lack precise information about either the date or the stages of composition. It has become orthodox in the present century, for reasons that are connected with interpretation of P.'s entire career, to assign the writing of the *Rep.* to a period somewhere between c.385 and 365 (cf. Ussher xvii n.1). This view is not impregnable, and it has been challenged most recently by Thesleff, who believes that P. was working on the dialogue at different times between the 390s and 350s (101–7; see *Phronesis* 34 [1989] 11–14 for a restatement). But Thesleff's case, like that of several 19th cent. scholars (cf. Adam I 345, 353), depends in large part on taking *Eccl.* as a parody of P.'s ideas (103-4), and to that extent it cannot provide independent support for this possibility. Although the full case cannot be argued here, I adhere to the majority view that it most unlikely that the ideas of *Rep.* 5 had been formulated by P. as early as the 390s.

(D)   If P. was not an influence on Ar.'s comedy, it remains open to us to suppose that Ar. was drawing on other sources of communistic and radical thinking. Some scholars would hypothesise one particular such source, common to both Ar. and P.: see e.g. Ussher xviii–xx, who leaves identity open, and Demand's article, which argues a highly speculative case involving both Socratic and Pythagorean circles; cf. the Introduction n. 13. But it is easier and preferable to believe that Ar. gleaned and amalgamated ideas from a variety of sources: the connection of 'messes', *sussitia*, with Sparta is one obvious detail (see n.

458c8–9); the theme of women being sexually 'shared' or 'in common', *koinai* (Adam I 350, item 1), was already current in 5th cent. 'anthropological' thought about non-Greek peoples (see the Introduction, p. 10); and the idea of a society without need of law-courts no doubt reflects another strand of utopianism (cf. n. 464d7). These illustrations cover aspects of three of the four major points set out in (A) above, and leave untouched only the question of female rule. But the latter is anyway a rather different matter in *Eccl.* – where it represents older comic motifs of gender-reversal and 'women in charge' (*gunaikokratia*) – from P.'s proposal for female Guardians who work alongside men.

(E)   The question remains: did P. have *Eccl.* in mind when composing *Rep.* 5? The most prudent answer is that he may well, but need not have. It is certainly rash to say, with Adam I 354, that P. 'must' have known the play (cf. 346 for the same statement about Aristotle). It is much too easy to assume that individual works always had the prominence which they now possess for us. In P.'s time, ten new comedies were produced each year at the City Dionysia and Lenaea (cf. n. 475d7–8): thus, by (say) 475 some 170 comedies had been staged since the first (and perhaps the only) performance of *Eccl.* Nor were play-texts all that common. It obviously remains possible that P. remembered or knew something about *Eccl.* But nothing in *Rep.* 5, I believe, proves that he did so. In particular, the book's repeated references to the fear of laughter, and to the anticipated mirth of the witty (see n. 451a1, and esp. 452a-e), show that P. is aware of the *general* potential for comedy in the materials of his argument, not that he is alluding to any particular play from the comic stage. If he *were* thinking of something particular at 452a-e, it could not in fact be *Eccl.*, which does not include the theme of female soldiers or gymnasts (cf. (B) iv above). But it is more satisfactory, in any case, to interpret this and other similar passages in terms of broader features of vulgar humour, whether inside or outside the comic theatre (cf. nn. 452a4-5, 11).

(F)   I conclude, therefore: (i) that *Eccl.* and *Rep.* reflect a partially similar conception of social and sexual communism, but are also divergent in some equally important respects; (ii) that *Eccl.* predated any Platonic version of the arguments of *Rep.* 5; (iii) that insofar as Ar. used intellectual sources of material for his play (cf. *Eccl.* 571 for a hint, but often wrongly used to argue for a link with P.), these were various; (iv) that it is far from certain that P. had *Eccl.* in mind when writing bk. 5, though he certainly alludes to popular topics of humour about women and relations between the sexes.

Index

Note that separate references to a topic on successive pages have usually been grouped together.

(ii) Style & Language

CLASSICAL TEXTS

Editorial Advisor: Professor M.M. Willcock (London)

Published volumes

AESCHYLUS
THE EUMENIDES, edited by A.J.Podlecki
ARISTOPHANES, edited by Alan H.Sommerstein
ACHARNIANS
BIRDS
CLOUDS
KNIGHTS
LYSISTRATA
PEACE
WASPS
AUGUSTINE
SOLILOQUIES *and* IMMORTALITY OF THE SOUL, edited by G.Watson
CAESAR
CIVIL WAR Books I & II, edited by J.M.Carter
CASSIUS DIO
ROMAN HISTORY Books 53.1-55.9, edited by J.W.Rich
CICERO General Editor: Professor A.E.Douglas
TUSCULAN DISPUTATIONS 2 & 5, edited by A.E.Douglas
TUSCULAN DISPUTATIONS I, edited by A.E.Douglas
ON FATE with **BOETHIUS** CONSOLATION V, edited by R.W.Sharples
PHILIPPICS II, edited by W.K.Lacey
VERRINES II,1, edited by T.N.Mitchell
ON STOIC GOOD AND EVIL: (De Finibus 3 and Paradoxa Stoicorum)
    edited by M.R. Wright
ON FRIENDSHIP and THE DREAM OF SCIPIO: (De Amicitia and
    Somnium Scipionis), edited by J.G.F.Powell
EURIPIDES General Editor; Professor C.Collard
ALCESTIS, edited by D.Conacher
ELECTRA, edited by M.J.Cropp
HECUBA edited by C.Collard
ORESTES, edited by M.L.West
PHOENICIAN WOMEN, edited by E.Craik
TROJAN WOMEN, edited by Shirley Barlow
GREEK ORATORS
I ANTIPHON, LYSIAS, edited by M.Edwards & S.Usher
III ISOCRATES Panegyricus and To Nicocles edited by S.Usher
VI APOLLODORUS c. Neaira, edited by C. Carey
HELLENICA OXYRHYNCHIA
edited by P.R.McKechnie & S.J.Kern
HOMER
ODYSSEY I & II edited by P.V.Jones
JOSEPH OF EXETER
THE TROJAN WAR I-III, edited by A.K.Bate
LIVY
Book XXXVI, edited by P.G. Walsh